# Studies in the Assessment of Parenting

C............................................roversial
qu...........................................address
di...........................................f current
k

..............................................l experts
...............................................1gs, and
...............................................complex
...............................................e child's
...............................................er topics

•
•
•

S..............................................ture but
n..............................................logists,
s..............................................in child
c..............................................-to-day
cl.............................................eing of
cl

**Peter Reder** is a consultant child psychiatrist and a trained family therapist. He co-authored the books *Beyond Blame* and *Lost Innocents* and co-edited *Assessment of Parenting* and *Family Matters*.

**Sylvia Duncan** is a consultant clinical psychologist and accredited family therapist. She is co-author of *Beyond Blame* and *Lost Innocents*.

**Clare Lucey** is a consultant child and family psychiatrist. She co-edited *Assessment of Parenting*.

# Studies in the Assessment of Parenting

Edited by Peter Reder,
Sylvia Duncan and
Clare Lucey

Routledge
Taylor & Francis Group

LONDON AND NEW YORK

First published 2003
by Routledge
27 Church Road, Hove, East Sussex BN3 2FA

Simultaneously published in the USA and Canada
by Routledge
270 Madison Avenue, New York NY 10016

Reprinted 2005, 2007 and 2010

*Routledge is an imprint of the Taylor & Francis Group, an Informa business*

Typeset in Times by
Keystroke, Jacaranda Lodge, Wolverhampton
Printed and bound in Great Britain by
the MPG Books Group
Paperback cover design by Sandra Heath

*British Library Cataloguing in Publication Data*
A catalogue record for this book is available from the British Library

*Library of Congress Cataloging in Publication Data*
Studies in the assessment of parenting / edited by Peter Reder, Sylvia
Duncan and Clare Lucey.
        p. ; cm.
Includes bibliographical references and indexes.
 ISBN 1-58391-179-0 (hardback : alk. paper) -- ISBN 1-58391-180-4 (pbk.
: alk. paper)
 1. Parental influences. 2. Parenting. 3. Parent and child. 4.
Parenthood--Psychological aspects.
 [DNLM: 1. Parent-Child Relations. 2. Parenting--psychology. 3.
Child Abuse--prevention & control. 4. Child of Impaired Parents. WS
105.5.F2 S933 2003] I. Reder, Peter, 1946- II. Duncan, Sylvia, 1948-
III. Lucey, Clare, 1957-

RJ507.P35S786 2003
362.76--dc22
                                        2003018402

ISBN 13: 978–1–58391–180–8 (pbk)

# Contents

# Illustrations

## Tables

## Figures

# Contributors

**Tony Baker** is Consultant Child Psychiatrist at the Baker & Duncan Family Consultancy in Brookwood, Woking.

**Arnon Bentovim** is Consultant Child Psychiatrist and Director at the London Child and Family Consultation Service in Harley Street, London, Honorary Consultant Psychiatrist at Great Ormond Street Children's Hospital and the Tavistock Centre and is Honorary Senior Lecturer at the Institute of Child Health, London.

**Christopher Cordess** is Professor of Forensic Psychiatry in the School of Health and Related Research at the University of Sheffield, and is Director of Research and Honorary Consultant at Rampton Hospital Authority.

**Sylvia Duncan** is Consultant Clinical Psychologist at the Baker & Duncan Family Consultancy in Brookwood, Woking.

**Liz Fellow-Smith** is Consultant Child and Adolescent Psychiatrist in the Children and Families Consultation Service and Medical Director for the West London Mental Health Trust in Southall.

**Geraldine Fitzpatrick** is Consultant Child and Adolescent Psychiatrist and Clinical Director at St George's Hospital in London. She is also Honorary Senior Lecturer at St George's Hospital Medical School.

**David P.H. Jones** is Consultant Child and Family Psychiatrist at the Park Hospital for Children in Oxford.

**Clare Lucey** is Consultant Child and Adolescent Psychiatrist for the Children & Families Consultation Service in Southall.

**Begum Maitra** is Consultant Child and Adolescent Psychiatrist at the Child and Family Consultation Centre, London.

**Peter Reder** is Consultant Child and Adolescent Psychiatrist at the Child and Family Consultation Centre, Director of the Centre for Relationship Studies, London and Honorary Senior Lecturer at the Imperial College of Science, Technology and Medicine.

**Claire Sturge** is Consultant Child and Adolescent Psychiatrist at Northwick Park Hospital, Harrow.

**The Rt Hon. Lord Justice Thorpe** sits at the Royal Courts of Justice in London.

**John Triseliotis** is Emeritus Professor at the University of Edinburgh and Visiting Professor and Senior Research Fellow at the University of Strathclyde.

**Helen L. Westcott** is Lecturer in Psychology in the Faculty of Social Sciences at the Open University in Milton Keynes.

# Preface

Soon after the 1989 Children Act was implemented (in 1991), it became apparent that little had been published to help mental health and other professionals undertake parenting assessments in complex child care court cases. Two of us (Peter Reder and Clare Lucey) decided to edit a book, bringing together contributions by acknowledged experts, which addressed the theory and practice of assessments in the context of family proceedings. It was published by Routledge in 1995 as *Assessment of Parenting: Psychiatric and Psychological Contributions*.

Since then, there have been further developments in our knowledge about parenting breakdown and guidance on how professionals should respond to it. For example, the government has produced an assessment framework to guide social workers and practitioners continue to debate the relative merits of the Children Act. A link between child maltreatment and parental mental health problems has become recognized, while child neglect and abuse by 'induced or fabricated illness' is more widely discussed. In addition, the theoretical principles and clinical approaches reported in the original book have had time to be tested in everyday practice and new controversial questions have emerged. We concluded that this was an appropriate time to plan a companion volume, not as a second edition that would replace the original book, but one that would complement it because it addressed new issues or reconsidered certain topics in a different way. The aim has therefore been for minimal overlap between the two books.

We approached psychiatrists, psychologists and social workers who had long experience of undertaking parenting assessments and providing expert opinions to courts and/or considerable academic involvement in the issues. A leading judge in the Family Division of the High Court also agreed to contribute. All chapter titles were posed as questions which the authors were invited to argue through, with reference to theoretical and research literature, as well as their own practice experience. The issues at the centre of each question were chosen for different reasons. Some were identified because we felt they needed a fresh consideration or it was timely to bring together developments in knowledge, theory or practice on that topic. Many were challenging dilemmas that we had faced in our own attempts to assist courts. The chapter topics come together under the following Part headings: I: Principles and Practice; II: The Child's Perspective; III: Assessing Parents; IV:

Recommendations; and V: Judgments. Since the book is not intended to be a comprehensive handbook, it does not cover the types of child abuse or aspects of parenting breakdown that are well represented elsewhere in the literature.

We originally intended the book to be based around a set of case studies but decided to seek advice about the inclusion of clinical material, since issues of confidentiality and consent have become particularly intricate. Our conclusion was that authors should include such material only with written informed consent but that heavily disguised, brief vignettes would be acceptable.

Thanks are due to the authors for finding time in their busy schedules to consider the questions we posed and to compose their responses. We appreciate the time and effort this required, especially since all the chapters went through a number of redraftings as we urged authors to go a bit further in their response to the challenging topics.

The contents should be of interest to a spectrum of professionals involved in child welfare and family court work. This includes social workers, children's guardians, adult and child psychiatrists, clinical psychologists, solicitors, barristers and judges, as well as those training for such professions. Our hope is that the book, as a complement to the first one, will usefully inform the process of assessing parenting and advising courts whether parents are satisfying children's needs and promoting their welfare.

**Peter Reder**
**Sylvia Duncan**
**Clare Lucey**
(September 2002)

# Part I

# Principles and practice

# Chapter 1

# What principles guide parenting assessments?

*Peter Reder, Sylvia Duncan and Clare Lucey*

Parenting assessments are a planned process of identifying concerns about a child's welfare, eliciting information about the functioning of the parent/s and the child, and forming an opinion as to whether the child's needs are being satisfied. This book focuses on assessments undertaken as part of Family Proceedings in order to advise courts making decisions about children's future care. Commonly, these are hearings under the 1989 Children Act to consider whether a child has suffered significant harm as a result of the parenting they have received and whether an Order should be made to safeguard their future care. Alternatively, the hearing may be part of Matrimonial Proceedings around disputed contact arrangements between separated/divorced parents.

Assessments under the Children Act will have been preceded by front-line 'initial' and 'core' assessments in accordance with the *Framework for the Assessment of Children in Need and their Families* (Department of Health, Department for Education and Employment and Home Office, 2000; Department of Health, 2000a; Horwath, 2001; Gray, 2001). As its title indicates, this framework is concerned with ascertaining which children/families are 'in need' (of services), only a small proportion of whom are likely to require a child protection plan. Its core premise is that families referred to social services should be helped to remain intact and the assessment philosophy is inclined towards identifying those interventions which might help them do so. Thus, it is intentionally focused on screening referrals and selecting families that might require more detailed assessment. It allows for the possibility that services might be introduced concurrently with the assessment.

The philosophy and context of parenting assessments for court are different. The families have already been identified as showing major problems, the authority of the court adds a new dimension to the tradition of partnership between family and professionals, the assessor remains neutral throughout as to the relative strengths and weaknesses of the family, there is no bias towards any type of intervention or assumptions about the viability of the family unit, and distinction is made throughout between assessment and intervention.

Nonetheless, the spirit of the Children Act pervades all levels of assessment. The desirability of keeping families intact if possible is clear, so that cases brought before the court are expected to demonstrate that every attempt has been made to do so and all reasonable interventions have been offered and tried. A sense of partnership is now reflected in the custom of joint instruction to experts. In addition, all assessments and recommendations are expected to prioritize the child's needs and the child's perspective must be fully represented. The notion of significant harm to the child's welfare and development remains a core criterion for deciding whether parenting has broken down (Bentovim, 1998; Duncan and Baker, Chapter 5).

In this opening chapter, we shall consider some of the core principles which underpin assessments for court. We shall discuss premises about parenting and parenting breakdown and the way that parenting assessments have been approached for different purposes. We shall then offer a framework to guide assessments for court and suggest how this might best be used in practice. Where relevant, indication will be given to subsequent chapters of the book which discuss issues in greater detail.

## PREMISES ABOUT PARENTING

Parameters of 'good-enough' parenting are socially constructed, since the concept depends as much on subjective impressions, culture-bound beliefs (see Maitra, Chapter 3) and context-related thresholds of concern (Dingwall et al., 1983) as on objective qualities. We have argued elsewhere (Reder et al., 1993) that, even at the most severe end of the spectrum of parenting, the concept of 'child abuse' is an evolving one, with changes in definition and recognition over time. Criteria for considering what constitutes child abuse arise out of a number of social and historical contexts, such as social attitudes to children and families, theories and knowledge about child development and family functioning, and professional practice in relation to them. The ever-changing interrelationship between these dimensions is punctuated and reflected at intervals by political initiatives and changes in legislation.

A recent example is the debate about whether it is permissible to smack children, in which informed commentators hold discrepant views (e.g. Larzelere, 1996; 2000; Waterston, 2000a; 2000b; Trumbull, 2000). Conventions and legislation also vary between different countries, although some social attitudes have changed following publicity about research which showed that smacking may be counterproductive and that alternatives are effective. The relationship between advances in knowledge, public opinion and legal changes is complex. In 1979, Sweden passed legislation which abolished corporal punishment as a legitimate child-rearing practice but, according to Roberts (2000), it is erroneous to believe that the legal changes altered public opinion, since there is good evidence that support for corporal punishment had significantly declined prior to 1979. Even so, it was a ruling of the European Court of Human Rights that prompted initiatives to change British legislation (Department of Health, 2000b). Meanwhile, Cawson et al. (2000) found that 72 per cent of a sample of 18–24 year olds in the UK recalled experiencing physical forms of discipline during childhood.

Jones (2001) proposed that 'parenting' refers to activities and behaviours of primary caretakers necessary to achieve the objective of enabling children to become autonomous. In our view, the purpose of parenting is to facilitate the child's optimal development within a safe environment. More specifically, according to Hoghughi (1997), the core elements of parenting are:

- *Care* (meeting the child's needs for physical, emotional and social well-being and protecting the child from avoidable illness, harm, accident or abuse);
- *Control* (setting and enforcing appropriate boundaries); and
- *Development* (realizing the child's potential in various domains);

and, in order to be effective, the parent needs to have:

- *Knowledge* (e.g. how the child's care needs can best be met, the child's developmental potential, how to interpret the child's cues, sources of harm);
- *Motivation* (e.g. to protect, to sacrifice personal needs);
- *Resources* (both material and personal); and
- *Opportunity* (e.g. time and space).

These key facets of parenting must be achieved within the evolving relationship between parent and child. The child is not a passive recipient of parental input, nor is the parent a mechanical or ubiquitous provider. For example, at one moment, the child will demand care from the parent and, later, feel satiated and claim rest. At the same time, the child's impulses, behavioural tendencies and attitudes will be modified by the parent's reactions and role modelling. The child and parent will elicit feelings in each other and both will attribute meaning to their experiences within the relationship. Thus, each evokes responses from the other in a reciprocal manner, through interactions that are influenced by personal qualities of each individual and by other relationships and events. The nature of their interactions varies as the child develops and the parent accommodates to this, whilst also needing to respond to changes in their own life. As in other relationships, the behaviour of one participant is bound to affect the other, even if that behaviour is hostility, indifference, rejection, or prolonged absence. Furthermore, like all relationships, the parental one is continuous in the sense that each participant carries an image of it in their mind, even when they are apart. However, it is important to recognize that the emotional relationship does not automatically depend on the blood link between child and adult, since it is primarily a function of their interpersonal history together, not their genetic history (Goldstein *et al.*, 1973; Schaffer, 1998).

As Quinton and Rutter (1988) noted:

> parenting is now understood not only to involve what parents do with their children and how they do it, but also to be affected by the quality of the parents' relationships more generally, by their psychological functioning, by

their previous parenting experiences both with other children and with a particular child, and by the social context in which they are trying to parent. (p. 8)

They went on to identify the task of parenting as being concerned with the provision of an environment conducive to children's cognitive and social development, using skills appropriate to the handling of their distress, disobedience, social approaches, conflicts and interpersonal difficulties. Such skills are reflected in the parents' sensitivity to their children's cues and needs, as they change over the course of development. In addition, parenting is described as a social relationship, which is therefore affected by the parent's previous experiences of being parented, by their current psychological state, by the child's characteristics and by interaction with a broader social network.

Belsky and Vondra (1989) offered a coherent systemic model to describe the multiple determinants of parenting, in which individual, historical, social and circumstantial factors combine to shape parental functioning:

> the model presumes that parenting is directly influenced by forces emanating from within the individual parent (personality), within the individual child (child characteristics of individuality), and from the broader social context in which the parent–child relationship is embedded – specifically the marital relations, the social networks, and occupational experiences of parents. Further, the model assumes that parents' developmental histories, marital relations, social networks, and jobs influence their individual personalities and general psychological well-being and, thereby, parental functioning and, in turn, child development. (pp. 156–7)

Belsky and Vondra (1989) reported an extensive review of research which identified the factors promoting optimal parenting behaviours and, in turn, outcomes for children. Even though the various studies may have used different measures of outcome – ranging from indices of children's psychological, cognitive and behavioural development, parent–child interaction and parental attitudes and behaviours – there was good consistency in the findings that allowed Belsky and Vondra to construct a table of advantageous factors (see Table 1.1). They noted that parental competence is multiply determined and that the factors are interrelated, although the parent's personal psychological resources are the most crucial. Maltreatment was considered to be the consequence of an interaction between stress (vulnerability or risk) factors and support (compensatory) factors. Based on these principles, we have constructed a simplified model for understanding child abuse and parenting breakdown, as shown in Figure 1.1.

No single attribute of the parent, child or family determines the quality of the parenting relationship, since it is multi-determined. Schaffer (1998) and Golombok (2000) have reviewed relevant outcome literature and concluded that family structure or individual parental attributes matter far less to children's development

*Table 1.1* Belsky and Vondra's (1989) summary of factors contributing to optimal child care outcomes

## Parent

*Sensitivity*, including:

> sensitivity to the child's capabilities, developmental tasks and cues
> capacity to empathize and a nurturant orientation
> realistic expectations and appropriate ascription of child's intentionality

*Psychological maturity*, with:

> a stable sense of self, self-esteem and an internal locus of control
> belief that own psychological needs are being met
> capacity to show affection
> ability to enable others
> active coping styles
> recognition of effects of one's own behaviour

*Mental health*, including:

> warmth, parent-initiated interactions and spontaneity
> environment stability and organization

*Developmental history* of:

> affectionate parenting
> intact family

## Child

*Physical*, including:

> obstetric and developmental health

*Temperament*, such as:

> easy to parent
> reinforces parent's sense of control

## Context

*Support*, from:

> partner
> social network
> employment

---

than the quality of relationships within families and with the wider social world. They report that research has allowed the following inferences to be drawn.

- Being the child of a single parent is not *per se* a risk factor for the child's development and welfare. Exposure to continuing parental conflict is more harmful than the fact of divorce/separation or the nature of custody arrangements and it is the associated financial hardship that often renders single parental status problematic.
- Fathers are just as capable of effective and sensitive parenting as mothers, so that if both divorced parents apply for prime responsibility to care for their child, it is not the parent's sex but their individual circumstances that matter.

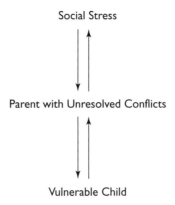

Figure 1.1 A model of parenting breakdown

Source: Reder and Duncan (1999).

- The father's presence in, or absence from, the home does not make a significant difference in itself to a child's gender identity, sex role development, or general psychological outcome.
- Being cared for by homosexual partners (whether early or late in childhood) makes no difference to the young person's gender identity or psychological stability.
- Consanguinity confers no emotional advantage to the child over pregnancy achieved artificially, although there remains an absence of studies on surrogacy.
- Step-children are more likely to show problems if their family was reconstituted later in their upbringing.
- The figure whom the child regards as their parent depends much more on their social, not their genetic, relationship.
- It is the totality of a child's experience that is relevant to their emotional development and well-being rather than single events at any particular period in their development, however upsetting those events may have been or how early in life they occurred.
- While consistency of experience is important for children, they do have considerable recuperative powers and capacity to form new relationships. Breaks may leave a child vulnerable but do not necessarily produce lasting pathology. It is continual disruption that is developmentally harmful.

In summary, the following statements about parenting form the basis of our theoretical and clinical work:

- Parenting is a constellation of behaviours, attitudes, emotions and responsibilities directed by an adult to a child;

- The aim of parenting is to facilitate the child's optimal development within a safe environment;
- Parenting initially serves to ensure the child's survival and gradually aims towards ensuring their autonomous functioning;
- Parenting is a continuous process over many years;
- Different parental behaviours are necessary at different times in the child's life;
- Parenting involves a relationship between adult and child, to which both contribute;
- A child's parenting and the family relationships in which it occurs is a fundamental contributor to their future psychological well-being;
- Other close relationships affect the parent–child dyad;
- Everyone has the potential to parent satisfactorily but this potential may be influenced by past and present experiences;
- Parameters for acceptable and unacceptable parenting are socially constructed and differ between cultures and over a society's history;
- Most societies demand the right to intervene if parenting in a family is believed to be unacceptable;
- Substitute caretakers can compensate for deficiencies of natural parents.

## APPROACHES TO PARENTING ASSESSMENTS

We shall now consider how assessments of parenting have been approached from three different perspectives: for research purposes; in everyday clinical practice; and by those offering opinions to courts about parenting breakdown. It will be apparent, even from this selected review, that elements of approaches utilized in research and clinical practice have informed frameworks used in family proceedings.

### Assessments devised for research

Quinton and Rutter's (1988) study of the intergenerational continuities of parenting breakdown serves as a good example of a research-based approach. The study used standardized interviews and both unstructured and prompted observational methods (see also Dowdney *et al.*, 1985). Interviews included detailed accounts of the child's behaviour and the parental responses to it. Particular attention was paid to interactions over issues of: *control*; *peer and sibling disputes*; *fears and anxieties*; and *play*. Note was made of how typical episodes began and were resolved and measures were devised to rate *parental warmth, sensitivity, consistency* and *effectiveness*. Direct observations were made in the home of play and social interaction, noting the frequency and sequences of interactional episodes around *discipline, the child's distress* and *the child's attempts to gain the mother's attention*. Good parenting outcomes were associated with high or moderately high sensitivity and warmth, absent or infrequent shouting or smacking, and control strategies that were moderately to firmly effective, consistent and predictable.

As another example, Tyler *et al*. (1997) adapted rating scales devised by other researchers in order to measure caregiving by substance misusing parents towards 6-month-old infants. The eight scales used addressed areas of: *social engagement*; *stimulation*; *facilitation of development*; *quality of physical contact*; *frequency of expressed negative regard*; *delight with infant*; *maternal intrusiveness*; and *sensitivity*. Ratings were made from the video-tape of a session in which the parent was invited to feed, play, watch television, clean the house, talk to a friend, or interact directly with the child.

The University of Minnesota Mother–Child Interaction Research Project (e.g. Pianta *et al*., 1989) illustrates how a range of specific measures can be used to create an overall picture and how different factors become more relevant as the child develops. Thus, prenatal assessment included questionnaires regarding the mother's *feelings about the pregnancy*, *knowledge of child care* and *expectations of the child*. In the early months of the child's life, scales were used to measure the *environmental stress* on the mother and her *enjoyment of the baby*. During the first year, *security of attachment* and ratings of the mother's *style of discipline* were assessed, going on through the following year to observational ratings of *quality of care* in the home, further ratings of the mother's knowledge of normal development and inventories addressing the quality of *social*, *emotional* and *cognitive stimulation* provided. Various combinations of these measures were repeated as the child became older.

A different research approach is necessary when studying child maltreatment, since parameters of parenting must first be identified, followed by threshold criteria of inadequate care. Cawson *et al*. (2000) investigated the prevalence of child abuse and neglect in the United Kingdom using a retrospective, questionnaire-based method with young adults. Table 1.2 presents an adapted summary of the study's criteria for defining physical abuse, physical neglect, emotional maltreatment and sexual abuse. Physical abuse and neglect were grouped into three categories of severity: 'serious', 'intermediary' and 'cause for concern', while the severity of other types of abuse was usually determined by a cumulative score. Severe physical abuse, for example, was recorded if any identified maltreatment occurred regularly, led to physical effects lasting more than a day, and/or led to physical injury. The authors cautioned that this was not an exhaustive list of maltreatment criteria since, for example, the young adults studied could not be expected to recall accurately physical neglect experienced when an infant.

## Assessments developed in clinical settings

Kumar and Hipwell (1996) reported the Bethlem Mother–Infant Interaction Scale, devised for use in their mother and baby psychiatric unit. In addition to general clinical observations, seven subscales were chosen which described:

*Table 1.2* Modified summary of maltreatment criteria used in a retrospective, questionnaire-based prevalence study by Cawson *et al.* (2000)

**Physical abuse**
Hit with a hard implement
Hit with a fist or kicked hard
Shaken
Thrown/knocked down
Beaten up
Grabbed around the neck and choked
Deliberately burned/scalded
Threatened with a knife or gun

**Physical neglect**
Went hungry because no food in the house/no one got meals ready
No one looked after you/took you to a doctor when ill
Not taken for medical/dental checks
Had to go to school in dirty clothes
Had to look after yourself because parent/s had personal problems or went away
Allowed to go into dangerous situations/places
Physical conditions of the home dangerous
Allowed at home overnight without an adult (before aged 10)
Allowed to stay out overnight without parents knowing whereabouts (before aged 14)
Looked after younger sibling/s while parents out (before aged 12)
Allowed to go to shops without an adult (before aged 10)

**Emotional maltreatment**

*(1) Psychological control and domination*
    Parent unpredictable
    Not allowed freedom of speech
    Not allowed freedom to mix with other people
    Not allowed freedom of thought/belief

*(2) Physical acts of domination*
    Mouth washed out with soap
    Made to miss a meal/go hungry
    Made to eat/drink something to make you sick
    Locked in a room or cupboard
    Shut outside on a cold day
    Always made to do the worst jobs in the house
    Nose rubbed in wet sheets

*(3) Humiliation*
    Regularly made to feel embarrassed
    Humiliated in front of other people
    Regularly shouted/screamed/sworn at
    Regularly called stupid/lazy
    Told was wished dead/never been born

*(4) Withdrawal*
    No demonstrations of affection
    Left out of treats given to others

continued

*Table 1.2* continued

*(5) Antipathy*
Parent obviously disliked/resented you
Parent seemed to want to hurt/upset you deliberately

*(6) Terrorizing*
Was sometimes really afraid of parent
Threatened with being sent away/thrown out

*(7) Proxy attacks*
Physical violence between caretakers
Parent deliberately broke treasured possession
Parent got rid of your pet/had healthy pet put to sleep

**Sexual abuse**
Pornographic photos/videos taken of you
Shown pornographic material
Made to watch other people performing sex acts
Someone exposed their sexual organs to you to shock you or excite themself
Hugged or kissed in a sexual way
Someone touched or fondled your sexual organs
Someone got you to touch their sexual organs to arouse them
Someone put their finger/tongue/an object into your vagina/anus
Someone attempted oral sex/sexual intercourse/anal intercourse with you
You had oral sex/full sexual intercourse/anal intercourse

1   *Eye contact* (e.g. its regularity, associated facial expressions, and responsiveness to the baby's state);
2   *Physical contact* (e.g. its appropriateness and sensitivity to the baby's state);
3   *Vocal contact* (e.g. how initiated, its responsiveness and harmony with the baby);
4   *Mood* (e.g. in the baby's presence, appropriateness to the baby's state);
5   *General routine* (e.g. regularity and reliability, whether it requires external intervention);
6   *Physical risk to the baby* (e.g. carelessness, roughness, declared fears of harming the baby); and
7   *Baby's contribution to the interaction* (e.g. health, alertness, responsiveness, whether 'difficult').

A clinical procedure for assessing parenting was devised by Mrazek *et al.* (1995). The Parenting Risk Scale consisted of a semi-structured Stress and Coping Interview and identified five key dimensions of parenting:

1   *Emotional availability* (degree of emotional warmth);
2   *Control* (degree of flexibility and facilitation);
3   *Psychiatric disturbance* (presence, type and severity);
4   *Knowledge base* (understanding basic child care and development); and
5   *Commitment* (adequate prioritizing of child care responsibilities).

Information was also gathered on:

- the quality of the parents' *marriage*;
- recent *life stressors*;
- the parents' social *support network*;
- the *emotional climate* in the home;
- whether there were *attributions of negative traits* to the child;
- any *inappropriate expectations* of the child;
- evidence of *use of the child to meet the parents' emotional needs*; or
- apparent *lack of support for the child's increasing autonomy*.

The Parent/Child Game (Jenner and McCarthy, 1995) has been another attempt to elicit in the clinical setting elements of successful parenting. By observing struc-tured play sessions, scores are made of the ratio of parental behaviour which is *child-centred* (e.g. praise, attention) to that which is *child-directed* (e.g. commands, criticism). This tool is primarily of use to monitor the effectiveness of behavioural parenting interventions, although some claim has also been made for its con-tribution to assessments in parenting breakdown (Jenner, 1997). Gardner (1997) has warned, however, that parent–child interactions observed in structured or artificial settings may not be representative of those normally taking place at home. There have been other significant clinical strategies for working with families around parenting issues, most notably those developed by Webster-Stratton (e.g. 1991). However, although their efficacy has been well researched, these approaches remain essentially tools for intervening in dysfunctional parenting in a clinical setting, rather than assessing the nature, causes, extent and consequences of parenting breakdown.

## Assessments of parenting breakdown

A number of authors have discussed the assessment of parenting breakdown, including: Steinhauer (1983), Bentovim (Bentovim and Bingley, 1985; Bentovim, 1987; 1998), Sturge (1992), Tufnell (Tufnell, 1993; Tufnell *et al.*, 1996), Glaser (1993), Wolkind (1994), Iwaniec (1995), Herbert (1996), Budd and Holdsworth (1996), Kennedy (1997), Black *et al.* (1998), Sheldrick (1998), Azar (Azar *et al.*, 1995; 1998), Howe *et al.* (1999) and Jones (2001). In addition, Oates (1984), Swadi (1994), Göpfert *et al.* (1996), Jacobsen *et al.* (1997), Henry and Kumar (1999), Jenuwine and Cohler (1999) and Drummond and Fitzpatrick (2000) have focused on the assessment of parenting provided by adults with mental health or substance misuse problems. Reder and Lucey's (1995) *Assessment of Parenting* brought together contributions from psychiatrists and psychologists involved in child care court cases.

A spectrum of styles is represented in these publications. For example, Wolkind (1994) and Sheldrick (1998) emphasized the value of child psychiatrists assessing whether the child shows evidence of a psychiatric disorder and clarifying to the court the possible origins of that disorder within a developmental framework. Bentovim (1987) and Tufnell (1993), on the other hand, reported a modified systemic approach in which interactional processes were highlighted, while Kennedy's (1997) work was based on psychoanalytic principles. Howe *et al.* (1999) advocated using the framework of attachment theory when taking the history of past and current parental functioning, in order to hypothesize the parent's internal working models of self and others. Azar *et al.* (1995; 1998) recommended using a cognitive framework to understand parenting competency.

Nonetheless, all agree that parenting assessments depend on identifying the needs of children, ascertaining whether they are being met, appraising the impact of any identified deficiencies on the child's functioning and development, describing the nature and likely origins of the adult's difficulties in fulfilling their parental roles, and considering whether change is possible. Azar *et al.* (1998) termed this a 'functional–contextual perspective', which demanded a focus on the developmental capacities and needs of a specific child and the 'match' of parental capacity to provide responses within the range of those developmental needs. Azar *et al.*'s main categories of skills required to care for children were:

- *Parenting* (e.g. child management);
- *Social cognitive* (e.g. problem solving);
- *Self-control* (e.g. impulse control);
- *Stress management* (e.g. coping capacities); and
- *Social* (e.g. empathy).

They recommended that the assessment should address factors relating to:

- *The parent*;
- *The child*;
- *Parent–child interaction*; and
- *Systemic issues.*

In order to assess specifically for emotional abuse and neglect, Iwaniec's (1995) approach included completion of an 'event-recording of parent–child-interaction', which covered *the reactive and proactive behaviour of the child* (e.g. playing freely, coming for help, responding to affection), *of the father/mother* (e.g. making eye contact, holding the child, answering the child's questions), and *of the siblings* (e.g. participation in activities). Checks of the *physical care* of the child involved their clothing's appropriateness and cleanliness, hygiene, sleeping arrangements and facilities, safety precautions, and medical attention. Nutritional checks included its adequacy, prioritization and emotional accompaniments.

Budd and Holdsworth (1996), Jacobsen *et al.* (1997), Azar *et al.* (1995; 1998) and Greene and Kilili (1998) have pointed out that many evaluators look for *optimal* parenting abilities, whereas evidence of *minimally adequate* parenting competence should be the more appropriate standard. Iwaniec (1995) and Azar *et al.* (1998) also emphasized the importance of identifying parenting strengths and potential resources as well as weaknesses, together with the parent's capacity to engage in a therapeutic process and work towards change. Even so, there are 'no operational definitions, no quantitative criteria, litmus test, or established assessment strategies to determine whether parenting meets, approximates, or exceeds the minimum in any particular case (Greene and Kilili, 1998: p. 54). Therefore, in order that the many facets of parenting can be encompassed within the assessment and balanced out, we shall propose an overall framework to guide the work.

## A REVISED FRAMEWORK FOR THE ASSESSMENT OF PARENTING

In *Assessment of Parenting*, Reder and Lucey (1995) proposed a framework to guide assessments in child care court cases. It was based on previously published clinical guides, theoretical premises about the essential needs of children and risk factors for child abuse identified through research. The framework consisted of a series of themes for the assessor to consider, although not all of them were likely to be of equal weight in any particular case. It was not intended as a checklist and we did not offer threshold criteria for what might be considered inadequate parenting, for the reasons discussed above. Practitioners reported that they found the framework a valuable guide to their assessments (e.g. Swadi, 1994; Westman, 2000).

Since then, our own practice has suggested the need for some modifications to this framework. In particular, we have revised its main headings so that they are are consistent with those used by Budd and Holdsworth (1996), Belsky and Vondra (1989) and Azar *et al.* (1998). Thus, our themes are now grouped together under: *The Parent (and Parent–Child Relationship)*; *The Child (and Child–Parent Relationship)*; and *The Context (and Family–Context Interaction)*; see Table 1.3. We have also attempted to incorporate the concepts described by others for assessing parenting, as outlined above. Despite the different terms used, it is evident that there is considerable overlap between the themes that have been suggested. In elaborating on this framework, we shall indicate where we have discussed some of the themes in greater detail in other publications, or where they are dealt with more fully in subsequent chapters of this volume.

### The parent (and parent–child relationship)

#### *Personal functioning*

The parent's own childhood *history of being parented* will have laid crucial foundations for their capacity to be a parent and the nature of their *relationships with others*, including partners and other potentially supportive people. Adverse

Table 1.3 A revised framework to guide the assessment of parenting (this should not be used as a checklist, since some factors are more relevant to one case than another)

| Parent (and parent–child relationship) | Child (and child–parent relationship) | Context (and family–context relationship) |
|---|---|---|
| *Personal functioning*<br>Childhood experiences of being parented<br>History of relationships with others<br>Unresolved care/control conflicts, including impulse control<br>Resilience factors<br>Sense of personal agency<br>Sensitivity to relationship stresses<br>Psychological mindedness<br>Potential for change<br>Mental health problems | *Evidence of significant harm*<br>Harm to physical and emotional well-being<br>Harm to physical, emotional, cognitive, social, moral and sexual development<br>Resilience factors | *Family functioning*<br>Discord or violence between parental couple<br>Child's involvement in discordant family relationships<br>Executive effectiveness<br>Tolerance of transitional stresses |
| *Relationship to the parenting role*<br>Provision of basic physical care<br>Provision of age-appropriate emotional care<br>Provision for behavioural needs<br>Knowledge of, and attitude to, the tasks of parenting<br>Commitment to the parenting role<br>Age appropriate expectations of child<br>Approaches to discipline<br>Acceptance of responsibility for own parenting behaviour | *Contribution to the parenting relationship*<br>Temperament<br>Activity<br>Illness or disability<br>Emotional or behavioural problems<br>Rejection or testing out of parental figure's commitment<br>Trigger for parent's emotional crisis | *Social stresses*<br>Poverty, unemployment, isolation, discrimination, or geographical dislocation<br>Repertoire of responses to social stresses<br><br>*Potential for stability*<br>Partner relationships<br>Accommodation |
| *Relationship with the child*<br>Feelings towards child<br>The meaning of the child<br>Interest in child's well-being and experiences<br>Capacity for empathy with child, including identifying with the child's experiences<br>Child's essential needs recognized and given primacy<br>Child viewed as person in own right | *Attitude to parental figures*<br>Feelings and behaviour towards parental figures<br>Descriptions of experiences<br>Conflicts<br>Wishes for future<br><br>*Sufficient understanding*<br>Age<br>Cognitive development<br>Complexity of the issues<br>Influence of personal and interpersonal conflict | *Relationships with others*<br>Relationship with extended family<br>Integration in community<br>Willingness to cooperate with professionals<br>Preparedness to utilize interventions offered<br>Ownership of personal contribution to evolution of relationships with others |

experiences of being cared for when a child, such as abuse or severe rejection, may lead to *unresolved care and control conflicts* (see Reder and Duncan, Chapter 12) in which the person grows up with conflicts about closeness to others and reliance on them, or about feeling controlled by others and capacity for self-control. These become manifest in adult life as, for example, unstable partnerships in which each threatens to leave the other or frequently does so, excessive dependency on other people or agencies, a suspiciousness that other people are trying to control them, a determination to control partners, or poor impulse control and a proneness to erupt into violence. These characteristics clearly have implications for child care as well as parental partnerships.

However, not everyone who has experienced maltreatment in childhood will develop such problematic behaviours (Friedman and Chase-Lansdale, 2002; Reder and Duncan, 2000; Reder, Chapter 13) and there may be evidence of *resilience factors*. The most important of these are: a history of support from a significant adult (such as a non-abusing parent, a partner, or a therapist); areas of success in personal functioning (such as at school or in sport); readiness to recall adverse childhood experiences; and recognition of the link between the way they were parented and how they in turn function as a parent. Resilience factors are likely to provide the person with a sense of *personal agency*, in which they feel they have control over their life and a *capacity to tolerate relationship stresses*. They may also be relevant to the person's capacity to use professional interventions and their *potential to change* problematic parenting and relationships.

Concrete thinking or proneness to act without thought can impede parenting. *Psychological mindedness* refers to a person's capacity to appreciate that relationships involve personal feelings and have meanings for all those involved. This includes some capacity to reflect on motivation for behaviour, to weigh up different aspects of a psychological conflict, to tolerate feelings, to judge another person's character, and to think ahead and imagine what life might be like if certain events occurred. It clearly has relevance for the parent's capacity to use 'understanding' therapy, but also more generally for their capacity to empathize with their child, understand the child's mental states, and help the child link thoughts and feelings, in what Fonagy (2001) referred to as developing 'a mentalizing capacity', an important component of secure attachment.

A parent's personal functioning can also be affected by *mental health problems*, including substance misuse. They particularly impact on children through changes in the parent's behaviour and the family atmosphere (see Duncan and Reder, Chapter 11).

### Relationship to the parenting role

The history of concerns about child care will indicate the degree to which the parent has anticipated and consistently *satisfied the child's age-appropriate physical, emotional and behavioural needs* – see Table 1.4 (adapted from Kelmer Pringle, 1978; 1986; Department of Health, 2000a; Duncan and Reder, 2000). This is likely to relate to the parent's *knowledge of the tasks of parenting* (such as appropriate feeding regimes for a baby) and *attitude to them* (for instance, whether the tasks are considered a chore), so that an overall *commitment to the parenting role* is important. The parent's attitude also includes whether they have *age-appropriate expectations* of the child's physical, emotional and cognitive development (such as sphincter control, frustration tolerance and understanding of right and wrong). Parents have various opportunities to acquire such child care knowledge, most especially from their own experiences of being parented but also from other relatives, friends and professional advisors. One feature that deserves highlighting is the parent's *approach to discipline* and limit setting, since physical chastisement is considered to be physically abusive, threats of extreme punishment to be emotionally abusive and lack of limit setting to be neglectful. Parents also need to *accept responsibility for their parenting behaviour* by acknowledging any problems observed by others, owning responsibility for the part they have played in them rather than blaming others, and not expecting the child to be responsible for their own care or protection.

### Relationship with the child

The parent's emotional relationship with the child includes their *feelings towards the child*, both positive and negative, together with acknowledgement of the basis for those feelings, since they might be displaced from another relationship. The parent's feelings may be influenced by *the meaning of the child* (Reder *et al.*, 1993; Reder and Duncan, 1995), which reflects how the child holds a special psychological significance for their parent because they are, consciously or unconsciously, associated with other key figures or conflictual events. Examples might be the child whose birth coincided with the loss of a close family member, whose characteristics remind the parent of another person, whose conception was unwanted, or who is expected to love the parent in order to compensate for emotional traumas from the

*Table 1.4* The essential needs of children

| Physical | Behavioural | Emotional |
|---|---|---|
| Nutrition | Stimulation/interaction | Affection/empathy |
| Warmth/shelter | Exploration/learning | Availability |
| Health/cleanliness | Socialization/role model | Consistency |
| Safety | Limit-setting/self-control | Reality testing |
| Contact/comfort | Rest | Building of self-esteem |
| | | Attachment/autonomy |
| | | Individual identity |
| | | Advocacy |
| | | Adaptation to change |
| | | Containment of feelings |

*Source*: Adapted from Kelmer Pringle (1978; 1986), Department of Health *et al.* (2000), Duncan and Reder (2000).

past. Some meanings can dominate the parent–child relationship and be associated with maltreatment, such as if a difficult birth left the mother feeling helpless and damaged by the baby, or when the parent perceives the child as failing to make up for emotional deficiencies in their life.

Parents also need to demonstrate a genuine *interest in the child's well-being and experiences* and a *capacity for empathy with the child*, in which they are able to put themself in the child's place and appreciate how the child experiences events. The parent must *recognize the child's essential needs* and *give them primacy* over their own personal wants (such as sacrificing a night out if there is no available baby sitter, or separating from a partner who has abused the child). In order to do this, the parent must *view the child as a person in their own right*, who has different needs, emotions, experiences and expectations from them.

## The child (and child–parent relationship)

### Evidence of significant harm

Adverse parenting may affect all domains of a child's *physical and emotional well-being* and assessment will need to consider the following developmental lines: *physical*; *emotional*; *cognitive*; *social*; *moral*; and *sexual* (Fitzpatrick *et al.*, 1995; Duncan and Baker, Chapter 5). Since children are affected differently by emotional trauma *resilience* factors should also be identified, especially the influence of a supportive adult, areas of success in their life, their self-esteem and their capacity to make sense of experiences (Reder and Duncan, 2000).

### Contribution to the parenting relationship

Assessors must acknowledge that some children are harder to parent than others by virtue of a fractious *temperament*, high *activity* levels, *illness* or *disability*, or some other personal characteristic. However, the task of parenting is to accommodate to such variations. Children who have previously experienced abuse or rejection may be especially difficult to care for because of *emotional or behavioural problems*, *rejection* of parental figures, or because they relentlessly *test out the commitment* of substitute parents towards them. Furthermore, disclosure of a crisis in the child's life (such as sexual abuse) may *trigger an emotional crisis* for their parent, such as a mother who has never previously disclosed that she, too, was sexually abused at a similar age (Reder and Lucey, 2000).

### Attitude to parental figures

The child's attitude to adults who have carried parental responsibilities towards them is a crucial component of the assessment, since it encapsulates the principle that parenting must be considered from the child's perspective. The child's attitude includes not only their declared *feelings* about those figures but also their observable *behaviour* in their presence, such as willingness to engage in conversation or play with them, readiness to turn to them for support, sense of trust in them, or fear, anger, or indifference towards them. Children's *accounts of their family and caretaking experiences* should generally be considered as valid and reliable (see Westcott and Jones, Chapter 6). However, it will also be necessary to ascertain whether they have been coerced into expressing a particular view or whether they are struggling with loyalty or other *conflicts* about a parental figure. Children should be asked about their *wishes for the future* and their views balanced against their capacity to understand the issues and their implications (see below).

### Sufficient understanding

The concept of sufficient understanding describes a young person's capacity to comprehend and reach informed and rational judgements about issues which affect them. This is partially a function of their chronological *age* but also depends on their level of *cognitive development*, the *complexity of the issues*, and the influence of associated *personal and interpersonal conflicts* (Reder and Fitzpatrick, 1998; Reder and Duncan, Chapter 7).

## The context (and family–context interaction)

### Family functioning

Family relationships are the immediate context for the child's experiences. The most significant aspects of family functioning which adversely affect children's welfare are: the degree of *discord or violence* between the parental couple (see Sturge, Chapter 10); whether the *child is caught up in discordant family relationships*, such as each parent soliciting for their loyalty (see Lucey *et al.*, Chapter 15); the *executive effectiveness* of the parent/s, in which everyday tasks are carried out and necessary decisions made – by mutual consensus if there is a parental couple; and the family's *tolerance of transitional stresses*, such as when members leave or enter it.

### Social stresses

Social stresses are well recognized as reducing parents' tolerance of relationship tensions, including between them and their child. Common factors include poverty, unemployment, isolation from the community, discrimination and geographical dislocation (see Maitra, Chapter 3). In addition, it is necessary to consider the parent's coping mechanisms and *repertoire of responses* to such stresses.

### Potential for stability

While it is important to assess the parent's capacity to change their problematic behaviour, as discussed above, their ability to provide the child with sufficient stability is equally relevant. The most significant areas are stable partner relationships, which offer the possibility of continuity of care, and reliable living circumstances, which provide security of accommodation, rather than relentless geographical mobility from one community to another.

### Relationships with others

The nature of a parent's *relationship with their extended family*, especially their own parents, is significant. A positive relationship enables them to avoid social isolation and receive help and support with parenting tasks, while unresolved conflicts between them are likely to impinge on the parent's interactions with their own children (see Reder and Duncan, Chapter 12). *Integration in the community* is also relevant for the availability of practical and emotional support. The family's genuine *willingness to cooperate with professionals* and *preparedness and ability to utilize interventions* offered to them indicates whether change is possible and whether monitoring of the child will be permitted. A positive sign is if the parents *accept ownership of the part they have played in the evolution of relationships* with others, rather than repeatedly blame everyone else for any problems that have occurred (see Bentovim, Chapter 14).

## USING THE FRAMEWORK

It has been necessary to separate out each factor in order to present this framework. However, it should be apparent that there is considerable interrelationship between the various elements. For example, the functioning of the family as a unit is significantly determined by the personal functioning of constituent parental figures, while a parent's willingness to cooperate with professionals has a considerable bearing on their potential for change.

It is important to re-emphasize that this scheme is *not* intended to constitute a checklist which assessors run through exhaustively during the interviews and then use to comment on each item in turn in their report. As in other clinical settings, the assessment process should be flexible and tailored to the specific circumstances of the case, so that the assessor progressively selects from a more comprehensive spectrum of factors those that appear to be most relevant to the family in question and their problems. The assessment should therefore be dynamic in the sense that information may emerge during its course which suggests that additional factors need addressing. Hence, the scheme is meant first to identify a set of factors that are particularly relevant to parenting in general and to parenting breakdown in particular. Second, the scheme attempts to collate these through an interactional framework. In practice, certain factors will emerge as much more relevant than others for detailed scrutiny in a particular case, depending on the nature of the problems and the family's history, while some factors will have a different significance for families from dissimilar cultural backgrounds. As Azar *et al.* (1995;

1998) stressed, parenting assessments should focus on whether there is a minimally adequate match between the developmental needs of a specific child and the parental capacities to provide responses within the range of those developmental needs taking into account the family's circumstances. Hence, the selection of most relevant factors and the appropriate balance between them is guided by the central assessment aims, which are: to represent a specific child's experiences; to describe the functioning of that child's particular family; and to provide an opinion as to how the child's life might be improved.

It is evident from the framework that we primarily take an interactional perspective when approaching parenting assessments in child care cases. For instance, any diagnostic formulations about the child's or the parent's mental state are not considered to be the *conclusions* of the assessment but *preludes* to a fuller consideration of the origins of these difficulties, an understanding of their connection to emotional and relationship conflicts, and their impact on others in the family. Furthermore, we are not relying merely on a snapshot of current behaviour and functioning as reflected in a relatively small number of interviews but are integrating information from a variety of sources (see Reder, Duncan and Lucey, Chapter 2).

## CONCLUSIONS

Parenting assessments in family proceedings under the 1989 Children Act (or its equivalent in other parts of the United Kingdom) are detailed appraisals of a parent's capacity to care for their child. The assessment process is complex and addresses a range of dimensions of the adult's functioning, including their past and current behaviour, influences from the past on their psychological make-up and ways of relating to others and their relationship with their child. Their living context must also be addressed, especially the current support networks and relationship with partner/s, while the child's perspective is an essential further consideration. No single dimension, taken in isolation, adequately describes someone's current functioning as a parent or predicts their future capacities. The assessment must balance positive and negative aspects and address whether change is possible in the future. The decisions the court will make about the child's future care will have a critical impact on the rest of their lives and it is an onerous responsibility on experts to provide balanced, informed, reasoned and careful advice to assist the court in their task.

In the next chapter, we go on to discuss how these principles can be translated into practice.

## References

Azar, S.T., Benjet, C.L., Fuhrmann, G.S. and Cavallero, L. (1995) Child maltreatment and termination of parental rights: can behavioral research help Solomon? *Behavior Therapy* 26: 599–623.

Azar, S.T., Lauretti, A.F. and Loding, B.V. (1998) The evaluation of parental fitness in termination of parental rights cases: a functional-contextual perspective, *Clinical Child & Family Psychology Review* 1: 77–100.

Belsky, J. and Vondra, J. (1989) Lessons from child abuse: the determinants of parenting, in D. Cicchetti and V. Carlson (eds) *Child Maltreatment: Theory and Research on the Causes and Consequences of Child Abuse and Neglect*, Cambridge: Cambridge University Press.

Bentovim, A. (1987) A family therapy approach to making decisions in child care cases, in A. Bentovim, G. Gorell Barnes and A. Cooklin (eds) *Family Therapy: Complementary Frameworks of Theory and Practice*, London: Academic Press.

Bentovim, A. (1998) Significant harm in context, in M. Adcock and R. White (eds) *Significant Harm: Its Management and Outcome*, 2nd ed., Croydon: Significant Publications.

Bentovim, A. and Bingley, L. (1985) Parenting and parenting failure: some guidelines for the assessment of the child, his parents and the family, in M. Adcock and R. White (eds) *Good-Enough Parenting: A Framework for Assessment*, London: British Agencies for Adoption and Fostering.

Black, D., Harris Hendriks, J. and Wolkind, S. (eds) (1998) *Child Psychiatry and the Law*, 3rd ed., London: Gaskell.

Budd, K.S. and Holdsworth, M.J. (1996) Issues in clinical assessment of minimal parenting competence, *Journal of Clinical Child Psychology* 25: 2–14.

Cawson, P., Wattam, C., Brooker, S. and Kelly G. (2000) *Child Maltreatment in the United Kingdom: A Study of Prevalence of Child Abuse and Neglect*, London: NSPCC.

Department of Health (2000a) *Framework for the Assessment of Children in Need and their Families: Practice Guidance*, London: The Stationery Office.

Department of Health (2000b) *Protecting Children, Supporting Parents: A Consultation Document on the Physical Punishment of Children*, London: Department of Health.

Department of Health, Department for Education and Employment and Home Office (2000) *Framework for the Assessment of Children in Need and their Families*, London: The Stationery Office.

Dingwall, R., Eekelaar, J.M. and Murray, T. (1983) *The Protection of Children: State Intervention and Family Life*, Oxford: Blackwell.

Dowdney, L., Skuse, D., Rutter, M. and Mrazek, D. (1985) Parenting qualities: concepts, measures and origins, in J.E. Stevenson (ed.) *Recent Research in Developmental Psychopathology*, Oxford: Pergamon.

Drummond, D.C. and Fitzpatrick, G. (2000) Children of substance misusing parents, in P. Reder, M. McClure and A. Jolley (eds) *Family Matters: Interfaces Between Child and Adult Mental Health*, London: Routledge.

Duncan, S. and Reder, P. (2000) Children's experiences of major psychiatric disorder in their parents: an overview, in P. Reder, M. McClure and A. Jolley (eds) *Family Matters: Interfaces Between Child and Adult Mental Health*, London: Routledge.

Fitzpatrick, G., Reder, P. and Lucey, C. (1995) The child's perspective, in P. Reder and C. Lucey (eds) *Assessment of Parenting: Psychiatric and Psychological Contributions*, London: Routledge.

Fonagy, P. (2001) *Attachment Theory and Psychoanalysis*, New York: Other Press.

Friedman, R.J. and Chase-Lansdale, P.L. (2002) Chronic adversities, in M. Rutter and E. Taylor (eds) *Child and Adolescent Psychiatry*, 4th ed., Oxford: Blackwell Science.

Gardner, F. (1997) Observational methods for recording parent–child interaction: how generalisable are the findings? *Child Psychology & Psychiatry Review* 2: 70–4.

Glaser, D. (1993) Emotional abuse, in C.J. Hobbs and J.M. Wynne (eds) *Clinical Paediatrics: International Practice and Research, Volume 1, Number 1: Child Abuse*, London: Baillière Tindall.

Goldstein, J., Freud, A. and Solnit, A.J. (1973) *Beyond the Best Interests of the Child*, New York: The Free Press.

Golombok, S. (2000) *Parenting. What Really Counts?* London: Routledge.

Göpfert, M., Webster, J., Pollard, J. and Nelki, J.S. (1996) The assessment and prediction of parenting capacity: a community-oriented approach, in M. Göpfert, J. Webster and M.V. Seeman (eds) *Parental Psychiatric Disorder: Distressed Parents and their Families*, Cambridge: Cambridge University Press.

Gray, J. (2001) The Framework for the Assessment of Children in Need and their Families, *Child Psychology & Psychiatry Review* 6: 4–10.

Greene, B.F. and Kilili, S. (1998) How good does a parent have to be? Issues and examples associated with empirical assessments of parenting adequacy in cases of child abuse and neglect, in J.R. Lutzker (ed.) *Handbook of Child Abuse Research and Treatment*, New York: Plenum.

Henry, L.A. and Kumar, R.C. (1999) Risk assessments of infants born to parents with a mental health problem or a learning disability, in A. Weir and A. Douglas (eds) *Child Protection & Adult Mental Health: Conflict of Interest?* Oxford: Butterworth-Heinemann.

Herbert, M. (1996) *Assessing Children in Need and their Parents*, Leicester: BPS Books.

Hoghughi, M. (1997) Parenting at the margins: some consequences of inequality, in K.N. Dwivedi (ed.) *Enhancing Parenting Skills. A Guide Book for Professionals Working with Parents*, Chichester: Wiley.

Horwath, J. (ed.) (2001) *The Child's World: Assessing Children in Need*, London: Jessica Kingsley.

Howe, D., Brandon, M., Hinings, D. and Schofield, G. (1999) *Attachment Theory, Child Maltreatment and Family Support: A Practice and Assessment Model*, Basingstoke: Macmillan.

Iwaniec, D. (1995) Assessing emotional abuse and neglect, in *The Emotionally Abused and Neglected Child: Identification, Assessment and Intervention*, Chichester: Wiley.

Jacobsen, T., Miller, L.J. and Pesek Kirkwood, K. (1997) Assessing parenting competence in individuals with severe mental illness: a comprehensive service, *Journal of Mental Health Administration* 24: 189–9.

Jenner, S. (1997) Assessment of parenting in the context of child protection using the Parent/Child Game, *Child Psychology & Psychiatry Review* 2: 58–62.

Jenner, S. and McCarthy, G. (1995) Quantitative measures of parenting: a clinical-developmental perspective, in P. Reder and C. Lucey (eds) *Assessment of Parenting: Psychiatric and Psychiological Contributions*, London: Routledge.

Jenuwine, M.J. and Cohler, B.J. (1999) Major parental psychopathology and child custody, in R.M. Galatzer-Levy and L. Kraus (eds) *The Scientific Basis of Child Custody Decisions*, New York: John Wiley.

Jones, D. (2001) The assessment of parental capacity, in J. Horwath (ed.) *The Child's World: Assessing Children in Need*, London: Jessica Kingsley.

Kelmer Pringle, M. (1978) The needs of children, in S.M. Smith (ed.) *The Maltreatment of Children*, Lancaster: MTP Press.

Kelmer Pringle, M. (1986) *The Needs of Children: A Personal Perspective*, London: Routledge.

Kennedy, R. (1997) Assessment of parenting, in *Child Abuse, Psychotherapy and the Law*, London: Free Association Books.

Kumar, R. and Hipwell, A.E. (1996) Development of a clinical rating scale to assess mother–infant interaction in a psychiatric mother and baby unit, *British Journal of Psychiatry* 169: 18–26.

Larzelere, R.E. (1996) A review of outcomes of parental use of nonabusive or customary physical punishment, *Pediatrics* 98: 824–8.

Larzelere, R.E. (2000) Child discipline: weak evidence for a smacking ban (letter), *British Medical Journal* 320: 1538–9.

Mrazek, D.A., Mrazek, P. and Klinnert, M. (1995) Clinical assessment of parenting, *Journal of the American Academy of Child & Adolescent Psychiatry* 34: 272–82.

Oates, M. (1984) Assessing fitness to parent, in *Taking a Stand: Child Psychiatrists in Custody, Access and Disputed Adoption Cases*, London: British Agencies for Adoption and Fostering.

Pianta, R., Egeland, B. and Erickson, M.F. (1989) The antecedents of maltreatment: results of the Mother–Child Interaction Research Project, in D. Cicchetti and V. Carlson (eds) *Child Maltreatment: Theory and Research on the Causes and Consequences of Child Abuse and Neglect*, Cambridge: Cambridge University Press.

Quinton, D. and Rutter, M. (1988) *Parenting Breakdown: The Making and Breaking of Inter-generational Links*, Aldershot: Avebury.

Reder, P. and Duncan, S. (1995) The meaning of the child, in P. Reder and C. Lucey (eds) *Assessment of Parenting: Psychiatric and Psychological Contributions*, London: Routledge.

Reder, P. and Duncan, S. (1999) *Lost Innocents: A Follow-up Study of Fatal Child Abuse*, London: Routledge.

Reder, P. and Duncan, S. (2000) Abuse then and now, in P. Reder, M. McClure and A. Jolley (eds) *Family Matters: Interfaces Between Child and Adult Mental Health*, London: Routledge.

Reder, P., Duncan, S. and Gray, M. (1993) *Beyond Blame: Child Abuse Tragedies Revisited*, London: Routledge.

Reder, P. and Fitzpatrick, S. (1998) What is sufficient understanding? *Clinical Child Psychology and Psychiatry* 3: 103–13.

Reder, P. and Lucey, C. (eds) (1995) *Assessment of Parenting: Psychiatric and Psychological Contributions*, London: Routledge.

Reder, P. and Lucey, C. (2000) The impact of children on their parents, in P. Reder, M. McClure and A. Jolley (eds) *Family Matters: Interfaces Between Child and Adult Mental Health*, London: Routledge.

Roberts, J.V. (2000) Changing public attitudes towards corporal punishment: the effects of statutory reform in Sweden, *Child Abuse & Neglect* 24: 1027–35.

Schaffer, H.R. (1998) *Making Decisions about Children*, 2nd ed., Oxford: Blackwell.

Sheldrick, C. (1998) Child psychiatrists in court: their contribution as experts in child care proceedings, *Journal of Forensic Psychiatry* 9: 249–66.

Steinhauer, P.D. (1983) Assessing for parenting capacity, *American Journal of Orthopsychiatry* 53: 468–81.

Sturge, C. (1992) Dealing with the courts and parenting breakdown, *Archives of Disease in Childhood* 67: 745–50.

Swadi, H. (1994) Parenting capacity and substance misuse: an assessment scheme, *ACPP Review & Newsletter* 16: 237–44.

Trumbull, D.A. (2000) Child discipline: parents need techniques for behavioural control (letter), *British Medical Journal* 320: 1539.

Tufnell, G. (1993) Judgements of Solomon: the relevance of a systems approach to psychiatric court reports in child care cases, *Journal of Family Therapy* 15: 413–32.

Tufnell, G., Cottrell, D. and Georgiades, (1996) 'Good practice' for expert witnesses, *Clinical Child Psychology & Psychiatry* 1: 365–83.

Tyler, R., Howard, J., Espinosa, M. and Simpson Doakes, S. (1997) Placement with substance-abusing mothers vs. placement with other relatives: infant outcomes, *Child Abuse & Neglect* 21: 337–49.

Waterston, T. (2000a) Giving guidance on child discipline: physical punishment works no better than other methods and has adverse effects, *British Medical Journal* 320: 261–2.

Waterston, T. (2000b) Child discipline: author's reply (letter), *British Medical Journal* 320: 1540.

Webster-Stratton, C. (1991) Strategies for helping families with conduct disordered children, *Journal of Child Psychology & Psychiatry* 32: 1047–62.

Westman, A. (2000) The problem of parental personality, in P. Reder, M. McClure and A. Jolley (eds) *Family Matters: Interfaces Between Child and Adult Mental Health*, London: Routledge.

Wolkind, S. (1994) Legal aspects of child care, in M. Rutter, E. Taylor and L. Hersov (eds) *Child and Adolescent Psychiatry: Modern Approaches*, 3rd ed., Oxford: Blackwell.

## Chapter 2

# How are assessments conducted for family proceedings?

*Peter Reder, Sylvia Duncan and Clare Lucey*

Much has already been written about the practice of court work, including invaluable advice to expert witnesses from lawyers, judges and mental health professionals (e.g. Carson, 1990; Expert Witness Group, 1997; Black *et al.*, 1998; White, 1998; Wall, 2000; Taylor, 2000; Myers and Stern, 2002), recommendations about preparing court reports (e.g. Tufnell, 1993; Tufnell *et al.*, 1996) and reflections on cross-examination (e.g. Reder *et al.*, 1993; Henderson, 2002; Manarin, 2002). It is not our intention to reprise the issues taken up in these publications. Instead, this chapter will address how experts might understand their relationship to the legal process and, in the light of that, conduct assessments and formulate opinions that are helpful to the court.

While many different professionals may be required to offer opinions in complex child care cases – such as social workers, children's guardians, paediatricians and pathologists – for the purposes of this chapter we shall focus the discussion on our own professions of psychology and psychiatry. The world of 'mental health', perhaps more than any other, can appear to be very discrepant from that of 'the law' and these differences may generate considerable discomfort for those who do not appreciate them. Therefore, before discussing practical aspects of parenting assessments, we shall offer some thoughts about the context of this work, in which two apparently different worlds come together in order to consider the welfare of a child.

## THE CONTEXT OF FAMILY PROCEEDINGS

Mental health professionals who are new to court work almost invariably find the experience disorienting, emotionally draining and intellectually debilitating. However much advice they may have received previously, they are unprepared for the unfamiliarity of the world which they have entered, with its unique traditions, language, communication styles, preoccupations and procedures, let alone the unusual physical layout of the buildings and the rooms (see Minuchin, 1984; King and Trowell, 1992; Etchegoyen and Adams, 1998). Similarly, a barrister making a professional visit to a psychiatric hospital or having the opportunity to observe a child psychotherapy session might be equally confused by the customs, language and beliefs on display. While there are many obvious differences between the two systems of 'the law' and 'mental health', the initial disorientation that accompanies representatives of either one experiencing the other masks important areas of similarity. Indeed, we shall argue that customary descriptions of the two systems represent over-generalized caricatures and that each system readily accommodates to the other in the common aim of child welfare.

## The world of 'the law'

The legal system can be characterized as pursuing the resolution of dichotomies, in the sense that courts must decide between two alternative options – such as whether a defendant is guilty or not guilty, whether certain evidence is admissible or not admissible, whether an application for an Order under the Children Act should be granted or refused. In resolving such dilemmas, it relies on the principle that 'truth' will emerge from the balancing of dichotomous propositions. Blom-Cooper wrote (Inquiry Report, 1987) of the fundamental legal premise 'based in part on the fundamental dialectical approach that the truth will most likely emerge if each interested party is allowed to put his or her own case, from their own perspective. Truth will emerge, so it is claimed, from the opposing thesis and antithesis' (p. 8). Through adversarial debate, opposing arguments, or versions of events, are presented to the judge (or jury in criminal proceedings), who will determine which one is valid. The court therefore concerns itself with opposing explanations and the possible evidence for each one.

In order to maintain impartiality, each piece of evidence is open to examination from one party's perspective and cross-examination from the perspective of other parties. Because of the importance of the matters before them, courts allow for erudite advocates to represent the opposing parties' arguments and formalize the proceedings so that each is given fair opportunity. Since each element of the propositions and counter-propositions is open to scrutiny, advocates prefer to be able to present scrupulously recorded detail and unequivocal knowledge. They develop their arguments by dissecting issues into categories and focusing down on minutiae in an apparently fragmentary fashion, simplifying explanations to the association between a minimal number of factors.

These adversarial formalities as a means of resolving dichotomies lead many to view the world of 'the law' as being reductionist, concerned with 'facts' and precision and promoting the belief that a single truth can be discovered if the searches are sufficiently rigorous. In atmosphere, they experience it as rule bound, hierarchical and intolerant of ambiguity.

## The world of 'mental health'

King and Trowell (1992) have pointed out that psychiatry and psychology are neither exact sciences nor capable of accurately predicting outcomes and the world of mental health is often criticised for being imprecise, over-thoughtful and indecisive, riddled with unsubstantiated theories, lacking a good evidence base and falling prey to personal opinions and guesswork (see Schaffer, 1998). One problem is that psychological explanations for human behaviour and difficulties have been informed by numerous different theoretical frameworks – behavioural, systemic, psychoanalytic, cognitive, attachment, group processes, and so on – some of which exist more in the domain of metaphor than demonstrable validity. Passionate devotees of each of the different models can be found and it may be a lottery as to which explanation for a problem is forthcoming.

For instance, there is a philosophy held by a number of mental health professionals that 'truth' does not exist and that each individual's understanding of the world is a unique personal construction (e.g. Burr, 1995; Boscolo and Bertrando, 1996). Hence, it is necessary to believe in individually valid versions of experience and multiple 'truths'. Furthermore, since phenomena are multi-determined and our knowledge keeps changing, current understanding about an issue is best seen from this perspective as a punctuation in time, an explanation that is more or less useful for now but is likely to need reviewing and future modification. In any case, people exist in relationship with others and therefore the behaviour of individuals must be considered in the context in which it occurs. This contextual focus means that notions of unilateral causality (i.e. that one person in isolation has caused an event) are deemed invalid.

Nonetheless, most practitioners would acknowledge that psychological problems are multi-determined, with varying possible contributions from inheritance, experience, internal mental processes and interpersonal relationships and it can be extremely difficult to disentangle the relative contributions of each. It is considered necessary to integrate information from multiple sources, especially about an individual's past and their current functioning, in order to reach a tentative formulation about the nature and origins of their problems. However, since any one of the contributory factors may change over time, it is usually considered wise not to offer hard-and-fast predictions for the future.

Because the world of mental health also includes the world of 'therapy', its ethos may appear to many outsiders as ultra-democratic, overinclusive and integrationist, with excessive tolerance of complexity and uncertainty, an inability to define anything simply because of assumptions that everything is interdependent, and governed by unlimited curiosity.

## Convergence between 'the law' and 'mental health' in pursuit of child welfare

Are these portrayals of the world of 'the law' and mental health' valid? Probably less so than might at first appear. The law, contrary to popular belief, can be remarkably imprecise. For example, how often do NHS staff request clear guidance from their Trust's legal advisor about a complex clinical matter, only to be told that the law is equivocal and open to various interpretations? Similarly, the notion of 'significant harm' was introduced with the Children Act and so could be considered a legal, rather than a psychological, term. Yet the definition and parameters of 'significant' remain stubbornly elusive. Within mental health systems, on the other hand, reductionist philosophies appear to have become the most prevalent. For example, there is now a preoccupation with evidence-based practice, which advocates that only interventions which have been subjected to formal statistical research and which can demonstrate measurably beneficial outcomes should be selected. Many general psychiatrists and some child psychiatrists (see Angold, 2002) focus their attention on diagnostic precision, so that their assessment histories elicit facts rather than experiences and their formulations emphasize descriptions rather than explanations.

The second question is whether the two worlds are really so discrepant. The answer is that in the field of child welfare, each system continues to learn from and adapt to the other and there are many areas of convergence. For instance, it was overzealous pursuit of a diagnosis (of child sexual abuse) that contributed to events culminating in the Cleveland Inquiry. It required the intervention of a judge, Butler-Sloss (1988), as chair of the inquiry, to remind all practitioners that no single test is 'diagnostic' of sexual abuse and that their interviewing style with children should be open-minded rather than determined to discover what they believe to be the truth. In family proceedings, opinions from mental health experts are often considered to be critical contributions to the court (Wall, 2000) and some judges value psychoanalytic and allied frameworks, seeing them as a means of understanding unconscious and developmental processes (Wall, 1997). In general, family courts are equally concerned with attributing meaning to events being described and recognizing children as thinking, feeling and immature persons.

When it comes to mental health assessments, we would suggest that professionals adopt a mind-set that is complementary to the one that underpins the legal profession. We found ourselves using exactly the same Socratic philosophy described by Blom-Cooper (Inquiry Report, 1987) to describe a 'dialectic mind-set' that should underpin all assessments (Reder and Duncan, 1999; 2000), including those of parenting ability. The only difference is that the aim is to arrive not at 'the truth' but a closer understanding of the problem – see Figure 2.1. The process is seen as a continuous one in which different hypotheses about the available information are compared, out of which a synthesis – or a 'best fit so far' – emerges. This will be compared with additional hypotheses that are constructed as the result of further information becoming available (e.g. through the assessment), so that the meaning attributed to the accumulating information is refined or changed. The assessment also requires criteria against which to compare findings and to weigh up whether a critical threshold of concern has been reached. The action or intervention which follows must then must be monitored against criteria of failure and success. Reference to literature containing theoretical frameworks, research findings or practical experiences informs the process at each stage.

Sturge (1992), Azar et al. (1995) and Sheldrick (1998) have therefore identified the following aspects of child mental health professionals' expertise that are

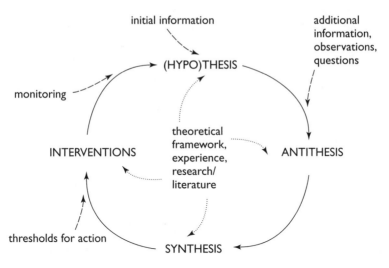

*Figure 2.1* Assessment within a dialectic mind-set

*Source*: Reder and Duncan (1999).

especially beneficial in court work. First, their training is scientifically based and grounded in the philosophy of hypothesis-testing, systematic inquiry, drawing inferences from available information and making use of research evidence. Second, they are conversant with normal and abnormal development and the factors which contribute to them, as well as with the nature of relationships and interactional processes. Third, they are well placed to consider the impact of events on the immature and developing child and to represent the young person's perspective on events. Fourth, they are skilled at talking with children and with their parents and making sense of what they say. Fifth, they are trained to assess for, and to provide, a range of therapeutic interventions relevant to children's welfare and parenting effectiveness.

## MENTAL HEALTH EXPERTS IN FAMILY PROCEEDINGS

How, then, can mental health professionals capitalize on this expertise while also accommodating appropriately to the legal system? They principally need to recognize that the ultimate concern of all professionals involved in family proceedings is to secure an optimal outcome for the child in question, even though the court's rituals will shape how this is decided and the different lawyers will be arguing that this is best achieved by satisfying the claims of their respective clients. They must remain aware that their task is to advise the court and help it reach a judgment. Therefore, their clinical role at this stage is limited to assessment and not to provision of therapeutic help to the family. They must accept that they are not 'in control' of the case, cannot determine its outcome, their opinion may or may not be accepted and their aim is not to 'win' the case.

Mental health professionals should also expect to make modest adjustments to their customary role and practices in order to engage successfully in court work. The request for their involvement will have come through a letter of instruction, which outlines the help required by the court and represents a different form of contract from that implicit in everyday NHS or private referrals. The letter spells out in detail the specific questions being posed and what range of interviews has been agreed. It is then for the expert to finalize their contract with the instructing solicitor, such as how the fees will be paid, and, if necessary, to negotiate which questions are reasonable for them to address and lie within their area of expertise. This agreement must then be adhered to.

Another area of difference from everyday clinical practice is the need to keep more detailed records of all information pertinent to the case. For example, full notes of interviews and any telephone conversations will be necessary, especially the exact words used in statements which might need to be quoted verbatim in the final report. Therefore, unlike interviews in other contexts, records should be contemporaneous – i.e. written during the conversation. Accurate starting and ending times of interviews may need to be reported during cross-examination, and secretaries will need to record carefully all communications outside the meetings, such as reasons given for failure to attend an appointment. It is also advisable to send copies of appointment letters to all solicitors.

The assessment should be aimed at providing an opinion on the questions posed. However, this does not mean being diverted away from a dialectic mind-set and becoming reductionist or simplistic. Courts recognize the complexity of psychological functioning and of family relationships and expect this to be represented in the proceedings. An assessment is therefore useful if it weighs up different alternative explanations for the family's problems and supports coherent argument between different possible outcomes for the parent and child.

In order to ensure that the clinical assessments are satisfactory, relevant and acceptable within the court context, they should consist of the following elements.

## Reading and collating the papers

Before seeing any of the parties in the case, it is helpful to compile a genogram of the child's family and then collate a chronology of events, based on information contained in the court documents. The intention is progressively to weave together details about significant events and relationships in the family's history, concerns about child care and other problems that have come to professionals' attention, interventions that were attempted, whether they were of any benefit, and so on – as depicted in Figure 2.2. This chronology comes up to date with a picture of the present child welfare problems, the current living arrangements and reasons for any recent changes in caretaker. This provides a summary of other people's

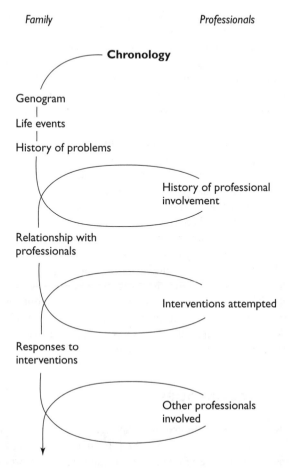

*Figure 2.2* Collation of information to generate a case chronology

*Source:* Reder and Duncan (1999).

observations and concerns, together with a preliminary account of the family background and the family's responses to professional input. Some of this information can be taken as fact but, at this stage, much of it has the status of tentative, second-hand data that allow preliminary hypotheses to be constructed about the problems but need to be checked with the family and compared with their account.

## Interviewing

At least one interview with each relevant adult and child is necessary, although more may be needed to overcome initial hostilities or reservations and to ensure that histories are covered in sufficient detail. At the beginning, it is essential to clarify with each person the context and nature of the interview and that, because it will result in a court report, its contents are not confidential. Assessors tend to keep the interviews relatively unstructured but guide the conversation into appropriate areas. The interviewing style is essentially similar to that used in other clinical assessments, although differences include a more active questioning, a more rigorous pursuit of details and greater preparedness to confront inconsistencies. It is possible to structure details about family history by constructing a genogram with each adult, using a white-board if this is available, and this often provides opportunities to make occasional linking comments in order to test hypotheses and the person's psychological mindedness.

Generally, assessment sessions with children are also unstructured and employ the interviewing techniques discussed by Westcott and Jones in Chapter 6. Play or drawing material is made available, depending on the child's age. Observation of contact between parent and child may take place in the consulting room or at a neutral contact centre and is an opportunity to see how they interact, such as how they greet each other, the quality of their play, whether the child is afraid of the parent, or whether the parent has thought of bringing any child-centred material, such as toys. Most assessors believe that at least one interview conducted in the family home elicits a wide range of useful information about family life and relationships in action, since the setting is less artificial than a professional office and it is possible to observe the state of the house, sleeping arrangements, whether there are child-centred play materials, and so on.

## ASSESSMENT TECHNIQUES

Within this overall structure, a number of issues need to be addressed about assessment techniques. These include whether the informal interview and observation techniques most commonly employed are adequate for court proceedings and whether more structured procedures have a place.

### Interviews

Cox and Rutter (1985), Cox (1994) and Angold (1994) have reviewed the evidence relating to diagnostic interviewing with parents and children in child mental health services. Structured interviews have been shown to elicit more relevant factual and diagnostic information but flexible supplementary probing is necessary to clarify the meaning of initial answers and open questions are also required when beginning to explore new areas. Experienced clinicians are able to obtain more relevant information generally. It has also been shown that reliable and valid measures of even subtle aspects of family life and relationships can be elicited from one family member at interview.

Even though parenting assessments have a different focus from diagnostic interviewing, there is support for assessment interviews which balance an open style with guided questioning. However, Milner *et al.* (1998) warn that assessors in child protection work need to be aware of possible sources of bias, such as those emanating from gender differences or personal experience, when interpreting interviews. Further discussions about interviewing children can be found in Kennedy (1992), Jones (1992), Aldridge and Wood (1998), Mordock (2001), Westcott and Jones (Chapter 6) and Reder and Duncan (Chapter 7).

## Children's drawings and play

There is now an extensive literature on the inferences that can be made from children's drawings. Clinical experience (e.g. King and Trowell, 1992; Dale, 1992) has suggested that some aspects of children's drawing are more suggestive of abusive experiences (such as phallic-like objects or a figure seemingly tied up) but are never in themselves conclusive. Instead, they should be considered as guides to further exploration through discussion or other techniques, such as play. Sometimes, the evolution of the child's drawing and the story that they construct around it are more revealing of their inner world and experiences than might be obvious from the finished picture.

Burgess and Hartman (1993) and Veltman and Browne (2002) have undertaken comprehensive reviews of research into children's drawings, concluding that, although there is consensus that children leave an imprint of their inner self in their drawings which is less susceptible to faking than verbal self-reporting, caution must be exercised in drawing specific inferences from them. For example, spatial relationships in a child's drawing of their family do give useful clues to interpersonal relationships between the figures depicted but this needs to be supplemented by additional information from other sources. Similar caution must be exercised in interpreting children's play, where explicit enactments of 'abusive' scenes may, but also may not, reflect previously abusive experiences (King and Trowell, 1992). Everson and Boat (1994) discussed the use of anatomically explicit dolls in assessment work with children and came to similar conclusions.

## Structured procedures

Some practitioners offer opinions to courts about parenting based on inferences drawn from traditional psychological tests of personality or intelligence. Brodzinsky (1993), Milner (1995), Budd and Holdsworth (1996), Jacobsen *et al.* (1997) and Azar *et al.* (1998) have all expressed concern, which we strongly endorse, that such instruments were not designed to evaluate child care competency or interactions with children. Originally developed to address specific clinical questions, they bear, at best, an indirect relationship to parenting issues and research has not examined their ability to predict parenting effectiveness. Furthermore, it must be emphasized that, even when a parent has learning disabilities, the most relevant issue is their parenting-specific skills – past, present and future – not their score on an intelligence test (Dowdney and Skuse, 1993). As Azar *et al.* (1998)

have pointed out, courts should be supplied with data that link parents' individual skills/deficits with their capacity to parent a particular child within the circumstances that are available to them. In particular, since 'no single offender profile has emerged for child physical or child sexual abuse, data from existing measures should not be used as conclusive evidence of abuse and should not be used in court proceedings as evidence that the individual has or has not abused a child' (Milner *et al.*, 1998: p. 103).

It is important with all protocols to remain aware of their primary purpose and their relative merits in different circumstances (e.g. Azar and Soysa, 1999). The pack of eight questionnaires and scales (Cox and Bentovim, 2000) produced to accompany the Department of Health *et al.*'s (2000) new *Framework for the Assessment of Children in Need and their Families* is an example. These protocols (see Table 2.1) were originally intended as general approaches to screening for emotional difficulties in children or family effectiveness, or else to help social workers include specific questions in their interviewing technique. If used with these purposes in mind, community-based practitioners may well find them useful. However, in our view, they are neither sufficiently specific nor sensitive to identify serious parenting breakdown in those families coming to family proceedings.

This pack has been complemented by *The Family Assessment* (Bentovim and Bingley Miller, 2001), which can generate a multidimensional profile of the family's competence, strengths and difficulties. Although it is proposed that this Department of Health sponsored tool has a wide application, the principal benefit appears to be providing the means by which workers might meet together with whole families and elicit information about various aspects of family life (e.g. *family organization, family character* and *family history*) and relationships (e.g. *communication, boundaries* and *alliances*). It remains to be seen how *The Family Assessment* might contribute to family proceedings assessments.

Another question arises about whether structured tests that have been devised to appraise aspects of parenting have a place in court work, since their aura of 'certainty' might appear to be suited to the world of 'the law'. Milner (1995), Heinze and Grisso (1996), Milner *et al.* (1998), Hansen *et al.* (1999) and Gershater-Molko and Lutzker (1999) have reviewed techniques more commonly used because of their greater validity and reliability and these are brought together in Table 2.2. The majority of these tests focus on specific aspects of the parenting relationship, such as the parent's expectations of the child's developmental attainments, or what arouses the parent's anger. As such, they have merit but they also carry with them a number of risks. The most obvious is the illusion of scientific objectivity that may be attributed to them, since a standard sequence of questions generating a numbered score can appear to offer clarity in a sea of complex and troubled relationships. Allied to this is the misbelief that formal tests are able to uncover aspects of psychological functioning that would otherwise remain undiscovered (Brodzinsky, 1993). Another concern is the confidence with which assessors might over-generalize from focal features of parental functioning and suggest that overall parenting capacities can be judged from one test of a specific feature of the parent

*Table 2.1* Structured procedures recommended for use with the Assessment Framework

| Procedure | Purpose | Technique | Factors assessed |
|---|---|---|---|
| Strengths and Difficulties Questionnaire (Goodman, 1997) | Screening for emotional and behavioural problems in children and adolescents | Caretaker's questionnaire | Pro-social, hyperactivity, emotional problems, conduct problems, peer problems |
| Parenting Daily Hassles Scale (Crnic and Greenberg, 1990) | To highlight areas for interview discussion | Caretaker's questionnaire | Frequency, intensity and impact of 20 parenting stresses |
| Home Conditions Scale (Davie et al., 1984) | Initial screening | Assessor's observations | 11 items of home cleanliness |
| Adult Well-being Scale anxiety, (Snaith et al., 1978) | To highlight areas for further discussion | Assessor's questionnaire | Parental irritability, depression |
| Adolescent Well-being Scale (Birleson, 1980) | To identify depression in older children and adolescents | Self-report questionnaire | How young person (aged approx. 7–16) feels about their life and themselves |
| Recent Life Events Questionnaire (after Brugha et al., 1985) | Aid to compiling a social history and further exploration | Self-report questionnaire | Impact of life events in last 12 months |
| Family Activity Scale (after Smith, 1985) | Aid to further exploration and to encourage relevant activity | Assessor's questionnaire | Child-centredness of environment provided for child |
| Alcohol Scale (Piccinelli et al., 1997) | Aid to introducing alcohol issues at interview | Self-report questionnaire | Impact of alcohol consumption on the parent and their parenting |

Source: Cox and Bentovim (2000).

*Table 2.2* Examples of structured procedures that may contribute to the assessment of parenting and parenting breakdown in family proceedings

| Procedure | Purpose | Technique | Factors assessed |
| --- | --- | --- | --- |
| Adult–Adolescent Parent Inventory (Bavelock, 1984) | To assess parent's attitudes to child and to parenting | Self-report | Parental expectations of child, sensitivity to child's needs, belief in corporal punishment, views of parent–child roles |
| Child Abuse Potential Inventory (Milner, 1986; 1990; 1995) | To screen for parent's potential to abuse physically | Self-report | Parental distress, rigidity, unhappiness, problems with child and self, problems with family, problems with others, ego-strength, loneliness |
| Child Well-being Scale (Magura and Moses, 1986) | To assess quality of child's care | Assessor's questionnaire | Whether parents are meeting child's needs for physical, emotional and psychological care |
| Childhood Level of Living Scale (Polansky et al., 1981) | To assess neglect of young children | Assessors rating | Parent's physical, emotional and cognitive care of child |
| Conflict Tactics Scale (Straus, 1979; Straus et al., 1996) | To assess conflict resolution between partners | Self-report | Use of reasoning, coercion, verbal or physical aggression during conflict with partner |
| Parent Behavior Checklist (Fox, 1994) | To assess maltreatment of young children | Assessor's questionnaire | Parental discipline, nurturing and expectations of child, including strengths and weaknesses |
| Parent–child Relationship Inventory (Gerard, 1994) | To assess parent's attitude towards parenting and their child | Self-report | Parental support, involvement, communication, limit-setting, autonomy, role orientation, satisfaction with parenting |
| Parent Opinion Questionnaire (Azar et al., 1984) | To assess parent's expectations of child's behaviours | Self-report | Expectations of self-care, help and affection to parents, family responsibility, being left alone, feelings, and punishment |

*Table 2.2* continued

| Procedure | Purpose | Technique | Factors assessed |
|---|---|---|---|
| Parental Anger Inventory (Hansen and Sedlar, 1998) | To assess anger experienced by maltreating parents | Self-report | Degree of anger evoked by child-related scenarios |
| Parental Locus of Control Scale (Campis *et al.*, 1986) | General assessment, but also relevant to maltreating parents | Self-report | Parental efficacy, responsibility, belief in fate, control of child's behaviour, child's control of parents |
| Parenting Stress Index (Lloyd and Abidin, 1985; Abidin, 1995) | To screen for dysfunctional parent–child relationships | Self-report | Potentially stressful characteristics of child (e.g. demandingness, mood, adaptability), of parent (e.g. competence, health), and of general life (e.g. isolation) |

or the parent–child relationship (Heinze and Grisso, 1996). A further caveat is that the capacity of parents involved in family proceedings to tailor their responses to suit vested interests is the same with structured questioning as with unstructured interviewing.

While many other assessment instruments have been suggested for use in child care court work, factors such as their validity, reliability, sensitivity and standardization remain unproven. Similar problems arise in relation to their relevance to parenting breakdown and child custody dilemmas in specific cases, as opposed to initial screening for possible risk of populations, and inability to offer recognized thresholds between adequate and inadequate parenting.

These reservations parallel those that apply to high-risk checklists for predicting future child abuse. Milner (1995: p. 48) observed that 'checklists and structured interviews typically do not provide information about which factors or group of factors provides the best prediction of child abuse; and the role of buffering variables is almost never discussed'. Similarly, Wilczynski (1997) pointed out that risk checklists are better at distinguishing between groups than individuals, generate too many false positives and false negatives, tend to be based on under-representative and poorly controlled samples, have poorly predictive clustering of factors, and rarely take buffering factors into account.

The two structured approaches which have received the greatest attention from practitioners and researchers, and are most commonly used in family proceedings assessments, are the Parenting Stress Index (PSI) (Lloyd and Abidin, 1985; Abidin, 1995) and the Child Abuse Potential (CAP) Inventory (Milner, 1986; 1989; 1994;

1995; Milner *et al.*, 1998). The PSI consists of 120 items relating to stresses in the child-rearing role, to which the parent indicates agreement or disagreement on a five-point scale. It has been shown to be reliable, valid, sensitive to changes resulting from treatment, and generalizable, but may generate false positives and is therefore recommended as an indicator of stresses that the evaluator should further explore verbally (Heinze and Grisso, 1996).

Milner's CAP Inventory has been the most extensively researched instrument and comprises a self-report questionnaire of 160 items, with a forced-choice 'agree/disagree' format, on the parent's attitudes towards the child and the task of parenting. It contains a *physical abuse* scale and factor scales addressing psychological difficulties (*distress*, *rigidity* and *unhappiness*) and relational difficulties (*problems with child and self*, *problems with family*, and *problems with others*). Later, scales were added to examine *ego-strength* and *loneliness*. In addition, it contains validity scales covering *lies*, *random responses* and *inconsistency*. The Inventory has proven reliability and validity but may err in eliciting false positives (Heinze and Grisso, 1996). Since it was intended as a screening tool for parental potential to abuse physically, Milner repeatedly cautioned against misrepresenting the Inventory's place in individual child maltreatment cases: 'The CAP Inventory abuse scale data must be used in conjunction with evaluation from other sources such as an interview, a case history, direct observations, medical data, and other psychological test data. Multiple types of evaluation data serve to increase the probability of making correct individual classification' (1989: p. 93); and again 'it appears that the best overall risk prediction can be obtained when risk assessment includes data from risk factors from as many sources as possible. These sources include structured parent interviews, collateral interviews, direct observations, and testing with multiple objective measures' (Milner, 1995: p. 61).

Hansen *et al.* (1999) also warned that practitioners should not offer scores on the CAP Inventory as a determining measure of whether a parent did or did not maltreat a child and recommended that 'professionals avoid reliance on any one measure and look for converging evidence across varying measures when attempting to understand parental behavior' (p. 145). Azar *et al.* (1998) suggested that different approaches could complement each other, giving examples of how concerning responses to items on structured assessment techniques might lead to further informal exploration. According to Budd and Holdsworth (1996: p. 11), 'most commentators recommend a multimethod, multisource, multisession approach to achieve a more comprehensive picture of parenting fitness', together with an assessment of parenting strengths and potential resources as well as weaknesses, while Kashani and Allan (1998) emphasized that the primary assessment tool in mental health to validate child abuse remains the semi-structured or unstructured interview.

## RESIDENTIAL ASSESSMENTS

Suggestions that a family should undergo a residential assessment may arise prior to an expert's involvement or as one of the expert's recommendations. Occasionally, a family is admitted to a residential unit for the purpose of providing the expert opinion. Residential units can offer observation of general parenting skills while at the same time providing supervision and monitoring of families in order to ensure the safety of the children.

The type of unit selected needs to reflect the nature of the questions being considered and the skill mix of the staff. They can be approximately divided into those which focus on basic parenting skills, whose staff mainly have a social work and child care background, and those which, in addition, include assessments of parental dysfunction. This may involve psychiatric and psychological assessments of the parents and their mental health problems, together with evaluation of their capacity and motivation to use psychotherapeutic interventions. In addition, the specialist unit may provide such interventions and monitor their effectiveness.

## Basic parenting skills

Most residential units aim to assess parental knowledge about child development, nutrition and the needs of children, as well as assessing practical daily life skills, such as ability to maintain a hygienic living environment, cook nutritious meals, budget appropriately, develop child-centred routines, establish boundaries, manage behaviour and provide stimulation. Some of these units are able to go beyond this to address issues that may be impeding a parent from providing optimal care. They provide opportunities for the parent to explore some of the difficulties originating in their own childhood, such as a history of abuse, separations and losses, as well as considering the impact of current problems, such as alcohol or drug misuse. The parent's response to interventions, which may range from therapeutic family work to direct child protection, forms part of the overall assessment, since it indicates their willingness to reflect and work on problems, cooperate with professionals and focus on the well-being and safety of the child.

The advantage of such units is that they allow for detailed observation of practical aspects of parenting and parental responses to practical advice and help. However, although it is often suggested that a residential assessment will provide more in-depth information about family functioning than a community-based assessment, it can be argued that they actually decrease the range of questions that can be addressed. A move into a residential unit constitutes an intervention for a family and will inevitably impact on their functioning. The family is separated from its local community and from the responsibility to provide many of their everyday needs. In addition, there is close emotional and practical support available 24 hours a day. However, many of the parents considered for such units are still suffering the consequences of major deficiencies in care when they were children, leaving them with unmet needs and unresolved emotional conflicts (see Reder and

Duncan, Chapter 12). Hence, this degree of containment and support has usually been absent from their lives and the assessment occurs in an artificial context.

Paradoxically, whereas parenting demands considerable psychological autonomy, parents can feel disempowered by the residential experience and controlled by it. In this respect, such a setting may not facilitate assessment of a parent's ability to take charge and to make a home for their children, nor their capacity to sustain supportive relationships in the community. It also offers them a degree of protection from factors which have interfered with their parenting ability at home, such as the availability of drugs or alcohol and volatile interactions with previous partners.

If a parent is still unable to meet their child's needs and/or care for them safely, despite the high level of support and containment that a residential assessment provides, then the unit could be said to have offered a unique opportunity to appraise this and to help make the case for the child to be placed permanently with a substitute family. However, experience suggests that a period of residential assessment usually confirms the parent's ability to provide good-enough care in a highly supportive environment but leaves unanswered the question of their ability to manage independently in the community, so that a second-stage assessment is often required once the family has returned home. This means uprooting the children from previously settled placements in foster families or residential homes, thus disrupting them once again, and also lengthens the assessment process and prolongs the period of uncertainty.

Residential assessment tends to be considered for those families where there is less certainty and where anxiety about the child's safety is greatest. We would argue they they should only be used where there is already reasonable confidence about a positive outcome.

## Parental dysfunction

There is only a small number of specialist units providing assessments of parenting problems and the psychological factors which underlie them, together with treatment programmes aimed at promoting long-term change in personal and family functioning. These include the Park Hospital for Children in Oxford (Byrne and Jones, 1998; Jones and Newbold, 2001) and the Cassel Hospital, outside London (Kennedy, 1997). The Marlborough Hospital in London (Schuff and Asen 1996; Asen, 2000) provides modified elements of a residential assessment through families attending a day programme.

Byrne and Jones (1998), from the Park Hospital, emphasized the importance of distinguishing assessment from treatment in such specialist units and of providing containment for families without encouraging their dependency. Kennedy (1997) described how the Cassel Hospital is staffed by qualified child and adult psychotherapists, who offer intensive psychotherapy to both parents and children, and nurses who focus on everyday family activities and parenting skills. Families may remain in treatment for up to a year. The core principle of the work is that helping families bear painful traumatic experiences and find words to express their distress may enable them to take charge of their lives rather than continue as victims of the past. In addition, they are better able to tolerate their child being dependent on them. Kennedy argued that the supportive counselling often on offer in other residential assessment units is insufficient to address the complex issues involved in parenting breakdown or the powerful feelings that can be evoked. However, the drawback of such a programme is that it is prolonged and expensive and, for families who are assessed as unable to resume care of their child, the parent and child must be separated once again, risking further emotional trauma and the delay in permanency planning.

### Post-natal mental health problems

Henry and Kumar (1999) identified one function of psychiatric mother and baby units as assessing actual or potential risk to infants within the context of maternal mental illness and associated problems. In admitting the mother and baby together, it is hoped to avoid attachment disruption. The assessments tend to take place over a relatively brief period during phases of acute mental illness and, while this enables an assessment of the immediate impact of the mother's disorder on her parenting, it allows little time for observing the mother's capacity to meet the child's developmental needs in the longer term. It will be necessary to complement this early assessment with information about the family in its wider context, such as the availability of a partner or extended family, environmental and financial stresses, and so on.

### Substance misuse

Recommendations may be made for parents with specific difficulties to participate in residential assessment/treatment programmes in their own right prior to any decision being made about their future care of their children. Typically, a substance misusing parent is required to undergo an in-patient detoxification programme followed by residential relapse prevention work, with decisions about resuming care of their child being based on whether they successfully withdraw from alcohol or illegal drugs. However, we believe that the risks to the child are potentially greater once the parent no longer is able to use substances to 'manage' their underlying emotional problems. Further therapeutic work will be needed to enable the parent both to gain insight into the origins of their substance dependency and to develop alternative coping strategies. The assessment should include their motivation and capacity to be involved in such work and whether sufficient progress is possible within the child's time scale.

### Induced or fabricated illness

In-patient assessment of suspected 'induced or fabricated illness' (Royal College of Paediatrics and Child Health, 2002) has been the subject of controversy in recent years (Samuels and Postlethwaite, 2001; Taylor and Nicholls, 2001). In selected cases, there is no doubt that covert video surveillance (i.e. without parental knowledge or consent) in a paediatric ward may be the only means of obtaining incontrovertible evidence that the parent is suffocating or otherwise deliberately attacking their child (Southall *et al.*, 1997). However, concerns of some parents and practitioners have led to the need for guidelines on the appropriate use of such assessment techniques (Department of Health *et al.*, 2002). The occasional need for hospital admission in order to undertake an assessment is acknowledged but the decision to do so should be arrived at through inter-agency discussion, with the police ultimately coordinating a criminal investigation.

## COORDINATED ASSESSMENTS

The specific problems discussed above are good examples of the benefit of assessments being coordinated between the various professionals involved. Coordination implies each practitioner or expert recognizing their optimal role in the case and the limits of their professional expertise, including understanding that another form of assessment may need to take precedence over theirs. For example, there will be some cases in which first-stage paediatric and forensic findings (e.g. about the nature, timing and likely origins of a child's injuries, or whether video-taping has demonstrated parental induction of illness) will be necessary in order to create the meaningful context for subsequent contributions from psychologists or psychiatrists (Jones and Newbold, 2001). Other cases may require parallel, though related, assessments from different experts, an example being coordination between paediatricians and child psychologists or psychiatrists when child neglect is suspected.

Again, when a parent is considered to be suffering from a mental health or substance misuse problem, the ideal assessment involves collaboration between adult and child mental health experts, in which each acknowledges the areas which they can best address and those which are beyond their skills. The adult psychiatrist can advise on the nature and prognosis of the parent's disorder, but it requires a child expert to comment on the impact of the parental behaviour on the child, as seen *from the child's perspective* (see Reder, Chapter 13). Drummond and Fitzpatrick (2000) described their collaborative approach to parenting assessments when a parent misuses drugs or alcohol, in which they

> clarify the different areas that each professional will address, followed by separate assessments . . . However, neither of these separate assessments can in itself provide the overall picture, and recommendations to the court must arise out of an ongoing conversation between the specialists, which bridges their different perspectives. This collaboration should allow them to draw inferences that highlight the adult's behaviour as a parent, the child's experiences of being parented in that way, and the likelihood of the parent's behaviour changing. (p. 142)

It is important to stress that this readiness to collaborate does not imply a readiness to modify inferences drawn from each respective assessment. The final recommendations to court should not be a compromise between different opinions, since it is the process of the assessment that needs coordination, not the conclusions. Opinions should be reached by taking account of all relevant information, which therefore includes that from other assessors. However, the nature of expert instruction is that each professional's assessment, opinion and recommendations are independent. Family proceedings allow for formal meetings between experts in order to clarify for the court those areas in which the experts concur and those where they diverge.

## ARRIVING AT AN OPINION

It is difficult to describe the process by which we arrive at a final opinion. Many other experienced experts to whom we have spoken agree that it is complex, time-consuming, detailed and hard to put into words. It is best thought of as a continuation of the assessment process, since it relies on the same 'dialectic' mind-set. The available information is reviewed and collated and various hypotheses considered. The parenting assessment framework outlined in Chapter 1 helps us reconsider which factors are particularly relevant to the case and refine the balance which we would accord them. The inferences drawn from the assessment are also measured, where possible, against acknowledged risk criteria and critical thresholds. This is a particularly onerous task since, as already discussed, high-risk checklists which itemize attributional factors rarely do justice to the nuance of an individual case. Furthermore, critical thresholds for parenting breakdown are especially difficult to define and most cases requiring expert opinions lie in the grey area between adequacy and failure of parenting.

For example, Jones (1997) has offered a summary of factors which usually indicate poor prospects for resumption of care by a maltreating parent. Translated into the framework for assessment we outlined in Chapter 1, the factors are:

1   Parent (and parent–child relationship);
- Abuse in childhood – not recognized as a problem;
- Pervasive problems with power, autonomy and expressions of affect;
- Personality disorder;
- Substance abuse;
- Paranoid psychosis;
- Learning difficulties;
- Poor competence in several domains (neglect and physical abuse/neglect);
- Denial of problems;
- Lack of empathy for child;
- Own needs before child;
- Severe, premeditated and/or sadistic abuse/neglect;

- Mixed abuse;
- Penetrative sexual abuse and/or long duration;
- Induced or fabricated illness.

2   Child (and child–parent relationship)
- Disordered attachment;
- Developmental delay with special needs;
- Very young child, requiring rapid parental change.

3   Context (and family–context relationship)
- Pervasive family violence;
- Lack of compliance;
- Social isolation;
- Lack of professional resources.

While this list may act as a preliminary guide, it should not be used as though it were a checklist, since it cannot capture the specifics of an individual case nor the interaction between factors. For example, only a few of the features may be present yet the profound impact of just one or two, such as the sadistic nature of abuse which the parent denies, might dominate the picture. Conversely, a number of these poor prognostic factors may be present, yet considerable strengths in the family could seem to compensate for them.

Gradually, the issues become reduced to a small number of either/or dilemmas which we need to consider. Usually, they mirror some or all of the questions itemized in the instruction letter. For example, one core concern might be whether a child would be safe enough if returned to a parent's care. Certain inferences we have drawn from the assessment are likely to be on the positive side in this equation, while others would be negative, so that the balance between them must be argued through. This might emerge more clearly through identifying the likely consequences of the child returning to the care of a parent who, say, does not wish for any therapeutic help despite many unresolved conflicts yet has managed to provide intermittent periods of warm, child-centred care. A series of 'if this . . . then that' formulations may then become apparent, leading to the final opinion.

The opinion, therefore, requires a considerable amount of thinking time, during which information is sifted through, factors considered and either/or alternatives weighed up. Some experts speak of the need to 'metabolize' the assessment over a number of days, during which they are reflecting on the case and clarifying their thinking. During that time, they may decide to consult the literature on certain matters, return to the letter of instruction to confirm that they are addressing all of the questions, or even discuss the case with a colleague. In our experience, it is especially important to have agreed a realistic date for submission of the report with the instructing solicitor that allows for this metabolizing process as well as time to compose the report. We would also resist requests to give preliminary opinions or to convey our views on just one of the questions, since we regard the report as a coherent document which argues through the complexities of the case, so that no one element should be taken out of context.

The potential for change in parental and family functioning is an important contribution to the final opinion. Recommendations for therapeutic intervention need to be realistic and based on an appraisal of the therapeutic potential of relevant family members, treatment efficacy, resource availability and the child's time scales. Whatever treatment is being considered, therapeutic potential includes such factors as acknowledgement that there are parenting and/or relationship problems that need to change, ownership by the parent of the part they played in the problem's development, and willingness to commit to a therapeutic process. Reviews of treatment approaches in child maltreatment and their effectiveness can be found in Gough (1993), Macdonald (2001) and Browne *et al.* (2002). Local NHS services can be offended to find that they have been 'prescribed' by an expert and written in to a court order without any prior consultation. Experts should always confirm first with any therapeutic centre being considered for recommendation that it is willing to be named in their report and in what way. Jones (1997) also emphasized that therapeutic components of care plans should identify the aims of the proposed treatment, criteria for its success and failure, and measures necessary for child protection during the course of the therapy. He further concluded that court orders can, in some circumstances, help motivate reluctant parents to accept help, while time scales for the child must take account of their age and developmental requirements, with younger children being more vulnerable to delays in permanency planning.

## CONCLUSIONS

Assessments by health or mental health experts in child care court cases involve work at the interface between two contrasting systems. Further complexities are that the assessments must be multidimensional and detailed and they need to emphasize the child's experiences of the parenting relationship and the strengths and weaknesses of the family. Opinions are reached by collating a wealth of information and weighing it up against recognized theoretical principles, research evidence and practice experiences.

Some cases pose particular dilemmas and the chapters which follow offer guidance on how they can be addressed.

## References

Abidin, R.R. (1995) *Parenting Stress Index – Manual*, 3rd ed., Odessa, FL: Psychological Assessment Resources.

Aldridge, M. and Wood, J. (1998) *Interviewing Children: A Guide for Child Care and Forensic Practitioners*, Chichester: John Wiley.

Angold, A. (1994) Clinical interviewing with children and adolescents, in M. Rutter, E. Taylor and L. Hersov (eds) *Child and Adolescent Psychiatry: Modern Approaches*, 3rd ed., Oxford: Blackwell.

Angold, A. (2002) Diagnostic interviews with parents and children, in M. Rutter and E. Taylor (eds) *Child and Adolescent Psychiatry*, 4th ed., Oxford: Blackwell Scientific.

Asen, E. (2000) Working with families where there is parenting breakdown, in P. Reder, M. McClure and A. Jolley (eds) *Family Matters: Interfaces between Child and Adult Mental Health*, London: Routledge.

Azar, S.T., Benjet, C.L., Fuhrmann, G.S. and Cavallero, L. (1995) Child maltreatment and termination of parental rights: can behavioral research help Solomon? *Behavior Therapy* 26: 599–623.

Azar, S.T., Lauretti, A.F. and Loding, B.V. (1998) The evaluation of parental fitness in termination of parental rights cases: a functional-contextual perspective, *Clinical Child & Family Psychology Review* 1: 77–100.

Azar, S.T., Robinson, D.R., Hekimian, E. and Twentyman, C.T. (1984) Unrealistic expectations and problem-solving ability in maltreating and comparison mothers, *Journal of Consulting and Clinical Psychology* 52: 687–91.

Azar, S.T. and Soysa, C.K. (1999) Legal and systems issues in the assessment of family violence involving children, in R.T. Ammerman and M. Hersen (eds) *Assessment of Family Violence: A Clinical and Legal Sourcebook*, 2nd ed., New York: John Wiley.

Bavelock, S.J. (1984) *Adult-Adolescent Parenting Inventory*, Eau Claire, WI: Family Development Resources.

Bentovim, A. and Bingley Miller, L. (2001) *The Family Assessment: Assessment of Family Competence, Strengths and Difficulties*, Brighton: Pavillion.

Birleson, P. (1980) The validity of depressive disorder in childhood and the development of self-rating scales, *Journal of Child Psychology & Psychiatry* 22: 73–88.

Black, D., Harris Hendriks, J. and Wolkind, S. (eds) (1998) *Child Psychiatry and the Law*, 3rd ed., London: Gaskell.

Boscolo, L. and Bertrando, P. (1996) *Systemic Therapy with Individuals*, London: Karnac.

Brodzinsky, D.M. (1993) On the use and misuse of psychological testing in child custody evaluations, *Professional Psychology: Research & Practice* 24: 213–19.

Browne, K.D., Hanks, H., Stratton, P. and Hamilton, C. (eds) (2002) *Early Prediction and Prevention of Child Abuse: A Handbook*, Chichester: Wiley.

Brugha, T., Bebington, P., Tennant, C. and Hurry, J. (1985) The list of threatening experiences: a subset of 12 life event categories with considerable long-term contextual threat, *Psychological Medicine* 15: 189–94.

Budd, K.S. and Holdsworth, M.J. (1996) Issues in clinical assessment of minimal parenting competence, *Journal of Clinical Child Psychology* 25: 2–14.

Burgess, A.W. and Hartman, C.R. (1993) Children's drawings, *Child Abuse & Neglect* 17: 161–8.

Burr, V. (1995) *An Introduction to Social Constructionism*, London: Routledge.

Butler-Sloss, Lord Justice E. (1988) *Report of the Inquiry into Child Abuse in Cleveland 1987*, Cm 412, London: HMSO.

Byrne, G. and Jones, D. (1998) Severe breakdown in the parenting of infants, in J. Green and B. Jacobs (eds) *In-patient Child Psychiatry: Modern Practice, Research and the Future*, London: Routledge.

Campis, L.K., Lyman, R.D. and Prentice-Dunn, S. (1986) The parental locus of control scale: development and validation, *Journal of Clinical Child Psychology* 15: 260–7.

Carson, D. (1990) *Professionals and the Courts: A Handbook for Expert Witnesses*, Birmingham: Venture Press.

Cox, A.D. (1994) Interviews with parents, in M. Rutter, E. Taylor and L. Hersov (eds) *Child and Adolescent Psychiatry: Modern Approaches*, 3rd ed., Oxford: Blackwell.

Cox, A. and Bentovim, A. (2000) *Framework for the Assessment of Children in Need and their Families: The Family Pack of Questionnaires and Scales*, Department of Health, London: The Stationery Office.

Cox, A. and Rutter, M. (1985) Diagnostic appraisal and interviewing, in M. Rutter and L. Hersov (eds) *Child and Adolescent Psychiatry: Modern Approaches*, 2nd ed., Oxford: Blackwell.

Crnic, K.A. and Greenberg, M.T. (1990) Minor parenting stresses with young children, *Child Development* 61: 1628–37.

Dale, F. (1992) The art of communicating with vulnerable children, in V. Varma (ed.) *The Secret Life of Vulnerable Children*, London: Routledge.

Davie, C.E., Hutt, S.J., Vincent, E. and Mason, M. (1984) *The Young Child at Home*, Windsor: NFER-Nelson.

Department of Health, Department for Education and Employment and Home Office (2000) *Framework for the Assessment of Children in Need and their Families*, London: The Stationery Office.

Department of Health, Home Office, Department for Education and Skills and Welsh Assembly Government (2002) *Safeguarding Children in whom Illness is Fabricated or Induced*, London: Department of Health.

Dowdney, L. and Skuse, D. (1993) Parenting provided by adults with mental retardation, *Journal of Child Psychology & Psychiatry* 34: 25–47.

Drummond, D.C. and Fitzpatrick, G. (2000) Children of substance-misusing parents, in P. Reder, M. McClure and A. Jolley (eds) *Family Matters: Interfaces between Child and Adult Mental Health*, London: Routledge.

Etchegoyen, A. and Adams, M. (1998) The role of unrecognised ambivalence: the mirroring of family conflicts within the professional and legal network, *British Journal of Medical Psychology* 71: 323–8.

Everson, M.D. and Boat, B.W. (1994) Putting the anatomical doll controversy in perspective: an examination of the major uses and criticisms of the dolls in child sexual abuse evaluations, *Child Abuse & Neglect* 18: 113–29.

Expert Witness Group (1997) *Expert Witness Pack: For Use in Family Proceedings*, Bristol: Family Law/Jordan Publishing.

Fox, R.A. (1994) *Parent Behaviour Checklist*, Brandon, VT: Clinical Psychology.

Gerard, A.B. (1994) *Parent-Child Relationship Inventory (PCRI): Manual*, Los Angeles, CA: Western.

Gershater-Molko, R.M. and Lutzker, J.R. (1999) Child neglect, in R.T. Ammerman and M. Hersen (eds) *Assessment of Family Violence: A Clinical and Legal Sourcebook*, 2nd ed., New York: John Wiley.

Goodman, R. (1997) The Strengths and Difficulties Questionnaire: a research note, *Journal of Child Psychology & Psychiatry* 38: 581–6.

Gough, D. (1993) *Child Abuse Interventions: A Review of the Research Literature*, London: HMSO.

Hansen, D.J. and Sedlar, G. (1998) *The Parental Anger Inventory: A Guide for Practitioners and Researchers*, Lincoln, NE: Clinical Psychology Training Program.

Hansen, D.J., Sedlar, G. and Warner-Rogers, J.E. (1999) Child physical abuse, in R.T. Ammerman and M. Hersen (eds) *Assessment of Family Violence: A Clinical and Legal Sourcebook*, 2nd ed., New York: John Wiley.

Heinze, M.C. and Grisso, T. (1996) Review of instruments assessing parenting competencies used in child custody evaluations, *Behavioral Sciences & the Law* 14: 293–313.

Henderson, E. (2002) Persuading and controlling: the theory of cross-examination in relation to children, in H.L. Westcott, G.M. Davies and R.H.C. Bull (eds) *Children's Testimony: A Handbook of Psychological Research and Forensic Practice*, Chichester: John Wiley.

Henry, L.A. and Kumar, R.C. (1999) Risk assessments of infants born to parents with a mental health problem or a learning disability, in A. Weir and A. Douglas (eds) *Child Protection & Adult Mental Health: Conflict of Interest?* Oxford: Butterworth-Heinemann.

Inquiry Report (1987) *A Child In Mind: Protection of Children in a Responsible Society, The Report of the Commission of Enquiry into the Circumstances Surrounding the Death of Kimberley Carlile*, London Borough of Greenwich.

Jacobsen, T., Miller, L.J. and Pesek Kirkwood, K. (1997) Assessing parenting competence in individuals with severe mental illness: a comprehensive service, *Journal of Mental Health Administration* 24: 189–99.

Jones, D.P.H. (1992) *Interviewing the Sexually Abused Child*, 4th ed., London: Gaskell/Royal College of Psychiatrists.

Jones, D.P.H. (1997) Treatment of the child and family where child abuse or neglect has occurred, in M.E. Helfer, R.S. Kempe and R.D. Krugman (eds) *The Battered Child*, 5th ed., Chicago: University of Chicago Press.

Jones, D.P.H. and Newbold, C. (2001) Assessment of abusing families, in G. Adshead and D. Brooke (eds) *Munchausen's Syndrome by Proxy: Current Issues in Assessment, Treatment and Research*, London: Imperial College Press.

Kashani, J.H. and Allan, W.D. (1998) *The Impact of Family Violence on Children and Adolescents*, Thousand Oaks, CA: Sage.

Kennedy, M. (1992) Not the only way to communicate: a challenge to voice in child protection work, *Child Abuse Review* 1: 169–77.

Kennedy, R. (1997) *Child Abuse, Psychotherapy and the Law*, London: Free Association Books.

King, M. and Trowell, J. (1992) *Children's Welfare and the Law: The Limits of Legal Intervention*, London: Sage.

Lloyd, B.H. and Abidin, R.R. (1985) Revision of the Parenting Stress Index, *Journal of Pediatric Psychology* 10: 169–77.

Macdonald, G. (2001) *Effective Interventions for Child Abuse and Neglect: An Evidence-based Approach to Planning and Evaluating Interventions*, Chichester: Wiley.

Magura, S. and Moses, B.S. (1986) *Outcome Measures for Child Welfare Services*, New York: Child Welfare League of America.

Manarin, B. (2002) Criminal responsibility and the mental health experts: the A, B, Cs of cross-examination, *Medicine, Science, & the Law* 42: 135–46.

Milner, J.S. (1986) *The Child Abuse Potential Inventory: Manual*, 2nd ed., Webster, NC: Psytec.

Milner, J.S. (1989) Applications and limitations of the Child Abuse Potential Inventory, in J.T. Pardeck (ed.) *Child Abuse and Neglect: Theory, Research, and Practice*, New York: Gordon & Breach Science Publishers.

Milner, J.S. (1990) *An Interpretive Manual for the Child Abuse Potential Inventory*, Webster, NC: Psytec.

Milner, J.S. (1994) Assessing physical child abuse risk: the Child Abuse Potential Inventory, *Clinical Psychology Review* 14: 547–83.

Milner, J.S. (1995) Physical child abuse assessment: perpetrator evaluation, in J.C. Campbell (ed.) *Assessing Dangerousness: Violence by Sexual Offenders, Batterers, and Child Abusers*, Thousand Oaks, CA: Sage.

Milner, J.S., Murphy, W.D., Valle, L.A. and Tolliver, R.M. (1998) Assessment issues in child abuse evaluations, in J.R. Lutzker (ed.) *Handbook of Child Abuse Research and Treatments*, New York: Plenum.

Minuchin, S. (1984) Family dismemberment: a day in court, in *Family Kaleidoscope: Images of Violence and Healing*, Cambridge, MA: Harvard University Press.

Mordock, J.B. (2001) Interviewing abused and traumatised children, *Clinical Child Psychology & Psychiatry* 6: 271–91.

Myers, J.E.B. and Stern, P. (2002) Expert testimony, in J.E.B. Myers, L. Berliner, J. Briere, C.T. Hendrix, C. Jenny and T.A. Reid (eds) *The APSAC Handbook on Child Maltreatment*, 2nd ed., Thousand Oaks, CA: Sage.

Piccinelli, M., Tessari, E., Bortolomasi, M., Piasere, O., Semenzin, M., Garzotto, N. and Tansella, M. (1997) Efficacy of the alcohol use disorders identification test as a screening tool for hazardous alcohol intake and related disorders in primary care: a validity study, *British Medical Journal* 514: 420–4.

Polansky, N.A., Chalmers, M.A., Williams, D.P. and Buttenwieser, E.W. (1981) *Damaged Parents: An Anatomy of Child Neglect*, Chicago: University of Chicago Press.

Reder, P. and Duncan, S. (1999) *Lost Innocents: A Follow-up Study of Fatal Child Abuse*, London: Routledge.

Reder, P. and Duncan, S. (2000) A required mind-set for child protection practice: comments on Munro (1999), *Child Abuse & Neglect* 24: 443–5.

Reder, P., Lucey, C. and Fellow-Smith, E. (1993) Surviving cross-examination in court, *Journal of Forensic Psychiatry* 4: 489–96.

Royal College of Paediatrics and Child Health (2002) *Fabricated or Induced Illness by Carers*, Report by the Working Party of the Royal College of Paediatrics and Child Health, London.

Samuels, M. and Postlethwaite, R.J. (2001) Confirming factitious illness, in M. Eminson and R.J. Postlethwaite (eds) *Munchausen Syndrome by Proxy Abuse: A Practical Approach*, London: Arnold.

Schaffer, H.R. (1998) *Making Decisions about Children*, 2nd ed., Oxford: Blackwell.

Schuff, G.H. and Asen, K.E. (1996) The disturbed parent and the disturbed family, in M. Göpfert, J. Webster and M.V. Seeman (eds) *Parental Psychiatric Disorder: Distressed Parents and their Families*, Cambridge: Cambridge University Press.

Sheldrick, C. (1998) Child psychiatrists in court: their contribution as experts in child care proceedings, *Journal of Forensic Psychiatry* 9: 249–66.

Smith, M.A. (1985) The Effects of Low Levels of Lead on Urban Children: The Relevance of Social Factors, unpublished PhD thesis, Psychology Department, University of London.

Snaith, R.P., Constantopoulos, A.A., Jardine, M.Y. and McGuffin, P. (1978) A clinical scale for the self-assessment of irritability, *British Journal of Psychiatry* 132: 164–71.

Southall, D.P., Plunkett, M.C.B., Banks, M.W., Falkov, A.F. and Samuels, M.P. (1997) Covert video recordings of life-threatening child abuse: lessons for child protection, *Pediatrics* 100: 735–60.

Straus, M.A. (1979) Measuring intrafamily conflict and violence: the Conflict Tactics (CT) Scales, *Journal of Marriage and the Family* 41: 75–88.

Straus, M.A., Hamby, S.L., Boney-McCoy, S. and Sugarman, D.B. (1996) The revised Conflict Tactics Scales (CTS2): development and preliminary psychometric data, *Journal of Family Issues* 17: 283–316.

Sturge, C. (1992) Dealing with the courts and parenting breakdown, *Archives of Disease in Childhood* 67: 745–50.

Taylor, D. and Nicholls, M. (2001) Munchausen's Syndrome by Proxy – the legal perspective, in G. Adshead and D. Brooke (eds) *Munchausen's Syndrome by Proxy: Current Issues in Assessment, Treatment and Research*, London: Imperial College Press.

Taylor, K. (2000) *A Practical Guide for the Expert Witness*, Burnley: TM Publications.

Tufnell, G. (1993) Psychiatric reports in child care cases: what constitutes 'good practice'? *Association of Child Psychology & Psychiatry Review & Newsletter* 15: 219–24.

Tufnell, G., Cottrell, D. and Georgiades, D. (1996) 'Good practice' for expert witnesses, *Clinical Child Psychology & Psychiatry* 1: 365–83.

Veltman, M.W.M. and Browne, K.D. (2002) The assessment of drawings from children who have been maltreated: a systematic review, *Child Abuse Review* 11: 19–37.

Wall, The Hon. Mr Justice (1997) *Rooted Sorrows: Psychoanalytic Perspectives on Child Protection, Assessment, Therapy and Treatment*, Bristol: Family Law/Jordan Publishing.

Wall, Mr Justice (2000) *A Handbook for Expert Witnesses in Children Act Cases*, Bristol: Family Law/Jordan Publishing.

White, R. (1998) Significant harm: legal implications, in M. Adcock and R. White (eds) *Significant Harm: Its Management and Outcome*, 2nd ed., Croydon: Significant Publications.

Wilczynski, A. (1997) *Child Homicide*, London: Greenwich Medical Media.

# Chapter 3

# Would cultural matching ensure culturally competent assessments?

*Begum Maitra*

At first glance, the question of cultural matching between professional assessor and family being assessed is one that a minority ethnic psychiatrist, such as the author (South Asian, Hindu), might least wish to be asked publicly. For, either answer ('yes' or 'no') is easily open to being misunderstood unless the interrogator is willing to do a number of things – to be patient, to adopt the position of multiple disadvantage that many minority cultures occupy, and to identify and question the cultural assumptions of Western psychology.

It would be impossible to do justice to all the factors that contribute to cultural difference in a single chapter. Admittedly, the variables of social class and gender may not be separated in reality from the subjective experience of ethnic culture, and will inevitably appear in the discussion that follows. However, this chapter will primarily look at ethnic variations in parenting strategy, the reciprocal systems of belief, practice and expectation that connect the (ethnic) group with parents, children, and neighbouring groups. This chapter will look specifically at the problems of cultural matching when assessing risks to children. The author wishes to emphasize the distinction between assessment of risk and therapeutic interventions, since the outcome of therapy is not as crucially reliant on cultural competence as is child protection work. The longer time frames of therapy, the emphases on negotiation (of priorities and therapeutic modality), acceptance of trial and error, and the fact that the onus is placed on the therapist to join the family in its belief systems before change can occur, allow for a range of acceptable intermediate outcomes. The context of risk assessments is far less forgiving, and errors are often irreversible (Azar and Benjet, 1994).

## 'EXPERTISE' AND ETHNICITY: CLINICAL EXAMPLES

This section will consider four clinical vignettes from the author's experience, selected to examine different professional–family ethnic pairings and the questions they raise. First, when the family and the professional are from the same cultural background, is personal cultural experience the same as cultural 'expertise'?

Second, when a minority ethnic family (culturally matched with the author) is assessed by a white British professional, what constitutes cultural training? Third, if the family and the professional are from different minority ethnic groups (West African and South Asian respectively), how much advantage is gained from being a minority ethnic professional? Fourth, with a minority ethnic professional and a white British family, does mainstream training address the variety of white British culture? Three of these families (vignettes 1, 2 and 4) were examined in the context of care proceedings. The need to protect client confidentiality requires that the vignettes be brief, disguised, and schematic rather than descriptive. There is a tension between this and the need to show whether, and how, culture is relevant to considerations of harm to the child/ren in that particular case. Finally, references to what 'South Asians' might do, or 'West Africans' might believe, are not intended to suggest that these broad terms indicate homogeneous cultures, or that these cultures are fixed in any way.

## 1. South Asian professionals, South Asian family

A South Asian child, born prematurely due to antenatal problems that threatened the mother's life, was removed into foster care at the age of about one year with severe failure to thrive. In the paediatrician's view this was directly attributable to the parents' failure to attend appointments regularly, and to take professional advice about feeding their daughter. It was agreed by the large network of professionals that the parents undoubtedly loved this, the youngest, of their five children. Prolonged and detailed observations were carried out by a family centre of how the parents fed this child, and reports commented critically on 'force-feeding', on the absence of clear meal-times, and associated routines. Observers noted that the child was not seated on a (high-) chair, at a table, nor was she encouraged to use cutlery or to feed herself. The mother, it was noted, sat on the floor and finger-fed the child seated on her lap, or followed the child about the room with a plate of food when she refused to eat.

The seriousness of risk to this child was undoubted. The criteria for significant harm were satisfied, and indeed this was conceded by the parents' solicitor in the care proceedings. While the impairment of health and development was clearly attributable to the overall quality of care provided by these parents, more information was needed to decide whether the child should be permanently removed. Predictions of future risk (if the child remained with the birth family), and of the parents' capacity to change (to provide care that did not risk her future health) required the formulation of a hypothesis to explain why this child had suffered the particular kinds of harm that she had. Several expert opinions had been obtained but none of these offered much contextual information, or any explanatory hypotheses. Whereas the formulation had identified a harmful event (or events), perpetrator/s (to whom responsibility was attributed), and seriously adverse consequences, future predictions were made impossible without a detailed understanding of cultural meanings, motivations, and emotional responses.

### Why this child?

None of the four older children in this family had suffered failure to thrive, nor from any other nutritional or major health difficulty. Were gender and birth order significant in this child's case? As the third daughter at the end of a large sibling group could it be that the parents had wilfully neglected her, perhaps as a form of passive infanticide? A reading of the cultural literature on infanticide by exposure or neglect, and especially of female children, shows that it is well known in many parts of the developing world (Miller, 1987; Scheper-Hughes, 1987a), where socio-economic factors contribute to a preference for male children, and where medical care (birth control, abortion) is either not easily available, or runs counter to religious belief. Scheper-Hughes (1987b) describes the relationship between mothers' perceptions of the child's temperament and activity levels, folk diagnoses, and especially folk explanations for infant deaths. She makes an important distinction between the motivation, social cause, expressive content and outcome of 'failure to thrive', passive infanticide, and malicious child battering and abuse. Infanticide, abortion and 'selective neglect' of babies often entail a failure to recognize the child/foetus as a *person*; child *abuse* (which only relatively rarely leads to death), on the other hand, is often fuelled by a malicious and/or envious rejection of the *child*.

This discussion merely hints at the breadth of reading required about passive forms of neglect/harm in a range of cultures. Only with a wide-based understanding of the complex underlying motivations may the professional begin to look for evidence within the particular culture, and family. In the case described, did prematurity and the severe complications during pregnancy mark this child in her parents' eyes as a child destined to die? These are highly sensitive areas that are not easily accessible on interview. The level of probing necessary requires intimate cultural knowledge, and the greater ease of emotional communication possible in the family's mother tongue. (Interviews conducted through an interpreter would not have allowed sufficient rapport to develop in the limited time available.) Information emerged that the parents had in fact refused medical advice to abort this pregnancy, their choice being based on a different thread within the mesh of religious/cultural ideas about abnormal birth experiences and fate/divine will – namely, that the continuation of the pregnancy despite difficulties indicated Allah's will. And when faced with the threat of losing their child through legal proceedings, they struggled to bear a prolonged and often humiliating assessment (though not without outbursts of anger and despair) in order to have her returned to their care. No evidence was found to suggest that this child was unwanted, or given less value than her siblings.

### Feeding strategies: faulty parenting or faulty cultural practice?

Oddly, little curiosity was expressed about the fact that the allegedly appalling feeding techniques recorded had not produced health/nutritional deficits in the four older children. The South Asian observer is unlikely to find this surprising, since direct experience would show that, allowing for variations due to individual preference and social class, millions of South Asian children in their countries of origin are fed in much the same way as this child. Professional trainings rarely introduce such knowledge and the dissonance between personal experience and Western training may merely add to the difficulties of the non-Western professional seeking acceptance in a highly competitive profession.

These feeding strategies are applied to children up to the ages of 5–6 years (or sometimes older), and epitomize cultural beliefs about the nature of children and the properties of foods, and demonstrate connections between food-linked practices and children's emotional/socialization needs (Dwivedi, 2000). Feeding routines form part of larger adult–child behaviour patterns (such as the indirect communication of affection through distinctive qualities of touch, tone of voice and other non-verbal exchange) and routines (such as sleeping arrangements), that provide both care and the enculturation of children (Lancy, 1996). It is worth noting that South Asian feeding and sleep routines foster dependence on adults, with resultant 'attachment behaviour' that might appear problematic to Western observers looking for successful separation and developing autonomy. Similar patterns have been described among other cultural groups in Africa and South America (Harwood et al., 1995; LeVine et al., 1996). Cultural difference in the quality of physical contact is an area that is somewhat harder to demonstrate. Prolonged skin contact, with a firmness of touch that may appear forceful to other cultures, is part of the intense and indulgent maternal focus on babies and young children, manifest in finger-feeding, massage, and other South Asian styles of child care. Equally, prolonged feeding routines, in which the child is allowed to play while the mother cajoles her into eating, are components of a very particular style of developing parent–child attachment that relies more on physical reciprocities than on the eye contact and verbal exchanges said to be more typical of middle-class Western child-rearing. Comparing US and Mayan (Mexican) communities, Morelli et al. (1992) make similar links between infants' sleeping arrangements (Mayan infants sleep with a parent/other adult) and the need of American children for attachment objects and bedtime routines that ease the transition to sleeping alone.

## Why had the parents failed to take medical advice?

Azar and Benjet (1994) discuss the wide variety of reasons why non-compliance with a range of professional expectations (translated in the British context to care plans, contact arrangements and cooperation with alternative carers/professionals) may be misinterpreted by the mainstream professional as poor parenting. In this vignette, records showed that the parents had never refused home visits by health professionals and placed great reliance on their (South Asian) GP, whom they visited frequently, but that their attendance at hospital follow-up (paediatric) appointments deteriorated as time went by. How do such families understand the different roles of GP, health visitor, dietitian, community and hospital paediatric teams, neonatologist, and so on? Which professionals (and advice) do they find more 'user-friendly', and which ones do they avoid? Continued ignorance of Western systems, however frustrating to professionals and however dire its consequences, when identified in otherwise caring parents, requires very different therapeutic approaches compared to parents who intend to cause harm (effectively, to cause death). Without skilled assessment of the overall quality of parental investment in the child, non-compliance may not be safely read as indicating callous disregard or harmful intention.

## Professional, and cultural, expertise

Senior professionals involved in this case, who claimed experience of working with South Asians in their area, had nevertheless failed to pick up (or comment on) the obvious cultural misinterpretations of feeding routines. How might this be understood? At least one of these senior professionals belonged to a minority ethnic group, though not the same as that of the family. While personal experience of non-Western cultural patterns may facilitate awareness/interest in the variability of child-rearing practices, it may just as easily not do so. Equally, the mere fact of exposure to minority ethnic populations (in the catchment area) may not stimulate curiosity or lead to increasing cultural competence. Without a rigorous effort to understand the network of pragmatic and symbolic meanings, of overt and covert intentions, 'other' cultural practices will merely seem exotic or misguided. And it is a rare individual client (or family) who will have the linguistic and conceptual skills, as well as the capacity to stand outside their cultural world, in order to describe and explain it to a naive observer.

Among the numerous mental health professionals who had assessed the family were three South Asian workers, who occupied relatively junior positions within their institutional hierarchy. How easy would it be for these workers to voice dissenting opinions, to question the assumptions made by their supervisors about *their* culture, to risk appearing ignorant of local practice (about feeding, for example) especially when Western norms have acquired the status of 'good practice'? Two cultural experts (senior South Asian child psychiatrists) were instructed in this case and both agreed that, while the criteria for significant harm had been met, and were attributable to the quality of parental care, the combination of circumstances (related to prematurity, maternal health, concurrent family stressors, and the particular relationships between the parents and health agencies) that had cumulatively led to serious failure to thrive could not recur to cause similar risk. The court recommended rehabilitation of the child to her family.

## 2. 'Western' professionals, South Asian family

A South Asian mother agreed to undertake the care of four children born to her husband's white lover, who had died of a drug overdose. Despite her proven ability to provide excellent care (as shown by her own children), and despite the well-known difficulties of finding alternative families for sibling groups, the Local Authority recommended that these children should be placed in permanent foster/adoptive families. The expert and the social worker were both white immigrants from former British colonies. The social worker's concerns were: that the South Asian woman had been coerced by her husband into offering child care; that the resentment and hostility she was likely to feel towards these children would impair her ability to care for them; that she would be unable to address the children's cultural needs arising out of their 'white cultural heritage'; and that the jealousy between the two sibling groups would cause these children serious harm. The expert's opinion that the children should be placed in an adoptive family was based on the finding of insecure attachments between these children and their only remaining parent, their father.

The personal and professional experience of both the mental health expert and the social worker were likely to have included exposure to some South Asian and other non-Western cultures and to cultural variations in relationship patterns. The family's culture appeared in the social worker's report as a source of potential difficulties, masking the true intentions of the wife and limiting her ability to address the mixed heritage of the children. The issue of culture was not addressed in the expert's report. Despite the acknowledgement of limited cultural information on this family, it was assumed that some emotional responses would be universal – namely, implacable hostility towards the children of a lover and between sibling groups born of two partners to the same spouse.

### Women in patriarchal cultures

In his discussions with the author the social worker defended his reading of the cultural issues at stake based on 'cultural training' he had received. In the author's view, this was unhelpfully brief and superficial, allowing the confusion of disparate categories of information (Western feminist accounts of the oppression of women in 'traditional Asian culture', Western cultural beliefs about infidelity, and assumptions about the impact of infidelity on the self-esteem of women irrespective of culture; see discussion of similar concerns in Maitra, 1996). Little attempt had been made to confirm these assumptions through direct observation/interview of the couple or their children.

The author's interviews with this South Asian woman and her husband's family demonstrated her struggle to balance personal feelings of hurt and betrayal, with respect for her husband's sense of paternal responsibility (especially since it risked the condemnation of his family and the community), against the compassion she felt for these motherless children. Her decision to prioritize the children's needs above her own had earned her the support and respect of her husband's family and of her own children. Awareness of the roles women accept in traditionally polygynous communities (whether or not polygyny continues in current practice) and the routine care of co-wives' children makes this woman's willingness to take in her husband's children somewhat less remarkable (and less suspect). There are important differences between co-wives and mistresses and it would be unwise to assume that all South Asian women will care for children born of an illicit relationship, or to take declared altruistic intentions (based on cultural ideals) at face value. Detailed interviews based on a thorough knowledge of cultural reper-toires are necessary to understand the individual's interpretations of cultural rules and ideals and of the choices available to them. The power of such decision-making by women lies in their ability to achieve several aims without openly criticizing men or flouting male authority. In seeking the support of elders (and importantly, these were elders in her husband's family) she both made her husband's mis-demeanour public, and made it less reprehensible by joining with him to legitimize these children. She also gained the respect and gratitude of her husband and his family and re-structured the balance of power between her husband and herself. To see this as 'coercion', or as accommodation to male power, would miss the complexity of real relationships within patriarchal systems.

### The dangers of sibling rivalry

South Asian myth and legend abound with exemplary stories of sacrifice, duty and obligation between siblings. These might be understood as cultural solutions to common conflicts, acknowledging and correcting for divisive forces that might otherwise interfere with family cohesion and group goals. In this particular family, the children born of the marriage were able to talk about the gains and losses of acquiring 'new brothers and sisters'. The cultural ideal was here reinforced by the children's high regard for their mother, their acceptance of her decision, and the approval it had from their elders. Rivalrous feelings, when these arose, would not be given prominence and would be jointly discouraged by the group.

The mixed-race children were eventually placed in the care of their father and his wife.

## 3. South Asian professional, West African family

A 12-year-old boy of West African origin was seen in a child and family consultation service after a serious overdose. He insisted that he wanted to die because his mother did not love him. He recounted, with a mixture of sadness and dramatic relish, a story of being beaten and kicked. When asked about physical evidence (bruises, marks) of these apparently serious assaults he brushed this away. The significant risk of further self-harm and of emotional and physical abuse, together with the fact that there were no other adult family members who might have mediated, made it necessary to refer the family to the local child protection agency for assessment. When this was discussed with the boy's mother she flew into a rage, accused him of lying and ingratitude, and threatened to send him back to her family in Africa. The mother refused to attend further appointments, complaining that the author, being Asian, did not understand African culture, where physical chastisement was an acceptable means of ensuring that children were properly brought up. She dismissed her son's overdose as attention-seeking and his sadness (named thus by the author) as resentment because she could not afford the games/trips he wanted. She pointed out that he had more material luxuries than she or his contemporaries in Africa had and that returning him to Africa would both show him the realities of life and contain his increasing disobedience within a network of close adult supervision.

What degree of exposure to the culture of a family, or to 'allied' cultures, confers adequate knowledge? And what additional sources are relevant? The personal and professional bank of information that the author could draw upon (intimate knowledge of a cluster of South Asian cultures, experience of being a minority ethnic person in Britain, an 18-month sojourn in West Africa, clinical work with families from many parts of Africa, and a fairly broad reading of the literature *in English* on child-rearing and family function in a number of African cultures) did not prevent the rapid breakdown of trust in this case. Though a display of cultural affront may be used as a ploy to hold professionals at bay, especially when a parent has some awareness that their own behaviour may be at fault, the failure to engage this mother could not be attributed (at this stage) to the mother alone. The mental health professional's role in assessment of risk cannot ensure parental compliance in the same way that legal proceedings often do. Forced compliance, and restrictions on time, further complicate the gathering of detailed, reliable information about relationships that improve predictions of future risk. The success of assessment tasks (such as reading emotional conflict accurately, probing cultural beliefs, reassuring, drawing accurately on cultural parallels, and culturally viable alternative strategies) depends on subtle nuances of language, emotional expression, and knowledge that cannot be achieved without a degree of cultural match, or through prolonged cultural exposure and specific efforts to bridge the gap with professional training. In the absence of an appropriate West African colleague to refer to how can we identify the cultural issues relevant here?

### 'Acceptable' physical punishment?

Does physical punishment occur more commonly in certain ethnic communities, such as Asian, African and African Caribbean (Arnold, 1982)? Levinson (1981) notes that 90 per cent of parents in the United States use physical punishment. British law is clear that physical punishment may not be used in schools or other child care institutions. Explicit guidance on acceptable forms of chastisement by parents/carers is based on an assortment of beliefs about what causes harm and has an uneven evidence-base. Professionals tend to accept 'smacking', but without description one is often reliant on the language used by the child/adult witness. 'Hitting', 'beating' and 'slapping' arouse alarm more regularly, often with little consideration of the use of these terms by non-English speakers. This is not to say that adults do not minimize severe punishment or attempt to rationalize it away (e.g. 'It never did me any harm'). Other features that are likely to precipitate investigations include evidence of marking of the skin, reports of blows to the head/face, use of objects (stick or belt), or allegations of fear/humiliation being inflicted on the child. In considering the account given above, it was unclear whether the child's account was exaggerated and, if so, to what degree. False allegations about physical abuse cannot be ruled out. It is not unknown for angry, resentful children to exaggerate/fabricate complaints, calling in external agencies in a bid to influence the balance of power within the family. However, distinctions between true and false accounts must be based on detailed interviews and cannot rely on idealizations, whether of children or of culture.

### Interpreting emotion

How accurate is a reading of emotion across cultures? Cultural patternings of facial and verbal expressions of emotion (tone of voice, emphasis, use of expletives) are learned in early life and form the basis of social competence within the group. White (1993) discusses emotional attribution within a culture, and its embeddedness in a complex understanding of identities and scenarios of social action. When identifying emotion across cultures, while the broad categories might be correct, error is more likely in finer attributions (of nuanced meaning and action consequences). Variations in how anger is displayed, the influence of gender, how much is masked, and in which contexts, may not be easily read without prolonged exposure to the particular culture (and social class). In the case discussed, it would be difficult to be certain of the mother's emotions without simultaneous observation by a West African colleague conversant with variations due to class and regional difference, and skilled at differentiating between intensity of emotion (especially in the case of anger, which is more likely to be modified in social exchange), mixed emotional states (e.g. anger laced with contempt, outrage, betrayal, hurt), ambivalence, and other motivational states. Without joint exploration and feedback it is equally difficult to rule out misinterpretation between mother and child, the son's expressive repertoire (and comprehension skills) having developed at least in part within a peer culture alien to the parent's.

### Culture and punishment

Many cultures, including those in West Africa (Jahoda, 1982; Nsamenang, 1992; Lancy, 1996), aim to instill emotions such as 'fear' (of elders, especially parents, teachers, older siblings, extended family and community elders) or shame (through teasing or mockery) as a deterrent to disobedience and to teach a proper regard for adult authority. Such socialization experiences ensure the continuity of cultural models of desired behaviour, and children acquire a sense of justifiable and appropriate punishment. They may view even quite severe physical punishment as unremarkable if they are not treated any differently from their peers/siblings and, *if within that culture's understanding of esteem and affection*, they are assured of adult love and concern. Levinson (1981) showed that the availability of alternative caretakers in extended or polygynous households was accompanied by lower rates of physical punishment of children in those societies. However, as Lancy (1996) notes, rural–urban differences in society's expectations of parents (from more laissez-faire, shared caring with other adults in rural settings to urban expectations that parents will ensure certain standards of children's behaviour) contribute to a sharp rise in rates of child abuse/abandonment when rural African families migrate to cities.

In the case described, the mother's angry threat to send her child back to Africa might be understood as containing multiple messages: to the child, a threat of rejection and a promise of more strict discipline; to the professional, the mother's parental right to make decisions about her child, her access to preferred sources of help (her culture of origin), and rejection of therapy and professional expertise/ authority.

### Culture and adult authority: state and family

In countries where the state provides little assistance to parents for child care, parental authority over their children is perhaps only ever challenged directly by those above the parent in the family hierarchy. Immigrant children in British schools are exposed to a range of Western cultural ideals (autonomy, egalitari- anism, individualism, gender equality, scientific knowledge, professional expertise, particular styles of emotional expression) that challenge the status and authority of parents and community elders. Demands for acculturation into the emotional styles dominant within their peer groups may cut at the very basis of emotional exchange within the family. In the pitched battles that ensue between parent and child, it would be unwise to take what is often emotional rhetoric at face value. Equally, it would be wise to remember that the child's wishes will often sound more reasonable than the parents' because his language (if not the underlying intention) draws from the same world of meanings and values as the Western professional's.

## 4. South Asian professional, White British family

A white British family had been known to child protection agencies for over two decades. Several of the older children had been placed in the care of the local authority after recurrent injuries, allegations of physical abuse by the parents, and of sexual abuse by persons within the family's social network. Care proceedings for the youngest two children were triggered by similar concerns of uncontrolled bullying among the siblings, school non-attendance, lack of adult supervision (shoplifting and the 6-year-old found on the streets at midnight). Despite high levels of professional support the mother's attention to the children's (and her own) health, emotional and educational needs remained inadequate. All the professionals involved (social worker, guardian, child psychiatrist) were agreed that this had caused significant harm to the children's intellectual and emotional development. However, a stalemate ensued when the children refused to comply with proposals for foster care and residential schooling. Professional concern about using coercion on children raised interesting questions about the nature and severity of harm, and about different cultural expectations of parents within white British communities.

How might the local authorities' unusual degree of tolerance in this case be understood? In a number of workshops presented by the author, child protection and mental health professionals found it very difficult to formulate hypotheses to explain the cause of this family's 'dysfunction'. Azar and Benjet (1994) discuss the biases that make professionals discount abuse suspicions in persons resembling themselves – that is, from the same class and culture. Lancy (1996) compares non-Western agrarian societies, which see children primarily as economic assets, with Western 'child-centered' societies, in which the high level of parental involvement in rearing small numbers of children is a result of the opprobrium heaped on parents for failures of child-rearing. He admits that this might be less true of social classes other than the middle class. To what class might the family described above be allocated? Entirely dependent on the welfare state, and apparently ascribing little value to the aspirations promoted by mainstream British society (for education, employment, financial betterment, certain styles of interpersonal relationships), this family nevertheless seemed sufficiently familiar to British professionals not to attract a label of specific deviance, or to feature in professional training.

The commonest explanations of parenting deficit locate it in the individual, as attributable to the effects of disorder (learning disability, mental/physical illness) or trauma (recent, early, or overwhelming). In this case, vague, uncorroborated accounts of domestic violence in the distant past were insufficient to explain the pattern of parenting incapacity. Observations made of the mother's personal appearance, intellectual ability and social skills suggested a lower than average level of function, but did not fit a definable pattern or reach a significant degree of dysfunction in areas other than housekeeping and parenting.

Azar and Benjet (1994) and King and Piper (1995) discuss the American and British child welfare and legal systems respectively, commenting on their openness to personal and cultural bias due to inconsistent laws, poorly specified theoretical models based on inadequate research and a continuing confusion of 'optimal' with 'good-enough' environments for children. What constitutes harm to children continues to be defined by middle-class concerns, relegating numerous groups within the mainstream to a sort of hinterland with little attempt to enquire into the child-rearing goals of these groups. The invisibility of British culture (and within-culture variability) in professional training and in professional discourse within Britain is not surprising. However, without an explicit focus on this subject child welfare policy risks remaining ineffectual for children and families such as the one described.

## IS MATCHING POSSIBLE?

If it is possible to draw a single conclusion from these vignettes it may be that culturally expert assessments require more than culturally matched experts. Personal experience through enculturation is a valuable asset, but many additional skills are necessary before such information may contribute usefully to professional expertise. But first, two questions need to be considered. What is the availability of minority ethnic experts? And, to what extent is cultural competency a goal of their training?

## The populations

The 1991 UK census data (Balarajan and Raleigh, 1992) on the ethnic composition of the general population show that 94 per cent were White, 2.9 per cent Asian, 1 per cent Black Caribbean, 1 per cent Chinese, 0.4 per cent Black African and 0.4 per cent Black Other. Population estimates based on a recent Labour Force Survey (Office of National Statistics, 2000) show rising growth rates and increasing numbers of children in these communities, concentrated in a small number of cities. Based on the growth rates of ethnic communities Scott et al. (2001) report the following increases in the numbers of children between 1992–94 and 1997–99: 13 per cent (Pakistani), 30 per cent (Bangladeshi), 49 per cent (Black Mixed) and 28 per cent (Other Mixed).

Barn (1993) shows that Black children between 0 and 19 years, who form only 3.08 per cent of the total number of children in Britain (see Table 3.1), continue to be over-represented in the population looked after by local authorities. In a recent Department of Health study (2001), they formed 7 per cent of the looked-after population. Asian children, who make up 5.96 per cent of the total population of children, constitute 2 per cent of the looked-after population. Table 3.1 shows that very small numbers of health professionals and guardians are Black. While Asian children might be more easily matched with Asian health professionals, this would not be true with guardians.

## The experts

Brophy, Wale and Bates (1999) collected data from children's guardians in England and Wales on cases in court proceedings involving experts. Sixteen per cent of these cases concerned minority ethnic children but, not surprisingly, very few of these children had been matched with guardians from the same ethnic category. They found that over half the guardians reported the use of experts (by all parties) in at least 40 per cent of their cases in the previous year; guardians and local authorities usually gathered paediatric and psychiatric reports on children and parents, irrespective of ethnic group. Guardians usually sought expert opinions on minority ethnic children/parents from child and family psychiatrists (52 per cent), followed by paediatricians (35 per cent) and psychologists (26 per cent). There was very little use of cultural advisors or advocates.

*Table 3.1* Ethnicity of child population and experts (%)

|  | White | Black | Asian | Mixed | Other |
|---|---|---|---|---|---|
| **General population children (0–19 yrs)** (Office of National Statistics, 2000) | 88.1 | 3.08 | 5.96 | 1.97 | 0.84 |
| **Guardians** Brophy et al., 1997 | 94 | 2 | 1 | 1 | 2 |
| **Child psychiatrists** Royal College of Psychiatrists (personal communication) | 68.3 + 4.3 other | 0.16 (+ other) | 8.56 | – | – |
| **Adult psychiatrists** (Decker, 2001) | 64.5 | 6 | 17.7 | – | – |
| **Paediatricians** (Decker, 2001) | 64.4 | 5.2 | 20.5 | – | – |

Note: The National Institute of Social Workers was unable to provide data on the ethnic breakdown of social workers. Figures do not necessarily add up to 100 percent.

Brophy *et al.* (1999) have undertaken an extensive series of studies of experts in child protection litigation and have explored how much training they had received in cultural matters. They comment on the failure of social work training, both at basic and post-qualification levels, to integrate an understanding of the dynamic nature of culture in child protection work. The Social Services Inspectorate report on services for minority ethnic children and families (O'Neale, 2000) concluded that the quality of services to these families was heavily dependent on the quality of social work intervention. Families often experienced difficulty in accessing services because they did not understand the role of social services, particularly if English was not their first language. With regard to assessments, the report noted that these 'were often partial and rarely covered parenting capacity, the child's needs and family and environmental issues. In some instances the safety of ethnic minority children was being compromised because physical and sexual abuse had not been identified and properly dealt with as a child protection issue' (p. 4). While this concern is rarely made explicit it is likely that the more vocal the ethnic community the greater the reluctance of statutory agencies to pursue allegations of dangerous care.

In their survey of guardians, Brophy *et al.* (1999) found that just over half the sample of guardians had undertaken some equal opportunities training, and many felt that it did not focus on their work with minority ethnic children and wanted more training in this area.

The educational goals of higher training for psychiatrists (Royal College of Psychiatrists, 1998: p. 34) simply includes as core knowledge and skills, 'Knowledge of the impact of cultural, social and family influences on the genesis, maintenance and management of psychiatric disorders and the cultural aspects of psychiatric practice in a multi-ethnic society'. There is little to say how this will be achieved, or how competency in the area of culture/ethnicity will be rated.

In their study of 17 consultant child psychiatrists, Brophy *et al.* (2001) noted that half claimed to have had some training on the assessment of black and minority ethnic families. However, this consisted of fairly minimal input, namely a study day provided by the Royal College of Psychiatrists, a study day with a legal practitioner, and 'some training' offered by a London teaching hospital. Of the remainder some had 'informed themselves' because of the ethnic composition of their catchment areas. Others were divided in their views about the universal applicability of the conceptual frameworks they employed and some admitted to a sense of unease when working with black groups or children of mixed parentage 'because I think they would prefer to have a black psychiatrist, and I think where possible they . . . should find someone who parents find appropriate' (p. 51).

The higher specialist training for child psychiatrists must include in the 'Core Experience': 'Experience in developing skills in the assessment, formulation and treatment of all the main psychiatric disorders encountered in children and adolescents, *sensitive to the ethnic origin and cultural background of children and families*' (Royal College of Psychiatrists, 1999: p. 6; my emphasis). Again, it is left unclear how this sensitivity will be taught, or by whom, and how it will be assessed. 'Culture' is not mentioned at all in the context of assessing 'children and their families where child abuse is suspected'. The emphasis remains disappointingly linear and old-fashioned, with culture being seen as merely influencing the manifestations of disorder rather than the experiential contexts of both the client and the psychiatrist.

Drawing these elements together it would appear that, while black and mixed-race children are over-represented in court proceedings, the professions that undertake assessments of risk have minimal core training in assessing risk across cultural difference. In a significant proportion of these complex and potentially problematic cases, expert opinions may not be requested and reports are based largely on the premises of one discipline, social work (though many guardians may have additional training relevant to child care work: Brophy *et al.*, 1999). The small numbers of senior black/minority ethnic professionals in health and social services and the small numbers of black/minority ethnic guardians suggest that black or mixed-race children are usually assessed by white professionals. When black/minority ethnic workers are available they are likely to be poorly placed to counter the errors that might arise due to the dominant (Western) cultural bias. Brophy *et al.* (2001) noted that guardians were satisfied with child psychiatrists' expert opinions, but their research did not enquire whether this included the experts' attention to matters of culture or race. Given that the minority ethnic child's voice was likely to be heard through the reports of white guardians and white experts, it is difficult to know who, if anyone, should decide whether or not culture had been appropriately and adequately addressed.

## THE COMPONENTS OF CULTURAL COMPETENCE

If child protection policy and practice are to change so that assessments of black and minority ethnic children and families might be more skilled and accurate, change must also occur in those academic disciplines that inform risk assessments. Among the barriers to such change is a deep-rooted reluctance to question the universal claims of Western culture and indigenous (Western) psychology. While this conservatism may be understandable, and common to most societies, it is one face of institutional racism. The Macpherson Report (1999: p. 27) quotes Dr Benjamin Bowling:

> Institutional racism is the **process** by which people from ethnic minorities are systematically discriminated against by a range of public and private bodies. If the result or **outcome** of established laws, customs or practices is racially discriminatory, then institutional racism can be said to have occurred. Although *racism is rooted in widely shared attitudes, values and beliefs*, discrimination can occur irrespective of the intent of the individuals who carry out the activities of the institution . . . However, some discrimination practices are the product of **uncritical** rather than unconscious racism. That is, practices with a racist outcome are not engaged in without the actor's

knowledge; rather the actor has *failed to consider the consequences of his or her actions for people from ethnic minorities*. Institutional *racism affects the routine ways in which ethnic minorities are treated* in their capacity as employees, witnesses, victims, suspects and members of the general public. (My emphases)

Lau (1991), writing soon after the introduction of the 1989 Children Act, suggested the need to understand 'one's own ethnocultural roots and value systems'. While she provided prompts that might yield important cultural information, the impossibility of carefully arguing the relevance of culture in an arena as complex as this, and of containing it within a single chapter, seems painfully obvious. The very next paper in the same volume (Jones *et al.*, 1991) discusses developmental phases and tasks and the nature of attachment with no reference to the extensive literature on the cultural variability within these areas. Over a decade later, it would be difficult to point to signs of progress. Talk of culture largely remains an 'add-on' to the main subject, which is a discussion of assumed human psychological universals.

## Recent attempts

There have been a number of attempts to improve professional training for work with, and the provision of, services to black/minority ethnic children and families. Recent guidance for social workers within the *Framework for the Assessment of Children in Need and their Families* is contained in a section on 'Assessing Black Children in Need and their Families' (Dutt and Phillips, 2000). It attempts to extend the scope of discussion beyond the usual inventory of practices (e.g. dietary customs and care of skin/hair) but continues to treat culture as potentially problematic (if not accorded sufficient respect) and child protection policy as though it were culture-free.

The Training Manual published by the 'Race' and Culture Special Interest Group of the British Psychological Society (Patel *et al.*, 2000) is a welcome (though uneven) combination of theoretical critiques, practical ideas and annotated bibliographies. The Royal College of Psychiatrists has recently published the conclusions of an advisory group on training in transcultural psychiatry (Moodley, 2002). This lists the knowledge, skills and attitudes of a 'well-trained and culturally competent psychiatrist', incorporating critically important developments in theory to British psychiatry, which has significantly lagged behind family therapy and psychology training. Recommendations made for the basic specialist training curriculum, endorsed by the College, include suggestions for how this knowledge and these skills could be taught, assessed and examined and they acknowledge the need for trainers to seek colleagues more experienced in this area for formal joint training sessions.

While significant difficulties lie ahead if psychology and allied disciplines in Britain are to be revamped and genuinely relevant to a polyphonic world, perhaps this is a time for cautious optimism.

## CONCLUSIONS

A lot more data are needed about the long-term effects of adverse experience, about the protective/malign influence of real-life environments, and the role of culture in ascribing meanings to the available choices, before realistic developmental goals and reliable indicators of what constitutes long-term, significant harm (as opposed to those based on idealized children in optimal environments) may be defined. Until this baseline reflects the position of the minority ethnic child as part of culturally specific adult–community–child networks (rather than the sentimentalized individual with endless rights and few responsibilities), risk may best be assessed by appropriately trained, senior, bi-cultural professionals with an interest in debating (both within their disciplines and between relevant disciplines) the relative weights to be given to potentially competing needs.

Matching alone guarantees no more than personal experience, and this cannot encompass more than a fraction of the cultural information held by a society (Roberts, 1987). However, personal experience is a crucially important first step in appreciating the high costs of misunderstanding culture in this particular field – namely, the devastation of a community's hopes for its future. The interested professional must look for relevant literature, widening the net to include cultural psychology, ethnographic studies and contemporary debates around identity and ethnicity. They should bear in mind that most of the literature available in English is based on work by European or American researchers and contains the potential for bias in descriptions of other cultures. Active steps also need to be taken to seek consultation with cultural communities so as to avoid simplified, or idealized, accounts of traditional practice and equally to seek debate with a peer group of experienced clinicians on how the culturally relativist stance might be translated into practice. The expert must be alert to the cultural assumptions within their hypotheses and seek to check their relevance against observation and interview. They must have the personal strengths, and sufficient authority within their organization, to tolerate a position of some discomfort among their peers, since it would be naive to imagine that one might question dominant cultural assumptions without arousing some hostility. Finally, faced with the emotive pressures of such work it is important for the minority expert to remain scrupulously within the guidelines laid down for experts, but be willing to venture into uncharted territory when presenting their individual reading of cultural material to the court. They must support this with evidence clearly demonstrated in the assessment and with detailed argument to show the relevance of culture in the particular case and how it influences a reading of the best interests of the child.

## References

Arnold, E. (1982) The use of corporal punishment in child rearing in the West Indies, *Child Abuse and Neglect* 6: 141–5.

Azar, S.T. and Benjet, C.L. (1994) A cognitive perspective on ethnicity, race, and termination of parental rights, *Law and Human Behaviour* 18: 249–68.

Balarajan, R. and Raleigh, V.S. (1992) The ethnic populations of England and Wales: the 1991 Census, *Health Trends* 24: 113–16.

Barn, R. (1993) *Black Children in the Public Care System*, London: Batsford.

Brophy, J., Bates, P., Brown, L., Cohen, S., Radcliffe, P. and Wale, C.J. (1999) *Expert Evidence in Child Protection Litigation. Where Do We Go from Here?* London: The Stationery Office.

Brophy, J., Brown, L., Cohen, S. and Radcliffe, P. (2001) *Child Psychiatry and Child Protection Litigation*, London: Royal College of Psychiatrists/Gaskell.

Brophy, J., Wale, C.J. and Bates, P. (1997) *Training and Support in the Guardian ad Litem and Reporting Officer Service – Research Report*, London: Department of Health and the Thomas Coram Research Unit.

Brophy, J., Wale, C.J. and Bates, P. (1999) *Myths and Practices: A National Survey of the Use of Experts in Child Care Proceedings*, London: BAAF.

Decker, K. (2001) Overseas doctors: past and present, in N. Coker (ed.) *Racism in Medicine: An Agenda for Change*, London: King's Fund.

Department of Health (2001) *Statistical Bulletin: Children Looked after in England: 2000/2001*.

Dutt, R. and Phillips, M. (2000) *Assessment of Black Children in Need and their Families: Practice Guidance*, London: Department of Health.

Dwivedi, K.N. (2000) Cultural aspects of feeding: some illustrations from the Indian Culture, in A. Southall and A. Schwartz (eds) *Feeding Problems in Children: A Practical Guide*, Oxford: Radcliffe Medical Press.

Harwood, R.L., Miller, J.G. and Irizarry N.L. (eds) (1995) *Culture and Attachment: Perceptions of the Child in Context*, New York: The Guilford Press.

Jahoda, G. (1982) *Psychology and Anthropology*, London: Academic Press.

Jones, D.P.H., Bentovim, A., Cameron, H., Vizard, E. and Wolkind, S. (1991) Significant harm in context: the child psychiatrist's contribution, in M. Adcock, R. White and A. Hollows (eds) *Significant Harm: Its Management and Outcome*, Croydon: Significant Publications.

King, M. and Piper, C. (1995) *How the Law Thinks about Children*, 2nd ed., Aldershot: Arena.

Lancy, D.F. (1996) *Playing on the Mother-ground: Cultural Routines for Children's Development*, New York: The Guilford Press.

Lau, A. (1991) Cultural and ethnic perspectives on significant harm: its assessment and treatment, in M. Adcock, R. White and A. Hollows (eds) *Significant Harm: Its Management and Outcome*, Croydon: Significant Publications.

LeVine, R.A., Dixon, S., Levine, S., Richman, A., Herbert Leiderman, P., Keefer, H.C. and Brazelton, T.B. (1996) *Childcare and Culture: Lessons from Africa*, Cambridge: Cambridge University Press.

Levinson, D. (1981) Physical punishment of children and wifebeating in cross-cultural perspective, *Child Abuse and Neglect* 5: 193–5.

Macpherson, W. (1999) *The Stephen Lawrence Inquiry: Report of an Inquiry by Sir William Macpherson of Cluny*, London: The Stationery Office.

Maitra, B. (1996) Child abuse: a universal 'diagnostic' category? The implication of culture in definition and assessment, *International Journal of Social Psychiatry* 42: 287–304.

Miller, B.D. (1987) Female infanticide and child neglect in rural North India, in N. Scheper-Hughes (ed.) *Child Survival – Anthropological Perspectives on the Treatment and Maltreatment of Children*, Dordrecht: D. Reidel.

Moodley, P. (2002) Building a culturally capable workforce – an educational approach to delivering equitable mental health services, *Psychiatric Bulletin* 26: 63–5.

Morelli, G.A., Oppenheim, D., Rogoff, B. and Goldsmith, D. (1992) Cultural variation in infants' sleeping arrangements: questions of independence, *Developmental Psychology* 28: 604–13.

Nsamenang, A.B. (1992) *Human Development in Cultural Context: A Third World Perspective*, vol. 16, Cross-Cultural Research and Methodology Series, Newbury Park: Sage.

Office of National Statistics (2000) *Labour Force Survey*.

O'Neale, V. (2000) *Excellence not Excuses: Inspection of Services for Ethnic Minority Children and Families*, London: Department of Health.

Patel, N., Bennett, E., Dennis, M., Dosanjh, N., Mahtani, A., Miller, A. and Nadirshaw, Z. (2000) *Clinical Psychology, 'Race' and Culture: A Training Manual*, London: BPS Books.

Roberts, J.M. (1987) Within cultural variation, *American Behavioural Scientist* 31: 266–79.

Royal College of Psychiatrists (1998) *Higher Specialist Training Handbook*.

Royal College of Psychiatrists (1999) Child and Adolescent Psychiatry Specialist Advisory Committee (CAPSAC) Advisory Papers.

Scheper-Hughes, N. (1987a) Introduction: the cultural politics of child survival, in N. Scheper-Hughes (ed.) *Child Survival – Anthropological Perspectives on the Treatment and Maltreatment of Children*, Dordrecht: D. Reidel.

Scheper-Hughes, N. (1987b) Culture, scarcity, and maternal thinking: mother love and child death in northeast Brazil, in N. Scheper-Hughes (ed.) *Child Survival – Anthropological Perspectives on the Treatment and Maltreatment of Children*, Dordrecht: D. Reidel.

Scott, A., Pearce, D. and Goldblatt, P. (2001) The sizes and characteristics of the minority ethnic populations of Great Britain – latest estimates, *Population Trends* 105 (Autumn): 6–15.

White, G.M. (1993) Moral discourse and the rhetoric of emotions, in C.A. Lutz and L. Abu-Lughod (eds) *Language and the Politics of Emotion*, Paris: Cambridge University Press.

# Part II

# The child's perspective

# Chapter 4

# What is the relevance of attachment to parenting assessments?

*Tony Baker*

## INTRODUCTION

Clinicians who are commissioned as expert witnesses to assess families are often asked to give an opinion about the attachment of a child to their parents or other key relatives. The issue central to the proceedings will turn on whether the child has suffered significant harm and the question about attachment is usually given prominence when the court is considering the care plan for the child. The quality of the child's attachments to birth parents is then considered to have predictive value if there is to be an attempt at rehabilitation or continuing direct contact, even when there has been a finding of maltreatment.

This chapter will propose that assessing attachment has wider relevance to an assessment of parenting, on the basis that the child's attachments to their parents are a direct consequence of the care that they have provided during infancy and afterwards. If the attachment has been secure, it can be presumed that the parents (or some other key persons) have been, at least for some period, available to meet the child's needs in a way that was sensitively responsive and promoted healthy development. If the attachment process has been disrupted for any reason, without a subsequent reparative process, then the consequent insecurity will persist and even deepen. An indication will be given of the importance of attachment status as a foundation of the child's social and emotional development, with implications that extend beyond childhood into adolescence and adulthood. A spectrum of typologies of disrupted attachment will be described, together with the inferences that can be drawn from them about the parental care that the child has received. However, there is often an assumption that *attachment* is synonymous with *relationship* rather than one important aspect of it and the difficulty of distinguishing attachment-specific care from parenting in general will be discussed.

When requesting the clinician to assess the child's attachment to his or her parental figures, there is an assumption that attachment systems are assessable. Attachment *per se* may be assessable in isolation in children under 2 years old but when children are older than this, there are so many other aspects to their relationships that it would be difficult to compartmentalize the assessment in such a narrow way. The assessor will also need to take account of the child's personal history, in particular with a view to providing an understanding of the effects of trauma, maltreatment, or neglect on the child's overall development (see Duncan and Baker, Chapter 5). A 'narrative approach' to appraising the child's attachment status as part of an overall assessment will be described.

## ATTACHMENT AS A TRI-PHASIC PROCESS

Bowlby coined the term attachment in his 1958 paper, which explored the nature of the child's tie to his mother, and he elaborated later in his trilogy *Attachment and Loss* (1969/82; 1973; and 1980). Having observed that a process occurred between mothers and their infants, Bowlby explored the functions of this special relationship and the benefits to the child of establishing a state of secure attachment to the mother.

Since then, a number of factors associated with attachment have become accepted into the body of professional wisdom. It appears that the attachment process is related to survival, not only in terms of the individual infant but also as a way of ensuring an evolutionary advantage in terms of species or gene survival. Attachment serves a function in ensuring that the child is protected from predators and environmental dangers, as well as ensuring that the child's basic needs for food, comfort and relief of distress are met. Coupled with the concept of attachment giving the child advantages, it has been noted that their moves towards separation, independence and autonomy are promoted by a parent who remains available when they begin to explore the horizons of their environment and start learning through independent experiences.

This traditional model of attachment focuses on the specifics of the infant–mother tie in the early months of life. My own clinical practice suggests that the development of discriminant attachment at about 6 months of age, while (potentially) quite evident at infant observation, does not give the whole picture towards the development of secure attachment. The importance of routines in the day-to-day care of babies has also been recognized but not specifically linked to attachment. The following account is my attempt to make sense of the attachment process that is observable in three distinct phases, in which consistency of routine, then person, and then place have successive primacy.

### The first phase

The newborn baby is sentient but not cognizant, and their first stage of learning is through their sensory perceptions. To prime the attachment process, the infant is born with an instinctual fear of abandonment. The earliest fear is related to physical abandonment because the baby has no means to obtain the resources for their own nurture and protection. Primed with this fear, the baby is likely to be rapidly overwhelmed with anxiety by novel sensory experiences. The development of a secure attachment offers resilience to traumatic experiences when the parent offers a containing and sensitive response to the child.

The infant begins to recognize patterns by which they are able to anticipate sequences of primary care-giving. The parents play their part by establishing routines as they manage the child's physical and sensory environment. Patterns of care-giving that quickly reduce distress and induce comfort become established as predictable and reliable. The parents' responses to the baby create a context in which the innate fears of infancy are addressed and resolved in ways that the baby can learn to recognize from their own perspective. The baby learns to distinguish between associations of sensory discomfort, which give rise to attachment seeking behaviour ('find me: save me!'), and associations with sensory pleasure or comfort, which give rise to reinforcing signals to the parent (eye gazing, smiling, and cooing/verbalizations). The child uses every sense to fathom their world so that they acquire a sensory memory to recognize that which is familiar and safe as well as novel and worrying.

When the parents' responses are inconsistent or confuse the sensory recognition system that the baby is developing so that they are unable to establish a reliable sensory database, they are likely to remain in a default mode of anxious arousal, giving a repeating and unrequited distress signal. The attachment then becomes insecure.

This first phase in the attachment process can be called the sensory phase in which the infant becomes attached to routines that reliably meet their needs for comfort and pleasurable feelings. When these are intense, they create a strong antidote to the default position of anxious arousal. While babies can sense the identity of care-givers as familiar through smell, sound and touch in the early months of life, it seems that infants develop reliable visual recognition of care-givers at about 6 months of age. This coincides with development of the capacity to distinguish between familiar and strange people and to respond differently to them. Strangers may evoke distressed attachment behaviour after 6 months of age, or so.

## The second phase

The second phase concerns the establishment of attachment to people who can be relied upon to meet the infant's needs within consistent patterns and routines. The child develops a sense of belonging and trust as the first building blocks in social relationships through the attachment figures meeting a wide repertoire of needs. These range from nurture and protection to healthy stimulation of pleasure and education, especially in language development and communication skills (verbal and non-verbal).

Being able to discriminate between familiar attachment figures and strangers, the child can now operate their distress signals in more precisely targeted ways towards a specific person. It is after this phase has begun that the most useful descriptive observations can be made within an assessment process. Inconsistency and insensitivity will generate insecurity and anxiety, leading the child to make more demands in search of an unambiguous response or they may regress back to the first sensory phase of operation.

## The third phase

When the toddler becomes independently mobile and begins to explore their world, moving out of sight and sound of attachment figures, it becomes important to be able to recognize places that are familiar and associated with safety and pleasure. New places will be explored if an attachment figure is close by and their responses to the new environment can be monitored. They will still be using their entire sensory database to discover familiar perceptions, as much to seek pleasure as to avoid signals of danger. The child's early cognitive skills will also facilitate the process.

## ATTACHMENT AND PARENTING BEHAVIOUR

Reder and Duncan (2001) reviewed the literature relating poor and dangerous parenting with early family experiences, including the parent's own attachments. In particular, Solomon and George (1996) have suggested a crucial connection in the intergenerational progression to either good-enough or adverse parenting by linking the parent's internal representational model of themselves as a protective care-giver with their own early attachment experiences. There is also evidence that mothers with unresolved attachment pathology may not respond satisfactorily to their own infant's distress, but whether this is directly related to their own experience or a more complex dynamic related to their flawed adult personality is unclear. However, Rutter (1997) argued against linking all relationship qualities in adulthood with persistence of attachment-related dynamics. He concluded that a parent's early experiences of selective attachments seem to be associated with the greater capacity to be a well-functioning parent but the link, although important, is by no means inevitable. Only moderate-strength associations have been found between insecure attachment in infancy and psychopathology in later life and between the quality of parenting and an infant's attachment relationships with parents. However, the association strengthens between disorganized insecure attachments and later pathology, including pathological parenting.

Healthy maternal bonding is the inseparable mirror image to successful infant attachment and it can be conceptualized as the mother making emotional space for the child within her psyche. This is a process that may begin before conception and it can be strongly influenced by the mother's previous antenatal, obstetric or gynaecological history. The bonding process relies on the maternal fantasies about the life growing within her and her anticipation and expectations of the infant's birth and the realization of her motherhood. Reder and Duncan (1995) described the concept of the child-to-be developing a meaning for the mother, which may or may not be shared with her partner or other close relatives. If the realization of birth, motherhood and baby do not provide a close enough match with her prenatal fantasies, and if the child acquires a negative meaning (linked to anxiety or depression), the bonding process may become limited or pathologically flawed.

This, in turn, will influence the mother's response sensitivity to her infant's attachment behaviours.

## IMPLICATIONS OF ATTACHMENT FOR THE CHILD'S WELL-BEING AND DEVELOPMENT

Main and Hesse (1990) hypothesized that fear lies at the root of attachment disorganization. This hypothesis is explored and developed extensively by Solomon and George (1999a) and their co-contributors in the light of their earlier research (1995 and 1996). Fear is introduced into the relationship by *frightened* as well as *frightening* mothers. In studies of children with disorganized attachments, where there was not a history of physical child maltreatment, there was a strong association with the mother having an unresolved attachment issue from her own childhood. In addition to poor social adjustment, controlling or aggressive behaviour problems, low self-esteem, poor play competence, it has been shown that this group of children is likely to have enduring problems into adolescence, including a greater tendency to react to stress by dissociation.

Others have looked at the longer-term effects of attachment disorder and psychopathology. This has been extensively reviewed by Dozier *et al*. (1999), who reported a higher incidence of psychiatric conditions such as depression, anxiety, schizophrenia, dissociative disorders, and personality disorders (especially borderline personality and antisocial personality). Greenberg (1999) has also reviewed the associations between attachment problems and psychopathology in childhood and between protective factors and risk factors leading to maladaptive psychological and social growth.

Attachment disorders are increasingly being diagnosed and described as the *product* of faulty early parenting and the *cause* of current behaviour and socialization difficulties. The use of this diagnostic descriptor as a catch-all can lead to difficulties. However, there is undoubtedly a group of children who have a severe problem in relating to others, in the absence of an autistic spectrum disorder, in that they do not make any attachment or they make superficial and indiscriminate attachments. The diagnosis cannot be made simply on current observation and there will be a history of disruption, fearful relationships, specific maltreatment or neglect.

## A PROPOSED TYPOLOGY OF ATTACHMENT DYSFUNCTION

Attachment security was defined by Ainsworth *et al*. (1978) as 'the state of being secure or untroubled about the availability of the attachment figure'. To be able to describe a child as secure in their attachment to a particular care-giver, it is necessary to observe the child in the presence of that adult in a context that is likely to give rise to attachment behaviour – that is, when the child is stressed and in need of protection, comfort or reassurance. This is possible in early childhood using Ainsworth *et al.*'s (1978) Strange Situation Test, a research tool which requires an observer to code interactions between child and parent through a formulated series of separations and reunions involving a stranger. Ainsworth and her colleagues found that some infant responses were indicative of a secure attachment, while others reflected an insecure attachment, which they called *avoidant* and *ambivalent/resistant*. Main and Solomon (1990) later described a further category, *disorganized/disoriented*, as their research had identified a significant discrete group that did not match Ainsworth's types.

Solomon and George (1999b) give an excellent critical review of the research tools that have evolved since Ainsworth's report of the Strange Situation in early childhood. What is to be drawn from this analysis is that there is a variety of research approaches to assessing attachment but there is no standardized approach for the use of clinicians generally.

My own clinical experience has suggested the following types of attachment dysfunction, the last four of which have not been described before:

- Never having been attached, i.e. *unattached*
- Now detached after having been attached, i.e. *detached*
- Avoidant under stress, i.e. *avoidant*
- Regressed and dependent with clingy separation anxiety, i.e. *dependent*
- Alternately avoidant and dependent i.e. *ambivalent*
- Compulsive care-giving towards parent, i.e. *reversed*
- Confuses intimate care with sexual arousal and sexualizes approaches to care-giver, i.e. *erotic*
- Controlling, chaotic, bizarre and destructive in serial placements, i.e. *malignant*.

The key concept which links these types is that attachment relationships are based on *needs*, and they become dysfunctional by distortion of the mechanisms for perceiving needs, meeting needs or identifying who meets whose needs and how. These descriptors are attachment-based but also incorporate other contaminating or distorting factors in the child's broader developmental story of social and emotional development. A summary of each type will be given.

## The unattached child

The unattached child is one who, from earliest infancy, has been subjected to severe neglect by unresponsive carers, sometimes compounded by extremes of physical violence, and who fails to develop attachment relationships. The child's undifferentiated ego suffers severe assaults and subsequently they protect themselves from all people, remaining instead in a world of self-stimulation. The child shows repetitive stereotyped behaviour patterns that are not integrated with events in the external environment, which Rutter *et al.* (1999) described as quasi-autistic. Another manifestation of the unattached child can be seen in the pre-school years as indiscriminate approaches to others in a way that is shallow and devoid of normal social meaning. Other people are used as functional objects to gain attention and contact, but in a mechanistic way. The abandonment inherent in severe neglect renders the child unable to develop an internal working model of relationships that includes any sense of belonging, trust or true relationship in the conventional sense.

## The detached child

The child who is detached is one who has experienced an attachment relationship, whether secure or insecure, but their attempts to obtain a sensitive response have been frustrated repeatedly by neglect, inconsistency, emotional abandonment and a combination of physical and emotional abuse. The child's meaning to the parent may have been positive until they made a move towards autonomy. If the infant is temperamentally challenging or in other ways a poor match with the mother's bonding fantasy, her disappointment may result in rejection and punishment of that source of her disappointment.

Behaviourally, the detached child becomes a self-caring toddler who is actively resistant to being cared for, even when removed from the birth family into foster care. While such children may be able to interact, they are unable to form relationships based on a sense of belonging or trust and care-givers' approaches are rejected, either coldly or with highly aroused distress.

## Avoidant attachment

The child with an avoidant type of attachment disorder is one who manifests an obvious anxious reaction to stress, but retreats when approached by the attachment figure. Such a child may relate in an appropriate way when not under stress and copes with social interactions neutrally when receiving primary care by a parent. The distress of the child is associated with high arousal and the avoidant response ('leave me alone!') has its origins in inconsistent and disproportionate responsiveness of their parent(s).

This is most likely to occur when the attachment figure has resonated with the child's distressed arousal in a way that is out of control and so they fail to meet the infant's needs. Such a situation may arise particularly if the child was premature or suffered from serious illness or injury in early life, which required special sensitivity in the parents' responses.

## Dependent attachment

Children with a dependent type of attachment disorder manifest their insecurity by separation anxiety, becoming clingy and easily upset, and repeatedly pursuing proximity. The parent reciprocates by offering the child an exaggeratedly sensitive response that reinforces the child's regressive need for closeness. The child's internal working model evolves an internal characterization of itself as being incapable of independent exploration or separation without high arousal. The parent is unable to tolerate the child's distress and probably also responds to distress themselves by regression, with loss of ordinary coping skills and a need to be rescued. There may be a parental history of separation anxiety and exaggerated arousal responses, highly dependent relationships and other types of problematic dependency (e.g. alcohol/substances) and addictions/compulsions (e.g. eating/oral gratification).

## Ambivalent attachment

Ambivalent attachment reflects the child's response to inconsistent primary care. The emotional context is one of high arousal on the part of the parents, with high expressed emotion throughout the family environment. Thus the child is exposed to extremes of both positive and negative arousal. The parents include the child in their own dramas and they respond with overwhelming closeness, overanxious protectiveness and a tendency to lose control in frustration, anger and distress.

In situations where the child develops an ambivalent pattern of attachment, the meaning of the child may be influenced by high maternal anxiety about her own and the baby's safety and an over-idealized view of family life, which is never realized. The greater the over-protectiveness and smothering, the more the child's regression and dependency is reinforced; but the more the child is exposed to a highly charged negative environment, the more they will respond by avoidance. Domestic violence with dramatic oscillations between separation threats and reconciliations creates a typical context for ambivalent attachment, as does parental mental illness, such as bi-polar affective disorder.

## Reversed attachment

In older children, a pattern of reversed attachment may arise when the child devotes their energy to meeting the parent's needs. Such a child is born into a family with a highly dependent parent and carries a prescribed role – for instance, to give the parent status, to be a comforter to the parent's distress, or to be a conflict regulator in the family. The child with reversed attachment closely monitors the parent's mood, learns to respond with compliance to the parent's demands and manages to cope by suppressing their own needs, having learnt not to make demands.

The signs of reversed attachment in a child are anxiety, lack of self-confidence, low self-esteem, lack of ego-differentiation, and preoccupation with the parents' well-being and comfort. School refusal may be a significant later feature, as is personal neglect, since the child's needs are subjugated to the parents' needs. A typical context will be a primary attachment figure who is isolated in the community, lacking extended family support and who shows other dependency behaviours, including psychosomatic illnesses, alcohol or substance abuse. The child is manipulated by the parent's emotions and is given undue responsibilities in the home from an early age.

## Erotic attachment

Erotic attachment disorder can typically be seen in children who approach opposite-sex parents in a sexualized way, seeking proximity as if for comfort or affection but then using it to become sexually aroused. This type of behaviour will be transferred to other adults in a caring or attachment role, for instance other adult relatives, teachers, nurses, foster carers or residential social workers.

An obvious link can be made to early (pre-school) sexual abuse by a parental figure, where the child is 'invited' into intimacy with the parent. Such children will usually experience their own sexual arousal as gratifying rather than painful or aversive. It can be understood that if children's needs for comfort and reassurance are repeatedly confused by sexual stimulation through intimacy, then sexual arousal and gratification may become part of their repertoire for meeting comfort needs. Further confusion arises later in puberty when they are managing their sexual arousal, which is then directed towards the mother-figure or her substitute. There is undoubtedly a conditioning factor to this type of attachment disorder, but it can be seen that the problems arise specifically when the need for comfort and relief of distress/arousal are distorted by sexual associations. The preoccupying mind-set of confusion between sex and violence may be set at a very early age but can have a major role in the development of sexually sadistic behaviour directed towards older women.

Erotic attachment disorder is not confined to boys. Its manifestation in girls can be seen in the anxious preoccupation that they may have about intimacy and sexual contact with adult males who have a caring or authority role. Women with this type of attachment disorder often give histories of multiple sexual abuse throughout childhood and adolescence, where sexual contact becomes a principal strategy towards meeting a range of needs.

## Malignant attachment

Malignant attachment disorder describes the ultimate manifestation of disorganized attachment systems. The child is initially excited and aroused by closeness with the adult, even though it is for the purpose of enhancing the parent's experience rather than the child's. The parent's expectations of the child may be far beyond his or her ability to cope with the 'exciting' experience and he/she fails, becomes upset and spoils the adult's enjoyment. The child is then punished in some way and left to cope with their own distress in a context of rejection.

The pervasive nature of this type of experience may include: tickling games that become sadistic; receiving 'presents' that the parent breaks; play-fighting or rough and tumble games that end when the child is hurt and cries; sexual abuse that the child experiences with pain and distress (e.g. choking); or any experience in which the child is required to participate with enthusiasm but ends in their distress, the parent's anger and disappointment, and the child being blamed, punished and rejected. The child's capacity to distinguish between positive and negative sensory experiences is diminished by the repeated re-enactment of 'nice' becoming 'nasty'. The child learns that enjoyment and fun always lead to pain and rejection, no matter how much the parent smiles at the outset. The child therefore cannot trust their own or others' judgement.

The term malignant is appropriate because the child transfers their expectations of parents, based on an internal working model, to all new care settings. Such children are described as destructive, overactive, controlling, chaotic and unable to enjoy any experience. Well-meaning foster carers find that whatever good activities they arrange, the child always spoils the fun. It is as if the child cannot bear to wait for the 'nice' experience to become 'nasty' and they take control of the waiting by ensuring a bad outcome that inevitably leads to their rejection. This accounts for the multiple placements of some children whose malignant behaviour cannot be tolerated as it is transferred from care setting to care setting. Each disruption of placement deepens the attachment disorder as the child's internal working model is reinforced. Labels of conduct disorder yield to diagnosis of sociopathy or even psychopathy as the child lurches from placement to placement.

## A NARRATIVE APROACH TO THE ASSESSMENT OF ATTACHMENT

Clinicians are often asked to assess attachment status of children who have already been separated from their parents with subsequent restriction of contact. While the separation itself may be a stressor, any findings may be attributable as much to the child's subsequent experiences as to the child–parent relationship and attachment. Even children who had been securely attached prior to the separation may have become insecure by the traumatic nature of their attachment disruption. Some children as young as 5 years of age are known to have had as many as twenty placements, and it seems to be almost redundant to assess attachment in such a context of disruptions. None of the available research assists with assessing the attachment status of this group of children who have been removed from their primary care-givers. Behavioural and emotional observations will inevitably represent the impact of primary and secondary trauma as well as the insecurity arising from repeated disruptions in care.

A 'narrative' approach to assessment uses the tri-phasic model as a frame of reference and traces through the history of the child's early experiences. The assessor gathers information about the three phases and any other experiences or factors that would interfere with the successful negotiation of the phases. For instance, what is known about the mother's care routines in the early months, whether there were any circumstances which would have caused disruption of routines consistency and stability (e.g. parental illness or substance misuse), whether a consistent attachment figure was available, and what consistency of place or family home has occurred.

It is important to assess the parental bonding to provide a context for the attachment narrative. Interviews with both parents, if they are available, and the grandparents can be very illuminating in providing subjective data that could be compared with the more objective professional observations that may be found in antenatal, postnatal or social services records. Such a detailed assessment process will allow an assessor to formulate hypotheses about the meaning of the child to members of the birth family, which could be tested in subsequent interviews.

In addition, there will be a history of concerns about the child or other children in the family. Social services workers will usually provide a detailed chronology of the history of concerns and statements will be available about the family background, often with accounts of the child's known or presumed experiences in their birth parents' care. Other professional observers may be able to add to the narrative of the child's life story prior to the assessment. Minutes of Child Protection Conferences will also give details of presumed or actual neglect, poor care or known maltreatment. There will be descriptions from a variety of sources of the child's behaviour, relationships and interactive responses. The assessor then has the task of processing the information that has been obtained and separating, if possible, what behaviours or developmental observations may relate to the child's attachment to their birth parents and what can be attributed to trauma.

The narrative will yield an opportunity to the assessor to formulate the quality of the child's experiences and whether or not the child has had any period of secure attachment and sound development. A parent's capacity to respond sensitively to any known trauma the child may have suffered will also be assessable, and it can be postulated whether the child has developed resilience in the context of a secure child–parent attachment. If the child has had experiences likely to cause an insecure attachment, it will be important to assess whether there has been a significant level of fear-inducing experiences with frightened and/or frightening parents, leading to the possibility of attachment disorganization.

## Assessing the child

Observation of contact between child and parents is a necessary part of the assessment process. For children up to 4 years of age, a period of observation should include an opportunity to observe the parent meeting the child's needs through an ordinary primary care task, such as preparing a meal, or play. It is very important to observe greeting and parting behaviours.

However, simple observation of children with their parents does not assess either attachment or maternal sensitivity if there is no stress introduced during the period of observation. Natural stresses may arise during the observation and the assessor will be able to note parental awareness and response sensitivity. In an assessment setting, whether home or clinic/centre, the clinician can use a modification of the

Strange Situation Test. With pre-school and school-age children, it is possible to devise a projective technique that taps into the child's internal working model of relationships with care-givers, using representational and symbolic images of children in stressful situations. The child draws on their internal working model in shaping their response when asked to describe what is happening in a picture or to complete a standardized story stem. A method I favour is to invite the child to listen to a story. In order to engage the child in this process, I tell the story while drawing a simple picture of a house to show the bedrooms, the upstairs bathroom/toilet (with a light on), the kitchen and the sitting room. The child is told that a child lives in the house with their parent. The child is asked to help with the names of the people and the child's age (they often give their own name and their mother's name but the age of the child in the story may be younger than their actual age). I then describe a situation with parent and child in their beds and asleep at night. A thunder-storm occurs, blotting out the moon and creating a great noise of thunder, rain and wind. There is a power cut, the child wakes up and is frightened by all the noise and the darkness and they wet the bed. I then imitate a child crying aloud, 'Mummy! Mummy! Mummy!' or ('Daddy! . . .') observing the child's non-verbal response to the sudden cries of distress. The child is then invited to say what happens next in the story.

The child's responses will be informed by their own experience of a parental figure when they were in distress. The non-verbal behaviour may be as telling as the child's version of events. Children with a disorganized attachment may attempt from the outset to control my story stem and at the point of high distress may freeze, grimace and be unable to manage their facial expression as they switch un-controllably between laughing and showing fear. Some children throw themselves about, hit themselves or show other bizarre responses. The verbal response may be to disengage angrily from the whole process, to become silent or to be able to complete the story.

The assessor's task is then to interpret the child's story completion to the court in a way that reflects their internal working model. A useful exercise is to postulate the genesis of different types of insecure attachment and compare these with what is known or believed to have been the child's experience with primary attachment figures. The objective is to formulate the child's attachment profile by comparing the narrative with what is observable in the child's current care context. Patterns of history and current behaviour may provide a match that can then form the basis of an assessment report, noting resilience to attachment disruption as well as vulnerability to change.

## CRITICAL PERIODS AND REPAIR OF DISRUPTED ATTACHMENTS

Bowlby introduced the concept of critical periods for the formation of attachments with primary carers. It was thought that a secure attachment needs to be established between 6 months of age and 18 months and this is a helpful guide in terms of assessing whether a normal attachment process has been followed. However, when a child's attachment has been disrupted or rendered pathologically insecure, they may still be available for attachment in the sense that they still attempt to find a person who might be available to meet their needs. This is more probable if the young child has had a secure attachment, for instance to a parent who has died. A child who has never attached at all, or who has become detached, will need convincing that a person who is offering to meet their needs can be trusted to provide a sense of belonging.

This is more likely to occur if the tri-phasic model described above is followed. The attachment-disrupted child can only engage with this process if they are able to surrender the management of their environment (i.e. their sensory world) to an attachment figure who is consistent, reliable, patient and at the same time firmly in control. The adult will need to enter the child's world and be prepared to understand the value to them of their own survival strategies. Once this has been established, even if the child begins to use the adult in a mechanistic and self-serving way, the child may then be able to use their cognitive skills to decide whether to acknowledge the adult as a person who might meet their basic needs. It may be that the process of attachment will be distorted in this reconstructive exercise, in that the child may find it easier to attach to places where they feel safe before they are prepared to trust a person again.

It is unhelpful to consider a child's availability for rehabilitation to parents who were failed attachment figures simply in terms of their chronological age. Children who have developed insecure attachments prior to removal from home may automatically seek to secure an attachment to substitute carers, for instance emergency foster carers, and experience repeatedly demonstrates that children will ask temporary carers if they can live with them 'for ever' and call them 'mum and dad'. Children are generally optimistic and seek attachments and a sense of belonging even when they have been severely maltreated and neglected. This optimism declines fairly rapidly if they are moved from placement to placement, and it should be said that it is the quality of a child's experience of alternative care that is likely to enhance or erode their capacity to attach anew.

Resilience is improved if there has been a positive experience of attachment to secondary figures, such as grandparents or older siblings. An older child may even be able to make transitional attachments to temporary carers if there is a clear plan to find new parents and a home in which they can belong and be safe. This is a concept that requires honesty on the part of the carers and social worker, who become the child's transitional attachment network. It should be remembered that maintenance of secondary attachment figures and places while a child is in a transitional placement will do much to preserve in them a sense that other parts of their world can remain intact, even when there has been a disruption of their primary attachments. Clearly, the role of routines is extremely important in helping the child to manage and develop a healthy understanding of where they are in the world. Even very young children can be helped to understand through simple explanations what is happening and what is going to happen. The child's cognitive competence is a major factor in expediting attachment processes at older ages, but children who have had to cope with disappointment and broken guarantees may soon learn to mistrust specific people and, ultimately, the world at large.

In looking at care plans for rehabilitation or permanent substitute care, assessors will be helped by a clear understanding of the child's availability for attachment and, if this is limited, how the situation can be remedied within the care plan.

## CONCLUSIONS

The quality of the child's attachment to their parental figures is an essential component of the child–parent relationship and has profound implications for the child's later adjustment towards separation, autonomy and emotional well-being. An important aspect of the assessment of attachment is its link to significant harm. Evidence of attachment disorder can be attributable to the care provided by parents but caution should be exercised in making this link if, by the time of the assessment, the child has had multiple placements and if there is a history of trauma in substitute care. In these situations, the narrative of the child's life story of disruption will bear close study if the assessment seeks to offer the court valid evidence of significant harm as an attachment disorder.

There are no absolutes in child psychology and children's development is a complex interweaving of many related and overlapping strands. The types of attachment disorder discussed above are not mutually exclusive, and it can be helpful to present the child's attachments as an attachment profile, using clinical descriptions that are derived from the narrative. This involves a combination of retrospective analysis of the child's presenting attachment behaviours at the assessment with the narrative assessment of the parental bonding, the meaning of the child and the child's social development, taking into account the traumas or maltreatment that the child is known to have to have suffered. Parental response sensitivity, the child's resilience and the child's availability for a relationship that is defined by their own dependence will all be factors that should be taken into account when formulating a prognosis for rehabilitation, permanent family placement and the viability of a therapeutic reparative intervention.

Children's attachment is an important part of an assessment of families, especially in Care Proceedings, but it is an imprecise science that depends on a careful analysis of history, observation and specific investigations that are tailored to the child's age and circumstances. There is more to attachment than the child's tie to their mother and attachment cannot be assessed as an isolated feature of a child's relationships with their parents. The relevance of attachment is most clearly seen when it is used as a basis for care planning.

# References

Ainsworth, M.D.S., Blehar, M., Waters, E. and Wall, S. (1978) *Patterns of Attachment: A Psychological Study of the Strange Situation*, Hillsdale, NJ: Erlbaum.

Bowlby, J. (1958) The nature of the child's tie to his mother, *International Journal of Psycho-Analysis* 39: 350–73.

Bowlby, J. (1969/82) *Attachment and Loss: Vol. 1. Attachment*, New York: Basic Books.

Bowlby, J. (1973) *Attachment and Loss: Vol. 2. Separation*, New York: Basic Books.

Bowlby, J. (1980) *Attachment and Loss: Vol. 3. Loss*, New York: Basic Books.

Dozier, M., Chase Stovall, K. and Albus, K.E. (1999) Attachment and psychopathology in adulthood, in J. Cassidy and P.R. Shaver (eds) *Handbook of Attachment: Theory, Research, and Clinical Applications*, New York: The Guilford Press.

Greenberg, M.T. (1999) Attachment and psychopathology in childhood, in J. Cassidy and P.R. Shaver (eds) *Handbook of Attachment: Theory, Research, and Clinical Applications*, New York: The Guilford Press.

Main, M. and Hesse, E. (1990) Parents' unresolved traumatic experiences are related to infant disorganization status. Is frightened and/or frightening parental behaviour the linking mechanism? in M.T. Greenberg, D. Cicchetti and E.M. Cummings (eds) *Attachment in the Preschool Years: Theory, Research, and Interventions*, Chicago: University of Chicago Press.

Main, M. and Solomon, J. (1990) Procedures for identifying infants as disorganized/disoriented during the Ainsworth Strange Situation, in M.T. Greenberg, D. Cicchetti and E.M. Cummings (eds) *Attachment in the Preschool Years: Theory, Research, and Interventions*, Chicago: University of Chicago Press.

Reder, P. and Duncan, S. (1995) The meaning of the child, in P. Reder and C. Lucey (eds) *Assessment of Parenting: Psychiatric and Psychological Contributions*, London: Routledge.

Reder, P. and Duncan, S. (2001) Abusive relationships, care and control conflicts and insecure attachments, *Child Abuse Review* 10: 2–17.

Rutter, M. (1997) Clinical implications of attachment concepts: retrospect and prospect, in L. Atkinson and K.J. Zucker (eds) *Attachment and Psychopathology*, New York: The Guilford Press.

Rutter, M., Anderson-Wood, L., Beckett, C., Bredenkamp, D., Castle, J., Grootheus, C., O'Connor, T.G. and the ERA Study Team (1999) Quasi-autistic patterns following severe early global privation, *Journal of Child Psychology & Psychiatry* 40: 537–49.

Solomon, J. and George, C. (1996) Defining the caregiving system: toward a theory of caregiving, *Infant Mental Health Journal* 17: 183–97.

Solomon J. and George C. (1999a) The measurement of attachment security in infancy and childhood, in J. Cassidy and P.R. Shaver (eds) *Handbook of Attachment: Theory, Research, and Clinical Applications*, New York: The Guilford Press.

Solomon, J. and George, C. (eds) (1999b) *Attachment Disorganisation*, New York: The Guilford Press.

Solomon, J., George, C. and De Jong, A. (1995) Children classified as controlling at age six: evidence of disorganized representational strategies and aggression at home and school, *Development and Psychopathology* 7: 447–64.

# Chapter 5

# What are the significant dimensions of harm to a child?

*Sylvia Duncan and Tony Baker*

## INTRODUCTION

The Children Act 1989 introduced the concept of significant harm as the threshold justifying compulsory intervention in family life in the best interests of the child. A court may only make an Order if it is satisfied that the child is suffering, or is likely to suffer, significant harm and that this harm is attributable to a lack of adequate parental care or control. There are no absolute criteria on which to rely when judging what constitutes significant harm and government documents (e.g. Department of Health *et al.*, 1999) offer only indirect guidance, indicating that it may be a function of the extent, duration, frequency, severity or characteristics of the abuse or neglect, or the degree of threat or sadism involved. Often, 'significant harm is a compilation of significant events, both acute and long-standing, which interrupt, change or damage the child's physical and psychological development . . . [and] . . . it is the corrosiveness of long-term emotional, physical or sexual abuse that causes impairment to the extent of causing significant harm' (ibid., p. 8).

Neglect describes omissions in care which are less readily observed and the effects of which are often more subtle, long-term and non-specific (i.e. open to various other explanations). Although neglect is now the commonest reason for a child's name to be entered on the Child Protection Register, we have the impression that it is the least common grounds for proceedings to be initiated under the Children Act: instead, statutory agencies tend to rely on the co-existence of other forms of maltreatment in order to strengthen their case.

In this chapter, the impact of maltreatment and neglect on the development and emotional health of children will be considered as an aid to appraising whether there is evidence of significant harm. We shall focus on the child, bearing in mind that this information must be integrated with an assessment of the parental figures and family in order to formulate an overall opinion to the court (see Reder, Duncan and Lucey, Chapter 1). We shall argue that, whilst the type of maltreatment may give rise to very specific damage to the child, such as a physical injury or serious growth delay, it is the accompanying psychological impact on the child which shapes both their immediate response and the likely long-term impact on them.

Much has been written about the impact of child maltreatment on children (e.g. Briere, 1992) and we do not intend that this should be a comprehensive treatise on all the possible sequelae. We propose that, of all the psychological dimensions which are affected by abuse and neglect, the most significant is the child's emotional development and therefore it should form the core of any assessment of the child. The model that we use allows for not only an evaluation of the immediate harm to the child but consideration of the likely long-term consequences as well.

## THE CONCEPT OF HARM

Harm is broadly defined in terms of impairment to health and development. While it is widely accepted that maltreatment has serious consequences for children, the relationship between maltreatment and its developmental outcomes is still being debated. There is some evidence that different types of maltreatment are associated with different sequelae (Crittenden, 1985; 1988; Egeland and Sroufe, 1981). However, there is a growing consensus that the psychological maltreatment that accompanies other forms of abuse is at the core of negative developmental outcomes for children (Garbarino, 1980; Brassard et al., 1987; Farber and Egeland, 1987; Garrison, 1987; Navarre, 1987; Claussen and Crittenden, 1991; Gibbons et al., 1995; Erickson and Egeland, 2002). Not only does psychological maltreatment often occur concurrently with physical maltreatment, some would say it is inherent within any act of parental abuse and many of the negative effects of maltreatment are psychological in nature (Brassard et al., 1987).

Parental behaviour alone is an inadequate predictor of the likely damage to the child. Whilst it is important to know what the child's experience has been, other factors will also influence the extent and nature of the harm done. For example, the resilience of children is known to vary (Rutter, 1985; Reder and Duncan, 2000). There is also a need to adopt a developmental perspective which recognizes that the appropriateness of parental behaviours will vary with the child's age and that outcome will be displayed differently according to their developmental stage (Aber and Zigler, 1981; Erickson and Egeland, 1987; Garbarino et al., 1986). Trickett & McBride-Chang (1995) reviewed research on the impact of different forms of maltreatment in a bid to understand how the experience of child abuse or neglect interferes with development at the time it is experienced and how it may affect the resolution of later developmental tasks. They concluded that maltreatment may have a cumulatively negative impact on competence and that, with age, children tended to become more aware of the difference between themselves and their peers, compounding the original problems.

Child neglect, in particular, is known to have a potentially devastating impact on all aspects of a child's development, including their physical growth and health, self-esteem, attention, impulse control and reactivity, socialization, peer relationships, and learning capacity (Helfer, 1987; Erickson and Egeland, 2002). The younger the child, the more profound are the consequences of neglect

(Erickson and Egeland, 2002). Indeed, neglect of a young child's physical needs can prove fatal (Bridge Child Care Consultancy Service, 1995).

When assessing what harm, if any, a child has suffered it is necessary to consider all aspects of their functioning, to include their *emotional, cognitive, physical, social, moral* and *sexual* development in comparison with other children of a comparable age. Each of these dimensions will be considered in turn, although greater emphasis will be placed on the child's emotional development and its interplay with their cognitive development.

In this chapter we will adopt a developmental perspective which draws on available developmental, attachment, psychoanalytic and systemic theory and research knowledge but is largely the product of our clinical observations of abused and neglected infants, children, adolescents and adults. An understanding of the emotional development of children and the association between emotional and cognitive development underpins this assessment framework.

## Emotional development

Emotional development embraces feelings in response to events or experiences as the child progresses from the dependency of infancy to the autonomy of adulthood Children are not born with a full emotional repertoire and their emotional reactions become more complex as they grow up. There has been much debate about emotional states and drives as being independent of cognition. Common sense would lead us to recognize in ourselves that what we think shapes how we feel, and vice versa, so that key milestones in cognitive and social development provide a foundation for staged emotional growth and a widened repertoire of emotional experience.

Events may be experienced cognitively or sensorily or both. Emotions may be precipitated by external changes or may arise out of the child's own internal process of perception. We would suggest that, as the child grows over the years, it is possible to observe a widening repertoire of emotional responses and, when exposed to trauma, children progressively develop four main internal emotional drives: *anxiety; guilt, anger*; and *grief*. In this section we shall explore the ways in which these emotional states arise, are defended against to ensure psychological survival, and may be manifest in the history or presentation of children being assessed as part of family proceedings.

### Anxiety

The new-born infant has a physiological capacity to be aroused by new stimuli, which increases circulating adrenaline levels and produces an alert state with increased muscle tone and activity. When the stimulus is discomforting, the baby will generate a cry from the outset of life. The cry alerts the parent or carer and the infant begins to learn experientially that they have not been and will not be abandoned. Fear of abandonment is an instinct that shapes behaviour from cradle to grave. Physical abandonment is the unconscious preoccupation of the infant, while social abandonment through rejection is the subconscious concern of older children and adults. The parent's competence and willingness to deal with the crying baby in a contained way will shape their response pattern to further uncomfortable events. Thus, parent and child are dealing with trauma from the very beginning of life in each novel situation. Secure attachment (see Baker, Chapter 4) offers the baby a resolution strategy to deal with the earliest arousal of anxiety or fear of abandonment. Regression to infantile attachment behaviour may occur whenever the relatively autonomous child feels insecure or threatened. Anxiety, then, is the first response to trauma. For the infant or pre-school child who lacks the cognitive capacity to understand their experience it is the primary emotional response underlying any symptoms they may manifest.

Anxiety will lessen if the child receives physical comfort and age-appropriate information about their situation. They will need to know that the situation can be managed in a contained way by someone who takes charge, that their attachments to persons and places are intact and that they are not abandoned, as well as being given an explanation about the traumatic incident and what will happen next.

In the absence of these different elements to resolve the anxiety or fear, the child may develop any of the following: *regression* (as illness or loss of developmental competence); *aggression*; *hyperarousal* (agitation, sleeplessness or hyperactivity); *phobic avoidance*; *confusional states*; *preoccupation with the trauma* (evidenced by dreams and nightmares, incessant talking about the event or re-enactment through play); or *physical symptoms* (asthma, enuresis, etc.). Regression can be as severe as loss of language or other previously acquired competencies, or loss of social skills and other age-appropriate coping behaviour. Clingy behaviour, school refusal or loss of self-care skills may be short-term problems, which, if unresolved, will be the precursor for more entrenched insecure or dependent attachment. Infantile rages and early childhood aggressive tantrums are most probably the manifestation of severe anxiety rather than anger, as is usually suggested. Parental inconsistency or indecisiveness, lack of routines and chaotic rearing styles and inappropriate behavioural cueing of events will all predispose to this type of response in a baby or young child.

Perry (1997) has shown that deprivation of optimal developmental experiences may lead to the underdevelopment of cortical, sub-cortical and limbic areas of the brain which ordinarily modulate the more primitive, less mature reactive impulses, resulting in persistent hyperkinetic states of arousal. The similarities between attention deficit hyperactivity disorder and post-abuse hyperarousal with aggression and violent preoccupation can create considerable diagnostic difficulty (Haddad and Garralda, 1992).

Children may draw attention to themselves through preoccupation with a traumatic event. Thus, children who are violent or sexual in their play may well be trying to gain mastery and understanding over something that they know of as anxiety-laden but which is beyond their understanding. Preoccupation with death may also be seen in children who have witnessed extreme domestic violence when they believed that one of their parents might die. Terr (1991) reports that some children who have been exposed to traumatic events relating to a preverbal period of development will exactly re-enact those experiences in their play, even though they have no conscious memory of what they are known to have witnessed.

When a child has been terrorized by abuse, they may unconsciously protect their psyche through emotional numbing or by dissociating from the event and repressing memory of it. This may only re-emerge through triggering 'flashbacks', which amount to a reliving of the experience, either in nightmare states or sometimes while awake. Terr (1991) described a sense of foreshortened future in children with such post-traumatic stress disorder. This can be seen to be a logical development if the child is unconsciously held in a frozen state of uncertainty about their survival because the traumatic material will not have been consciously processed.

## Guilt

Guilt as an internal emotional state should not be confused with the social construct of blame. Guilt arises out of a combination of factors, including the development of power and relative autonomy, increased cognitive understanding of the relationship between cause and effect, and the capacity to feel a sense of responsibility in relation to events. This capacity typically begins to emerge as the child approaches school age and extends their range of emotional response to any traumatic event.

Guilt does not replace anxiety but rather compounds it. In the face of maltreatment, the child tends to assume that they were responsible for the events. This is internally driven and dependent on the developmental age of the child as they begin to move into a more egocentric stage of development. However, in addition, abusers often rationalize their behaviour by blaming the victim and a susceptible child may easily be induced to believe that they are responsible. That responsibility is sometimes related to the keeping of a secret, for instance about the cause of injuries, on the understanding from the child's point of view that, if they were to tell the truth, the situation for the abuser or the family would be made worse. They may also be made to believe that unless they comply with the maltreatment then another, perhaps more vulnerable member of the family, may suffer. If the abuser demonstrates their manipulative, violent or destructive power, the child may feel that they alone have the power to obtain reasonable and kind behaviour from them. Thus, the child is given the illusion of power to make things happen, or not, when the power actually rests with the adult who uses it without taking responsibility (see Bentovim, Chapter 14). Children may also be led to believe that they deserve a particular type of maltreatment or humiliation. In whatever way a child's compliance and silence are obtained, the fact that they did not protect themselves or a sibling, that they did not tell someone who could protect them, and that they believed the abuser's lies are all experienced as foundations for later guilt.

When children are trapped with guilty feelings they develop a negative self-image, regarding themselves as a bad, shameful person. They are driven to silence, fearful of the judgements of others, and may become quiet and withdrawn, isolated from their peers, with no sense of fun and freedom. Unresolved guilt can sometimes lead to a depressed state in which the child has no energy, is unable to sleep, eat, concentrate and learn, or make friends.

Guilt can also lead individuals to develop irrational beliefs about their own power and how it may cause a desired effect. This is seen at its most obvious in obsessive-compulsive ritual disorders, which can arise in the aftermath of severe trauma. Two types of ritual behaviours are seen, which have different cognitive drives. In compulsive cleansing rituals the individual can be seen to be trying to undo their 'guilty' past. Sometimes these rituals are very complex and demand perfection in their execution and therefore need to be repeated very often. Because they are irrational they never lead to sustained relief of guilt and each day increasing time may be taken up with this type of behaviour. The other drive for obsessionality arises from the almost superstitious belief that certain rituals will protect others from harm. This is akin to magical thinking that is seen in most 4- to 6-year-old children who assume that, because they wish for something, the mere act of wishing increases the likelihood that it will happen.

The most common unconscious defences against guilt seen in children during assessment are rationalization and/or becoming a 'supergood' child. Rational-ization involves changing the meaning of what has happened, so that the altered cognitions modify the emotional response. The 'supergood' child is driven to behave perfectly so that they are never in a position of being judged as bad. When such children become the focus of a child protection inquiry their teachers are often unable to reconcile the suspicions or allegations with the apparently well-adjusted, helpful child that performs so well in the classroom. What marks these children out is their lack of a sense of fun or enjoyment.

## Anger

Rudimentary expressions of anger in response to unwanted experiences occur even in babies and can be seen in the angry protests of infants separated from their attachment figures. However, a later, more organized experience of anger arises out of a sense of unfairness or injustice and, in order to be able to conceptualize it, a child will need the cognitive ability to make comparisons and to understand about rights. This capacity rarely emerges before the age of about 9 or 10 years, although the language of unfairness may precede it. Anger can be resolved if the child has a concept of rights, can make a protest that is acknowledged by an authority figure and is helped to formulate a strategy to redress the past rights abuses and protect their future rights. In order to experience anger at their maltreatment, a child must realize that they have been wronged, that trust has been betrayed and that their damaging experiences were unnecessary, whether deliberately malicious or not. Anger may be directed at unprotecting adults as well as the responsible parties, triggered by the realization that they have suffered harm.

If anger cannot be satisfactorily resolved, the child may realize that they have had to suffer a compromise to their personal rights. To commit to such a compromise is to surrender self-esteem. Properly contained assertion and protection of rights through advocacy is an effective way to prevent erosion of children's self-esteem after abuse. If a child has no sense of their rights and no experience of advocacy being initiated on their behalf, they will not express their anger. If they have acquired the concept of themselves having rights but are unable to voice a protest because it would not be safe to do so, they may internalize their anger and remain passive to an external observer or even become frankly depressed. If this is sustained, the anger may become somatized and be expressed as psychosomatic disorders, or expressed through acts of self-harm. Paradoxically, self-cutting or other forms of self-mutilation involving the skin may give a feeling of relief and this can become the habitually preferred method for a person to release their angry energy.

Anger that has been internalized for a long period may erupt with a trigger event, with loss of temper control and destructive acts, such as trying to spoil the life of others in revenge for their own perceived harm. When a young person doubts that there can be any justice for them, they may feel compelled to enact their anger by taking away the rights of others, through destructiveness, stealing or other antisocial behaviour.

### Grief

The emotional drive of grief arises out of a sense of irretrievable loss. Such loss can only be conceptualized if the individual can compare the current reality, after a traumatic event, with the way their life would have been if the event had not taken place. This capacity generally develops during the teen years and requires a capacity to compare the concrete with the abstract. People find it hard to cope with loss of significant elements in their life and the initial response to loss is often denial. The next step in addressing loss is to arrive at a point of acknowledgement, during which a person may believe that they can be compensated or that the loss can be recovered. Pursuit of compensation claims, litigation and 'justice' may become a major preoccupation, which may extend this phase. Such activity, even if it is psychologically internalized rather than enacted, will delay movement into the next stage of acceptance of irretrievable loss. Acceptance demands a conscious appraisal of what has been lost, which gives rise to sadness and emotional pain. Once the pain is mastered the individual can move on to the stage of re-evaluation, when they redefine their life through incorporating the loss without it dominating and organizing their life.

While denial of loss is characterized by emotional numbing or the presentation of a false persona ('I'm fine'), acknowledgement of loss can give rise to anger and a wish for revenge, which leaves the individual feeling bitter and incomplete. When acceptance of loss is realized, the pain may become so intolerable that the individual seeks anaesthesia through alcohol or drugs. When the 'anaesthetic' wears off, the pain resurfaces unchanged and mastery is not achieved.

Children come to experience a range of losses in the aftermath of maltreatment. Grief is a later emotional phenomenon and some losses will not be realized until adulthood. Loss of family life, loss of childhood, loss of innocence and loss of educational achievement are all common descriptions of loss after abuse. Some may have to cope daily with loss through disability after severe physical injuries sustained through physical abuse or neglect. In our view, the hardest loss to bear following any form of maltreatment is loss of value as a child in the eyes of parents who deliberately or neglectfully hurt them rather than loving and protecting them. That hurting is equally damaging whether it occurred through wilful neglect, indifference, malice or sexual objectification. The loss of love, care and value can give rise to a sense of desolation, which inhibits recovery and growth and is often manifest as a belief that it would be better not to exist at all, leading to suicidal attempts. There may be a constant search for comfort and compensation from external sources, such as alcohol, drugs, power, transient sexual relationships, pregnancy, stealing or holding a belief that it is impossible to survive without a partner on whom to depend.

### Emotional harm

In accordance with this model, the emotional consequences of adverse care for a child at any specific time will be directly related to their developmental age and the behavioural manifestation of this will vary accordingly. The emotional harm to a child who has been maltreated can be long-term. It may persist into adulthood as the memory of the experience takes on new and different meaning with increased cognitive maturity and increased range of emotional responsiveness. Each phase compounds the existing impact by adding another layer to it. We would therefore argue that any assessment of the harm suffered by a child as the result of mal-treatment or neglect, and any decisions about their current and future needs, must be based on the immediately observable indications of the damage and should also take a developmental perspective, with a projected view of the likely future impact. Such a model also helps to inform recommendations regarding treatment needs.

## Cognitive development

Cognitive development is concerned with aspects of mental function which include perception, memory, learning, application of facts and ideas, imagination, reasoning and understanding, as well as communication, problem solving and obtaining a meaning of self which informs a person's beliefs and judgements. Cognitive acquisitions are a function both of the brain's anatomical development and of psychological processes.

Early brain development is constantly modified by environmental influences and, in a review of available research, Glaser (2000) concluded that there is considerable evidence for changes in brain function in association with child abuse and neglect. Neglect and failure of environmental stimulation during critical periods of brain development may lead to permanent deficits in cognitive and other abilities. Other studies indicate that early experiences shape the neural connections in the brain, giving rise to chronic cognitive changes which are not amenable to subsequent remediation. Glaser highlighted the function of a secure attachment relationship to protect the developing neural structures from the deleterious effects of high levels of stress. Once again, we see evidence of the close interrelationship between cognitive and emotional development.

Maslow (1954) proposed that a hierarchy of needs exists for the fulfilment of human development and self-actualization, basic needs demanding fulfilment before higher order needs can be met. The implication is that, if our available energy is taken up dealing with survival in the face of basic physiological or environmental danger, we have less psychological and physical energy available to develop at the higher levels in terms of self-esteem and cognitive development. Therefore, cognitive development will suffer in conditions where the quality of care provided by parental figures does not provide safety and nurturance. The evidence is consistent that physically abused and neglected children show delays in cognitive development and poor academic progress, with neglected children probably suffering the most (Trickett and McBride-Chang, 1995).

While Terr (1991) found that single episodes of major trauma may give rise to a specific post-traumatic stress disorder of childhood, she also found that in those circumstances the child's ability to learn was not impaired in spite of severe symptoms. On the other hand, in line with Maslow's experience, it is recognized that chronic anxiety and fear, chronic pain and preoccupation will impair learning and restrict the capacity to think. The most striking example of this is the inability of chronically abused children to progress beyond concrete conceptualization into abstract thinking modes. Poor performance in comparison with peers leads to loss of confidence and self-esteem and the child who is being humiliated or derided at home will quickly feel defeated at school and eventually they will lose all hope of succeeding. Parents who neglect to respond to a child's sounds or who do not reflect the child's attempts to speak will impede language development. It can be seen that neglect and/or ignorance of the child's need for parental involvement will delay the child's competence in communication skills with an associated impact on their social and emotional development.

An important aspect of cognitive development is in the area of finding a meaning for experiences. As the child gains wider knowledge of the world and the expectations and norms of their culture, they may reflect on their own experiences in a way that leads them to change their perceptual understanding of what has happened. What may have seemed usual at 6 years of age will come to be perceived differently when they are 12 or 16 or 26 years old. This change in perception is likely to then have a different emotional impact, giving rise to alternative attitudes and judgements about their childhood and their parents. Assessments for court therefore also need to consider whether therapy could help a child move on from their abusive experiences.

## Physical development

Physical development is concerned with dimensions of growth and physical ability in terms of sensory and motor function and healthy bodily function. To establish whether a child has suffered significant physical harm, there is generally a need for assessments undertaken by both paediatricians and mental health professionals. Paediatricians are best placed to assess the nature and extent of any impairment to the general health or physical development of a child and to proffer opinions about the likely causes of any damage sustained. It needs to be said that a child who is severely disabled or scarred as a result of maltreatment will carry an additional emotional burden, which may have an impact on their social and emotional adjustment through life. In addition, the knowledge of having been physically injured by a parent, even where there is no permanent damage, may have a lasting emotional impact.

It is well recognized that persistent poor emotional care can lead to inhibited physical growth even in the presence of an adequate diet (Erickson and Egeland, 2002). Failure to thrive in infancy may be the only alerting sign of emotional abuse or neglect. At the other end of the spectrum, obesity can also be associated with the poor quality of the child's diet and/or comfort eating. Overeating and foraging behaviours may also be a consequence of starvation or a child's attempt to overcome chronic emotional deprivation. Inadequate emotional care or emotional abuse can also create a state of chronic anxiety in childhood which can lead to a somatizing disorder in which the symptoms of anxiety are manifest in bodily change such as eczema, psoriasis, asthma, headaches, abdominal pain or bowel disorders. There may also be delay in achieving developmental milestones such as bladder and bowel control. The evidence that any such disturbance is induced by anxiety is usually found by rapid recovery or developmental progress when the child is removed to an environment that offers safety, containment and safe attachment.

## Social development

Social development demands the acquisition of the wide range of capacities necessary for the establishment of mutually rewarding relationships with others. Evidence of distortion of social development can be seen in the impaired capacity of a child to belong, to trust, to use power constructively, to communicate, to play at an age-appropriate level, to learn about danger, to develop self-care skills, to respond to the boundary setting of its primary carers, to learn social rules, to develop an appropriate moral code and to invest in healthy aspirations.

The foundations of relationship skills are laid down in a stepwise sequence, where particular competences are built on previously acquired capacities. Safety, containment and a secure attachment are prerequisites for successful growth in all areas of social development and so it may be affected by any form of maltreatment. There are also thought to be critical periods during which specific experiences are required for optimal organization and development of the brain. Atypical patterns of neural activity during these sensitive periods are believed to result in compromised function in other brain-mediated functions such as empathy, attachment and affect regulation (Green, 1983). Social development can therefore be adversely distorted by both the emotional and the physical sequelae inherent in child maltreatment. Babies and young children will not have the knowledge to evaluate the quality of their relationships and they are likely to accommodate to even gross levels of abuse and neglect because they have no comparisons to make. The evidence of that neglect may be seen in their demeanour, which may vary from abject misery through frozen watchfulness, to the absence of usual attachment or separation behaviour for the child's age. Baker (Chapter 4) has described in more detail the ways that attachment problems of the abused child manifest in social difficulties.

## Moral development

Moral development includes developing the competence to differentiate right from wrong and to be aware of the implications for self and others of any particular choice. Trustworthiness, honesty, integrity, honour and social responsibility are all functions of moral development and the value that is placed on these by the prevailing culture will influence a child's development in this respect. Maltreatment can lead to the child adopting the amoral codes of the abusive subculture, rejecting usual societal codes in favour of ones which bring them a greater sense of approval and belonging within the context in which they are living. The process of rationalization necessary to achieve this modifies the meaning of the maltreatment and may help to alleviate any guilt and responsibility the child may be feeling.

## Sexual development

Sexual development is concerned with biological gender and identity and the expression and gratification of sexual drives. In general terms, it can be seen that sexual adjustment arises out of a complex interplay of physical characteristics and interpersonal and environmental influences. Sexuality may be precociously advanced, distorted or suppressed through emotional or physical maltreatment or neglect. Sexual activity may be used by the young person to provide some compensation for loss of power or status that they feel in their primary relationships. Some teenage girls will seek pregnancy in order to become the mother of a baby that will love them unconditionally and make up for the deprivations of their life (see Reder and Fitzpatrick, Chapter 8). Teenage boys might seek both comfort and control through sexual partnerships in which their female partner becomes to them a possession without autonomy or separate identity.

The growing child develops a set of expectations in relation to sexual ideals, which may be based on their view of their parents' sexual relationship(s). These influences may shape their own theory of sexuality, which in turn affects their relationships with men, women and other children. Cognitive distortions will lead to false assumptions being made about the sexual interests and boundaries of others. Because sexuality is such a fundamental aspect of personality, it is not surprising that healthy sexual adjustment is very vulnerable to child maltreatment even in the absence of frank sexual abuse.

## PRACTICAL APPLICATIONS

In our view, the child mental health expert is best placed to describe the impact on the child of their experience of being parented. By utilizing a developmental model, as described, the assessor can then attribute meaning to the child's behaviour, which helps not only to understand the origins of any disturbance but also to provide an indication of how their situation might progress if no action is taken to protect them. In addition, it offers ideas about the future difficulties one might expect them to develop as their understanding of their experiences increases in complexity. As such, it gives a means of assessing both the current and the likely harm and can offer guidance with regard to the treatment needs of the child.

The young child who responds with anxiety and confusion to maltreatment may give clues about the nature of their experience in their play, their drawings and their spontaneous communications. It is helpful to adopt a non-directive approach to the assessment of children of this age, offering a safe space for them to bring their anxiety, whilst carefully observing the content of their play for clues about the basis for this. It can help the child if the assessor suggests that their play appears to be trying to answer questions that they are struggling with. Frequently, children will be assisted to verbalize their questions if given such an opening and go on to reveal something about their experience of living with their parent(s).

Children who are experiencing guilt associated with anxiety tend to be bossy and controlling; they resist the authority of others (including the assessor) and prefer to make their own choices about what they do. An understanding that such behaviour is likely to be driven by insecurity and guilt can enable an assessor to identify this with the child as a possible explanation for their behaviour. Frequently, this frees the child to speak more openly about their experiences. It is unhelpful to rush into telling the child that they should not feel guilty, as this will merely serve to increase their defences and ensure that they do not speak further. Guilt is inevitable but it is important to let the child know that they were not responsible and should not be blamed for what was done to them.

Professionals often impose their own emotional agenda on children, forgetting that their vision will vary from that of the child, due to differences in their respective stages of emotional development. Professionals, for example, often express anger about what is thought to have been done to a child and attribute this anger to the child as well. However, anger may take a long time to emerge and the absence of anger should not be taken as a sign that the abuse did not take place or was not serious. The child will need not only to have the capacity to measure their experience against that of others but have a safe place where any anger can be received without the risk of rejection or retaliation. For the older child who has a sense of justice, acknowledging the unfairness of their situation and endorsing their right to be angry can often free them to speak more openly.

It is of course helpful when the child can be facilitated to share their own account of their experiences and we know that they can give reliable accounts (see Westcott and Jones, Chapter 6). For those who remain unable to speak it will be even more important to carefully collate information from various sources to build up a picture of their behaviour over time which offers clues about their emotional state. It then becomes possible to link their behaviour to available information regarding their care. This forms the basis on which the court will decide if the threshold criteria for the making of an Order have been met.

Whilst the harm experienced by children who have suffered maltreatment and neglect may fall into clusters of symptoms which correlate with recognized psychiatric diagnostic categories, in our view it is generally more helpful to simply list and describe the symptoms, giving explanations, where possible, for the association between the harm and the care the child has received, with specific reference to the probable emotional origin of the damage sustained. This descriptive approach allows the assessor to give an opinion about the seriousness and extent of the harm inflicted on the child, as a means of helping the court decide whether or not this amounts to significant harm. In psychological terms, exactly how much harm constitutes significant harm is not clearly defined but the assessor will be expected to give an opinion as to whether or not there has been a gross impact on the child's development and well-being.

## CONCLUSIONS

The effects of child maltreatment and neglect can be seen in a broad spectrum of dimensions. A child's age will determine their immediate response patterns but consideration also needs to be given to long-term mental health and developmental effects. The child's understanding of their experiences may change significantly through childhood, adolescence and adulthood and it needs to be recognized that the cognitive change in itself may have an impact on relationships, emotional welfare, personality and moral development. Children have a capacity to experience anxiety whenever they perceive a threat to their survival but they do not experience guilt until they have the competence to measure the effects of their own power and choices. Anger following traumatic events is determined by the child's ability to make concrete comparisons and conceptualize personal rights and feel a sense of injustice. Grief after loss is related to the competence for abstract thinking and this emotion does not arise until the child has a notion of irretrievability. Losses in childhood may not be recognized until adulthood. It is not helpful for adults to project an adult emotional agenda on children who may be delayed in development, in any event, by their experiences of maltreatment.

# References

Aber, J.L. and Zigler, D. (1981) Developmental considerations in the definition of child maltreatment, in R. Rizley and D. Cicchetti (eds) *New Directions in Child Development: Developmental Perspectives in Child Maltreatment*, San Francisco: Jossey-Bass.

Brassard, M., Germain, R. and Hart, S. (1987) *Psychological Maltreatment of Children and Youth*, New York: Pergamon.

Bridge Child Care Consultancy Service (1995) *Paul: Death through Neglect*, London: Islington ACPC/Bridge Child Care Consultancy Service.

Briere, J.N. (1992) *Child Abuse Trauma: Theory and Treatment of the Lasting Effects*, Newbury Park, CA: Sage.

Claussen, A.H. and Crittenden, P.M. (1991) Physical and psychological maltreatment: relations among types of maltreatment, *Child Abuse & Neglect* 15: 5–18.

Crittenden, P.M. (1985) Maltreated infants: vulnerability and resilience, *Journal of Child Psychology & Psychiatry* 26: 85–96.

Crittenden, P.M. (1988) Relationships at risk, in J. Belsky and T. Nezwarski (eds) *Clinical Implications of Attachment*, Hillsdale, NJ: Lawrence Erlbaum.

Department of Health, Home Office and Department of Education and Employment (1999) *Working Together to Safeguard Children*, London: The Stationery Office.

Egeland, B. and Sroufe, L.A. (1981) Developmental sequelae of maltreatment in infancy, in R. Rizley and D. Cicchetti (eds) *New Directions in Child Development: Developmental Perspectives in Child Maltreatment*, San Francisco: Jossey-Bass.

Erickson, M.F. and Egeland, B. (1987) A developmental view of the psychological consequences of maltreatment, *School Psychology Review* 16: 156–68.

Erickson, M.F. and Egeland, B. (2002) Child neglect, in J.E.B. Myers, L. Berliner, J. Briere, C.T., Hendrix, C. Jenny and T.A. Reid (eds) *The APSAC Handbook on Child Maltreatment*, 2nd ed., Thousand Oaks, CA: Sage.

Farber, E.A. and Egeland, B. (1987) Invulnerability among abused and neglected children, in E.J. Anthony and B.J. Cohler (eds) *The Invulnerable Child*, New York: The Guilford Press.

Garbarino, J. (1980) Defining emotional maltreatment: the message is the meaning, *Journal of Psychiatric Treatment and Evaluation* 2: 105–10.

Garbarino, J., Guttman, E. and Seeley, J.W. (1986) *The Psychologically Battered Child*, San Francisco: Jossey-Bass.

Garrison, E.G. (1987) Psychological maltreatment of children: an emerging focus for enquiry and concern, *American Psychologist* 42: 157–9.

Gibbons, J., Gallagher, B., Bell, C. and Gordon, D. (1995) *Development after Physical Abuse in Early Childhood: A Follow-up Study of Children on Protection Registers*, London: HMSO.

Glaser, D. (2000) Child abuse and neglect and the brain – a review, *Journal of Child Psychology & Psychiatry* 41: 97–116.

Green, A.H. (1983) Dimensions of psychological trauma in abused children, *Journal of the American Academy of Child & Adolescent Psychiatry* 22: 231–7.

Haddad, P.M. and Garralda, M.E. (1992) Hyperkinetic syndrome and disruptive early experiences, *British Journal of Psychiatry* 161: 700–3.

Helfer, R.E. (1987) The litany of the smouldering neglect of children, in R.E. Helfer and R.S. Kempe (eds) *The Battered Child*, 4th ed., Chicago: University of Chicago Press.

Maslow, A.H. (1954) *Motivation and Personality*, New York: Harper Row.

Navarre, E.L. (1987) Psychological maltreatment: the core component of child abuse, in M.R. Brassard, R.B. Germain and S.N. Hart (eds) *Psychological Maltreatment of Children and Youth*, New York: Pergamon Press.

Perry, B.D. (1997) Incubated in terror: neurodevelopmental factors in the 'cycle of violence', in J.D. Osofsky (ed.) *Children in a Violent Society*, New York: The Guilford Press.

Reder, P. and Duncan, S. (2000) Abuse then and now, in P. Reder, M. McClure and A. Jolley (eds) *Family Matters: Interfaces between Child and Adult Mental Health*, London: Routledge.

Rutter, M. (1985) Resilience in the face of adversity: protective factors and resistance to psychiatric disorder, *British Journal of Psychiatry* 147: 598–611.

Terr, L.C. (1991) Childhood traumas: an outline and overview, *American Journal of Psychiatry* 148: 10–20.

Trickett, P.K. and McBride-Chang, C. (1995) The developmental impact of different forms of child abuse and neglect, *Developmental Review* 15: 311–37.

# Chapter 6

# Are children reliable witnesses to their experiences?

*Helen L. Westcott and David P.H. Jones*

Perceptions of child witnesses, in the eyes of both professionals and the public, have undergone major changes over the years. At different points in time, child witnesses have been denigrated as totally unreliable and prone to fantasy (e.g. Heydon, 1984), whereas at others they have been rehabilitated as much more reliable and accurate than previously believed (Spencer and Flin, 1993). In the United Kingdom (and in many countries around the world), the 'discovery' of child sexual abuse in the 1980s had a profound influence on policy and practice in relation to children's testimony (Bottoms and Goodman, 1996). Legal and procedural innovations were implemented to increase the numbers of children able to testify in criminal courts, most notably through 'livelinks' and video-taped evidence-in-chief introduced as a result of the Criminal Justice Acts of 1988 and 1991 (see Westcott, Davies and Spencer, 1999 for a review). Similar developments occurred within family proceedings, where, although children rarely testify, their accounts are of critical importance to decision making. The British government published its now internationally regarded guidance on 'how to' interview child witnesses for criminal proceedings, *The Memorandum of Good Practice* (Home Office in conjunction with the Department of Health, 1992) – revised as *Achieving Best Evidence* in 2002 (see also Jones, 2003). Interviews made according to this guidance, and according to the influential Cleveland Report (Butler-Sloss, 1988), are used regularly to inform child care proceedings too.

The increased awareness of child sexual abuse also had a significant – if not dominating – influence on psychological research in relation to children's testimony. In the United States, psychologists were already beginning to become interested in child witness issues again (e.g. Goodman, 1984), but the specific problems associated with interviews of suspected child sexual abuse victims came to shape the research agenda. Specifically, psychologists became particularly interested in the way in which children responded to different sorts of questions, and in the degree to which they were susceptible to information put to them in leading or misleading questions – the concept of *suggestibility* to which we turn in just a moment. This chapter aims to review research findings and clinical observations relevant to the question posed by the title 'Are children reliable witnesses to their experiences?' It is important to acknowledge at the outset, however, that in so doing it will be necessary to summarize the conclusions of some of the debates that have emerged among psychologists and professionals researching this issue (e.g. Ceci and Friedman, 2000; Doris, 1991; Lyon, 1999).

## WHAT DO WE MEAN BY RELIABLE?

We must, first, unpick the term 'reliable'. The Oxford Dictionary defines the adjective as 'that may be relied on; of sound and consistent character or quality'. In the legal context, these aspects are typically conflated when we consider a 'reliable' or 'unreliable' witness; psychologically, however, we must address them more specifically, for different social and cognitive processes are implicated. Three strands of research are relevant:

1   That related to the accuracy of witnesses' statements;
2   That related to the consistency of witnesses' statements over time;
3   That related to witnesses' capacity to be deceptive.

We must also note that children's accounts may be reliable, yet incomplete. The accounts of young children and those with learning disabilities are particularly likely to be partial accounts of the event(s) at issue, and so, even though accurate, of limited value to practitioners (Baker-Ward and Ornstein, 2002). Faced with incomplete accounts, yet potentially concerning information, practitioners attempt to gain a fuller picture of a child, which may lead them to choose inaccurate methods (see below).

We must further acknowledge at the outset that the credibility of children's accounts – or the readiness of others to believe them – is not necessarily related to their reliability (accuracy) or consistency. It is beyond the scope of this chapter to review research findings relating to credibility, most of which stem from experimental simulations of criminal court cases involving children, with mock jurors reporting on what aspects of the child or his/her account they found believable (e.g. Leippe *et al.*, 1993).

While the standards of proof in criminal proceedings are different from family proceedings, the same principles apply to the assessment of the histories given by children. Indeed, courts hearing child care cases may make 'findings of fact' that abuse did occur as a preliminary to considering issues of significant harm and placement.

## THE ACCURACY OF CHILDREN'S STATEMENTS

Research relating to this aspect of reliability has tended to receive the most attention, particularly the notion of suggestibility (e.g. Ceci and Bruck, 1993; 1995). It is also the area where the psychological processes underpinning memory and interviewing become most complex and interrelated (see reviews in Westcott, Davies and Bull, 2002). Under free report conditions, that is when children are asked only the most general of questions (e.g. 'What happened that day?') and are not subjected to any pressure or misleading influences by the interviewer, then children's responses are typically highly accurate (over 80 per cent and often over 90 per cent accurate). The problem, especially in a legal context, is that such reports are also typically very brief (perhaps no more than 20 per cent of the total amount of possible information available). Consequently children are questioned further, and it is then that problems with inaccuracies can arise.

## Impact of different questioning styles on children's accuracy

Lamb and his colleagues have extensively researched questioning styles used with child witnesses in interviews for suspected abuse, in Israel, Sweden, the United States and the United Kingdom (see Poole and Lamb, 1998; and Lamb *et al.*, 2002, for reviews). Patterns of questioning are remarkably similar across these countries, and Lamb *et al.* have proposed a typology of questions that, they argue, accounts for 90 per cent of interviewer utterances in investigative interviews:

* *Open questions* or imperatives (also known as general questions and invitations)
* *Facilitators*
* *Directive questions* (also known as specific or focused questions)
* *Option-posing questions* (also known as closed or forced-choice questions)
* *Suggestive questions* (also known as leading and misleading questions).

An *open question* does not prescribe the witness's response in any specific way, and, because of this, is most likely to get the most accurate information from a witness's memory. Many of the 'Wh-' questions – 'what', 'when', and 'where' – would be classified as open questions, for example 'And then what happened?', or 'What happened after that?'. However, 'why' questions are less straightforward as they can be perceived by witnesses as imputing blame rather than 'fact-finding' (e.g. 'Why didn't you tell anyone?').

Lamb and his colleagues have found throughout their studies of child witness interviews that open-ended questions lead to responses that are three to four times longer, and three times richer in relevant details, than responses to other types of questions. *Facilitators*, such as 'okay', 'hmm', or restatements of the witness's previous utterance, are designed to encourage the witness to continue their account. Since they too are non-leading and non-specific, they can also be effective at maintaining the witness's narrative without decreasing the accuracy of the information that derives from their use.

*Directive questions* direct the witness to search their memory for further details or aspects of the event that the witness has mentioned previously. They may be open-ended or cued invitations, for example 'Tell me what the girl looked like' asked in an interview when the child being interviewed has mentioned a girl already, but not what she looked like. Focused questions may increase the number of details provided by the witness, but usually reduce the accuracy of the witness's account overall.

*Option-posing questions*, such as 'Was the car blue or brown?', limit the response the witness can provide (here, to 'blue' or 'brown'), and may also focus on aspects of the event that the witness has not already mentioned. In this way, they may also be considered 'leading' or 'suggestive', but the term *suggestive question* is usually reserved for questions posed by interviewers which strongly suggest what response is required from the witness, or assume details which the witness has not yet provided. Suggestive questions are those seen as most problematic by both psychologists and lawyers in terms of the limited value (and even damage) they can add to a witness's account. The possibility that the witness is not answering from memory at all, but rather is simply repeating information contained in the question, cannot be discounted. Suggestive questions are linked by psychologists to the concept of suggestibility (see below).

Unfortunately, Lamb *et al.* have found that, like lawyers at criminal court, investigative interviewers do not yet have the balance of questioning right in most interviews. Typically, they use too few open questions, and too many focused and option-posing questions, thus reducing the potential accuracy of the children's accounts. Although interviewers also use leading questions, the percentage may not be as high as some commentators suggest (Sternberg *et al.*, 2001, in a study of recent UK interview transcripts, found that police interviewers used on average 5 per cent leading questions), and certainly not as high as the number of leading and inappropriate questions used by lawyers questioning children in criminal cases (e.g. Davies and Noon, 1991; Davies *et al.*, 1995; Goodman *et al.*, 1992; Kranat and Westcott, 1994). There are no systematic studies of questioning styles used by professionals in family proceedings. However, case-based accounts, such as those of Cleveland (Butler-Sloss, 1988) and Orkney (Clyde, 1992) in the United Kingdom, and clinical experience (e.g. Ceci and Bruck, 1995) suggest that the picture is broadly similar to that described in the context of criminal investigation.

## Concept of suggestibility

Fundudis (1997) defined suggestibility as 'the act or process of impressing something (an idea, attitude or desired action) on the mind of another' (p. 151). In 1974 Loftus and Palmer carried out a classic study which investigated the effect of misleading questions on witness memory. Interestingly, this experiment was carried out with *adult* witnesses, yet the term suggestibility has become much more associated with *children's* testimony, and has compounded historical stereotypes of children as unreliable fantasists.

In a typical psychological experiment, the participant will either witness or participate in an event (e.g. Loftus and Palmer showed a video-tape of a car accident), and are later questioned individually about what happened. Usually, there will be a mixture of question types, with some open questions (e.g. 'What happened on the video?'), and others more directive (e.g. 'What colour was the car?'). Further, some questions will attempt to mislead the witness, by suggesting something different to what they witnessed (i.e. containing a false supposition). For example, it may be suggested that a protagonist performed an act which they had not, or that they were wearing clothing which they were not, or that a car was a different colour to the one seen in the video. From such experiments, psychologists have proposed three possible theoretical mechanisms that may underlie suggestibility effects (Wright, 1995):

- The original memory becomes overwritten or *destroyed* by the suggested information, such that it does not exist or that a 'blended memory' containing both original and suggested information is created;
- The misinformation is reported by the witness because the vital information did not enter into memory in the first place – thus the suggested information has *supplemented* the original memory rather than destroyed it;
- Both the original and suggested information *co-exist* in memory, but when the witness is questioned the most recent (misleading) information is reported. In certain circumstances, however, it is possible to retrieve the original correct information from memory.

No one single mechanism is likely to explain all of the effects which suggestibility research has demonstrated (Davies, 1999). The overall implication of these theoretical models for children's reliability in reporting seems to be that, depending on the circumstances in which they are reporting their experience, children may recall (a) information originally encoded about an experience, or (b) suggested information encoded after their experience (i.e. information someone may deliberately or unintentionally have suggested to them, but which was not in their original memory), or (c) a mixture of information blended from their experience *and* from subsequent suggestions. One of the further problems facing children is that they often experience difficulties in trying to identify the source of information in their memories (e.g. from experience *vs* from someone's suggestion) under conditions which make such source monitoring difficult (see Lindsay, 2002, for a review of children's source monitoring).

## Suggestibility and interviewing practice

Ceci has carried out a number of studies examining suggestibility in pre-schoolers, in relation to interviewing practice (Ceci *et al.*, 2002 offer a review). It is important to remember that these youngest children (i.e. under fives) are the most vulnerable to suggestion, due to their developing cognitive and social skills. Older children and young people behave much more similarly to adult witnesses in experimental studies. Nonetheless, Ceci *et al.* have found that young children can be suggestible in the following circumstances:

- When the interviewer repeatedly makes false suggestions (through misleading questions) and creates stereotypes about a person (Leichtman and Ceci, 1995);
- When they are asked repeatedly to visualize fictitious events (Ceci, Huffman, Smith and Loftus, 1994; Ceci, Loftus, Leichtman and Bruck, 1994);
- When they are asked about personal events that happened a long time previously and their memory has not been 'refreshed' since (Bruck, Ceci, Francoeur and Barr, 1995);
- When they are suggestively asked to use anatomically detailed dolls to re-enact an event (Bruck, Ceci, Francoeur and Renick, 1995);
- When they are questioned by a biased interviewer who pursues a 'hypothesis' or line of questioning single-mindedly (White, Leichtman and Ceci, 1997);
- When questioned in an over-authoritative manner, and/or by an adult with perceived high status (Ceci and Bruck, 1995; Poole and Lamb, 1998).

In sum:

> [W]hen children are interviewed by unbiased, neutral interviewers, when the number of interviews as well as the number of leading questions are kept to a minimum, and when there is an absence of threats, bribes and peer pressure, then children's reports are at considerably less risk for taint. (Bruck, Ceci and Hembrooke, 1998)

Ceci and his colleagues contend that such practices can be common in interviews with child witnesses, especially pre-schoolers (e.g. Ceci and Friedman, 2000), a contention that has been challenged by other researchers (e.g. Lyon, 1999). Regardless, there are important pointers for practitioners who must question child witnesses.

---

### Implications for practice

In order to promote the accuracy of children's accounts, interviewers should:

- Use approaches and questions which invite free report from the child;
- Note that directive questions may be necessary to establish detail, but they should be non-leading and preferably paired with open-ended questions and invitations;
- Avoid leading questions;
- Not pressurize or use coercive techniques;
- Take care with the use of adult authority;
- Maintain neutrality, but not indifference;
- Manage any bias and presumptions held about the child's experiences, and strive to maintain an open mind;
- Know the circumstances in which children are vulnerable to suggestion.

---

## THE CONSISTENCY OF CHILDREN'S STATEMENTS OVER TIME

A common approach used during cross-examination in courts is to highlight inconsistencies in a witness's account, thereby implying that the witness is un-reliable and that their evidence should be disregarded (e.g. Stone, 1985). In fact, such a tactic does little to help determine whether a child's account is reliable or not, and indeed clouds a number of issues associated with the child's recall and the type of questioning they have experienced. There is good reason to believe that in many cases inconsistencies in reports indicate a genuine experience (Fivush, 2002). Several interrelated aspects of consistency are considered here:

- Consistency of reports across interviews *vs* consistency within the same interview;
- The effects of repeated questioning within the same interview;
- Questioning about a repeated event *vs* about a single experience.

Simple repetition of information is beneficial to maintaining information in memory (e.g. Powell and Thomson, 2002). If a child is asked only the most general, open-ended questions, then their reports *across* different interviews – including over delays of considerable time – are likely to be highly accurate, but also incon-sistent in that different details will probably be reported in different interviews. The exact reasons for this inconsistency are unclear, but may, for example, reflect cognitive factors such as younger children's limited understanding and skills in structuring their recall (Baker-Ward and Ornstein, 2002; Fivush, 2002). Thus 'just because children may select different aspects of an event to report during different recall interviews, it is not necessarily the case that the newly reported information is incorrect' (Fivush, 2002, p. 59). If, however, the newly reported (inconsistent) information in a subsequent interview is elicited *only* in response to specific or directive questions, then it may be inaccurate, since, as we have already seen, specific questions are typically associated with an increase in errors in children's reports.

*Within* an interview, however, inconsistent answers to the same question are more problematic, and probably reflect social psychological processes: most obviously that the child will assume, since the interviewer is repeating the question, that the answer s/he provided the first time must somehow be wrong, or not what the interviewer wanted (Moston, 1987). It is thus important that if an interviewer wishes to question the child about an aspect of their experience on more than one occasion within the same interview, then they should use different forms of the same question, feign ignorance such as 'I don't get it. You said that . . .', or seek clarification, such as 'I think I know what you mean but just help me on (this or that) a bit better . . .', or, 'I just want to make sure I understand you . . .'.

Often in psychological research, children are being repeatedly questioned about a one-off event. In many cases, however, such as child sexual abuse, children will experience the event repeatedly. This raises its own set of issues about consistency, since there may be some aspects of the repeated event that are consistent across its various occurrences, and others that are unique to particular occasions. The more frequently an event is experienced, and the greater the number of unique aspects across the repeated events, then the more difficult it is for the child to keep track of which details were experienced on any particular occasion (see Powell and Thomson, 2002 for a review). It therefore follows that a child who has experienced a repeated event may give 'inconsistent' responses as a result, but that does not necessarily mean that s/he is being unreliable. However, there is an increased likelihood that the child will acquiesce to misleading 'yes/no', option-posing questions about aspects that varied across the repeated experience. This places a significantly raised cognitive load on both interviewer and child in interviews about repeated events. Asking the child to distinguish between occasions can help, for example, by asking the child to describe the first, last or most memorable occasion. Similarly, helping the child to focus on one particular event, or letting the child select the one that seems most salient to them, can assist. Conversely, 'leap-frogging' between different occasions of the repeated event (or simply between different aspects of the same event, which is another common cross-examination practice, e.g. Brennan and Brennan, 1988) poses serious problems for the child witness, and is damaging to the accuracy and consistency of their account. Again, then, the consistency of children's reports is largely influenced by how they are questioned and by the nature of their experiences.

Unfortunately, research on other questions likely to be of interest to the court – how consistent and accurate are children's reports about perpetrator identity, frequency of events, and estimates of time – offers little by way of assistance. In most child abuse cases, the identity of the alleged perpetrator is not in question, and s/he is likely to be known to the child. By contrast, most research on children's eyewitness identification accuracy has involved experimental simulations requiring the identification of strangers (e.g. Davies, 1996 for a review). Psychological research on children's estimates of frequency and duration would suggest that interviewers should exercise caution when asking children how many times an event occurred, or how long ago an event took place (e.g. Davies and Westcott, 1999). Such questions require complex cognitive skills (e.g. the handling of abstract concepts) and measurement abilities which are unlikely to be present in a child before the age of 7 years. Interviewers can assist by making such questions, where necessary, as simple and as 'concrete' as possible. For example, instead of asking how long ago an event occurred, an interviewer might ask if it occurred in school time or during the school holidays.

---

Implications for practice

In order to improve the consistency of children's accounts, interviewers should be aware that:

• More than one session or interview may enable the child to describe further information, especially if the child has experienced an event repeatedly;
• If an interview is of good quality and contains many open and few leading questions then no reduction in accuracy is likely to come from further interviews;
• If many leading or suggestive techniques are used, then accuracy declines sharply;
• They must take care when repeatedly asking about the same issue during a single interview. If this is required, methods should be used which avoid suggestion or which might lead the child to assume a particular response is sought;
• Adverse events which occurred repeatedly present particular challenges for practitioners. Techniques should be used which allow the child to describe different aspects of their overall experience, and assist them to distinguish memorable occasions;
• Children have difficulty responding to questions which contain abstract concepts or require measurements of frequency or duration.

---

## CHILDREN'S ABILITY TO BE DECEPTIVE

Vrij (2000) defines a lie as 'a successful or unsuccessful deliberate attempt, without forewarning, to create in another a belief which the communicator considers to be untrue' (p. 6). Thus, the speaker's intention to deceive is paramount, such that if a child makes an erroneous statement by mistake, then such a child would not be lying. Although this distinction may seem obvious, it is particularly important in a legal context, since we have already referred in this chapter to a number of factors which increase the likelihood of children making erroneous statements – for example: asking the same question twice in one interview; repeated questioning about a fictious event; misleading questions; and difficulties in monitoring the source of information in memory.

It is an indication of the competing stereotypes associated with children's deception – 'children never lie' vs 'children are fantasizing all the time' – that deception research with children and adults has taken divergent paths (mirroring divergent paths of suggestibility research with adults and children). In adult deception research, the assumption is that adults can and do lie on occasions, and research concentrates instead on the issues around detecting deceit. With children, however, deception research has focused on whether children can and do lie, and in what circumstances.

Research (reviewed by Vrij, 2002) suggests that children are capable of being deliberately deceptive at the age of 4 (e.g. Bussey, 1992), but also that before this age children may be able to misinform others in a rather simple manner, for example by refusing to answer a question which would reveal their deceit (e.g. Lewis, Stanger and Sullivan, 1989). The underlying requirement to be able to deceive is the ability to appreciate another person's mental processes since, in order to tell a lie successfully, then a child must convince another person that what they are saying is true (Oldershaw and Bagby, 1997). This ability improves with age, as cognitive skills and social experience increase.

Children will lie for at least five different reasons (DePaulo and Jordan, 1982; Saarni and von Salisch, 1993; see Vrij, 2002):

- To avoid negative consequences (e.g. punishment);
- To obtain a reward;
- To protect their self-esteem;
- To maintain relationships (e.g. 'white lies');
- To conform to norms and conventions.

It appears that the above list represents a developmental progression, such that children's first lies are told to avoid punishment, and it is not until children are much older that they tell lies to maintain norms. Experimental research (e.g. Ceci and DeSimone Leichtman, 1992) has shown that even very young children will lie to protect people whom they love, a finding that is supported by research with child victim witnesses (see Wade and Westcott, 1997 for a review). Children and young people who underwent investigative interviews for suspected child abuse made it clear that they often revealed only part of their experiences in interviews, or 'minimized' the details, to protect non-abusing carers whom they knew would be upset by their disclosures. Of course, such altruistic motives are easily misconstrued at court, and are used to challenge the child's reliability.

From his review of the literature on deception in relation to children and the forensic context, Vrij (2002) draws the following conclusions:

> [E]ven young children [will lie] when they have motives to do so. Initially, children will lie when they anticipate punishment, perhaps when they are threatened by someone not to disclose the truth. Older children may also lie to gain reward. Children are also willing to lie when someone else (especially someone they like) asks them to lie.
>
> It remains unclear how skilful children are at lying . . . however, it seems doubtful whether children at a very young age are capable of spontaneously telling elaborate lies which sound plausible and convincing. It is more likely that they will conceal information, or that their lies will contain only a few words. The fact that children at a very young age are already capable of telling

one word lies renders a style of interviewing requiring only one word answers undesirable. (p. 89)

Vrij's final sentence again underlines the unfortunate fact that typical questioning practices in criminal court, where lawyers actively seek to restrict witnesses' responses (e.g. Henderson, 2002), make it more difficult to know whether a child's account is reliable or not. This problem is compounded by research findings which show that children's lies are easier to detect when listening to their voices, rather than looking at their faces (e.g. Shennum and Bugental, 1982), and that introverted and socially anxious children (as many may be in the courtroom) are less likely to be believed by observers, irrespective of whether they are accurate or truthful (e.g. Vrij and van Wijngaarden, 1994).

---

Implications for practice

- Knowledge of the reasons why children lie can help alert the practitioner to the potential for it to occur;
- Children's lies may be in the direction of minimizing or denying that abuse has occurred, as well as providing false accounts that it has;
- The use of open questions seeking detailed responses (rather than questions requiring just a 'yes', 'no' or one-word answer) can help make it more difficult for a child to maintain deceit.

---

## FROM INITIAL SUSPICIONS TO COURT PROCEEDINGS

### Erroneous concerns and cases of maltreatment

It can be seen from the above that there are several opportunities for error to occur in the journey from initial concern to a court hearing. Children, their carers, and professionals may each be confused as to what has occurred. Both children and adults sometimes lie. Carers and professionals can leap to erroneous conclusions, and this may be reflected in their questioning and style of communication with children. Some questioning techniques are more error prone than others. All these considerations are especially important for child sexual abuse, where concerns and conclusions are more heavily reliant upon what the child says. However, they may also be relevant in other kinds of maltreatment such as physical abuse. In any one of the ways noted above, a false positive conclusion about maltreatment can arise. Such situations have also been called 'false allegations', but we prefer the terms 'erroneous concern' or 'erroneous case' because they are less pejorative, and do not imply any particular motivation or mechanism leading to the error.

Erroneous concerns and cases have the potential to result in substantial harm and serious consequences for the child and any adult involved. These include unnecessary separation of child and parent, parental imprisonment, loss of job and reputation. It is probable that there is considerable psychological harm deriving from erroneous conclusions about child abuse. Mere suspicion is not necessarily harmful to the child or the adult involved, unless the full panoply of protection measures follow, without caution or further exploration. Fortunately, many concerns which turn out to be erroneous are investigated by social services and other agencies without negative consequences for a child or adult (Jones and McGraw, 1987; Oates *et al.*, 2000).

Approximately 40 per cent of sexual abuse concerns become substantiated by an agency following assessment (Ceci and Friedman, 2000). In a recent study (Oates *et al.*, 2000), 43 per cent of 551 concerns were substantiated; 2.5 per cent were deemed erroneous, and made by children; 34 per cent erroneous by adults (some of these were parents, other non-relatives and, less commonly, professionals); while 21 per cent remained inconclusive, following assessment. The adult errors were mainly mistaken concerns, not deliberate lies. The study emphasizes the substantial burden of responsibility on professional agencies to conduct their assessments swiftly, with the least possible disruption and harm to children and adult carers, while at the same time remaining alert to the need to protect certain children from harm. In addition, the findings imply the need for professionals to maintain an open minded and unbiased approach. There have not been similar studies in the field of physical abuse or neglect.

Error can exist in the other direction too, leading to false negative conclusions about maltreatment. In such cases children may remain in unsafe situations, which affects their trust in others to support and protect them. Many concerns which are reported to social services departments remain unsubstantiated, and it is clear that a proportion of these are false negatives. Some will reappear after months or years, when the situation is clearer and abuse capable of being confirmed. Others are not re-reported, as we learn from the retrospective accounts of adults recalling childhood experiences.

---

### Implications for practice

- Erroneous or false accounts of maltreatment can occur;
- They occur because of mistaken concerns, beliefs, or conclusions, as well as because an adult or child lies;
- Errors from adults appear to be more common than those emanating from children;
- Practitioners must prevent erroneous concerns becoming translated into erroneous cases (false accounts) of abuse;

- The harmful effects of erroneous concerns can be kept to a minimum through high-quality assessments and investigations;
- Neutrality and the management of presumption and bias within assessment or investigation teams is a key requirement;
- False negative conclusions also occur, and leave children unprotected.

## Court proceedings

There are several implications of the issues discussed in this chapter for experts, including how they communicate with children; and how they construct and articulate their opinion about children's accounts for the court. We shall take these in turn.

### 1. Communicating with children

The expert involved in court proceedings should be well versed in existing guidance on good practice (e.g. Jones, 1992; 2003; Home Office, 2002; Wilson and Powell, 2001) as well as relevant research and the implications which derive from it, as discussed elsewhere in this volume. Practice implications can be summarized as a series of positive competencies and qualities to be either encouraged or avoided within practice, as shown below.

Positive competencies and qualities

*The professional should:*

- listen to and understand the child;
- impart genuine empathic concern;
- convey to the child that it is s/he who is 'expert' about the issues under assessment, not the professional;
- permit the child to freely recall his/her experiences;
- maintain professional neutrality and manage unhelpful emotions, views, and perspectives in all interactions with the child;
- operate within a context of continuing professional development and critical review of practice;
- clarify any ambiguous communication.

Qualities and approaches to avoid

*The professional should* not:

- employ leading questions or other techniques which are prone to error;
- apply excessive pressure or use coercive strategies when communicating with a child;
- maintain assumptions or biased views which affect assessment, decision making or reporting.

## 2. Communicating with the court

Guidance is available for experts undertaking and reporting on their work for courts (e.g. *Re H*, 2000; *Re D*, 1998). Any proposed direct work with the child should be planned with the full knowledge of the court. Particular care is needed in order to distinguish between: interview sessions which are linked with initial assessments (Department of Health, 1999; 2000); investigations of a possible crime (Department of Health, 1999; Home Office, 2002); as a contribution to a comprehensive assessment (Department of Health, 2000); or as therapeutic interviews (interviews conducted in the context of therapy, which only exceptionally become the source of material which may help the court in discovering facts – see *Re D*, 1998).

It will help the court if the expert sets out in the report the chronology through which concerns about maltreatment have unfolded, and the psychosocial context in which it occurred. The expert could usefully draw attention to the questioning style and techniques used by all those involved in the chain of events, if such information is available. This enables the court reporter to draw attention to both strengths and weaknesses in the child's account as it has unfolded, and as it has become presented to professional agencies.

Clearly, it would be beyond the expert's remit to provide an opinion on whether the child's account is truthful or believable. This is the preserve of the court. However, it is within the expert's role to point to those aspects of the case which increase confidence in the reliability of the account given, from a psychological perspective, as well as drawing attention to factors which reduce confidence. In addition, it can be useful to comment on the relative interaction between these factors, because many accounts of maltreatment have some elements of both. The boundary between the expert's and the court's territory will vary in relation to these issues. Hence it is preferable for the expert to establish the areas to be covered in his or her report, at preliminary direction hearings.

Sometimes, in contentious court cases the negative effect of one or two questions is raised as a basis for doubting the veracity of the entirety of the child's account. The expert can be helpful here in providing evidence from a psychological perspective about the relative likelihood that one or two examples of imperfect practice might lead to a completely erroneous account. Thus, the all-important neutrality and balance required during the practice of communicating with children is reiterated when analysing accounts and presenting evidence for the court's consumption.

## CONCLUSIONS

So, are children reliable witnesses to their experiences? In itself, this very question throws an interesting perspective on the issue of children's testimony, since it presupposes reliability to be a quality only present in the child, whereas, as we have seen, children's reliability is dependent both on them and on those adults who communicate with them. Nelson (1997), in a critique of the 'obsession' with children's reliability, contrasts the attention on children's evidence with that on adults' statements:

> We search extremely hard to find studies and reports on the reliability of evidence given by suspected adult abusers, or proposals on how we might devise tests and approaches which better discern truth from falsehood, fact from fantasy. Fantasising is, of course, a weakness of children, not of paedophiles. Adults need no competency test to ensure they know the difference between truth and lies. Yet strangely, almost every week we see uncovered abuses which continued for years or decades, where respectable adults had assured us nothing was going on, and stigmatised children protested their sufferings in vain. (pp. 155–6)

Walker (1993), too, was incensed by her observations of questioning child witnesses in a criminal trial. Asked to review the competency of a young witness she exclaimed:

> In short, there seemed to be nothing essentially wrong with this child's competence as a speaker or competency as a witness in a court of law. There did seem to be something very wrong, however, with the adults' competence at asking questions. (p. 67)

This chapter has amply demonstrated that, like adults, children can be reliable witnesses to their experiences but, at times, they can also be vulnerable to the deliberate or unintentional distorting influence of others. Many aspects of the context in which children are questioned can impact upon children's cognitive and socio-emotional psychological processes, and perhaps most profound of all is the potential influence of the interviewer. As Saywitz et al. (1993) have neatly summarized:

> Lying, fantasizing, and coaching are not the *only* reasons why a child's testimony might seem unbelievable or unreliable. Another plausible reason is

the mismatch between the linguistic, cognitive, and emotional worlds of children and adults, a mismatch that obfuscates communication with child witnesses. (p. 76)

This mismatch may be particularly pronounced when we consider the interventions by professional adult authority figures into the lives of some of the most disadvantaged and victimized children in our society. Psychological research still has a way to go before it can shed light on some of the fundamental motivational and individual difference factors that enable some children to remain steadfast in the face of considerable adversity, whereas others become damaged or react in other ways to similar experiences. Nor do we know enough about how these differences may subsequently impact upon children's reliability when questioned about difficult events. However, we do now know that children and young people can reliably describe adverse events they have experienced. The onus is upon the adult world to treat these memories with due care and respect, recognizing the pitfalls deriving from both zealous endeavour and woeful ignorance.

## References

Baker-Ward, L. and Ornstein, P.A. (2002) Cognitive underpinnings of children's testimony, in H.L. Westcott, G.M. Davies and R.H.C. Bull (eds) *Children's Testimony: A Handbook of Psychological Research and Forensic Practice*, Chichester: Wiley.

Bottoms, B.L. and Goodman, G.S. (1996) *International Perspectives on Child Abuse and Children's Testimony: Psychological Research and Law*, Thousand Oaks, CA: Sage Publications.

Brennan, M. and Brennan, R.E. (1988) *Strange Language: Child Victims Under Cross-examination*, Wagga Wagga, NSW: Riverina Literacy Centre.

Bruck, M., Ceci, S.J., Francoeur, E. and Barr, R.J. (1995) 'I hardly cried when I got my shot!' Influencing children's reports about a visit to their pediatrician, *Child Development* 66: 193–208.

Bruck, M., Ceci, S.J., Francoeur, E. and Renick, A. (1995) Anatomically detailed dolls do not facilitate preschoolers' reports of a pediatric examination involving genital touching, *Journal of Experimental Psychology: Applied* 1: 95–109.

Bruck, M., Ceci, S.J. and Hembrooke, H. (1998) Reliability and credibility of young children's reports, *American Psychologist* 53: 136–51.

Bussey, K. (1992) Children's lying and truthfulness: implications for children's testimony, in S.J. Ceci, M. DeSimone Leichtman and M. Putnick (eds) *Cognitive and Social Factors in Early Deception*, Hillsdale, NJ: Lawrence Erlbaum Associates.

Butler-Sloss, E. (1988) *Report of the Enquiry into Child Abuse in Cleveland in 1987*, London: HMSO.

Ceci, S.J. and Bruck, M. (1993) Suggestibility of the child witness: a historical review and synthesis, *Psychological Bulletin* 113: 403–39.

Ceci, S.J. and Bruck, M. (1995) *Jeopardy in the Courtroom: A Scientific Analysis of Children's Testimony*, Washington, DC: American Psychological Association.

Ceci, S.J., Crossman, A.M., Scullin, M.H., Gilstrap, L. and Huffman, M.L. (2002) Children's suggestibility research: implications for the courtroom and the forensic interview, in H.L. Westcott, G.M. Davies and R.H.C. Bull (eds) *Children's Testimony: A Handbook of Psychological Research and Forensic Practice*, Chichester: Wiley.

Ceci, S.J. and DeSimone Leichtman, M.(1992) 'I know that you know that I know that you broke the toy': a brief report of recursive awareness among 3-year-olds, in S.J. Ceci, M. DeSimone Leichtman and M. Putnick (eds) *Cognitive and Social Factors in Early Deception*, Hillsdale, NJ: Lawrence Erlbaum Associates.

Ceci, S.J. and Friedman, R.D. (2000) The suggestibility of children: scientific research and legal implications, *Cornell Law Review* 86: 33–108.

Ceci, S.J., Huffman, M.L.C., Smith, E. and Loftus, E.F. (1994) Repeatedly thinking about a non-event: source misattributions among preschoolers, *Consciousness and Cognition* 3: 388–407.

Ceci, S.J., Loftus, E.F., Leichtman, M.D. and Bruck, M. (1994) The role of source misattributions in the creation of false beliefs among preschoolers, *International Journal of Clinical and Experimental Hypnosis* 62: 304–20.

Clyde, J. (1992) *The Report of the Inquiry into the Removal of Children from Orkney in February 1991*, Edinburgh: Her Majesty's Stationery Office.

Davies, G.M. (1996) Children's identification evidence, in S.L. Sporer, R.S. Malpass and G. Koehnken (eds) *Psychological Issues in Eyewitness Identifications*, Mahwah, NJ: Lawrence Erlbaum Associates.

Davies, G.M. (1999) Contamination of witness memory, in A.H. Heaton-Armstrong, E. Shepherd and D. Wolchover (eds) *Analysing Witness Testimony: A Guide for Legal Practitioners and Other Professionals*, London: Blackstone Press.

Davies, G.M. and Noon, E. (1991) *An Evaluation of the Live Link for Child Witnesses*, London: Home Office.

Davies, G.M. and Westcott, H.L. (1999) *Interviewing Child Witnesses under the Memorandum of Good Practice: A Research Review*, London: Home Office Policing and Reducing Crime Unit.

Davies, G.M., Wilson, C., Mitchell, R. and Milsom, J. (1995) *Videotaping Children's Evidence: An Evaluation*, London: Home Office.

Department of Health, Home Office and Department for Education and Employment (1999) *Working Together to Safeguard Children: A Guide to Inter-Agency Working to Safeguard and Promote the Welfare of Children*, London: The Stationery Office.

Department of Health (2000) *Framework for the Assessment of Children in Need and their Families*, London: The Stationery Office.

DePaulo, B.M. and Jordan, A. (1982) Age changes in deceiving and detecting deceit, in R.S. Feldman (ed.) *Development of Nonverbal Behaviour in Children*, New York: Springer-Verlag.

Doris, J. (1991) (ed.) *The Suggestibility of Children's Recollections*, Washington: American Psychological Association.

Fivush, R. (2002) The development of autobiographical memory, in H.L. Westcott, G.M. Davies and R.H.C. Bull (eds) *Children's Testimony: A Handbook of Psychological Research and Forensic Practice*, Chichester: Wiley.

Fundudis, T. (1997) Young children's memory. How good is it? How much do we know about it? *Child Psychology and Child Psychiatry Review* 2: 150–8.

Goodman, G.S. (1984) Children's testimony in historical perspective, *Journal of Social Issues* 40: 9–31.

Goodman, G.S., Pyle, L., Jones, D.P.H., Port, L. and Prado L. (1992) Testifying in court; emotional effects of criminal court testimony on child sexual assault victims,

*Monographs of the Society for Research in Child Development* 57 (5, Serial No. 229): 1–161.

Henderson, E. (2002) Persuading and controlling: the theory of cross-examination in relation to children, in H.L. Westcott, G.M. Davies and R.H.C. Bull (eds) *Children's Testimony: A Handbook of Psychological Research and Forensic Practice*, Chichester: Wiley.

Heydon, J. (1984) *Evidence: Cases and Materials*, London: Butterworths.

Home Office (2002) *Achieving Best Evidence in Criminal Proceedings: Guidance for Vulnerable or Intimidated Witnesses, Including Children*, London: Home Office Communication Directorate.

Home Office in conjunction with the Department of Health (1992) *Memorandum of Good Practice on Video Recorded Interviews with Child Witnesses for Criminal Proceedings*, London: HMSO.

Jones, D.P.H. (1992) *Interviewing the Sexually Abused Child: Investigation of Suspected Abuse*, 4th ed., London: Gaskell.

Jones, D.P.H. (2003) *Communicating with Vulnerable Children: A Guide for Practitioners*, London: Gaskell Press.

Jones, D.P.H. and McGraw, J. M. (1987) Reliable and fictitious accounts of sexual abuse to children, *Journal of Interpersonal Violence* 2: 27–45.

Kranat, V.K. and Westcott, H.L. (1994) Under fire: lawyers questioning children in criminal courts, *Expert Evidence* 3: 16–24.

Lamb, M.E., Orbach, Y., Sternberg, K.J., Esplin, P.W. and Hershkowitz, I. (2002) The effects of forensic interview practices on the quality of information provided by alleged victims of child abuse, in H.L. Westcott, G.M. Davies and R.H.C. Bull (eds) *Children's Testimony: A Handbook of Psychological Research and Forensic Practice*, Chichester: Wiley.

Leichtman, M.D. and Ceci, S.J. (1995) The effects of stereotypes and suggestions on preschoolers' reports, *Developmental Psychology* 31: 568–78.

Leippe, M.R., Manion, A.P. and Romanczyk, A. (1993) Discernibility or discrimination? Understanding jurors' reactions to accurate and inaccurate child and adult eyewitnesses, in G.S. Goodman and B.L. Bottoms (eds) *Child Victims, Child Witnesses: Understanding and Improving Testimony*, New York: The Guilford Press.

Lewis, M., Stanger, C. and Sullivan, M.W. (1989) Deception in three-year-olds, *Developmental Psychology* 25: 439–43.

Lindsay, D.S. (2002) Children's source monitoring, in H.L. Westcott, G.M. Davies and R.H.C. Bull (eds) *Children's Testimony: A Handbook of Psychological Research and Forensic Practice*, Chichester: Wiley.

Loftus, E.F. and Palmer, J.C. (1974) Reconstruction of automobile destruction: an example of the interactions between language and memory, *Journal of Verbal Learning and Verbal Behavior* 13: 585–9.

Lyon, T.D. (1999) The new wave in children's suggestibility research: a critique, *Cornell Law Review* 84: 1004–87.

Moston, S. (1987) The suggestibility of children in interview studies, *First Language* 7: 67–78.

Nelson, S. (1997) The Memorandum: quest for the impossible? in H.L. Westcott and J. Jones (eds) *Perspectives on the Memorandum. Policy, Practice and Research in Investigative Interviewing*, Aldershot: Arena.

Oates, R.K., Jones, D.P.H., Denson, D., Sirotnak, A., Gary, N. and Krugman, R.D. (2000) Erroneous concerns about child sexual abuse, *Child Abuse and Neglect* 24: 149–57.

Oldershaw, L. and Bagby, R.M. (1997) Children and deception, in R. Rogers (ed.) *Clinical Assessment of Malingering and Deception*, New York: The Guilford Press.

Poole, D.A. and Lamb, M.E. (1998) *Investigative Interviews of Children: A Guide for Helping Professionals*, Washington: American Psychological Association.

Powell, M. and Thomson, D. (2002) Children's memories for repeated events, in H.L. Westcott, G.M. Davies and R.H.C. Bull (eds) *Children's Testimony: A Handbook of Psychological Research and Forensic Practice*, Chichester: Wiley.

*Re D (Child Abuse: Interviews)* (1998) *Family Law Reports* 2: 10–21.

*Re H (Children: Care Proceedings, Sexual Abuse)* (2000) *Family Court Reporter* 2: 499–511.

Saarni, C. and von Salisch, M. (1993) The socialization of emotional dissemblance, in M. Lewis and C. Saarni (eds) *Lying and Deception in Everyday Life*, New York: The Guilford Press.

Saywitz, K., Nathanson, R. and Snyder, L. (1993) Credibility of child witnesses: the role of communicative competence, *Topics in Language Disorders* 13: 59–78.

Shennum, W.A. and Bugental, D.B. (1982) The development of control over affective expression in nonverbal behaviour, in R.S. Feldman (ed.) *Development of Nonverbal Behaviour in Children*, New York: Springer-Verlag.

Spencer, J.R. and Flin, R. (1993) *The Evidence of Children: The Law and the Psychology*, 2nd ed., London: Blackstone Press.

Sternberg, K.J., Lamb, M.E., Davies, G.M. and Westcott, H.L. (2001). The Memorandum of Good Practice: theory versus application, *Child Abuse & Neglect* 25: 669–81.

Stone, M. (1985) *Cross-examination in Criminal Trials*, London: Butterworths.

Vrij, A. (2002) Deception in children: a literature review and implications for children's testimony, in H.L. Westcott, G.M. Davies and R.H.C. Bull (eds) *Children's Testimony: A Handbook of Psychological Research and Forensic Practice*, Chichester: Wiley.

Vrij, A. (2000) *Detecting Lies and Deceit: The Psychology of Lying and the Implications for Professional Practice*, Chichester: Wiley.

Vrij, A. and van Wijngaarden, J.J. (1994) Will truth come out? Two studies about the detection of false statements expressed by children, *Expert Evidence* 3: 78–84.

Wade, A. and Westcott, H.L. (1997) No easy answers: children's perspectives on investigative interviews, in H.L. Westcott and J. Jones (eds) *Perspectives on the Memorandum. Policy, Practice and Research in Investigative Interviewing*, Aldershot: Arena.

Walker, A.G. (1993) Questioning young children in court: a linguistic case study, *Law and Human Behavior* 17: 59–81.

Westcott, H.L., Davies, G.M. and Bull, R.H.C. (eds) (2002) *Children's Testimony: A Handbook of Psychological Research and Forensic Practice*, Chichester: Wiley.

Westcott, H.L., Davies, G.M. and Spencer, J.R. (1999) Children, hearsay, and the courts: a perspective from the United Kingdom, *Psychology, Public Policy, and Law* 5: 282–303.

White, T.L., Leichtman, M.D. and Ceci, S.J. (1997) The good, the bad, and the ugly: accuracy, inaccuracy, and elaboration in preschoolers' reports about a past event, *Applied Cognitive Psychology* 11: S37–S54.

Wilson, C. and Powell, M. (2001) *A Guide to Interviewing Children*, London: Routledge.

Wright, D.B. (1995) Misinformation methodologies: explaining the effects of errant information, in G. Davies, S. Lloyd-Bostock, M. McMurran and C. Wilson (eds) *Psychology, Law and Criminal Justice: International Developments in Research and Practice*, Berlin: Walter de Gruyter.

# Chapter 7

# How much should children's views count?

*Peter Reder and Sylvia Duncan*

## INTRODUCTION

The following vignettes represent common dilemmas faced by those assessing parenting. Children express views about their future care that the court must consider but it remains uncertain what validity should be placed on them. Questions might include whether the child is old enough to understand the issues, whether their views are excessively influenced by the vested interests of a parent, or whether the child's strong wishes should be respected if they are contradicted by the conclusions of professionals assessing their welfare needs.

> A 10-year-old girl and her 11-year-old brother had been removed from the care of their single father because of his chronic drug dependency and episodic neglect of their needs. Throughout numerous assessments, both children asserted that they had always been well looked after and insisted that they wanted to return to live with their father. Their views were respected but as the time approached for a trial reunification in a residential family assessment centre, the girl began to wet her bed and report frightening dreams and her challenging behaviour increased. Finally, she told her social worker that did not want to go in to the centre, although she was unable to say why.
>
> An 8-year-old-boy of mixed race had to move from the home of his white foster parents where he had lived for some years and his social worker was determined to place him with a black family. Despite his vehement protests that he felt he was white and wanted to be with a white family, the social worker insisted that he was black because 'society will see you as black' and she found a black foster family for him.
>
> A young teenage boy had not attended school for four years and he and his mother claimed that he was receiving adequate education by reading

newspapers and books in the local library. Many professionals were concerned that his mother suffered from a psychotic illness, that he identified with her disturbed ideas and that he was being recruited into an increasingly reclusive and paranoid existence. However, both mother and son resisted all attempts at assessment until a Child Assessment Order enabled him to be interviewed. He was articulate and well-informed and the only apparent expression of irrationality was vehement hostility to homosexuals and any professional who criticized his mother. He insisted that his mother was both sane and caring and he wanted to remain living with her as before.

The Children Act 1989 and The Children (Northern Ireland) Order 1995 require children's views to be taken into account by courts when making decisions about their future care. This is consistent with society's progressive respect for the child as an individual (de Mause, 1976) and with Article 12 of the United Nations Convention on the Rights of the Child 1989, which proclaims that a child who is capable of forming his or her own views has the right to express them and for them to be given due weight in accordance with their age and maturity. However, neither the Children Act (and equivalent order in Northern Ireland) nor the United Nations Convention compels courts to implement children's wishes, but only to take them into account (Littlechild, 2001). Hence, practitioners interviewing children for child care proceedings will need to ascertain the child's views and wishes and also advise the court how much weight to accord those expressed opinions. This has become even more significant following implementation of the 1998 Human Rights Act in October 2000, since the Act emphasizes that everyone (that is, children and parents) has the right of respect for family life. Consequently, if a child expresses the wish to live separately from a parent or to have no further contact, this will need to be balanced with any contrary wishes of the parent, since each member of the family has equal rights under the Act (Cleave, 2001).

The concept of 'sufficient understanding' is relevant to this issue, even though it was primarily conceived as a parameter to guide young people's capacity to give consent to medical interventions (Reder and Fitzpatrick, 1998). The Law Lords' ruling in the *Gillick* case (*Gillick v West Norfolk and Wisbech Health Authority and the Department of Health and Social Security*, 1985) was a historic landmark, since, for the first time, doctors in England, Wales and Northern Ireland were granted discretion to prescribe medication (in this case contraceptives) to young people below the age of 16 years without the knowledge or consent of their parents (Dyer, 1985; Parkinson, 1986). Lord Scarman's ruling contained such phrases as 'provided she has sufficient understanding and intelligence', 'she must also have sufficient maturity to understand' and 'to enable him or her to understand fully what is proposed'.

The notion of the 'Gillick-competent child' has entered everyday medico-legal parlance, usually referring to a child who has 'sufficient age and understanding' (e.g. Lyon and de Cruz, 1993; White *et al.*, 1996; Department of Health, 2001). According to legal texts, 'Gillick-competence' to consent to treatment involves a capacity to understand the treatment's purpose, nature, likely effects, chances of success, risks and alternatives (Kennedy and Grubb, 1994). Similarly, the Age of Legal Capacity (Scotland) Act 1991 allows a person under the age of 16 years to consent to medical interventions provided that they are 'capable of understanding the nature and possible consequences of the procedure or treatment'. Even so, the psychological components of 'sufficient understanding' have remained loosely defined and the debate continues about children's consent in clinical situations (e.g. Devereux *et al.*, 1993; Pearce, 1994; Alderson and Montgomery, 1996; Honig and Bentovim, 1996; Reder and Fitzpatrick, 1998; Shaw, 1998; 1999; Bailey and Harbour, 1999; Honig and Jaffa, 2000; Oates, 2000; British Medical Association, 2001; Department of Health, 2001; Ford and Kessel, 2001).

In England and Wales, the 1989 Children Act reinforced the *Gillick* ruling and made it relevant to family proceedings by introducing a welfare checklist that courts must refer to before deciding whether to grant an Order. In particular, they must ascertain the wishes and feelings of the child concerned and consider them 'in the light of the child's age and understanding'. In other words, the child's views must be adequately represented so that the court can weigh them against their capacity to understand the issues at stake, as well as other evidence and opinions in the case. A parallel legal requirement, following the case of *Re M* 1994, is that solicitors are expected to take instruction from an 'intelligent' and 'articulate' child, even if he or she appears to be emotionally disturbed.

Here, we shall discuss the concept of sufficient understanding as it applies to children's views about who should care for them in the future or what contact they will have with a non-resident parent. We then consider how child mental health professionals might assess this. The chapter is intended to complement that by Duncan and Baker (Chapter 5) on assessing the psychological impact on children of *previous and/or current* parenting, and by Wescott and Jones (Chapter 6) on the reliability of children's disclosures about adverse care experienced *in the past*, by addressing children's capacity to contemplate their *future* circumstances.

## CHILDREN'S UNDERSTANDING

According to the British Medical Association (2001), the relevant tests of understanding are whether the individual is able to comprehend and retain information relevant to the opinion and weigh that information in the balance as part of a decision-making process free from undue external influence. Reder and Fitzpatrick (1998) have also argued that young people's understanding is not a single attribute, but is a composite of a number of factors. These include the meaning that they attribute to the available information and its relevance for them personally in the context of their past and present life circumstances. Also relevant is the child's awareness of the implications of any decisions, based on that meaning and relevance. Hence, their understanding will depend on: the *complexity of the issues* under consideration; their *cognitive development*; the *clarity and appropriateness of communication* with them; their *emotional state*; and the influence of *interpersonal conflict* on their thinking.

Each of these themes needs to be considered as part of an assessment, together with their mutual interaction. For example, parenting breakdown is likely to arouse strong emotions and tensions in children which will influence their cognitive functioning and capacity to make sense of the issues. However, since the child's cognitive development, the impact of personal and interpersonal conflict and the need for clear and appropriate communications are especially relevant to the assessment process, we shall consider them in greater detail here.

## COMPLEXITY OF THE ISSUES

Decisions about care or contact are complex issues for children, with multiple component factors which need to be identified, distinguished and weighed up. In addition, they may contain concepts at a high level of abstraction. Within the limits of their cognitive development (see below), the child will need to be assisted to separate out each element and render it meaningful.

The legal context is also a complicated one for children to grasp. Saywitz and Goodman (1996) reported that by 10 years of age most children understand the basics of the judicial process but younger children may have difficulty conceptualizing the decision-making role of the judge. However, even 5-year-olds appreciate the need to tell the truth during legal proceedings. For all children, the nature of the assessment interview as part of the legal process will need to be explained. The interviewer must make themselves relevant to the child by clarifying who they are and ensuring that the child is aware of the reasons for the meeting.

## COGNITIVE DEVELOPMENT

Children's cognitive ability is partially dependent on their chronological age, but their capacity to understand is also a function of genetic endowment, of any neurological trauma suffered and of the effects of environmental stimulation. Rarely would an assessor in child care proceedings need to resort to formal psychological tests to determine 'sufficient understanding'. However, the various cognitive factors that intelligence tests address can be identified as the basis for informal assessment. These include: knowledge; alertness to the environment; concept formation (i.e. the ability to place objects and events together in a meaningful group); richness of ideas; comprehension (including ability to reach solutions by drawing on past experiences); social judgement; reasoning (including the capacity to break a whole into its component parts and synthesize them into a coherent whole again); attention to, retrieval of, reflection upon and application of information (including the ability to differentiate essential from non-essential detail and size up the total situation); and planning ability (adapted from Sattler, 1982).

Piaget's work remains a cornerstone of our knowledge about children's cognitive development. He described children as actively constructing and reconstructing reality out of their experiences with the environment and he proposed that the way they conceptualize the world changes as their cognitive capacities progressively develop (e.g. Inhelder and Piaget, 1958; Piaget, 1969; and see also Hobson, 1985; Shaffer, 1989). In the 'pre-operational' stage, between the ages of approximately 2 and 7 years, children reason from the particular to the particular, so that when two events occur together, they assume that one event caused the other. They focus on a single aspect of a problem, ignoring other relevant information. They usually view the world from their own perspective and they have difficulty recognizing another person's point of view. Most children attain 'concrete operations' at the age of 6 or 7 years, in which they construct a lawful world, begin to organize their experiences in a more ordered manner and to reason logically about objects, events and experiences. They recognize that the effects of many physical actions are reversible. However, they still find it difficult to think about an abstract or hypothetical idea that has no basis in reality, so that their explanations are directly related to events in their real and immediate world, and they tend to accept the first solution to a problem that comes to mind. Even so, the child begins to extend their thought from the actual towards the potential, so that by 11 or 12 years of age, development of 'formal operations' enables most early adolescents to begin to think flexibly, to reason about abstract ideas and to test alternative solutions, especially around issues of significance to them. Hence, ideas about their present and future life can be contemplated.

Children's emerging sense of time is multi-determined and depends on a number of developmental lines: cognition; language; behaviour; and emotions. *Cognitively*, even young children can envisage themself being an adult, such as imagining what they want to be when they grow up, and 3-year-olds begin to understand the concept of cause and effect. Young children first understand the future as a recurrence of past events (Harner, 1982). By the age of 4 years, children can represent the order of daily activities and, by 6 or 7 years of age, annual regularities, although the more general concept of order and recurrence in life is not fully integrated until aged 8 or 9 years (Friedman, 1982). From approximately 4 years of age children begin to distinguish between reversible and irreversible events, and by 6 or 7 years of age they can comprehend that death is irrevocable (Speece and Brent, 1984). However, it is only during adolescence that they can fully conceptualize time, and therefore 'the future', as an abstract entity (Fraisse, 1976; Harner, 1982).

In the development of *language*, the words 'today' and 'tomorrow' and use of the past, present and future tenses have usually appeared by the age of 3 years, although may not always be used correctly until aged 5 or 6 years (Harner, 1982). Formative *behavioural* experiences also contribute to the child's sense of time, and parenting that has involved routines and consistency in daily life lays the foundation for both an expectation that needs will be met in the future and an internal working model of people as reliable figures now and in the future. *Emotionally*, Goldstein *et al.* (1973) and Arlow (1989) showed that children have an inbuilt sense of time based on the urgency of their instinctual and emotional needs. An infant's memory begins to incorporate the way in which parents satisfy wishes and needs and reappear after their disappearance, which in turn enables the child to develop the capacity to delay gratification and to anticipate and plan for the future. According to the clinical experiences of Goldstein *et al.* (1973), infants and toddlers cannot stretch waiting to more than a few days without feeling overwhelmed by the parent's absence; most children under the age of 5 years find parental absence of more than 2 months beyond comprehension and for most young school-aged children the absence of more than 6 months can be similarly experienced. Thus, the child's sense of the passage of time depends on what part of the mind does the measuring, whether it is the sensible and reasoning part or the impulsive, egocentric part.

These principles allow us to define the following range of questions about cognitive and intellectual functioning that need to be considered during interviews with children seeking to elicit their views.

## Cause and effect

Is the child able to trace through the practical consequences of decisions about their care arrangements (e.g. that living with their mother means attending such-and-such a school, or only seeing their father on selected days)? How much does the child recognize that actions and, therefore, decisions have consequences? If so, does the child realize that, in some circumstances, the consequences may be permanent (e.g. choosing to terminate a pregnancy) but other decisions are reversible and could be modified at a later date (e.g. which parent to live with, or changing their name)?

## Self and others

To what degree can the child distinguish the implications for themself personally from the consequences for significant others (e.g. a parent)? Also, can the child appreciate that societal standards influence individual behaviour (e.g. the expectation that children will receive education, usually by attending school)?

## Historical sense

Has the child an ability to consider issues within a temporal framework, with some sense of past, present and future? To what extent can the child project themself into the future and conceptualize that they will be different then from how they are now and that their actions will have a consequence for their life in the future? Also, is there some recognition that other people change over time?

## Cognitive complexity

Does the child show some capacity for abstract thinking? As a result, does the child appreciate that most issues tend to be multi-determined? Does the child appreciate the reasons why others have had concerns about their care and that caretaking choices need to be made? Does the child recognize the possibility of being able to choose between alternatives? If so, can the child balance the different factors in importance and attempt some sort of risk–benefit analysis?

## Reality testing

Is the child able to conceptualize the unknown in such a way as to test whether alternatives are realistic? Is the child's thinking clouded by a formal psychiatric disorder (e.g. psychosis)? Has a parent's disordered thinking or threats disturbed the child's sense of reality?

## APPROPRIATENESS OF COMMUNICATION

The literature on children's disclosures has some relevance to this topic, since it includes the degree to which children are suggestible (that is, their memory or statements are susceptible to parental interference or to overzealous interviewing by professionals) or their thinking is vulnerable to emotional influences. Such concerns are most relevant to criminal proceedings, such as a parent's trial on charges of sexual abuse, where the child's testimony needs to satisfy a jury 'beyond a reasonable doubt' whether events did, or did not, occur. In family proceedings, however, the court is weighing up 'on the balance of probability' whether a child has been significantly harmed and who should care for them in the future. Although assessments in these two contexts have different purposes and are governed by different legal criteria, they nonetheless have a common interest in representing the child as accurately as possible. We shall therefore start with a brief summary of the current position with regard to children as informants during assessment interviews.

Saywitz and Goodman (1996) considered that any individual's capacity to resist suggestion depends on, amongst other things, the type of information to be recounted, the conditions of the interview and the language used. Interviews were found to be more reliable when based on open-ended questions (perhaps followed by requests for more specific details) and a neutral atmosphere of curiosity rather than an interviewer who was intimidatory to the child, conveyed an accusatory attitude to another relevant individual or showed determination to elicit presumed information. Thus, 'even young children can under certain conditions provide accurate testimony, especially when interviewed in a supportive manner that does not involve highly suggestive accusatory contexts' (p. 303). Ceci and Bruck (1995) were similarly concerned that the use of negative words or tone of voice, or excessive prompting could influence children to distort their accounts. They recommended that interviewers should maximize the accuracy of children's recall by taking a neutral and 'scientific' approach – in other words, ruling out alternative hypotheses rather than setting out to prove their own favoured hypothesis. They also concluded that the absence of suggestive techniques allows even very young pre-schoolers to provide highly accurate reports and that, although 'young children occasionally make spontaneous, strange, and unfounded allegations . . . many of these allegations can be understood by sensibly questioning the child and parent further. Often, these statistically rare allegations reflect the child's source confusion or anxieties' (p. 235).

Goodman and Schwartz-Kenny (1992) discussed how children's cognition is not strictly age-bound, since their skills are more sophisticated in the context of familiar events, simple tasks, supportive surroundings and a favourable prevailing emotional climate. Feelings such as powerlessness could have significant adverse effects and, although older children have advanced cognitive skills and knowledge of the world which usually enables them to give more accurate reports, they also have insight into the significance of their statements for themselves or for others. Orbach and Lamb (2000) were able to demonstrate that, during investigative interviews with children as young as 5 years of age, open-ended questions inviting free recall, followed up if necessary by prompts based on what the child had already said, could elicit clear, detailed, consistent and uncontaminated information. They recommended that interviewers should listen actively in order to extract central details from the child's accounts that could be used as contextual cues later in the interview.

Waterman (1986), Steward *et al.* (1993), Fitzpatrick *et al.* (1995) and Westcott and Jones (Chapter 6) have discussed how time must be allowed for a child to respond to the question and toys or play material should be available to assist their communication. Allowance must be made for a younger child's limited ability to relate to 'why', 'when' and 'how' questions. Also, the younger child prefers shorter words and sentences, and complex concepts should be broken down into their component parts. Words must be chosen that are familiar to the child and not peculiar to the adult world, especially to the legal arena. As Saywitz and Goodman (1996) observed, 'Legalese contains lengthy compound sentences fraught with independent and embedded clauses and grammatical constructions that are beyond the comprehension and memory of many children under 8 years of age' (p. 304). A child is also prone to respond to the part of a question that they can make sense of, typically the beginning or the end of a long sentence, and, if young, cannot be relied upon to reveal that they have not understood.

Dent (1992) reported that children with learning difficulties can have particular problems with memory, rendering their accounts less complete or accurate, and that they are more suggestible than other children. They, too, respond optimally to free-recall questions and when answering general questions but are less reliable when responding to specific questions.

Equally relevant are practical issues of receptive and expressive language, such as the physical capacity of the child to hear and articulate, or the need for interpreters when the child's first language is different from the interviewer's.

## EMOTIONAL STATE

Anxious children do not fully concentrate on details of information, nor can they pay close attention during conversations. Their anxiety might be related to the context (e.g. an unknown place) or to the nature of the information (e.g. 'your mother has gone away and left you here'). Unhappy children also may not pay attention, either because of withdrawal or because they are preoccupied with other thoughts. Alternatively, a child may be confused by contradictory information and many well-meaning adults lie to children in an attempt to protect them from upset. In addition, although the court process and the assessment procedure may be experienced as a relief to some children, many others experience them as stressful.

## PERSONAL AND INTERPERSONAL CONFLICT

Because of their developmental immaturity, children and adolescents may form views that are significantly influenced by personal or interpersonal conflict. Even though they have been made intellectually aware of the various issues involved, emotional turmoil reduces their capacity to weigh them up. We shall discuss these in some detail in order to emphasize the importance of taking them into account when weighing up children's views about separated or divorced parents and maltreating parents.

Views that children express about which separated parent they would like to live with can be significantly coloured by the conflictual nature of the family relationships. Children are distressed by being the focus of parental battles, feeling that they have to choose between their parents, or knowing that they are not loved. They are vulnerable to uncertainty or ambiguity, especially when it concerns their sense of personal security and identity, and try to protect themselves from such anxiety. Some children develop polarized attitudes to separated parents, siding with the one considered 'good' and rejecting closeness with the one designated 'bad' (Kempe, 1987). In custody disputes, this polarized attitude is often an attempt to resolve an intolerable loyalty conflict, in which each parent invites the child to side with them against the other (e.g. by being especially generous with presents, lenient during contact visits or criticizing the other parent).

Children of separated parents frequently believe that they were responsible for the parental break-up, may be preoccupied with guilt and wish to make amends by reuniting the family, however unrealizable that is. They might expresss a hope for a fairy-tale solution, in which they find comfort in the company of an idealized absent figure, even if they have hardly known them. Johnston *et al.* (1989) found that older children were more enmeshed in parental divorce conflicts than preschoolers because they had developed the cognitive capacity for self-reflexive thinking and could simultaneously perceive the opposing views of their disputing parents.

Sometimes, children change their views about separated parents, not through a considered reappraisal of them, but in response to a minor recent upset which has introduced a temporary intolerable negative feeling (Kempe, 1987). Other children's attitudes to separated parents are dominated by their own developmental priorities and a young person entering adolescence may wish to live with the same-sex parent whom, they believe, will provide a role model for their gender identity.

Abused children may offer surprising views about their future. A common picture is the abused and insecurely attached child who has become pseudo-mature and compulsively self-reliant, as though they do not need anybody to care for them (Schofield, 1998; Howe et al., 1999). They find it difficult to tolerate mixed feelings about their parent/s or to recognize that they have good points as well as faults. At best, they appear indifferent to caretaking decisions, or else may reject a parent who offers hope of reasonable care. As a reaction to feeling helpless through many years of parental hostility or neglect, some try to assert a capacity to control decisions being made about their lives (e.g. by insisting they know what is best for them or threatening to make an unwelcome placement unworkable). Their apparent personal maturity masks an underlying lack of cognitive sophistication and an emotional turmoil that they have needed to deny. A variant to this picture is the child who shows role reversal and has become a compulsive caretaker as the result of insecure attachment (Crittenden and Ainsworth, 1989; Howe et al., 1999). Their protectiveness of their parent is manifest as defensive denial of their inadequate parenting and a concern to remain close to that parent. If the child's attachment pattern has become 'insecure-ambivalent', they may repeatedly change their attitudes to a parent (Schofield, 1998), oscillating between a description of them as 'absolutely wonderful' to dismissing them as 'absolute rubbish' (Howe et al., 1999: p. 225).

Other abused children cling desperately to anyone who provides even the minimum of care, with a rather hopeless sense that there is no possibility of anything better. In attachment terms, since fear intensifies proximity seeking, if there is no on else to turn to, the child clings even to an abusing parent (Rutter, 1997). They may also deny to themselves and to others that their parent was abusive, including supporting the parent's denials and rationalizations or withdrawing their earlier allegations, and now saying that they wish to remain in the same home environment. Green (1978) found that denial and splitting defence mechanisms, in which the fantasy of having a 'good' parent was sustained, were commonest when the child had been abused by the parent who provided most of the nurturing. Many abused children also feel guilty and responsible for causing their own maltreatment (Briere, 1992), which adds to their denial of the parent's behaviour.

Probably the most difficult conflicts to disentangle concern the child who has experienced episodes of maltreatment from a parent who has also provided intermittent periods of affectionate care. It may be that episodic parental mental health problems have resulted in neglect or physical abuse of the child, interspersed with satisfactory parenting (see Duncan and Reder, Chapter 11). Children find it difficult to tolerate extremes of inconsistency and may defend themselves by becoming withdrawn and passive, careful not to upset their parent by expressing any critical comments. In addition, they often experience a strong wish to remain with them because it is their belief, possibly true, that their parent is reliant on them for support. Similar difficulties occur following sexual abuse by a father who has progressively sexualized an apparently close and loving relationship with his daughter. The child's basic need for attachment and care appears to have outweighed the impact on her of the abuse (e.g. boundary confusion, secretiveness, denial of conflict, engagement in developmentally inappropriate behaviour, and betrayal of trust and power; see Finkelhor and Browne, 1986 and Duncan and Baker, Chapter 5). She expresses the wish to retain a positive bond with the father, as though unaffected by these other psychological traumata.

## ASCERTAINING CHILDREN'S UNDERSTANDING AND VIEWS

In the majority of child care cases, children's understanding can be assessed informally through unstructured interviews which the professional guides into particular areas. The child's capacity to comprehend their family circumstances and the issues that the court will consider, as well as their emotional relationship to them, can emerge during the general assessment, as described by Fitzpatrick *et al.* (1995) and elsewhere in this book.

The literature on children's suggestibility indicates that the interviewing style must be neutral and supportive and, in our opinion, professionals interviewing children as part of parenting assessments should adopt more of a 'listening' stance than an active questioning one, in which they create a facilitating atmosphere and are prepared to follow the child's leads. They should observe the child's behaviour or play and ask clarifying questions based on what the child says or does but often it will be necessary to allow the child freedom to bring material slowly into one or more meetings. A colleague told us about a session with a young child whose sibling had been killed. She sat quietly for some time and then swept all the toys on to the floor. The psychiatrist simply commented, 'They've gone on the floor.' This was repeated four times until the child volunteered: 'Just like my baby brother . . . when mummy knocked him off the table' and, for the first time, she revealed her anxiety that this could also have happened to her and that she still feared living with her mother.

This does not mean, however, that specific questions cannot be asked; the child's opinions about their future care can be sought directly, as well as their reasons for them. The child can be asked why they believe that a court is having to make such decisions about them and what they think went wrong in the past. A child who is muddled about this could be informed in simple terms and then their capacity to retain the information checked later in the interview. They can be asked to talk about the different options that they think are available and what each of these would be like for them. It is possible to ask the child directly whether they have been coerced by anyone to convey a particular view. The child's thoughts, feelings and relationships can be discussed in the usual way and, in effect, the parts of the interview eliciting the child's understanding are little different from those addressing other aspects of the child's functioning.

It is particularly important that the child mental health professional assesses the contribution of personal and interpersonal conflict to the child's views. Ezriel's (1952; 1956) notion of the 'feared catastrophe' can be helpful, since it describes how individuals defend themselves psychologically from uncomfortable conflicts and avoid awareness of stressful issues because they fear that, if they acknowledged them, something calamitous would happen (see also Reder, 1988). An example might be the child who clings to the remnants of an unhappy relationship with one parent, rather than facing the unknown of an alternative placement, because they fear that they might find themself alone in the world. Another illustration might be a child who insists on continued contact with a mentally ill parent because they fear that, in their absence, the parent might collapse and die and they would be responsible for their death.

Recognizing that children's views may be influenced by such fears, the assessor can explore hypotheses about them. They should already have made themself relevant to the child at the beginning of the first interview by explaining in age-appropriate language who they are and their role in relation to the child's circumstances and the court process. This will have created a context for the meetings, so that everything that arises during them can be understood as a communication about the child's experiences and views. Although this exploration is intended to elicit the underlying basis for the child's opinions, as opposed to their memory for events, it is equally important to avoid committing any errors of suggestion. Therefore, an indirect approach is necessary, using generalized comments (e.g. 'Sometimes children do worry that they will upset someone if they say what they really feel') or hypothetical situations (e.g. creating a play scenario in which the child can use dolls or other toys to demonstrate their relationship dilemmas). It then becomes possible for the assessor to wonder with the child whether they experience similar dilemmas and whether the conflicts and fears that have emerged in a displaced way might be relevant to them personally.

This might also help understand children's fluctuating opinions, for they may be having to contemplate alternative possibilities, both of which are associated in their minds with feared calamities. Furthermore, it can help make sense of some children's emphasis on what, to the adult, is a seemingly trivial or concrete issue, since behind the apparently minor consideration may lie a much more painful one which the child is unable to contemplate because it is associated with a fearful belief (e.g. 'my dad takes me to nice parks . . . so I want to live with him . . . because I would never see him again if I lived with mum').

Schofield (1998) recommended making an informal appraisal of the child's attachment status, since insecure attachment can manifest in the way children are able to be in touch with and express their feelings. For example, children with avoidant attachment patterns are liable to deny distress or emotional conflict, ambivalently attached children may express contradictory or unrealistic attitudes, and children with disorganized attachment may conceal their feelings or say what they believe the interviewer wants in order to escape the uncomfortable encounter.

A related concern is whether a child has expressed an opinion about one parent under duress from the other. Particularly difficult to unravel is a young child who implies during their parents' acrimonious divorce that one parent sexually abused them and that this is their reason for not wanting to live with them. Sometimes, it is the resident parent who first makes the allegation, based on the child's behaviour and state around contact visits. Faller (1998) and McGleughlin et al. (1999) have pointed out that such allegations are a rare feature of custody disputes but, if they occur, they tend to be validated in around two-thirds of cases. McGleughlin et al. (1999) concluded that the stress of parental conflict for the child, or the fear of losing one or both parents, can produce anxiety, separation problems, night-mares, somatic complaints, aggression or even sexualized behaviour, which should not be presumed to be indicative of sexual abuse unless there is additional compelling evidence. In these circumstances, MacFarlane (1986) believed that the absence of appropriate affect, use of 'adult' language and lack of convincing detail in the child's account of the alleged abuse is suggestive of coaching by one of their parents.

MacFarlane (1986) also suggested that, because the outcome of divorce is so important to most children, 'It is important to try to find out what a child wants to have happen, doesn't want, is afraid of, thinks will happen, and so on . . . For example, learning that a child believes she won't ever see her father again if she talks about sexual abuse, may provide more data to help clarify the child's motives – whether for talking about it or refusing to talk' (p. 126). Indeed, some children reveal previous sexual abuse at the point of parental divorce because they are 'genuinely terrified at the prospect of having to go and live alone with an abuser' (p. 133).

This illustrates that some children's fears are not imagined but real and based either on information that they have not yet revealed or overt threats that have been made to them. The child may have been threatened by the father who sexually abused them that they would be the cause of the family's break-up if they disclosed the abuse; a violent father may have warned that he would kill the child and/or her mother; or a parent might have repeatedly threatened to abandon the child if they did not remain loyal by speaking well of them and running down the other parent.

## CONCLUSIONS

The issue of children's views about their future care is a complex one and poses dilemmas at many different levels, including legal, psychological, ethical and practical. For instance, if the views of maltreated children can be significantly coloured by emotional conflicts, is it ethical to elicit them from the child only for the court to discount them? Or, how is it possible to balance out strong opinions held by a child, who does not have the cognitive means to weigh up the various issues, with their obvious ability to make an unwelcome placement unworkable? This review has pointed to psychological factors that should be considered by expert assessors but it cannot hope to resolve all the dilemmas, which must be debated and ruled upon case by case.

What direction can this chapter offer to assessors who might become involved in cases similar to those outlined in the opening three vignettes? The circumstances of the pre-adolescent brother and sister teach that children's conflicts may only emerge over time and that assessment inferences might need to be revised in the light of subsequent information. Different professionals might draw different inferences about the boy of mixed race. For us, it suggests that practitioners should not impose their own social assumptions on a child who is feeling helpless in the midst of considerable life changes and that certain beliefs of children can be respected even if they appear to the adult to be an artificial resolution of a dilemma. The adolescent boy who supported his mother's bizarre parenting behaviour exemplifies that the thinking of some young people can be distorted by their living experiences and their views should be overruled, despite their age.

Finally, we cannot leave this topic without mentioning the increasingly common question about a child's capacity to instruct a solicitor and thereby have their own counsel in court. This may particularly arise if the child does not wish their views to be represented through the Children's Guardian, or when the Children's Guardian intends to advise the court to overrule the child's wishes. It could be argued this is not so much a psychological issue as a human rights one and that everyone is entitled to be fully represented in court, including a child – so long as they comprehend the issues and the court process. The purpose of the hearing should then be to weigh up the child's views and the factors which may be influencing them, along with other evidence and opinions. A mental health expert might be invited to advise on what weight should be accorded to the child's views, as well as the views of all other participants in the case. These views would then be open to cross-examination by barristers for all the parties, including the child.

## References

Alderson, P. and Montgomery, J. (1996) *Health Care Choices: Making Decisions with Children*, London: Institute for Public Policy Research.

Arlow, J.A. (1989) Time as emotion, in J.T. Fraser (ed.) *Time and Mind: Interdisciplinary Issues*, Madison, CT: International Universities Press.

Bailey, S. and Harbour, A. (1999) The law and a child's consent to treatment, *Child Psychology & Psychiatry Review* 4: 30–4.

Briere, J.N. (1992) *Child Abuse Trauma: Theory and Treatment of the Lasting Effects*, Newbury Park, CA: Sage.

British Medical Association (2001) *Consent, Rights and Choices in Health Care for Children and Young People*, London: BMJ Books.

Ceci, S.J. and Bruck, M. (1995) *Jeopardy in the Courtroom: A Scientific Analysis of Children's Testimony*, Washington, DC: American Psychological Association.

Cleave, G. (2001) The Human Rights Act 1998 – how will it affect child law in England and Wales? *Child Abuse Review* 9: 394–402.

Crittenden, P.M. and Ainsworth, M.D.S. (1989) Child maltreatment and attachment theory, in D. Cicchetti and V. Carlson (eds) *Child Maltreatment: Theory and Research on the Causes and Consequences of Child Abuse and Neglect*, Cambridge: Cambridge University Press.

de Mause, L. (1976) *The History of Childhood: The Evolution of Parent–Child Relationships as a Factor in History*, London: Souvenir Press.

Dent, H. (1992) The effects of age and intelligence on eyewitnessing ability, in H. Dent and R. Flin (eds) *Children as Witnesses*, Chichester: John Wiley.

Department of Health (2001) *Reference Guide to Consent for Examination or Treatment*, Crown Copyright, London: Department of Health.

Devereux, J.A., Jones, D.P.H. and Dickenson, D.L. (1993) Can children withhold consent to treatment? *British Medical Journal* 306: 1459–61.

Dyer, C. (1985) Contraceptives and the under 16s: House of Lords ruling, *British Medical Journal* 291: 1208–9.

Ezriel, H. (1952) Notes on psychoanalytic group therapy, II. Interpretation and research, *Psychiatry* 15: 119–26.

Ezriel, H. (1956) Experimenting with the psychoanalytic session, *British Journal for the Philosophy of Science* 7: 29–48.

Faller, K.C. (1998) The parental alienation syndrome: what is it and what data support it? *Child Maltreatment* 3: 100–15.

Finkelhor, D. and Browne, A. (1986) Initial and long-term effects, in D. Finkelhor and associates, *A Sourcebook on Sexual Abuse*, Beverley Hills, CA: Sage.

Fitzpatrick, G., Reder, P. and Lucey, C. (1995) The child's perspective, in P. Reder and C. Lucey (eds) *Assessment of Parenting: Psychiatric and Psychological Contributions*, London: Routledge.

Ford, T. and Kessel, A. (2001) Feeling the way: childhood mental illness and consent to admission and treatment, *British Journal of Psychiatry* 179: 384–6.

Fraisse, P. (1976) *The Psychology of Time*, Westport, CT: Greenwood.

Friedman, W.J. (1982) Conventional time concepts and children's structuring of time, in W.J. Friedman (ed.) *The Developmental Psychology of Time*, New York: Academic.

Gillick v West Norfolk and Wisbech Health Authority and the Department of Health and Social Security (1985) 3 *All England Reports* 3: 402.

Goldstein, J., Freud, A. and Solnit, A.J. (1973) *Beyond the Best Interests of the Child*, New York: The Free Press.

Goodman, G.S. and Schwartz-Kenny, B.M. (1992) Why knowing a child's age is not enough: influences of cognitive, social, and emotional factors on children's testimony, in H. Dent and R. Flin (eds) *Children as Witnesses*, Chichester: John Wiley.

Green, A.H. (1978) Psychopathology of abused children, *Journal of the American Academy of Child Psychiatry* 17: 92–103.

Harner, L. (1982) Talking about the past and the future, in W.J. Friedman (ed.) *The Developmental Psychology of Time*, New York: Academic.

Hobson, R.P. (1985) Piaget: on the ways of knowing in childhood, in M. Rutter and L. Hersov (eds) *Child and Adolescent Psychiatry, Modern Approaches*, 2nd ed., Oxford: Blackwell.

Honig, P. and Bentovim, M. (1996) Treating children with eating disorders – ethical and legal issues, *Clinical Child Psychology and Psychiatry* 1: 287–94.

Honig, P. and Jaffa, T. (2000) Consent in relation to treatment of eating disorders, *Psychiatric Bulletin* 24: 409–11.

Howe, D., Brandon, M., Hinings, D. and Schofield, G. (1999) *Attachment Theory, Child Maltreatment and Family Support*, Basingstoke: Macmillan.

Inhelder, B. and Piaget, J. (1958) *The Growth of Logical Thinking from Childhood to Adolescence*, New York: Basic Books.

Johnston, J.R., Kline, M. and Tschann, J.M. (1989) Ongoing postdivorce conflict: effects on children of joint custody and frequent access, *American Journal of Orthopsychiatry* 59: 576–92.

Kempe, R.S. (1987) A developmental approach to the treatment of the abused child, in R.E. Helfer and R.S. Kempe (eds) *The Battered Child*, 4th ed., Chicago: University of Chicago Press.

Kennedy, I. and Grubb, A. (1994) *Medical Law*, 2nd ed., London: Butterworths.

Littlechild, B. (2001) Children's rights to be heard in child protection processes – law, policy and practice in England and Wales, *Child Abuse Review* 9: 403–15.

Lyon, C. and de Cruz, P. (1993) *Child Abuse*, 2nd ed., Bristol: Family Law.

MacFarlane, K. (1986) Child sexual abuse allegations in divorce proceedings, in K. MacFarlane, J. Waterman, S. Conerly, L. Damon, M. Durfee and S. Long (eds) *Sexual Abuse of Young Children: Evaluation and Treatment*, London: Holt, Rinehart & Winston.

McGleughlin, J., Meyer, S. and Baker, J. (1999) Assessing sexual abuse allegations in divorce, custody, and visitation disputes, in R.M. Galatzer-Levy and L. Kraus (eds) *The Scientific Basis of Child Custody Decisions*, New York: John Wiley.

Oates, L. (2000) The court's role in decisions about medical treatment, *British Medical Journal* 321: 1282–4.

Orbach, Y. and Lamb, M.E. (2000) Enhancing children's narratives in investigative interviews, *Child Abuse & Neglect* 24: 1631–48.

Parkinson, P.N. (1986) The Gillick case – just what has it decided? *Family Law* 16: 11–14.

Pearce, J. (1994) Consent to treatment during childhood: the assessment of competence and avoidance of conflict, *British Journal of Psychiatry* 165: 713–16.

Piaget, J. (1969) *The Child's Conception of Time*, London: Routledge & Kegan Paul.

Reder, P. (1988) 'Because': a suggested contribution to systemic and strategic therapy, *Journal of Family Therapy* 10: 75–81.

Reder, P. and Fitzpatrick, S. (1998) What is sufficient understanding? *Clinical Child Psychology and Psychiatry* 3: 103–13.

Re M (1994) *Family Law Reports* 1: 749.

Rutter, M. (1997) Clinical implications of attachment concepts: retrospect and prospect, in L. Atkinson and K.J. Zucker (eds) *Attachment and Psychopathology*, New York: The Guilford Press.

Sattler, J.M. (1982) *Assessment of Children's Intelligence and Special Abilities*, 2nd ed., Boston: Allyn & Bacon.

Saywitz, K.J. and Goodman, G.S. (1996) Interviewing children in and out of court: current research and practice implications, in J. Briere, L. Berliner, J.A. Bulkley, C. Jenny and T. Reid (eds) *The APSAC Handbook on Child Maltreatment*, Thousand Oaks, CA: Sage.

Schofield, G. (1998) Making sense of the ascertainable wishes and feelings of insecurely attached children, *Child & Family Law Quarterly* 10: 363–75.

Shaffer, D.R. (1989) *Developmental Psychology: Child and Adolescence*, 2nd ed., Pacific Grove, CA: Brooks/Cole.

Shaw, M. (1998) Childhood, mental health and the law, in J. Green and B. Jacobs (eds) *Inpatient Child Psychiatry: Modern Practice, Research, and the Future*, London: Routledge.

Shaw, M. (1999) Treatment decisions in young people: (1) the legal framework; (2) practical guidelines; (3) frequently asked questions and references. FOCUS Information Sheets 2, 3, and 4. London: Royal College of Psychiatrists' Research Unit.

Speece, M.W. and Brent, S.B. (1984) Children's understanding of death: a review of three components of a death concept, *Child Development* 55: 1671–86.

Steward, M.S., Bussey, K., Goodman, G.S. and Sayitz, K.J. (1993) Implications of developmental research for interviewing children, *Child Abuse & Neglect* 17: 25–37.

United Nations (1989) *Convention on the Rights of the Child 1989*, Geneva: United Nations.

Waterman, J. (1986) Developmental considerations, in K. MacFarlane, J. Waterman, S. Conerly, L. Damon, M. Durfee and S. Long (eds) *Sexual Abuse of Young Children: Evaluation and Treatment*, London: Holt, Rinehart & Winston.

White, R., Williams, R., Harbour, A. and Bingley, W. (1996) *Child and Adolescent Services. Safeguards for Young Minds: Young People and Protective Legislation*, London: HAS & Gaskell.

# Part III

# Assessing parents

# Chapter 8

# Can adolescents parent?

*Peter Reder and Geraldine Fitzpatrick*

It is customary to start with apparently dramatic statistics. In England and Wales in 1997, there were 8,300 known conceptions to women under the age of 16 years, resulting in 1,600 live births; 1 mother was aged 11, 3 were aged 12, 26 were 13 years old and 258 aged 14. Fifty-two per cent of the pregnancies were terminated. Little change has been recorded in the conception rate by this age group (approximately eight girls in every thousand below the age of 16 becoming pregnant) over the last 30 years. In 1997, there was a total of 46,316 live births to teenage mothers, with only 11 per cent occurring within a marital relationship (see Family Policy Studies Centre, 1999). The United Kingdom has the highest rate of teenage births in Western Europe (twice that of Germany, three times that of France and six times that of the Netherlands and Switzerland), while the United States has a rate more than twice that of the UK (Social Exclusion Unit, 1999).

Such figures have led many countries to regard teenage pregnancy as a major concern and the British government has set targets to reduce its prevalence through social, economic and educational measures (Social Exclusion Unit, 1999). However, with such a focus on it as a *social* issue, there is a risk that every pregnancy occurring to a young teenager will be presumed to be problematic. It is important also to focus on the *psychological* factors relevant to parenting by this age group and we therefore favour the term 'adolescent' over 'teenage' parent because it emphasizes that the developmental process through adolescence is the relevant issue, not simply childbearing before 20 years of age.

We shall summarize the personal and interpersonal developmental processes associated with adolescence and review whether there is evidence that infants born to young parents are at risk of significant harm (capitalizing on previous reviews by Brooks-Gunn and Furstenberg, 1986; Osofsky *et al.*, 1988; Furstenberg *et al.*, 1989; Lask, 1994; Trad, 1995; and Stevens-Simon and Nelligan, 1998). We shall then suggest how this can be assessed in specific cases. However, the social dimension cannot be ignored, since it forms the context for every case coming before the courts and we shall first briefly consider the process of adolescence as both a psychological and a social phenomenon.

## ARE ADOLESCENT PROBLEMS A SOCIAL CONSTRUCTION?

Adolescence is a process determined partly by physiological and psychological imperatives of human development and partly by society's attitudes to young people. Petersen and Offer (1979) observed that in the Western world, adolescence lasts much longer than in other societies, where adult responsibilities are assumed at a much younger age. They suggest that adolescence takes on much of the character of the society which creates it and that the lessons of history are that when society itself is in turmoil, adolescents have greater difficulty making the transition to adulthood.

Biologically, humans usually become capable of reproduction within a year of puberty and so can begin to conceive and bear children in very early teens. However, many societies believe that their young should postpone assuming parental responsibilities and instead practise sexual abstinence, use contraception, decide to terminate a pregnancy or place the baby for adoption. It is interesting to speculate why adolescent pregnancy has become such a concern in this country and elsewhere (Macintyre and Cunningham-Burley, 1993). For some, its association with single parenthood implies a breakdown of social order; for others the link with socio-economic hardship poses a political and economic dilemma. Several authors focus on a presumed health risk to mother and infant, or on the belief that it reflects the psychological improbability of 'children parenting children', while others remain troubled by the obvious evidence of sexual activity by young people. A number of commentators have wondered whether teenage pregnancy is more of a problem for professionals than for the mother, her child or the extended family (e.g. Phoenix, 1993; Campion, 1995; Jacobson *et al.*, 1995). However, rarely is there mention of the legal matter that pregnancy in a mother under the age of 16 is evidence of sexual intercourse with a minor.

## DOES THE ADOLESCENT PROCESS CONFLICT WITH PARENTHOOD?

Adolescence is the phase of development bridging childhood and adulthood, during which major physical, cognitive, emotional and interpersonal changes are negotiated. Some authors describe early, middle and late phases of adolescence but chronological age is not synonymous with developmental maturity and these are arbitrary divisions to which individual adolescents do not neatly adhere. Therefore, our preference is to identify the respective elements of development and consider the process as a continuum along a series of pathways (Steinberg, 1987; Trad, 1995).

The most significant *cognitive* change is from what Piaget termed 'concrete operations' to 'formal operations', characterized by the ability to think in abstract terms and to construct hypotheses about what might occur, to reason and use ideas flexibly, and to distinguish between fantasies and possibilities. There is the gradual understanding of social and ethical issues and capacity for introspection and to weigh up alternatives. *Emotionally*, there evolves a capacity to empathize with others rather than persist with egocentric attitudes, the realization that ranges of emotion are tolerable and that sexual and aggressive instincts can be translated into physical achievements. *Interpersonal* developments include relinquishing internal representations of the parents and seeking relationships outside the family, during which oscillations between dependence/independence occur. Other relationships are experimented with and these lead to an evolving sense of *personal* identity and autonomy.

Adolescence is a dynamic process, during which progression along all these developmental lines is unlikely to be smooth but unfolds irregularly with leaps forward followed by periods of temporary regression, phases of mixed experiences and periods of excessively strong beliefs or emotions. Thus, there may be episodes of passionate idealization or confusing ambivalence, shifts in senses of identity, rapid changes in mood, or dangerous risk-taking and experimentations. For a while, personal responsibility may be denied and all blame attributed to others, or an intense emotional investment in someone or something suddenly directed elsewhere. Relationships with family of origin are re-examined and tested anew, including the degree to which the parents can facilitate the process of individuation, identity formation and social experimentation.

It is only in the later stages of adolescence that a more stable adjustment can be expected to the somatic, emotional and cognitive changes that have preceded it. The needs of others are more consistently considered and more enduring and intimate relationships developed. Curiosity and self-reflection are sustained, events are anticipated, problems reasoned through and longer-term plans made.

Hamburg (1986), Pines (1988), Trad (1995) and Stevens-Simon and Nelligan (1998) compared the natural processes of adolescence with the psychological requirements of pregnancy and parenthood. The obvious *bodily* changes of pregnancy may conflict with the adolescent's adjustment to their new body image and some very young mothers resent what the foetus is doing to them. *Interpersonally*, the arrival of a new baby disturbs the adolescent's negotiations for independence from their own parents, since it creates the need for increased support, and this conflict may be resolved by either abdicating all responsibility to the grandmother or insisting on total isolation from her. Furthermore, pregnancy usually involves a process for the new mother of identification with her own mother, the reverse of the adolescent's momentum towards psychic separation from her. *Cognitively*, egocentricity contrasts with the more outwardly (or 'other person') focused period of maternal role attainment and, even when formal reasoning of cognitive development has begun, information processing and decision making are significantly impaired when dealing with matters highly charged with anxiety or personal stress. Instead, the young person is prone to narrow the range of perceived alternatives, ignore long-term consequences and come to precipitous decisions. *Socially*, the natural expectations of socializing, experimenting with outside interests or peer relationships, and indulging in periods of irresponsibility or self-centredness must be curtailed in order to focus attention on the needs of a demanding and helpless infant who requires constant attention and care.

*Emotionally*, the mother must acknowledge the needs of the baby, even while *intra-utero*, and Hatcher (1973) found that denial of the pregnancy was not uncommon among young adolescents, leading to postponement of antenatal care. The young mother must also become capable of distinguishing her own feelings and needs from those of the child, something that is not usually achieved until late in the adolescent process, while a reduced capacity to contain emotions can provoke frustration with the infant. Furthermore, any of the customary *beliefs* of invincibility, disregard for the consequences of their actions, tendency for risk-taking and short-term planning do not accord with the needs of babies. Occasional episodes of impulsivity or feeling out of control and blaming others may generate anger and beliefs that the child is causing the problems. Adolescents' propensity for personal experimentation and trying out different roles, identities and lifestyles similarly conflicts with the imperative to assume the identity of a reliable provider.

## IS THERE AN ASSOCIATION WITH PARENTING BREAKDOWN?

With so many years of professional, academic and political interest in the children of teenage parents, reflected in a voluminous literature, it might be expected that the accumulated evidence is clear. In fact, many of the findings have been equivocal, contradictory or confusing. One likely explanation is that the early studies of maternal age usually failed to control for associated socio-economic and educational factors and when later ones did, many of the associations disappeared (e.g. Garcia Coll *et al.*, 1987; Sommer *et al.*, 1993). Another is that a large proportion of the studies have been of black urban populations in the United States (Phoenix, 1993) and it remains questionable whether generalizations from those findings are valid or apply to the United Kingdom. Most importantly, very few studies have distinguished the ages of the mothers year by year, so that most investigations have compared 'teenagers' (i.e. all mothers under the age of 20 years) with older mothers; a serious limitation when the key issue is relevance of the mother's psychological development on her parenting capacity as she matures (Hatcher, 1973; Buchholz and Gol, 1986; Melhuish and Phoenix, 1988; Shapiro and Mangelsdorf, 1994).

Three aspects of this question will be considered. The first is whether there is evidence of adverse development in children born to adolescent mothers; the second is whether there is evidence for poor parenting by such parents; and the third is whether the prevalence of maltreatment is higher for these children.

## Child development

It has long been acknowledged that children of adolescent parents face developmental adversity from the outset, through the association with obstetric complications and low birth weight. However, even though infants born to mothers under the age of 16 years are twice as likely to be of low birth weight, well-controlled studies have demonstrated that this is not a function of the mother's immature physiology but the often associated poverty, poor education, unmarried status and inadequate antenatal care (McAnarney, 1987; Stevens-Simon and White 1991). Even so, the infant mortality rate is significantly higher amongst children born to very young teenagers (Baldwin and Cain, 1980) and an interpretation of the delay seeking antenatal care shown by some pregnant adolescents (Hatcher, 1973) is that they fail to recognize their responsibility to care for the foetus as a developing being.

Cognitive deficits and poor behavioural control are common findings in longitudinal studies of the children (e.g. Miller *et al.*, 1996), with the differences becoming more pronounced as they became older (Brooks-Gunn and Furstenberg, 1986). Long-term follow-up by the Baltimore team (Furstenberg *et al.*, 1987) of children born to mothers under the age of 18 years found 'what can only be described as massive school failure' (p. 148), with evidence of poor educational achievements and major behavioural problems. The girls were also more likely to become adolescent parents themselves (Brooks-Gunn and Chase-Lansdale, 1991).

## Parenting capacity

A team at the University of Notre Dame, Indiana developed a construct called 'cognitive readiness to parent', which included measures of the parent's child-centredness, knowledge and expectations of developmental norms and styles of interacting with a child. Adolescent mothers' scores were significantly poorer than adult mothers and this was associated with subsequent parental stress and poor intellectual, language and behavioural development of their children (Sommer *et al.*, 1993; Miller *et al.*, 1996). By contrast, an earlier study by Schilmoeller and Baranowski (1985) of middle-class adolescent mothers found their knowledge of developmental milestones and their child-rearing attitudes to be comparable to older mothers. Even so, they were significantly less verbally responsive or stimulating and more restrictive and punitive towards their children.

Other reliable reports have also indicated that teenage mothers vocalize significantly less with their children and provide less stimulation (Ragozin *et al.*, 1982; Brooks-Gunn and Furstenberg, 1986; Garcia Coll *et al.*, 1987; Parks and Arndt, 1990). McAnarney *et al.* (1986) demonstrated that the younger the adolescent mothers were the more they engaged in negative communications and the less they were accepting, sensitive or cooperative with their toddlers. They added the important rider that, on clinical observation, the younger mothers had enjoyed mothering their dependent infants but, as the children became ambulatory, they demonstrated impatience towards and intolerance of their play and exploration.

Using qualitative and quantitative methods to examine the experience of motherhood during adolescence, Flanagan *et al.* (1995) concluded that 'Although a mother's chronological age provides some index regarding her developmental and parental capacities, age alone offers the clinician little guidance given the significant individual differences among adolescent mothers' (p. 275).

## Child maltreatment

Many studies have focused on whether an association can be found between teenage parents and child abuse *potential*, as measured on Milner's (1986) Child Abuse Potential Inventory and, although this instrument is well researched with older parents, it is uncertain whether its validity extends to the lower age range. Nonetheless, high scores have frequently been reported (e.g. McCullough and Scherman, 1998; de Paúl and Domenech, 2000), especially in under 16s, who were found by Haskett *et al.* (1994) to have greatly elevated unhappiness scores and strong beliefs in physical forms of punishment. Using a different approach, Browne's detailed study of the relative predictive value of screening characteristics for child abuse and/or neglect, using discriminant function analysis, revealed that maternal age (less than 21 years at the time of the birth) ranked only ninth in order of importance (Browne and Herbert, 1997): however, we have already argued that dichotomizing at this age may not adequately reflect the nature of the problem.

Gelles (1986) and Connelly and Straus (1992) reviewed previous studies on the relation between maternal age and child physical abuse, concluding that empirical evidence failed to support an association. However, Connelly and Straus's (1992) own research with mothers (the youngest of whom began childbearing at the age of 16) produced a statistically significant relationship between the mother's age at the time of the child's birth and disclosure at structured interview of physical aggression to the child. Boyer and Fine (1992) investigated young adolescent mothers, many of whom had themselves been abused: by the time their child was approximately 2 years of age, 9 per cent reported that they had been contacted by child protective services and 5 per cent said that their child had been taken from them.

No association is apparent with fatal abuse. In a study of such cases notified to the Department of Health (Reder and Duncan, 1999) the average age of the identified perpetrators was 27 years: as far as could be judged, the average age at which the mothers first bore children was 19 years.

Bolton (1990) believed that the child maltreatment risk presented by adolescent mothers in the early years of parenting is overstated and the social and personal entrapment that they experience, which increases their stress and risk of abuse, is the same as that faced by adult parents who are poor and isolated. Buchholz and Korn-Bursztyn (1993) similarly concluded that, 'The degree of risk for maltreatment of children from adolescent parents, rather than being directly related to parental chronological age, is embedded within the additional factors of economic status, stress, isolation, knowledge of child development, as well as the woman's experience of motherhood' (p. 376). Zuravin's (1988) findings were consistent with the hypothesis that chronic socio-demographic stress mediates the relationship between young age at first birth and both child physical abuse and neglect.

When a link is found, the commonest one is with child neglect, especially when the mothers were below 16 years of age (Bolton and Laner, 1986). Stier *et al.* (1993) found that maltreatment occurred twice as commonly over 5 years to children born to mothers under the age of 19 years than to older mothers, although neglect was the only type that reached statistical significance: surprisingly, the occurrence of maltreatment was not higher among the very youngest members of the sample, although grandmothers were noted to be heavily involved in those children's care.

## WHAT CONSTELLATIONS OF ADVERSITY MAY OCCUR?

Our conclusion is that parental age is relevant, although we would not suggest that there is a specific transitional age which distinguishes risk from safety. Amongst the wealth of literature on teenage pregnancy, there has been little which separates out risks associated with particular years. Clinical impression and knowledge of adolescent psychological development suggest that pregnancy below the age of approximately 16 years should be regarded with more concern. However, as Haskett *et al.* (1994), Nitz *et al.* (1995), Flanagan *et al.* (1995), Luster (1998), McCullough and Scherman (1998) and Budd *et al.* (2000) observe, there are significant individual differences in the personal and parenting characteristics of teenagers and even more important are the social and interpersonal adversities which frequently accompany adolescent pregnancy. Therefore, when it comes to assessing the capacity to parent by an adolescent, it is necessary to consider not just their chronological age and cognitive development but also whether they are in the midst of a constellation of adversities, both social and emotional. In particular, once the child is born, the parent may continue to struggle with the same unresolved psychological conflicts and social hardship that made pregnancy at an early age more likely.

### Antecedents to adolescent childbearing

The question of whether a pattern of antecedent adversities is associated with adolescent pregnancy has been considered for some time. For example, Quinton and Rutter's (1984) study of parents with children in care pointed to a constellation of personal, interpersonal and social factors leading to adverse parenting. When compared with matched controls, significantly more of the mothers studied had become pregnant before the age of 19 years and had left home young for 'negative' reasons. The picture was of adolescents leaving home to escape intolerable family tensions and becoming pregnant and/or entering transient marriages to men with similar disadvantaged backgrounds. Indeed, the association with both socio-economic disadvantage and low educational attainment is the most consistent of all findings about teenage parenthood (for males as well as females), together with a frequently found background of parental disharmony, family dislocation and personal low self-esteem (Whitman *et al.*, 1987; Furstenberg *et al.*, 1989; Breakwell, 1993; Budd *et al.*, 1998).

A connection with experiences of childhood abuse is also recognized. Quinton *et al.* (1984) followed up girls who had been admitted to a children's home because of major parenting breakdown: compared with matched controls, a significantly larger proportion (42 per cent) had become pregnant by the age of 19 years. In a study of young women whose first pregnancies had occurred at a mean age of 15.7 years, Boyer and Fine (1992) found that 66 per cent had experienced forced sexual molestation, attempted or actual rape, over half of which was perpetrated by a family member: 11 per cent of those raped had become pregnant as a result. Overall, 71 per cent had experienced sexual, physical and/or emotional abuse. Herrenkohl *et al.* (1998) reported that physical abuse, with and without neglect, and sexual abuse all had significant relationships to teenage parenthood, with physical abuse having the more potent effect for females. The largest proportion of teenage parents was found among those who had experienced both abuse and neglect in early childhood. By contrast, de Paúl and Domenech (2000) reported no raised prevalence of childhood physical abuse in adolescent mothers, although their cut-off age was 21 years.

## Continuing adversities

Researchers have noted how constellations of adversity that preceded early pregnancy frequently continue afterwards. Crockenberg (1987) found that adolescent mothers who experienced rejection during childhood and were inadequately supported by their current partner were the ones more likely to exhibit anger and punitiveness towards their toddlers. Bolton (1990) considered that children were most at risk if their adolescent parents became pregnant to escape negative situations in their family of origin, were very young, were poor and did not have the continuing emotional and practical support from a caring family. Zuravin and DiBlasio (1996) compared adolescent mothers who neglected their children with those who did not, concluding that neglect was most likely if the mother had experienced sexual abuse in childhood, had run away from home, had been in trouble with the law and had resided with different caretakers. They were also more likely to have borne children at a younger age, to have had more obstetric complications and to have completed fewer grades in school. In Wurtz Passino *et al*'s (1993) study, the mother's prenatal adjustment predicted parenting stress and quality of relationship with the infant.

While it is clear that early childbearing can be associated with a background of social and emotional disadvantage which significantly reduces the educational and employment opportunities for the mother, the long-term environment in which the children will be raised may not always remain one of adversity. Long-term follow-ups in Baltimore (Furstenberg *et al.*, 1987; Brooks-Gunn and Chase-Lansdale, 1991) and in New Haven (Horwitz *et al.*, 1991) revealed that a substantial proportion of teenage mothers returned to education later in life and improved their economic circumstances.

A more optimistic picture also emerged from a longitudinal study by Wolkind and Kruk (1985) of teenage mothers in a deprived area of London. During pregnancy, they appeared to be a group of disadvantaged young women unprepared for motherhood and unwelcoming of their pregnancies. Follow-up for six years revealed that, compared with an older control group, no differences could be found on virtually every measure of their child care attitudes and practices.

An additional ingredient to the constellation of adversities for adolescent parents is the co-existence of risky sexual behaviour, substance misuse and mental health problems found amongst some groups of adolescents (Kessler *et al.*, 1997; Bennett and Bauman, 2000). A cluster of risk-taking behaviours may be apparent, including early unprotected sex and reckless use of drugs or alcohol, sometimes allied to criminal activity or prostitution (especially when there is a history of sexual abuse). Furthermore, adolescent mothers may have depressive and somatizing disorders which continue beyond the immediate postnatal period, with consequences for the parent–child interaction (Panzarine *et al.*, 1995; Trad, 1995; Irvine *et al.*, 1997).

## Children as contributors to stress

We believe that the age of the child can be a particularly important contributor to stress for adolescent parents, though only a few researchers have focused on this factor (Levine *et al.*, 1985; McAnarney *et al.*, 1986). A number of very young mothers seem able to care well enough for their younger babies, tending to regard them almost as 'dolls' whom they can dress up and show off to others. Their apparently satisfactory care is enhanced in the early months when family and professional support is at its maximum. Problems are more likely to arise when the child changes from a passive extension of the mother and enters the separation-individuation phase (Mahler, 1979) at about a year, showing increasing mobility, exploration, assertiveness and autonomy. Such behaviour may challenge the adolescent mother's expectations and tolerance, particularly if it coincides with reduction in external supports. Osofsky *et al.* (1988) suggested that these mothers are so entrenched in their own conflict about separation from family-of-origin that they have difficulty being sensitive to their child's autonomy.

In addition, greater concern will arise if the young parent quickly bears further children and there is accumulated evidence that successive pregnancies are the greatest stressor for this age group which increases the risk of maltreatment (Buchholz and Gol, 1986; Zuravin, 1988; Zuravin and DiBlasio, 1992; 1996; Connelly and Straus, 1992). However, although intentional repeat pregnancy occurs (Matsuhashi *et al.*, 1989), long-term follow-up suggests that these mothers may end having fewer children than they initially claim to have wanted (Furstenberg *et al.*, 1987).

## WHAT FACTORS SHOULD BE ASSESSED?

The issue with all research is translating general patterns discernible in population samples to the specifics of a particular case. This is even more difficult with regard to adolescent parenting because so many of the research findings are contradictory. Nonetheless, a reasonable inference seems to be that there is a proportion of adolescents for whom parenting will be problematic and they are likely to be those who are very young and/or have already suffered a range of psychosocial adversities which persist after the child is born, including lack of personal resources or of emotional, financial and practical support. This would be consistent with Landy *et al.*'s (1984) suggestion that teenage mothers seemed to fall into one of three groups: (a) the acting-out teenager who is from a highly disorganized family background (and whose child care skills may be suspect); (b) the young woman psychodynamically tied to her mother who has the baby to attain separateness (often with success); or (c) the teenager emotionally and sexually more mature (irrespective of chronological age).

The assessment of adolescent parents has not been considered by many authors, Trad (1995) being a notable exception. We believe that the following aspects of personal history, current functioning and future expectations are especially relevant and need to be highlighted during interviews.

### Psychological functioning

Informal assessment of the young person's cognitive and interpersonal functioning can be performed through an unstructured interview. For example, their capacity to construct hypotheses and to weigh up alternatives can be gauged though 'what if . . .' questions about the baby's development and needs and about their relationships with the child's other parent, their mother, and so on. They can be asked to talk through a decision that may need to be taken in the future in order to gain an impression of their sense of the future, how they approach decision taking and their sense of personal responsibility. Questions can be asked of their capacity to appreciate the child's feelings when experiencing everyday or unforeseen events. Their sense of identity can be indicated through questions about how they see themself now that they are pregnant/have a child and what, if anything has changed about their life. Reality testing will be apparent through, for example, questions which reveal a mother's over-romanticized beliefs about the intentions of the baby's father. Consecutive interviews may be necessary to indicate how stable these responses are.

## Awareness of an infant's development and expectations of their parenting role

Simple questions are possible about their reasonable knowledge of children and their needs. The basis for the young parent's awareness will also be relevant. Examples might include feeding, sleeping, mobility and limit setting, followed by enquiry about how the young parent's own parents fulfilled these needs when they were a child. They can be asked to describe how the child will/has impacted on their life, which will give a good impression of how much they prioritize the child's needs above their own.

Many young adolescent mothers imagine giving birth to a 'perfect' baby, one who is beautiful, passive and doll-like and accepting of their care without complaint. Sometimes there is a fit between the mother's expectations and the child's temperament but frequently the mother has to cope with a 'less-than-perfect' baby, who cries, is irritable, needs constant changing, or is a poor feeder. They will need to be asked about their emotional and practical responses to these events, or else to imagine what they would do in such circumstances (e.g. 'what would you do when you're tired and the baby cries in the middle of the night?'). Positive signs include that the parent both acknowledges that such events may occur and contemplates the possibility of developing strategies to cope with them.

## Unresolved care/control conflicts

Reder and Duncan (1999) coined the term 'unresolved care or control conflicts' to describe those individuals who had experienced maltreatment, emotional deprivation or rejection in childhood, the psychological scars of which intruded into subsequent relationships, most particularly with partners and offspring. They may, for example, become overdependent on others (or its counterpart, relentlessly distant from everyone), excessively sensitive to being left by a partner, or easily tip over into rages of frustration, especially when experiencing circumstances which feel out of their control. The baby's helplessness or inconsolable crying can reawaken these conflicts and lead to neglect or abusive assaults (see Chapter 12).

The young parent's history and current functioning should be explored for evidence of such conflicts. This includes how they were cared for by their parent/s, whether they were maltreated, neglected or rejected, and the evolving story of their relationship with their parent/s, and especially their mother. Their impulse control is especially important, as well as the circumstances which might provoke loss of control and aggression. Examples can be explored of temper outbursts, how arguments with others usually start and end, or whether there have been impulsive acts of walking out of an encounter in response to stress. Anti-authority attitudes, although common in adolescents, may also represent fears of being controlled by others and will have relevance for cooperation with professionals. Episodes which re-evoke unresolved conflicts also need to be considered, such as threats of being left by someone close, the actual loss of someone to whom they were close, or their baby's demands for attention.

## The meaning of the child

Reder and Duncan (1995) also described a facet of interpersonal relationships in which another person has a particular significance for someone, such as carrying certain expectations of role or behaviour or unwittingly being associated with unresolved conflicts and influences from their past. In particular, children may acquire an undeclared script or blueprint for their life that is consistent with themes in their parent's experiences but submerges their own personal identity and characteristics. Hence, the 'meaning of the child' includes the parent's overt and covert motivations for having a child, as well as conscious and unconscious determinants of their attitudes to, feelings about and relationship with the particular child.

It must first be recognized that starting to bear children during adolescence may be intentional, culturally consistent, conflict-free and the expected means of achieving maturity (Adler and Tschann, 1993). Furthermore, even though a pregnancy is unplanned, this is not synonymous with its being unwanted (Adler and Tschann, 1993; Macintyre and Cunningham-Burley, 1993). On the other hand, a number of authors have indicated conflictual reasons for some adolescents to become pregnant. Coddington (1979) reported an association with significant recent life changes, especially parental illness, death or separation or the death of a grandparent. Horwitz et al. (1991) highlighted attempts to resolve conflicts with the adolescent's family-of-origin. These could include: having a child as a reason to leave home; competitiveness with their own mother (or sister) who is pregnant; or an attempt to obtain closeness to a rejecting mother, such as by providing her with the 'gift' of a baby or inviting her approval.

The greatest attention has been on those young people who have experienced emotional deprivation or sexual abuse. Bolton (1990) suggested that pregnancy for them may be a means of generating some control and power in their lives, the illusion of creating a happy family life or the means of escaping the continuing abuse at home, while Buchholz and Gol (1986) mentioned attempts to overcome deprivation by identifying with the new baby as her own self, or the need to find someone to belong to. Rainey et al. (1995) found that a substantial number of teenagers who had suffered sexual abuse were actively trying to conceive (as did Butler and Burton, 1990; and Boyer and Fine, 1992) and they inferred that many had the need for self-validation because they believed that something was wrong with them as a result of the abuse. Some abused young mothers relate to their baby as though it were an idealized 'doll' because they unwittingly hope that the child will confirm that they were, after all, capable of creating something good.

The problem with any of these psychological meanings is not only that they can dominate the infant's identity but the child can be at risk of harm if they fail to fulfil the unspoken hopes. Stevens-Simon and Nelligan (1998) observed that, if the pregnancy was an attempt to overcome feelings of depression and loneliness, the mother may be particularly insensitive to the child's needs and misinterpret crying as rejection, while pregnancy as a means of pleasing and holding on to a boyfriend could lead to blaming the child if he leaves her. In addition, a child conceived following rape or incestuous abuse may well be consciously hated or cathected with considerable ambivalence.

Thus, the adolescent mother may need to be interviewed about the following areas: what are her feelings about the pregnancy/child; is there any link between these feelings and her own past experiences; what were the circumstances in which the pregnancy occurred; what else was happening in her life at the time; who is the father; what is her relationship with him; what is her expected future relationship with him; what expectations does she have of her relationship with the child and of the child with her; what difference has her pregnancy/child being born made to her life; how has her relationship with her mother/family-of-origin been affected by the pregnancy/birth; and so on. Adolescent fathers will need to be assessed in a similar way, including the nature and degree of emotional stress that they may be experiencing (Elster and Lamb, 1986).

## Ability to manage their life

In order for a young parent to assume primary responsibility for the care of their child, they must be able to manage their everyday life with some degree of autonomy. Their day cannot be haphazard or spent sleeping for long periods and their lifestyle must have sufficient consistency, such as no sudden or frequent moves of home. They must be able to plan ahead and remember appointments. Money management will include budgeting for essentials rather than spending money on superficial sources of gratification. They can be asked to describe their daily routine and how it did/will change with the baby's birth, using such examples as: what time they get up; do they pay electricity bills on time; do they still have enough money at the end of the week; what food and clothes do they buy; what housework do they do; and what appointments have they kept or missed.

## Network of relationships

An ability to manage their life is not incompatible with also using help from a network of family and friends. The Baltimore longitudinal study (Furstenberg and Harris, 1993) revealed that just 9 per cent of children of adolescent mothers had lived continuously with their father by the time they had reached late teens and only 13 per cent had maintained a strong bond with their non-residential father: however, the contact with the biological father made little difference to outcome for the child and what did was a close tie with their 'stepfather'. The study also suggested that co-residence of an adolescent mother with her own mother could be conflictual and have a negative impact on the young mother's parenting capacities (Brooks-Gunn and Chase-Lansdale, 1991). Over one third (36 per cent) of the teenage parents studied by Nitz et al. (1995) reported that their own mother was a source of conflict, while nearly one half (43 per cent) also found the baby's father a source of conflict. An often ignored factor is the impact of the father's parents, and Bolton (1990) reported evidence that adolescent pairs living with the father's parents, or receiving financial support from them, had the best outcome when the measure was subsequent maltreatment reports.

Clearly, the nature of such relationships is an essential component of an assessment, particularly if the (grand-)mother is to be considered as the infant's main caretaker or the mother's principal support. Support from the child's father appears important in the short term but may not be so crucial in the longer term to the child's well-being.

## Underlying psychopathology

Since adolescent pregnancy can be associated with substance misuse or depression, both of which have significance for child care, it is important to make enquiry about these mental health issues. Use of drugs should be questioned routinely.

## Interventions available

All assessments should include questions about whether the parent believes that they require any help, either practical or emotional. Osofsky et al. (1988) and Stevens-Simon and Nelligan (1998) reviewed interventions used in everyday clinical practice with young parents and concluded that educational input needed to be accompanied by multi-disciplinary work, both clinic- and home-based and continuing beyond the immediate post-partum period, addressing self-esteem, vocational goals and self-sufficiency skills. Their own programmes also focused on preventing school drop-out and repeat pregnancies and direct information-giving about child development. Anger management, attending to the infant's emotional needs and communicating with the child are common to many programmes (Budd et al., 1998), while Trad (1995) proposed an approach of 'previewing', in which the mother first was encouraged to predict how imminent developmental changes would affect her relationship with the infant and then subsequently rehearsed them. Landy et al. (1984) considered that any intervention should be tailored to the specific characteristics of the case and needs of the young parent and child, a number of which would require education and peer and professional support, some would require additional counselling, while more intensive psychotherapy was appropriate to others. The need to include the infant's father and peer support has been emphasized by many authors, including Furstenberg et al. (1989) and Budd et al. (1998), although the difficulties of engaging either parent or of achieving positive long-term results was noted by Budd et al. (1998). Chase-Lansdale et al. (1992) argued that existing programmes needed to be longer in order to achieve sustained improvement, even becoming involved with the children when they reached school age.

Much less has been written about parenting interventions for adolescent parents in the context of court proceedings. The current 'default' approach in this country seems to be in all cases to recommend residential interventions: rather loosely called assessments. While such programmes may have initial positive results, often reporting evidence of a good relationship between mother and baby, we have come to view these early findings with considerable caution. In our view, these first few months can give a falsely optimistic picture because the early idealization by the mother of a dependent baby remains, as does the excessive support of the family centre residents and staff. The truer test is after about a year, when the infant becomes less passive and the mother is left to her own resources.

## CONCLUSIONS

Even though adolescence is far from an ideal time to begin to take on the responsibilities of parenthood, individuals differ in their capacity to care for children and each case must be considered on its merits. The young parents who come before family proceedings courts usually have a background of considerable emotional and social adversity, which tends to be associated with a poorer outcome for the child, as well as for the parent. The possibility of child maltreatment, especially neglect, must be considered, although the risk does not appear to be as high as many have presumed. The core of the assessment should be the same as that undertaken with older parents (as discussed elsewhere in this book) but, in addition, special attention will need to be paid to the parent's cognitive and emotional development, their awareness of children's needs, their expectations of the child, and their capacity to manage practical aspects of their life.

## References

Adler, N.E. and Tschann, J.M. (1993) Conscious and preconscious motivation for pregnancy among female adolescents, in A. Lawson and D.L. Rhode (eds) *The Politics of Pregnancy: Adolescent Sexuality and Public Policy*, New Haven, CT: Yale University Press.

Baldwin, W. and Cain, V. (1980) The children of teenage parents, *Family Planning Perspectives* 12: 34–43.

Bennett, D.L. and Bauman, A. (2000) Adolescent mental health and risky sexual behaviour, *British Medical Journal* 321: 251–2.

Bolton, F.G. (1990) The risk of child maltreatment in adolescent parenting, *Advances in Adolescent Mental Health* 4: 223–7.

Bolton, F.G. and Laner, R.H. (1986) Children rearing children: a study of reportedly maltreating younger adolescents, *Journal of Family Violence* 1: 181–96.

Boyer, D. and Fine, D. (1992) Sexual abuse as factor in adolescent pregnancy and child maltreatment, *Family Planning Perspectives* 24: 4–19.

Breakwell, G.M. (1993) Psychological and social characteristics of teenagers who have children, in A. Lawson and D.L. Rhode (eds) *The Politics of Pregnancy: Adolescent Sexuality and Public Policy*, New Haven, CT: Yale University Press.

Brooks-Gunn, J. and Chase-Lansdale, P.L. (1991) Children having children: effects on the family system, *Pediatric Annals* 20: 467–81.

Brooks-Gunn, J. and Furstenberg, F.F. (1986) The children of adolescent mothers: physical, academic, and psychological outcomes, *Developmental Review* 6: 224–51.

Browne, K. and Herbert, M. (1997) *Preventing Family Violence*, Chichester: Wiley.

Buchholz, E.S. and Gol, B. (1986) More than playing house: a developmental perspective on the strengths in teenage motherhood, *American Journal of Orthopsychiatry* 56: 347–59.

Buchholz, E.S. and Korn-Bursztyn, C. (1993) Children of adolescent mothers: are they at risk for abuse? *Adolescence* 28: 361–82.

Budd, K.S., Heilman, N.E. and Kane, D. (2000) Psychosocial correlates of child abuse potential in multiply disadvantaged adolescent mothers, *Child Abuse & Neglect* 24: 611–25.

Budd, K.S., Stockman, K.D. and Miller, E.N. (1998) Parenting issues and interventions with adolescent mothers, in J.R. Lutzker (ed.) *Handbook of Child Abuse Research and Treatment*, New York: Plenum.

Butler, J.R. and Burton, L.M. (1990) Rethinking teenage childbearing: is sexual abuse a missing link? *Family Relations* 39: 73–80.

Campion, M.J. (1995) *Who's Fit to Be a Parent?* London: Routledge.

Chase-Lansdale, P.L., Brooks-Gunn, J. and Paikoff, R.L. (1992) Research and programs for adolescent mothers: missing links and future promises, *American Behavioral Scientist* 35: 290–312.

Coddington, R.D. (1979) Life events associated with adolescent pregnancies, *Journal of Clinical Psychiatry* 40: 39–48

Connelly, C.D. and Straus, M.A. (1992) Mother's age and risk for physical abuse, *Child Abuse & Neglect* 16: 709–18.

Crockenberg, S. (1987) Predictors and correlates of anger toward and punitive control of toddlers by adolescent mothers, *Child Development* 58: 964–75.

de Paúl, J. and Domenech, L. (2000) Childhood history of abuse and child abuse potential in adolescent mothers: a longitudinal study, *Child Abuse & Neglect* 24: 701–13.

Elster, A.B. and Lamb, M.E. (1986) Adolescent fathers: the under studied side of adolescent pregnancy, in J.B. Lancaster and B.A. Hamburg (eds) *School-age Pregnancy and Parenthood: Biosocial Dimensions*, New York: Aldine de Gruyter.

Family Policy Studies Centre (1999) *Teenage Pregnancy and the Family*, Family Briefing Paper 9, London: Family Policy Studies Centre.

Flanagan, P.J., McGrath, M.M., Meyer, E.C. and Garcia Coll, C.T. (1995) Adolescent development and transitions to motherhood, *Pediatrics* 96: 273–7.

Fursternberg, F.F., Brooks-Gunn, J. and Chase-Lansdale, L. (1989) Teenaged pregnancy and childbearing, *American Psychologist* 44: 313–20.

Furstenberg, F.F., Brooks-Gunn, J. and Morgan, S.P. (1987) Adolescent mothers and their children in later life, *Family Planning Perspective* 19: 142–51.

Fursternberg, F.F. and Harris, K.M. (1993) When fathers matter/why fathers matter: the impact of paternal involvement on the offspring of adolescent mothers, in A. Lawson and D.L. Rhode (eds) *The Politics of Pregnancy: Adolescent Sexuality and Public Policy*, New Haven, CT: Yale University Press.

Garcia Coll, C.T., Hoffman, J. and Oh, W. (1987) The social ecology and early parenting of Caucasian adolescent mothers, *Child Development* 58: 955–63.

Gelles, R.J. (1986) School-age parents and child abuse, in J.B. Lancaster and B.A. Hamburg (eds) *School-age Pregnancy and Parenthood: Biosocial Dimensions*, New York: Aldine de Gruyter.

Hamburg, B.A. (1986) Subsets of adolescent mothers: development, biomedical, and psychosocial issues, in J.B. Lancaster and B.A. Hamburg (eds) *School-age Pregnancy and Parenthood: Biosocial Dimensions*, New York: Aldine de Gruyter.

Haskett, M.E., Johnson, C.A. and Miller, J.W. (1994) Individual differences in risk of child abuse by adolescent mothers: assessment in the perinatal period, *Journal of Child Psychology & Psychiatry* 35: 461–76.

Hatcher, S. (1973) The adolescent experience of pregnancy and abortion: a developmental analysis, *Journal of Youth and Adolescence* 2: 53–102.

Herrenkohl, E.C., Herrenkohl, R.C., Egolf, B.P. and Russo, M.J. (1998) The relationship between early maltreatment and teenage parenthood, *Journal of Adolescence* 21: 291–303.

Horwitz, S.M., Klerman, L.V., Sung Kuo, H. and Jekel, J.F. (1991) Intergenerational transmission of school-age parenthood, *Family Planning Perspectives* 23: 168–72 and 177.

Irvine, H., Bradley, T., Cupples, M. and Booham, M. (1997) The implications of teenage pregnancy and motherhood for primary health care: unresolved issues, *British Journal of General Practice* 47: 323–6.

Jacobson, L.D., Wilkinson, C. and Pill, R. (1995) Teenage pregnancy in the United Kingdom in the 1990s: the implications for primary care, *Family Practice* 12: 232–6.

Kessler, R.C., Berglund, P.A., Foster, C.L., Saunders, W.B., Stang, P.E. and Walters, E.E. (1997) Social consequences of psychiatric disorders, II: teenage parenthood, *American Journal of Psychiatry* 154: 1405–11.

Landy, S., Cleland, J. and Schubert, J. (1984) The individuality of teenage mothers and its implication for intervention strategies, *Journal of Adolescence* 7: 171–90.

Lask, J. (1994) Parenting in adolescents, *ACPP Review & Newsletter* 16: 229–36.

Levine, L., Garcia Coll, C.T. and Oh, W. (1985) Determinants of mother–infant interaction in adolescent mothers, *Pediatrics* 75: 23–9.

Luster, T. (1998) Individual differences in the caregiving behavior of teenage mothers: an ecological perspective, *Clinical Child Psychology & Psychiatry* 3: 341–60.

McAnarney, E.R. (1987) Young maternal age and adverse neonatal outcome, *American Journal of Diseases of Childhood* 141: 1053–9.

McAnarney, E.R., Lawrence, R.A., Ricciuti, H.N., Polley, J. and Szilagyi, M. (1986) Interactions of adolescent mothers and their 1-year-old children, *Pediatrics* 78: 585–90.

McCullough, M. and Scherman, A. (1998) Family-of-origin interaction and adolescent mothers' potential for child abuse, *Adolescence* 33: 375–84.

Macintyre, S. and Cunningham-Burley, S. (1993) Teenage pregnancy as a social problem: a perspective from the United Kingdom, in A. Lawson and D.L. Rhode (eds) *The Politics of Pregnancy: Adolescent Sexuality and Public Policy*, New Haven, CT: Yale University Press.

Mahler, M. (1979) *The Selected Papers of Margaret S. Mahler, Volume 2: Separation-Individuation*, New York: Jason Aronson.

Matsuhashi, Y., Felice, M.E., Shragg, P. and Hollingsworth, D.R. (1989) Is repeat pregnancy in adolescents a 'planned' affair? *Journal of Adolescent Health Care* 10: 409–12.

Melhuish, E. and Phoenix, A. (1988) Motherhood under twenty, *Children & Society* 4: 288–98.

Miller, C.L., Miceli, P.J., Whitman, T.L. and Borkowski, J.G. (1996) Cognitive readiness to parent and intellectual-emotional development in children of adolescent mothers, *Developmental Psychology* 32: 533–41.

Milner, J.S. (1986) *The Child Abuse Potential Inventory Manual*, 2nd ed., DeKalb, IL: Psytec Inc.

Nitz, K., Ketterlinus, R.D. and Brandt, L.J. (1995) The role of stress, social support, and family environment in adolescent mothers' parenting, *Journal of Adolescent Research* 10: 358–82.

Osofsky, J.D., Osofsky, H.J. and Diamond, M.O. (1988) The transition to parenthood: special tasks and risks for adolescent parents, in G.Y. Michaels and W.A. Goldberg (eds) *The Transition to Parenthood: Current Theory and Research*, Cambridge: Cambridge University Press.

Panzarine, S., Slater, E. and Sharps, P. (1995) Coping, social support, and depressive symptoms in adolescent mothers, *Journal of Adolescent Health* 17: 113–19.

Parks, P.L. and Arndt, E.K. (1990) Differences between adolescent and adult mothers of infants, *Journal of Adolescent Health Care* 11: 248–53.

Petersen, A.C. and Offer, D. (1979) Adolescent development: sixteen to nineteen years, in J.D. Call, J.D. Noshpitz, R.L. Cohen and I.N. Berlin (eds) *Basic Handbook of Child Psychiatry, Volume 1: Development*, New York: Basic Books.

Phoenix, A. (1993) The social construction of teenage motherhood: a black and white issue? in A. Lawson and D.L. Rhode (eds) *The Politics of Pregnancy: Adolescent Sexuality and Public Policy*, New Haven: Yale University Press.

Pines, D. (1988) Adolescent pregnancy and motherhood, *Psychoanalytic Inquiry* 8: 234–51.

Quinton, D. and Rutter, M. (1984) Parents with children in care, II: intergenerational continuities, *Journal of Child Psychology & Psychiatry* 25: 231–50.

Quinton, D., Rutter, M. and Liddle, C. (1984) Institutional rearing, parenting difficulties and marital support, *Psychological Medicine* 14: 107–24.

Ragozin, A.S., Basham, R.B., Crnic, K.A., Greenberg, M.T. and Robinson, N.M. (1982) Effects of maternal age on parental role, *Developmental Psychology* 18: 627–34.

Rainey, D.Y., Stevens-Simon, C. and Kaplan, D.W. (1995) Are adolescents who report prior sexual abuse at higher risk for pregnancy? *Child Abuse & Neglect* 19: 1283–88.

Reder, P. and Duncan, S. (1995) The meaning of the child, in P. Reder and C. Lucey (eds) *Assessment of Parenting: Psychiatric and Psychological Perspectives*, London: Routledge.

Reder, P. and Duncan, S. (1999) *Lost Innocents: A Follow-up Study of Fatal Child Abuse*, London: Routledge.

Schilmoeller, G.L. and Baranowski, M.D. (1985) Childrearing of firstborns by adolescent and older mothers, *Adolescence* 20: 805–22.

Shapiro, J.R. and Mangelsdorf, S.C. (1994) The determinants of parenting competence in adolescent mothers, *Journal of Youth and Adolescence* 23: 621–41.

Social Exclusion Unit (1999) *Teenage Pregnancy*, London: The Stationery Office.

Sommer, K., Whitman, T.L., Borkowski, J.G., Schellenbach, C., Maxwell, S. and Keogh, D. (1993) Cognitive readiness and adolescent parenting, *Developmental Psychology* 29: 389–98.

Steinberg, D. (1987) *Basic Adolescent Psychiatry*, Oxford: Blackwell Scientific.

Stevens-Simon, C. and Nelligan, D. (1998) Strategies for identifying and treating adolescents at risk for maltreating their children, *Aggression and Violent Behaviour* 3: 197–217.

Stevens-Simon, C. and White, M. (1991) Adolescent pregnancy, *Pediatric Annals* 20: 322–31.

Stier, D.M., Leventhal, J.M., Berg, A.T., Johnson, L. and Mezger, J. (1993) Are children born to young mothers at increased risk of maltreatment? *Pediatrics* 91: 642–8.

Trad, P.V. (1995) Mental health of adolescent mothers, *Journal of the American Academy of Child & Adolescent Psychiatry* 34: 130–42.

Whitman, T.L., Borkowski, J.G., Schellenbach, C.J. and Nath, P.S. (1987) Predicting and understanding developmental delay of children of adolescent mothers: a multidimensional approach, *American Journal of Mental Deficiency* 92: 40–56.

Wolkind, S.N. and Kruk, S. (1985) Teenage pregnancy and motherhood, *Journal of the Society of Medicine* 78: 112–16.

Wurtz Passino, A., Whitman, T.L., Borkowski, J.G., Schellenbach, C.J., Maxwell, S.E., Keogh, D. and Rellinger, E. (1993) Personal adjustment during pregnancy and adolescent parenting, *Adolescence* 28: 97–122.

Zuravin, S.J. (1988) Child maltreatment and teenage first births: a relationship mediated by chronic sociodemographic stress? *American Journal of Orthopsychiatry* 58: 91–103.

Zuravin, S.J. and DiBlasio, F.A. (1992) Child-neglecting adolescent mothers: how do they differ from their nonmaltreating counterparts? *Journal of Interpersonal Violence* 7: 471–89.

Zuravin, S.J. and DiBlasio, F.A. (1996) The correlates of child physical abuse and neglect by adolescent mothers, *Journal of Family Violence* 11: 149–66.

Chapter 9

# Can parents with personality disorders adequately care for children?

*Christopher Cordess*

## INTRODUCTION

This chapter addresses the relevance of the diagnosis of personality disorder to the assessment of parenting capacity. The definition of personality disorder includes enduring patterns of inner experience and behaviour and embraces abnormalities of cognition, affectivity (emotional life), interpersonal functioning and impulse control. Failures or lapses in these areas clearly do not bode well in regard to parenting capacity. However, this chapter cautions against the assumption of inadequate parenting capacity in those suffering from the different types of personality disorder. It also cautions against the opposite assumption of adequate parenting ability in those who present as 'normal' but who are actually, in one way or another, 'pseudo-normal', or 'as-if', personalities and have underlying personality characteristics which may present a danger to children in their care.

The accurate assessment of personality is beset by numerous problems of conceptualization, definition and methodology. Also, although part of the definition of personality disorder is that it is an 'enduring state', adjustments can be made with treatment and considerable change may even be produced (Gunderson and Gabbard, 2000).

This chapter begins with a general consideration of risk, followed by an overview of different dimensional and categorical classifications of personality, and proceeds to contextualize these in relation to the specific capacities needed for 'good enough' parenting.

## RISK

'Risk' is the probability of an event, combined with the magnitude of the losses and gains that it would entail. Since the consequences of the losses (the likely negative effects to the child of neglectful or abusive parenting by a personality-disordered person) are high, even if the likely frequency (probability) is not, the threshold of risk is likely to be set relatively low. However, such threshold setting is a function of socio-political influences and cultural expectations and, in the contemporary setting of a society which is increasingly 'risk averse' and accustomed to lay blame wherever possible, professionals should be wary of being misused for ulterior, and in the matter of personality disorder, frequently moralistic purposes. A contemporary example is that of the frankly political creation of 'dangerous and severe personality disorder', which combines the entity of personality disorder with its occasional associate, 'dangerousness'. It is likely to fuel the stigmatization and marginalization of people with personality disorders and, as Douglas (1992) points out, stigma is a self-fulfilling prophecy. This new category has since been dropped in the 2002 Mental Health Bill, since it proved impossible to define, but the policy of 'capturing' this apparent group of people within a very widely defined, 'catch-all' definition of mental disorder lingers on.

The concept of 'risk' has its origins in the science of probability theory. It was originally a morally neutral term, referring equally to possibilities of losses or gains, of ill effects or benign effects. Now the use of the term 'risk', which is central to all debates about policy, including health policy and problems of parenting, has, to quote Douglas (1992), 'not much to do with probability calculations; the original connection is only indicated by arm waving in the direction of possible science; the word "risk" now means "danger"; "high risk" means "a lot of danger"' (p. 24). Public discourse about modern risks, Douglas continues, 'has fallen into an antique mode' (p. 26) and become confused with sin, danger and taboo in order to legitimize certain dominant points of view. In the paradigmatic case of child abuse and neglect, these confusions and their related urgencies abound and can dangerously skew good clinical judgement and decision making.

The subjective experience of their psychological deficits by the personality-disordered person is of being 'a failure', from which and for which they suffer through no fault of their own. Others, including children, may suffer indirectly and unintentionally or, more rarely, may suffer harm directly as a consequence of behaviour associated with the personality disorder. These differentiations are largely the subject of this chapter. The point is that, in labelling someone with the personality disorder 'tag', there is sometimes an element of disapproval of what may be little more than an idiosyncratic lifestyle or antisocial behaviour, independent of any actual disorder.

This chapter, therefore, will attempt to steer a balanced course and reach tentative conclusions within a subject matter which could not be of more serious import, but which too often becomes a projective screen for hysterical media outbursts, knee-jerk political reaction and righteous, moralistic prejudice. It recognizes, too, the preliminary and impoverished nature of the definitions of personality disorder, as well as their poor predictive power, and the many variables which determine abusive relationships, including environment, partners, family and community networks. Also relevant are individual child characteristics, including resilience. It follows that a diagnosis of personality disorder does not, of itself, dictate a particular course of action in regard to child care. One needs to make case-by-case judgements and decisions, at least some of which will fall short of perfection.

The rare reader who seeks absolutes and certitudes and direct predictable causal links in these matters may find this position frustrating, if not frankly provoking. This would appear to be part of the impetus driving current policies and legislative enactments of government in relation to the essential vagaries of the whole subject of mental health in general. As Mullen (2001) writes, 'Risk assessment and risk management have emerged as central elements not just in forensic practice but in all mental health practice' (p. 73). Along with this centrality frequently come unrealistic expectations and the consequential risk in itself of experts claiming the ability to make risk assessments and predictions which are just not possible. The trouble is that 'anyone who insists that there is a high degree of uncertainty is taken to be opting out of accountability' (Douglas, 1992: p. 30). The increased societal pressure towards 'positive' risk assessments, such as 'this parent is dangerous', also has the danger of creating unacceptable numbers of false positives. The fallibility of risk assessments is well addressed in Gigerenzer (2002).

It will not have escaped the notice of anyone involved in these matters, whether personally or professionally, that the 'cure' (taking children into 'care') in recent decades has turned out to have had at least as bad, if not worse, consequences than the 'disease' (the problem of relative failure of parenting). These issues are vast but, in this author's view, there is a whole social and psychological exegesis awaited upon how as a society we have failed to protect, indeed further abused, those who have been taken into 'care', and for whom we have accepted a duty of protection.

This is the context within which decisions about removal of children from their biological parents need to be assessed.

## DIAGNOSTIC APPROACHES TO PERSONALITY DISORDER

The origins of present-day concepts of personality disorder lie largely within the historical and more contemporary psychoanalytic study of character disorder. This includes psychodynamic concepts of 'narcissistic', 'schizoid', 'borderline', 'sadistic' and 'masochistic' typologies. Personality disorder today is more operationally defined, although the definitions are open to dispute and are often elusive. One reason is that people, their personalities and their 'personality disorders' clearly exist on a dimensional continuum but, for heuristic reasons, contemporary definitions require categorical 'boxes'.

Personality disorders are common in the general population, estimated to be present in approximately 10 per cent of people (Casey and Tyrer, 1986), while, in an urban family practice, 28 per cent of attenders have been estimated to have a personality disorder (Casey and Tyrer, 1990).

Personality disorder is defined as an 'enduring pattern of inner experience and behaviour that deviates markedly from the expectations of the individual's culture' (American Psychiatric Association, 2000). It is manifested in the areas of:

1    cognition – ways of perceiving and interpreting the world;
2    affectivity – range and intensity of emotion;
3    interpersonal functioning; and
4    impulse control.

The pattern of personality disorder is said to be inflexible and pervasive across a broad range of situations and leads to clinically significant distress as well as impairment in social, occupational and other areas of functioning. It has its onset in adolescence. Table 9.1 sets out the sub-types of different personality disorders in the Diagnostic and Statistical Manual (DSM-IV-R) (American Psychiatric Association, 2000) and the International Classification of Diseases (ICD-10) (World Health Organization, 1992) so as to make comparison and it shows three clusters based upon descriptive similarities. However, these clusters are rough and ready and not well validated. Actual people tend to fall across and between categories, which should therefore only be used as a guide. Each cluster has been given an overall heading ('Odd–eccentric', 'Dramatic–emotional' and 'Anxious–fearful') which, contrary to the more common trend, would appear to de-emphasize possible dangerousness.

*Table 9.1* Comparison of the features of personality disorder as presented in DSM-IV-R and ICD-10

| DSM-IV-R | ICD-10 |
| --- | --- |
| **Cluster A**<br>(Odd–eccentric) | |
| Paranoid<br>Schizoid<br>Schizotypal | Paranoid<br>Schizoid |
| **Cluster B**<br>(Dramatic–emotional) | |
| Antisocial | Dyssocial<br>Emotionally unstable:<br>  impulsive type |
| Borderline<br>Histrionic<br>Narcissistic | borderline type<br>Histrionic |
| **Cluster C**<br>(Anxious–fearful) | |
| Avoidant<br>Dependent<br>Obsessive–compulsive<br>Passive–aggressive | Anxious (avoidant)<br>Dependent<br>Anankastic (obsessive–compulsive)<br>Other |

*Source:* Adapted from Dolan and Coid (1993).

In any given individual with personality disorder, it is often the case that there are several sub-typologies which fit, along with elements of other sub-types. It should be noted in general terms, however, that the diagnosis of a particular psychiatric disorder of any type has little correlation with specific consequences of behaviour or effects upon a child. The significant variables are the social and interactional consequences of the subject's problems, especially hostility and marital disharmony (Rutter and Quinton, 1984).

There is an increasing trend, including in clinical practice, towards the application of quantitative measures of personality, in line with the increasing demands for 'evidence-based' practice. Whilst such instruments of assessment can be helpful in certain situations and are essential in research, they have limited and only adjunctive relevance in the individual clinical case, where individual variables may 'trump' the predictive value of measurements standardized within, and honed from, cohort data.

Clearly, in so far as personality disorder sub-types represent consistent behaviours and ways of interacting, they will effect parenting capacity and functioning variously. Those in Clusters A and B are more likely to be actively abusive or violent, but may also be neglectful. Those in Cluster C may be abusive by imposing rigidity, or by becoming dependent upon those they should be caring for, so that the child becomes a 'young carer' whose life is restricted by reversal of the usual adult–child caring process. It is frequently easier to assess and predict actual acts of violence (commissions) and less easy to assess the consequences of failures of care (omissions). Thus, these categorizations of personality disorders do not take us very far in regard to the practical assessment of parenting capacity or how it may be improved.

## THE CONTEXT OF THE PERSONALITY-DISORDERED INDIVIDUAL: A MORE USEFUL APPROACH

In the influential document *Working Together to Safeguard Children* (Department of Health *et al.*, 1999), a helpful framework for assessing children in need and their families is proposed in order to provide 'a systematic basis for collecting and analysing information to support professional judgements'. There are three main aspects:

1  the child's development needs;
2  the capacity of parents or care-givers to respond appropriately to these needs, including their capacity to keep the child safe from harm; and
3  the impact of wider family and environmental factors on the parents and child.

The parenting capacity of those considered to be suffering from personality disorder concerns the second, as well as, to a lesser extent, the third aspect. The first aspect is important in that a child with especially demanding physical, emotional or behavioural needs, such as a child who has suffered from cerebral palsy from birth, will need an especially resourceful parent. The assessor will make an individual personality assessment but will be mindful of the relevance of the child's special needs and environmental and social factors, as well as other potentially disinhibiting factors such as alcohol and drugs.

Thorpe (1997) writes:

> Of particular importance is an understanding of the adult psyche, since the safety and well-being of children depend upon adult commitment and consistency . . . Furthermore, within the unconscious lie the springs and forces of sexuality and dangerousness often unrecognised by the conscious, and sometimes elaborately and skilfully concealed by the external presentation. Similarly, it follows that the evaluation of the risk that an adult presents to children in his or her care is made most profoundly by the forensic psychiatrist. (p. 2)

In fact he refers in this context to the 'forensic child psychiatrist'. Whilst I would agree with this statement, I would wish to add that other disciplines have equal contributions to make and that the court functions to weigh all the evidence and the various witness statements, as well as the expert opinions in the balance. Fortunately, the momentous decisions that have to be taken in regard to the protection of children do not fall entirely upon the clinician.

Gallwey (1997) writes:

> in the Family Courts standard psychiatric diagnoses are often of limited value. The factors to be considered are less gross so a psychiatric diagnosis cannot easily be made. This is one reason why psycho-dynamic thinking and concepts are more commonly used by professionals working in this area. (pp. 134–5)

Gallwey describes what he calls 'a rough and ready guide' of six simple categories which 'are not far removed from psychiatric diagnostic categories but which represent in very broad ways how different individuals manage their emotional turbulence and conflicts' (p. 135). He adds that these different ways of organizing mental defences can be identified fairly easily and have some practical value in making the sort of judgements that are needed regarding safety, vulnerability and treatment. It should be emphasized that it is the mode of organizing mental defences and the likely stability of these defences – for example, under threat of provocation by extreme psychological or social stress, alcohol or drugs, or pathological relationships with partners – that is the focus of this categorization. The categories are:

1   Well-adjusted delinquents;
2   Poorly adjusted delinquents and frail neurotic personalities;

3    Over-defended personalities;
4    Psychotic personalities;
5    Pseudo-normal personalities; and
6    Those with a primary diagnosis of mental illness or organic disorder.

Gallwey (1997) comments:

> You may be puzzled by the first category which appears to be a contradiction in terms since delinquency by definition is social maladjustment. However, here I am referring to psychological adjustment within the individual for, in my view, much delinquent behaviour can be explained as a compensatory mechanism, a defence against anxiety and conflict which enables the individual to function without breaking down into neurotic turmoil or psychotic confusion. (p. 135)

Gallwey goes on to describe the precariousness of this situation:

> Provided that such individuals can, through their manipulation of the world, make up for the absence of a defensive imagination then they will feel psychologically 'safe'. Their lives may be dangerous, uncertain, full of contradiction and threatened with loss of liberty and yet they have an emotional equanimity which belies their perilous situation. If they try and behave better they may become disturbed. This is a frequent finding in the treatment of habitual delinquents and a real stumbling block when they attempt to settle down into family life. Often they manage to keep their criminality going as a separate split off activity. Since they rely on their delinquency as a means of emotional adjustment then if they try to give it up completely they become frightened, violent or behave catastrophically. In this state they represent an almost certain risk of harm to a child especially when their criminal adjustment is unsafe so the risk of violence or hazardous accident is very real. (p. 135)

In my opinion, in this context, Gallwey fails to address those well-adjusted delinquents who may be part of a subculture of criminality and who thereby achieve relative social and psychological stability and whose parenting capacities may therefore be quite adequate.

Those in Gallwey's category 2 (who most likely fall within Cluster B of the ICD-10 and DSM-IV-R classifications, or possibly Cluster A) are, as he describes, 'a real menace. Some of the worst cases of child neglect and child cruelty derive from delinquent individuals who are constantly decompensating into neurotic turmoil with rages and catastrophic behaviour' (p. 136). They overlap with 'psychotic personalities' (category 4) who may, he writes,

> be very hard to assess in terms of their safety in relation to others, including children. Paranoid personalities who rely heavily on projection of bad feelings

into others are highly suspicious and antagonistic to the world, can, particularly if they are intelligent, sustain a somewhat beleaguered way of life within the framework of their grandiosity and hostility to others. They of course make bad parents, they might be cruel or violent, but it may be very difficult to show that this is the case. (p. 137)

Those parents who appear 'normal' but have a history of major breaks with reality or of sexual or violent impulsive action may be regarded as having 'encapsulated' psychotic parts to their personality. They are similar to the group who Gallwey says

> operate on the basis of very profound splits within their personalities. This schizoid group lead double lives so that some highly abnormal, destructive, perverse or dangerous behaviour is carried on in a clandestine way. They present a convincing picture of normality and represent, par excellence, the 'pseudo normal parents'. When their perverse behaviour comes to light, as is the case with many sexual offenders towards children, they manage to appear regretful and express shame, but at the same time convey a self-congratulatory, high moral tone about themselves in the same breath. They quite subtly convey that although it is not right to have sex with children and maybe that on this occasion they went too far, nevertheless at the time their intentions were good and the whole thing grew out of their love and concern for their victim. They have a great capacity to deceive themselves as well as others and have very often managed to create a way of life in which they have much contact with children or are in positions of trust like clergy, teachers or youth workers. They often seem to have a powerful influence as if they are able to hypnotise people into believing their pseudo-goodness and the denial of what they have done, so that they are once more able to insinuate themselves into the situations where they can continue their abusive needs. (p. 137)

Although each of the categories of personality in Gallwey's typology may be related to abusive parenting, it is the 'pseudo-normal' personalities that are the most difficult to assess and predict.

> These are a group in whom one cannot make a diagnosis of personality disorder or detect any clear pathology, but in whom encapsulated areas of high disturbance may erupt under certain conditions precipitating brief psychotic episodes or violence, perverse or even homicidal behaviour. Such encapsulated disturbance is rather like an aneurysm in the brain which may suddenly rupture causing physical catastrophe to the individual, but which was previously completely silent and therefore never detected. (p. 138)

This situation presents enormous difficulty for assessment and is hard to detect 'although certain features of over-compliance and anxiety usually discovered only in retrospect after the occurrence of the catastrophe may indicate the hidden encapsulated disturbance' (p. 138). Typically, like the more obviously 'over-defended' sub-type, an abusive act is an isolated major and explosive act of violence (of 'encapsulated psychopathology') apparently 'out of the blue' or a serial enactment of a particular, purposive, perverse behaviour, such as in the factitious illness (or Munchausen syndrome by proxy) scenario.

A related schema, which addresses the patient's primary psychodynamic characteristics, is described by Dolan and Coid (1993). They identify the following factors:

1    the degree of identity integration;
2    the type of defensive operations habitually employed; and
3    the capacity for reality testing.

In this tripartite schema, the basic personality structure is considered in relation to: the ego (or the structure of 'self'); the defensive organization and manoeuvres, together with their stability or instability (as in the Gallwey classification); and the accuracy of the relationship between psychic and 'objective' reality.

I find this psychodynamic schema to be the most helpful theoretical structure around which to organize and ponder the actual interaction with the parent at interview. There may, in particular cases, be striking transferential and counter-transferential aspects to the interviews but there should be caution in weighing this data because of the inevitably highly charged nature of the interaction. Minimization of problems and relative denial of frankly abusive behaviour are understandable and very common, at least at first. They need to be distinguished from the lying or less conscious denial of the predatory sexual abuser or perpetrator of illness-inducing behaviour (see below).

Problems of definition arise in the case of child sexual abuse, since sexual deviation which results in the abuse of children has traditionally been considered distinct from personality disorder *per se* (for example, in its specific exclusion from the Mental Health Act 1983). Clearly, there may well be overlap and, from a psychodynamic theory point of view, the overlap of sexual and character pathology may be regarded as near total. However, from any less strict position, it has to be accepted that sexual variation in adults is infinite, that sexual deviation, however defined, is common, and that the sexual abuse of children is, by comparison (and only by comparison) relatively rare. There is, in this author's view, therefore, some merit in resisting the easy conflation of sexual deviations and personality disorder. However, proposals in the new Mental Health Bill (2002) would not do so and, instead, the widest possible definition has been given to 'mental disorder', which is effectively a 'catch-all'. It remains to be seen what future thinking and proposals entail.

## PARENT–CHILD INTERACTION

An especially influential way of conceptualizing the different normal and pathological modes of interrelationships between parent and child is that of attachment theory (Cassidy and Shaver, 1999). The attachment status of the parent to their own parents is reliably predictive of their later attachment to their own children. Equally, whilst attachment status of the child for the parent, of itself, will not determine final decisions about sufficient or acceptable parenting capacity, it can frequently be helpful as a way of thinking about the dynamic within a family system and within primary carer–child relationships (see Baker, Chapter 4). From a clinical perspective, avoidant and ambivalent insecure attachment patterns are common amongst the children of parents whom one is asked to assess in regard to, respectively, neglect or abuse and, although in day-to-day assessment, one is not afforded the luxury of the Strange Situation Test (Ainsworth *et al.*, 1978) or the Adult Attachment Interview (Main, 1990), theoretical knowledge about attachment status can help in conceptualizing relevant relationships.

It is important to gain some understanding of the predicament of the neglected child. Whereas violent acts are most commonly born of parental frustration and impulse (far more rarely do they result from a predatory, sadistic need), neglect may involve emotional 'cutting off'. This is akin to psychological dissociation, so that the child experiences a change from solicitous attachment to complete detachment. From a psychological point of view this may be experienced as an attack, since the normally expected psychological containment of the infant's or child's projections by the primary carer is ignored and they are received back, as it were, 'raw' by the dependent infant as projections coming from outside. Such lack of processing of psychological raw materials has been discussed by Bion (1970) and further developed in contemporary psychodynamic literature. It can be associated with difficulties in later life of an affective and perceptive nature, and, therefore, in extreme cases, the development of personality disorder, including borderline personality disorder.

## ASSESSMENT

For a complete assessment, more than one interview is usually needed to be conducted with the parent, as well as interviews with other informants if that is possible. Historical data from medical, school, employment and social services records also need to be examined. A history of violence, of markedly unstable relationships, or unstable economic or rapidly changing and inadequate housing will obviously be of relevance, but it is not possible to provide a comprehensive checklist of the 'good enough' parent, or the setting in which a parent may so function, since this determination depends upon so many different variables (see Reder, Duncan and Lucey, Chapter 1). By contrast, certain features, such as repeated physical or sexual abuse of the child, are more likely to exclude the parent from further consideration of parental adequacy. Clearly, such secondary aspects of the personality disorder as substance abuse, a propensity to dysphoric decompensation, anxiety or depression will be particularly relevant factors in the assessment.

The assessment process may be summarized as follows.

1   A full history of the parent's development, including school records, occupational, criminal, behavioural and relationship record, and medical records.
2   A history of all the children's developmental milestones and their school and medical records. It is important to obtain a comprehensive account of the clinical records as there may be instances of abnormal illness and abnormal consultation behaviour and presentation of the children at numerous Accident and Emergency departments out of the area.
3   Interviews, including not only the standard mental state examination but also some assessment of how the parent thinks and feels about their predicament, in which their continued care of their children is threatened, and their attitudes to the 'helping' services. Are they defensive? Do they locate blame externally? Do they dissociate (or 'cut off' emotionally)? Aspects of countertransference (the emotional reaction of the examiner to the person and their behaviour) of course colour all such interactions, but they are to be used as a technique of interpretation only cautiously, especially by those who are not psychodynamically trained.

The use of psychometric scales is largely the province of the psychologist, although, with the increasing emphasis on 'evidence-based' opinions, a range of quantitative risk assessment tools are being introduced. These must always be regarded as adjuncts to overall clinical judgement, rather in the way that medical investigations such as X-rays are to medical diagnosis. They must not be regarded as sufficient in themselves (see Reder, Duncan and Lucey, Chapter 2), nor should they be considered to be transparently accurate, since each case depends upon its own particular variables. Also, the validity and reliability of all risk assessment tools are necessarily questionable, since they seek to assess not only static but also dynamic (human) factors which are inherently only partially predictable. There is the universal problem, too, of moving from the empirical findings derived from group data to their application to the individual case.

Clearly, the gender of the parent has relevance to the assessment of the consequences of personality disorder. This may cut several ways. For example, an 'absent' but nonetheless materially providing father may have an acceptable influence upon the family system and the children if the mother is capable and has good support from her own parents. Equally, an especially capable father may compensate for the parenting deficiencies of the mother.

## ACKNOWLEDGEMENT AND DENIAL

Acknowledgement by a parent of occasional negative thoughts about their child is normal (see Winnicott, 1947). It is likely to be significant if they report only positive feelings with never a negative thought about their children and this may be seen as a degree of 'idealization' of self as a parent. In this context, admission to some negative thoughts or feelings is reassuring.

Munchausen syndrome by proxy behaviour shares with abusive sexual behaviour the clandestine and secretive element and, in practically all cases, some form of denial is in operation. It may be at a frankly conscious level (i.e. telling untruths) through to, in some cases, unconscious denial ('not knowing'). Although conscious, habitual lying does not entirely preclude the possibility of bringing about therapeutic change (see Bentovim, Chapter 14), it does make assessment even less accurate than it otherwise would be. It is also a major risk factor in its own right when assessing parental capacity. However, a degree of minimization of past difficulties or problem behaviour is to be expected. A sympathetic attitude at interview will frequently bring forth acceptance or admission of abusive behaviour. Confrontation will equally often cause a defensive reaction.

Even though conscious and repeated lying presents a risk factor in its own right, in my view there is only a secondary place to be given to the detection of, or challenge to, lying, since the clinician's responsibility is to make a clinical assessment not act as a detective. A large part of the assessment, however, relies on the detailed reading of documentation, which may include evidence of witnesses, suspicions of professionals, charges and Child Protection Conference reports and minutes. Discrepancies and obvious untruths will become apparent and can be challenged at points during the interview in as helpful a way as possible. There is no point in aggressive confrontation which is likely merely to increase the defensive denial. A distinction needs to be made between deliberate lying and less conscious forms of denial. These include failure to register a given incident in episodic memory, dissociation, splitting, repression or failure to recall. The latter may be caused by a high degree of emotionality, such as around a regretted, shameful act (as in psychogenic amnesia).

## TREATABILITY

The treatment of personality disorders is a complex matter. There is reason to believe, from clinical experience, that character traits such as impulsivity and suspiciousness, as well as disorders of mental state (e.g. dysphoria) can be improved by psychotherapeutic intervention. The provision of a stable, medium to long-term, therapeutic relationship may be emotionally containing in itself. Simultaneous practical adjustments to the context in which the parent–child relationship exists and, for example, increased support from self-help peer groups may also assist significant change.

There is, too, substantial evidence now for the efficacy of the different psycho-therapies upon the range of personality disorders: cognitive-behaviour therapies can reduce troublesome and delineated behaviours, for example through 'anger' management, and psychodynamic psychotherapy may improve global sympto-matology, such as in borderline and narcissistic disorders. Possible treatment settings range from out-patient, day hospital, a therapeutic community, to treatment even within secure settings. Bateman and Fonagy (1999) have reported on the impressive outcomes for the treatment of borderline personality in a day hospital – so-called 'partial hospitalization' (see also Gunderson and Gabbard, 2000).

Probably the most critical issue, and the most commonly asked, is whether the person with personality disorder is 'motivated' to change (Cordess, 2002). The question is complex and frequently goes to the heart of their disorder. Difficulties in interpersonal relationships, resulting in poor attachment to professionals and to therapeutic and supportive care, are frequently stumbling blocks. It may be difficult to overcome suspiciousness or sometimes frank paranoia of patients who have come under examination by child protection services. A psychotherapeutic approach which works specifically on these resentments and fears, and which seeks to understand the subjective experience of the 'failing' parent, can be effective in establishing an initial therapeutic alliance. This may be the single most useful therapeutic achievement with parents who feel angry and isolated and alienated by the 'system'. In technical terms this can be described as using interpretations of expectations and 'transference', and especially likely future 'negative transference' (i.e. antagonism to the therapist) in order to engage with the parent. Put another way, these people often have a life history of rejection and expect it to be repeated. Professionals need to be well trained not to fall into this predictable drama and merely add one further experience to the long list of failed relationships. Invariably, personality-disordered patients have a poor sense of self-worth and do not feel worthy of help. They have little experience of basic trust and they often feel too ashamed to 'own up' to the full extent of their feelings of failure and inadequacy as parents. In several cases of my own, for example, this has been the reason for non-attendance at meetings, including critical Child Protection Conferences, which has counted seriously against them, until the reasons behind the non-attendance could be aired and explained to those in authority.

All of these factors may appear to the superficial eye as a lack of motivation for change. Detailed elucidation of the particular impediments to engagement is essential at the outset of assessment and treatment, and then during its continuation.

For these parents, stability of professional personnel is a priority. Sadly, in badly under-resourced social work, child and family mental health, and community psychiatric teams, constancy and continuity of professionals are rarely available. It is also true that staff in such facilities have excessive case loads and are frequently under-trained and under-supervised, so that parents with personality disorders are more likely than not to have the experience of repeat rejections rather than having their disturbing character traits understood and addressed. The opportunities for such failure are all the greater because psychotherapeutic treatments for personality disorder are necessarily medium to long-term. It is unrealistic to expect that the characteristics of a lifetime will change substantially within a matter of months. A particularly important issue in the assessment of parents with personality disorder is whether they can begin to change within a reasonable time scale, bearing in mind the developmental needs of the child. Clearly this must be judged on a case-by-case basis but, if a 'therapeutic alliance' is under way within the first six months, a fair prediction should be able to be made of the likelihood of continued and meaningful engagement in treatment. Children may then, for example, be able to return to parental care, under supervision, while the parent's treatment continues.

Perhaps most important of all is that professionals and therapists should not take on the feelings of hopelessness and resentment that these clients so readily induce and then act them out (in psychodynamic terms an 'acting out of the counter-transference'). This is where training and supervision are absolutely essential, but far too commonly lacking.

## CONCLUSIONS

The short answer to the question posed by the title of the chapter is: yes, some people who are diagnosed as having a personality disorder can certainly adequately care for children, but some cannot. There are numerous variables which may be critical, including the type of personality disorder or personality characteristics, the parenting context, conflicts within the marital or parenting relationships (including, for example, domestic violence) and the responses to stresses and triggers within the dynamic of the whole system. Indeed it is frequently the case that someone who does not reach the threshold for the diagnosis of personality disorder *per se*, but who has particular personality characteristics (for example, a lack of empathic understanding and concrete thinking which lead them to offer little emotional nurturance but to rely excessively on material offerings to the child, such as 'bribing' with sweets) may prove not to be able to offer adequate parenting, whereas someone with an established personality disorder may be able to do so, especially with help.

I write partially from the point of view of a forensic psychiatrist, but clearly with a predominant underpinning of psychodynamic and systemic theory and practice. I would like to encourage more forensic psychiatrists to enter into the work of family assessments and treatments and the difficult, but rewarding, work of Family Courts. Few forensic psychiatrists choose this area of practice, which may be a function of a lack of training that many of them have received in the range of psychodynamic and systemic skills which are commonly part of the professional tool-box of, for example, the child psychiatrist. It may be due to a realization that the forensic psychiatrist's armamentarium of skills is just too unrefined for the judgements required in cases of child care, or it may come down to pragmatic or even financial concerns. Most likely, I think, is that the forensic psychiatrist has become accustomed to think rather linearly in terms of a medically related and diagnostic model, whilst problems of parenting by those considered to suffer from personality disorder or abiding problematic character traits require systemic, dynamic and contextualized consideration: in other terms, a multi-system and multi-axial approach.

There are boundaries of professional expertise to be drawn and observed but, equally, there are areas of professional overlap. In the medico-legal situation, which has the merit that it concentrates the mind and requires careful formulation and presentation of arguments, the forensic psychiatrist should take on the task of assessment of the personality and of possible risks of violence and active abuse. Also, they should make some assessment of the likelihood of improvement of parenting skills and the amelioration of risk within a time span that is realistic in terms of making decisions regarding long-term placement needs of the children. The forensic psychiatrist may make comment about the more obvious aspects of limitations of parenting capacity by neglect, such as lack of concern for the child as a separate individual, or, for example, the pathological influence of a parent's obsessive-compulsive personality disorder. They should, however, leave to the child psychiatrist or child psychologist the finer points of parent–child interaction, only some of which have been touched upon in this chapter.

In particular cases where deception and the clandestine are especially prominent, the forensic psychiatrist may have something useful to say about relative degrees of denial and the likelihood of management, support and therapeutic interventions being genuinely worthwhile. A careful reading of all available documentation will allow the clinician to compare the given history and 'facts' with the account of the same events given by the parent. The attitude of the parent will be all-important, including their reaction to perceived frank differences of opinion. The given accounts of professionals may be wrong in certain details and a realization of this should be acknowledged. However, major consistent discrepancies will become obvious and can be reflected upon and discussed with the parent.

## References

Ainsworth, M.D.S., Bleher, M.C., Waters, E. and Wall, S. (1978) *Patterns of Attachment*, Hillsdale, NJ: Erlbaum.

American Psychiatric Association (2000) *Diagnostic and Statistical Manual of Mental Disorders*, 4th ed., revised, Washington, DC: American Psychiatric Press.

Bateman, A. and Fonagy, P. (1999) Effectiveness of partial hospitalisation in the treatment of borderline personality disorder: a randomised controlled trial, *American Journal of Psychiatry* 156: 1563–9.

Bion, W. (1970) Container and contained, in *Attention and Interpretation*, London: Maresfield Reprints.

Casey, P. and Tyrer, P. (1986) Personality functioning and symptoms, *Journal of Psychiatric Research* 20: 363–74.

Casey, P. and Tyrer, P. (1990) Personality disorder and psychiatric illness in general practice, *British Journal of Psychiatry* 156: 261–5.

Cassidy, J. and Shaver, P.R. (eds) (1999) *Handbook of Attachment: Theory, Research, and Clinical Applications*, New York: The Guilford Press.

Cordess, C. (2002) Building and nurturing a therapeutic alliance with offenders, in M. McMurran (ed.) *Motivating Offenders to Change. A Guide to Enhancing Engagement in Therapy*, Chichester: John Wiley.

Department of Health, Home Office and Department for Education and Employment (1999) *Working Together to Safeguard Children*, London: The Stationery Office.

Dolan, B. and Coid, J. (1993) *Psychopathic and Antisocial Personality Disorders: Treatment and Research Issues*, London: Gaskell.

Douglas, M. (1992) *Risk and Blame: Essays in Cultural Theory*, London: Routledge.

Gallwey, P. (1997) Bad parenting and pseudo parenting, in The Hon. Mr Justice Wall (ed.) *Rooted Sorrows: Psychoanalytic Perspectives on Child Protection, Assessment, Therapy and Treatment*, Bristol: Family Law/Jordan.

Gigerenzer, G. (2002) *Reckoning with Risk*, London: Allen Lane.

Gunderson, J. and Gabbard, G. (eds) (2000) *Psychotherapy for Personality Disorders*, Washington, DC: American Psychiatric Press.

Main, M. (1990) *A Typology of Human Attachment Organisation Assessed in Discourse, Drawings, and Interviews*, New York: Cambridge University Press.

Mullen, P. (2001) The prediction and management of violence (editorial), *Criminal Behaviour and Mental Health* 11, Special Book Reviews Supplement: S73–S76.

Rutter, M. and Quinton, D. (1984) Parental psychiatric disorder: effects on children, *Psychological Medicine* 14: 853–80.

Thorpe, M. (1997) The impact of psychoanalytic practice on the family justice system, in The Hon. Mr Justice Wall (ed.) *Rooted Sorrows: Psychoanalytic Perspectives on Child Protection, Assessment, Therapy and Treatment*, Bristol: Family Law/Jordan.

Winnicott, D. (1947) Hate in the countertransference, in *Through Paediatrics to Psycho-Analysis*, London: Hogarth (1975).

World Health Organization (1992) *The ICD-10 Classification of Medical and Behavioural Disorders: Clinical Descriptions and Diagnostic Guidelines*, Geneva: WHO.

Chapter 10

# Can violent parents be fit parents?

*Claire Sturge*

## INTRODUCTION

Recently, there has been a major shift in how the children in households where there is partner violence are viewed. This has moved from seeing the impact on children as only relevant when they were, literally, caught in the cross-fire and injured, through concerns about the effect of children witnessing violence, to a recognition of the adverse effects on children of simply being part of such households.

## THE NATURE OF DOMESTIC VIOLENCE

There is a variety of definitions and one of the difficulties in reviewing research in this area is that the term may not be defined at all or is defined differently in different studies. Some focus on the nature of the problem, others on the behaviours exhibited, while others are concerned with the context. Terms also vary according to the attitude of authors: for example, 'woman abuser' as opposed to 'wife batterer', or use of 'domestically violent' to include both genders.

According to Emery (1989), domestic violence is 'aversively stimulated aggression' and Voris (1991) defined it as 'a malevolent act by one family member against another with the intent of causing physical, sexual or psychological damage'. Increasingly, reference in the literature to domestic violence includes any violence within the home and can, for example, focus almost exclusively on physical abuse to the child. However, Hester and Pearson (1998) considered that domestic violence involves one or more of the following behaviours towards a partner:

- physical abuse – assaulting, hitting, punching;
- sexual abuse – e.g. rape/buggery;
- emotional abuse – e.g. withholding love;
- psychological abuse – e.g. threats to injure the woman or child;
- threats to kill;

- verbal abuse – e.g. denigration;
- financial control.

Throughout this chapter, I am using the term domestic violence to refer specifically to violence between partners and not to other forms. For the sake of simplicity, I refer to this violence as inter-partner violence and, when such situations involve children, to the male partner as the father, even though it could of course be a subsequent partner of the mother's, such as a step-father. It is the father or male in the relationship, as research outlined below indicates, who is most likely to be the instigator of actual violence, although this is not always the case.

## THE PREVALENCE AND COURSE OF DOMESTIC VIOLENCE IN HOUSEHOLDS CONTAINING CHILDREN

Most prevalence figures are unsatisfactory in that studies are not epidemiological investigations but depend on the reporting of violence – usually in terms of police involvement or the seeking of help through victim support agencies. When studies of victims use local communities as control groups, considerable abuse is usually also found in that control group.

Little is known about the course of domestic violence, since longitudinal studies have not been undertaken apart from some short-term follow-up of cases reaching court. While violence is known to be highest in adolescent partnerships and those involving young women under the age of 30, we do not know what happens in terms of their later relationships and later life. Marriage appears to be a 'safeguard', with rates of violence towards women in cohabiting relationships being three times higher (Zalar, 2000). The picture is further complicated by the increase in violence in the first weeks and months after couples separate.

In domestically violent families with children, at least 50 per cent of the children witness the violence (McCloskey and Walker, 2000). In addition to this, there is 'inferred witnessing' where the child can see the sequelae of the violence – black eyes, a limping mother, angry silences between the parents. The child usually has an awareness of the aggressive atmosphere or can overhear or identify events signalling violence, such as noises or being told to go to their room. Most professionals assume that all children, even the very small, have some awareness of things being very wrong in the home where there is domestic violence and some authors refer to the 'double whammy' of the child's exposure to both the domestic violence and physical abuse (Pagelow, 1990).

Virtually no studies with robust methodology are available of the natural course of domestic violence. It appears that it is the men rather than the women who carry the violence from one relationship to another (Pagelow, 1984; Andrews and Brown, 1988). Investigations of the course of violence within a relationship over time are not encouraging (O'Leary et al., 1994). The study by Jacobsen et al. (1996) of 45 batterers found that 38 per cent separated or divorced over the 2-year study period and, of those couples remaining together, approximately half showed no reduction in the level of violence. Even in those cases where the level of aggression did reduce, only 7 per cent of the batterers achieved abstinence from violence and all the husbands in this group continued to emotionally abuse the partner.

High conflict domestic situations pre-separation tend to persist for considerable periods post-separation (Johnson, 1994). Risks to the mother are also increased after separation, with an increased prevalence of further violence (Keilitz, 1994; Kyriacou *et al.*, 1999), homicide (Wilson and Daly, 1993) and stalking (Walker and Meloy, 1998).

However, the mysteries are as many as the available information. For example, is a violent man violent in all his relationships or does the choice of partner or gradual maturing affect this? How many women succeed in leaving violent partners and staying out of violent relationships? What factors are important in such outcomes? For children, how do exposure, separation, followed by contact or no contact, memories of abusive acts and associated factors, such as economic deprivation, interact in producing poor outcomes?

## Aetiology

There is no simple explanation for domestic violence and many factors are known to play a part or to be associated with it. Cultural factors are relevant, with there being a higher acceptance of male-to-female violence in less developed communities and, within the UK, attitudes have changed rapidly during the last century (Ross, 1996; Rumm *et al.*, 2000).

For men the experience of living as a child in a household in which they witnessed domestic violence raises the likelihood of them being violent to their partners, although genetics in relation to aggressive traits may also play a part, since domestically violent men may be aggressive or antisocial in other areas of life. In terms of the general functioning of such men, there seems to be a combination of feelings of inferiority combined with beliefs that their masculinity is predicated upon their ability to dominate and control. Research suggests that male batterers have poor self-concepts, verbal skill deficits as compared with their wives, problems with assertiveness, especially with their wives, and a need to feel powerful (Geffner and Rosenbaum, 1990; Blacklock, 2001). Many of these men also exhibit features of pathological jealousy. It is not surprising, therefore, that alcohol abuse (and, to a lesser extent, drug misuse) triggers an episode of violence in such men, although this is not a necessary prerequisite.

Specific triggers to violence are usually trivial, ranging from such things as the dinner being cold, the children's toys not being tidied up, anger over the mother taking some independent decisions, such as going out separately or spending money, to suspicions of infidelity. It is common for a violent man to keep tight control of his partner both in terms of her movements and contacts and her source of money. Some women are denied even their own door key to prevent them going out or having access to a telephone.

## The issue of women's role in domestic violence

The first question is to look at ways in which women precipitate or contribute to the continuation of violence by their partner. The second is whether women perpetrate as much of the violence as the men. The third is how to view this violence. These are all controversial areas, with gender issues that are politically sensitive.

Women subjected to domestic violence usually show victim behaviours and may have histories of victimization. They may contribute to the violence in some situations by provocative talk and challenges and their very subjugated demeanour and responses can act to perpetuate the violence. However, the little information that is available indicates that women are more likely than men to make future non-violent relationships (Pagelow, 1984; Andrews and Brown, 1988).

While female violence within a domestically violent situation is relatively common, it differs from that of men in a variety of ways. Principal amongst these are that violence by women is less frequent, is unlikely to result in injuries, and can most commonly be interpreted as active efforts by the woman to resist the oppressive coercion of her partner. This context of self-defence or retaliation is very different from the context of male violence, which is usually one of punishment or control. Men are more likely to be the first and last to use violence in a dispute. Studies based on selected samples, such as reported incidents of domestic violence, women in battered women's hostels, or psychiatric patients, show a huge preponderance of male-to-female violence, of the order of 10:1. However, with the advent of mandatory arrest for domestic violence in some states of America, there has been a large increase in the arrest of women. One study of women incarcerated as a result of domestic violence showed that their violence had mostly been self-protective but in a very small minority of such women there were violent traits and power motivations similar to that seen in men (Hamberger and Potente, 1994). It therefore appears that men are more violent, more likely to injure, more frequently violent and more likely to be motivated by wishes to endorse their dominance than women. Jealousy is also much more likely to be a feature of male violence.

The commonest experience for children would be witnessing the male partner as the main perpetrator of the violence and as a serious threat to their mother. They may see some retaliatory violence or self-protective violence from the mother. They may experience her as goading the man on into violence and the one to blame. Very few studies have addressed the question of the differential impact on the children where the mother is violent compared to when she is not. One such study in a reasonably large sample (Ross, 1996) showed that while a single incident of domestic violence by a husband or wife gave a probability of 5 per cent of subsequent physical abuse to a child, the increasingly close relationship between partner violence and physical child abuse applied much more to father- than mother-instigated violence.

Where both parents are violent to each other, the child often comes to see one as more culpable than the other. If it is the mother who appears to be the provocative or violent one in the relationship, the child may feel even more at risk and unprotected, out of fear of her violence. Gender of the child in relation to that of the violent person must be relevant, but there are no studies to help understand how this might act.

## Effect on the child

It has been increasingly recognized both that children are almost invariably involved, directly or indirectly, by violence within their homes and that such experiences have far-reaching effects. Exposure for the child can be life-long, with the first increase in inter-partner violence occurring during the woman's pregnancy and at any subsequent time of stress in the family. This may account for the increase of partner violence when children reach adolescence but, as violence is greater towards younger women (Rumm *et al.*, 2000), it is younger children who are most exposed and for the longest periods. Research (reviewed by Kolbo *et al.*, 1996) indicates that most, if not all, children are seriously affected by exposure to domestic violence, particularly where it is repeated and continues over a period of time (which is the usual pattern).

If being in a nearby room is included, then over 90 per cent of children are involved in domestically violent incidents. Results from the studies of Jaffe *et al.* (1986) and Sternberg *et al.* (1994) indicate that the negative sequelae are similar whether the child is directly involved, is a bystander or is simply part of the household. The impact on the child results from direct and indirect exposure to the violence and the undermining of family functioning and can be seen as mediated by direct and indirect mechanisms.

Direct mechanisms include:

* modelling of aggressiveness as acceptable behaviour and as a way to resolve conflict;
* familial conflict heightening the likelihood of the expression of genetic vulnerability to aggressive traits;
* exposure to negative conflict management and high levels of criticism, leading to poor regulation of emotions, high reactivity and behaviour problems;
* emotional and physical trauma leading to post-traumatic symptoms.

Indirect mechanisms include:

* distortion of the parent–child relationship, with failure to feel safe or protected and the possible development of insecure attachment;
* excessive disciplinary practices, actual physical abuse, or other forms of maltreatment.

The co-occurrence of physical child abuse with domestic violence is high, while the prevalence of direct sexual abuse is only slightly raised. The studies of Rumm *et al.* (2000) and Ross (1996) paint a very alarming picture, indicating a direct correlation between the amount of inter-parental violence and the likelihood of physical abuse of the child. Ross found a nearly 1:1 relationship of physical abuse with domestic violence where there had been 50 or more incidents of domestic violence.

Additionally, associated or incidental factors need to be taken into account when considering the impact on a child. These include: genetic factors and factors innate to the child, such as temperament; the resilience of the child; the functioning competence of one or both parents irrespective of the violence; the effects of conflict between the carers irrespective of actual violence; and socio-economic factors.

Children within a domestically violent situation are in an impossible situation in which their needs cannot be met. There is an atmosphere of unpredictability and fear and the children will be hypervigilant for any signs of tension, raised voices or, where alcohol plays a part, signs of inebriation. They will be sensitive to all changes in atmosphere and liable to observe the mother for signs of injury. They will know that they are expected to keep secret whatever goes on in the family and are therefore at risk should they choose to disclose. They will not be able to bring friends home or share information with them, making them feel increasingly different and isolated.

When arguments start, they will have learnt to get out of the firing line and many children retreat to another room, using such devices as turning up the volume on the television to block out sounds. If they have younger siblings, they will feel some responsibility for protecting them. They will constantly fear for their mother's safety, imagining she will be injured or even killed. They will be ashamed of their own powerlessness to control the situation and children often describe fantasies of heroic acts trying to protect their mothers, only to admit that they were too scared to do so, but that is what they would have liked to have done. Some children do try to intervene, especially in the early stages of a relationship becoming violent, but then feel compelled to give up, while retaining fantasies about being strong enough to protect their mother. They may have a system of checking by peeping into the room and, as soon as the fight subsides, waiting for signs that the two parents are all right or go to check that they are. They have no one to turn to, since their expected main protector, the mother, also appears to be a powerless victim. As a result, they may lose trust and respect, and instead identify with the aggressor, becoming violent themself.

The child in a domestically violent situation is particularly affected by the behaviours of the victim parent. The mother commonly has difficulties in coping in many areas of her life. She is less attentive to her parenting, which can become seriously neglectful. Small children will be particularly vulnerable to the consequences of neglect, including physical neglect and failure to supervise and protect, so they may be left alone or with unsuitable carers or allowed to wander unsupervised. The mother often experiences an overwhelming sense of helplessness and worthlessness, which leads to difficulties in making decisions and failure to protect the child from the many adverse experiences. If continually victimized, she loses her authority as a parent and the child may even be encouraged to join in her humiliation.

There may additionally be the consequences of over-punitiveness and hostility experienced by the child, as well as those of actual physical abuse. The young child may also be injured during the inter-partner violence. The work of Terr (1991) indicates that, for young children, particularly under the age of 3 years, it is even more psychologically traumatic to see their carer assaulted than to be assaulted themself. The outward signs of the distress to the child may be seen in concentration problems and school failure, aggressive behaviours, especially in boys, peer relationship difficulties, withdrawal and general unhappiness. Anxiety disorders may occur and, in the longer term, antisocial behaviours, depression and self-harm. There is a link with boys growing up to be violent within the relationships that they form and, to a lesser extent, girls finding themselves in violent relationships.

There is little research on children's resilience to domestic violence. Work on the effects on children of marital conflict indicates that these are a function of the meaning of the conflicts for the child and the family more than the frequency or even physical characteristics of the conflicts. In addition, the meaning of conflicts for the child will reflect their cognitive appraisal, emotional reactions and coping skills (Crockenberg and Forgays, 1996; Davies and Cummings, 1994). Common sense and some studies suggest that children fare better where a good relationship with the mother is maintained and some good parenting experiences are available (Osofsky and Fenichel, 1993/94). Some children do show remarkable resilience (Christensen, 1995), but why is far from clear. While most mothers report a recognition of how the violent situation undermines their ability to parent, a few report an increased closeness with their child or children and more committed parenting (Osofsky and Fenichel, 1993/4).

The outcome for children exposed to domestic violence appears to be very similar to that of physically abused children. Like them, there is the likelihood of repetitive behaviour, in which they either become the aggressor in their own adult lives, including aggression in intimate relationships and violent offending, or the victims of others' violence.

## WHEN TO INTERVENE ON BEHALF OF A CHILD IN A VIOLENT SITUATION

This question needs to be addressed whenever domestic violence comes to the attention of the authorities and the situation involves a child – directly or indirectly. The police are required to complete a Form 78 if they attend a 'domestic incident' and a child is in the household. This is forwarded to social services, who are required to make enquiries. The extent of these is very variable but good practice would require a Core Assessment. The decisions would then be based, like other decisions for social services departments, on the identified needs of the child.

Parenting and child protection issues need to be assessed and should pay particular attention to:

- the overall quality of the parenting;
- the extent of the child's exposure and their perceptions and reactions to the violence;
- the possibility of there being in parallel over-punitiveness, physical abuse and/or sexual abuse;
- the severity and significance of emotional abuse (which is likely always to be present);
- the child's overall situation, including performance at school and social opportunities.

If a threshold of significant concern is reached, then the family can be offered help and support. Where the likelihood of cessation of violence is low, the mother may need to be challenged about remaining in the situation with her child and supported in considering separation. Court intervention may be necessary at an early or later stage, particularly where there is no movement towards protecting the children. While this may seem punitive towards the mother (and indirectly the children), such action may empower the mother in making decisions for the welfare of her child, such as a decision to leave her partner.

## IMPLICATIONS FOR PARENTING ASSESSMENTS

Where violence is confirmed, the questions are around what future part that violent parent should play in their child's life. This may arise in relation to parental care itself or post-separation contact.

It could be argued that, if the violence was directed at the mother and not the child, this has no direct relevance to parenting and does not reflect on the father's affection for his children or his ability to provide for their needs. The counter-argument is that such violence is an abrogation of the most basic aspects of responsible parenting, since it can be seen as:

- attacking the child's main carer, whom the father should be expected to protect and support;
- undermining the child's basic stability, sense of security, need for predictability, and capacity to feel safe and to trust their carers;
- undermining of attachments by attacking the child's 'secure base';
- creating an atmosphere of fear where the child has nowhere to turn, as they cannot rely on the violent parent or the victim parent;
- producing an environment of isolation and secrecy where the child experiences a sense of shame in respect of those outside the family;
- providing a role model in which poor self-control, degradation and violence are the norm and moral values are distorted;

- distorting roles, since the child may try to act as the protective figure to the victim parent (or to siblings) or become a conspirator with the violent parent in degrading her;
- exposing the child to the risk of direct injury during the episodes of parental violence or physical abuse (which may also continue post-separation).

If there is evidence that the child has been exposed to these traumas, then it can be argued that the violent parent's behaviour has lost him his position as a responsible parent and that he should have no rights unless he can demonstrate how he can be a positive and constructive influence in the child's life in the future. When reviewing research on the ill-effects of domestic violence on children, Johnson (1994) concluded that there is 'a formidable link between domestic unfitness and parental unfitness' and suggested some parents should have their parental rights terminated.

## IMPLICATIONS FOR POST-SEPARATION CONTACT

There is a considerable literature on contact and residence disputes in domestically violent situations but relatively little methodical research. Divorces marked with ongoing disputes – in and outside court – carry a high level of complaints of domestic violence, with around 65 per cent reported in several studies (e.g. Depner *et al.*, 1992; Johnson and Campbell, 1988). The children involved in such disputes have a high level of adjustment problems compared with the normal population or children of other separating couples (Johnson, 1994). In Johnson's study, court-ordered joint custody and frequent visitation were associated with particularly poor outcomes (although the variable determining this is unclear) and particularly intensely conflicted parents remained highly conflicted – i.e. the situation did not improve over the years. The adjustment of the child's main carer was the best predictor of outcome for the child. Taken together, the evidence is that, following significant domestic violence, protracted legal disputes are associated with poor child outcomes, court-ordered arrangements often fail, and both the mother and child have a significant risk of suffering further violence. Therefore, the assumption that contact must be in the child's interests must be questioned.

In the comparative study of practice in England and Denmark (Hester and Radford, 1996), considerable differences were found, with the Danish approach recognizing that agreement between parents is not always possible or even desirable. Lack of agreement is seen as an indication that parents may be unable to share parenting and that sole parental authority may be the best outcome. In the English part of the study, 'coerced agreement' to contact arrangements on mothers was frequent but rarely worked satisfactorily and the majority of women suffered further violent abuse from ex-partners, always linked to contact.

The starting points for considering giving a violent parent an active role in the child's life post-parental separation are similar to those discussed by Lucey, Sturge,

Fellow-Smith and Reder (Chapter 15) as pertaining to all contact issues. They would be:

- the child wishing him to have such a role;
- evidence of attachment of that child to the parent or of a healthy relationship between the two;
- acknowledgement of the violence and its effects on the child and the other carer, including some wish to repair any damage;
- evidence that the violent parent is seeking help in understanding and changing that behaviour;
- demonstration of what the parent can offer the child by way of positive experiences and appropriate models of behaviour;
- demonstration that the violent parent can support the child's current living arrangements, especially taking the victim parent's perspective into account and the degree of threat to the new family's stability posed by the continuing involvement of the violent parent.

The child needs to be given some opportunity to understand the situation in which they find themself. Often, contact is reintroduced to a child who has witnessed the violence with no acknowledgement of how they may have perceived this. They are left wondering whether the father should be seen as a bad man; whether they are meant to emulate him or be critical of him; whether they are expected to behave as though nothing has happened; and uncertain what account should be taken of how the mother feels about this man and the child's contact with him. The child needs validating as a person in terms of the acknowledgement of their perspective in the situation and facilitation of their making sense of it. Not to do so is to risk further undermining the child and adding to their confusions and distorted experiences.

One study indicates that, when children have contact with a violent parent, hand-over times not only provide opportunities for continued violence to the mother (verbal or physical), which the children witness, but they also experience a high level of violence themselves (Hester and Radford, 1996).

Generally, a circumspect position is advised regarding post-separation contact (Sturge, 2000) and one that does not assume that contact would be in the best interests of the child.

## ASSESSMENT OF CHILDREN AND THEIR FAMILIES

The structure of an assessment will vary with its purpose and particularly whether it is to establish evidence of significant harm as part of Care Proceedings or to consider the question of contact. In both circumstances, it needs to include:

- an assessment of the child;
- an assessment of each of the child's carers;

- an assessment of the domestically violent couple's relationship;
- an assessment of the child's relationship with each caretaker;
- exploration of alternative arrangements for the child's care.

## The child

There needs to be a general assessment of the child and their mental state. This will inform the assessor as to how the child views the violent parent, and may provide details of what the child has been exposed to directly and indirectly and whether the child has been harmed in relation to his or her development. This would also include the question of whether the child is showing any post-traumatic symptoms. The assessment should also clarify the child's treatment needs, as well as the question of whether the child needs to be removed from the violent household, or, where there is already a separation, whether contact will promote or undermine their well-being.

## The child's carer/s

Those involved in any litigation around domestic violence must be individually interviewed. The adult who seeks to be the child's main carer needs to be assessed in terms of their overall functioning and ability to parent. This will include an assessment of the effects of any violence to which they have been victim and the effect of this on their functioning and parenting. A life history which focuses particularly on relationships and experiences with others as a child and adult will give some picture of the pattern of the person's relationships and its relevance to the type of partner they chose, issues of dependency and their ability to function as independent agents able to fully protect their child.

## The violent caretaker

An assessment from a forensic specialist can be very useful in teasing out processes that lead to violence. This is usually a complex picture involving such issues as the role models and relationships in the perpetrator's own childhood, security of male identity, need for control, anger control, attitudes to women generally, and the relationship with the child's mother (see Cordess, Chapter 9).

## The couple

The couple's relationship needs assessing, whether or not they are still together. Inevitably the dynamics within this relationship are relevant to the violence and to the couple's ability to give due attention to the needs of the children. Sometimes, their 'battle' can be so all-consuming to the participants that winning or surviving it is prioritized over all else. In a study of 51 post-separation situations where the parents had joint custody (Steinman *et al.*, 1985) it was the parents' showing respect and appreciation of the bond between the child and the other parent, objectivity, ability to empathize with the child and former partner and the establishment of new role boundaries that predicted successful outcomes for contact.

With couples who have separated and are in litigation over contact, the assessment needs to include:

- recognition that the most severe violence (including murders) is often seen post-separation and that the drive to seek contact with the child can be the drive to seek continuing contact with, and power over, the child's mother;
- consideration of whether the separation is likely to be sustained, since a pattern is often found where the couple has repeatedly separated, even with charges pressed or injunctions obtained, only to reverse all this when the partner swears to reform, or, through violent threats, persuades the victim to change course. However, often the victim herself appears to change her own mind and return to the perpetrator of her own volition, claiming to have a deep love for him;
- appraisal of whether the violence is denied or minimized by the man and whether it is minimized by the child's mother.

Clearly, both predicting future violence and predicting the future course of the relationship are highly relevant to the consideration of the child's needs and the planning (see Reder, Chapter 13).

## Quality of the child's relationship with each carer

If appropriate, the child needs to be observed with each of their carers and the quality of the relationship and the nature of the attachment assessed. This will be relevant to assessing the importance to the child of each caretaker and what contribution that person can make to the child's sense of self, identity and security.

Good quality of care from the child's custodial parent predicts good outcome for the child and it could be argued that such children do not need contact with the other parent to achieve their healthy development and good adjustment. Where the care extended by the custodial parent is more questionable, the value of contact with the other parent is more complex. Either it should be banned in order to give the fragile parent the best chance of achieving good enough care, or the child needs the balance of the other parent to maximize her or his chance of a healthy development. This will clearly depend on individual circumstances.

## CAN DOMESTIC VIOLENCE BE TREATED?

A problem in all studies in this area is deciding what the desired outcome is: the cessation of violence and the family remaining together; the victim succeeding in leaving the marital home; or the protection of children. The aim may vary with the circumstances of each case, while value judgements and political views will colour what is seen as a good outcome. The combined efforts of many agencies may be necessary, involving: the police; the judiciary; the local community (such as religious groups and housing); social, education and health services raising awareness; accessible legal and other advice; the provision of alternative accommodation for battered mothers and their children (such as shelters); the offering of support groups, counselling and treatment to both the mothers and the children; and the availability of specialist treatment centres for the violent partner's aggressiveness (and any other associated problems, such as alcohol abuse).

There are numerous papers describing different types of intervention in domestic violence, although relatively few focus on treatments for the perpetrator of the violence or for the couple. Tolman and Edelson (1995) reviewed studies of the treatment of batterers. None was a controlled study comparing outcomes of different sorts of treatments but modest change can be demonstrated in the short term with a variety of interventions. Some studies indicate that change in parenting is particularly difficult to effect while the violent situation continues (Eckenrode *et al.*, 2000).

In terms of eliminating the violence, the general wisdom seems to be that it is very difficult to eradicate within a particular relationship. Indeed the risks of escalating domestic violence and murder are highest for reunited couples (Kyriacou *et al.*, 1999). The most frequently advocated approach is that the couple should separate, with appropriate legal safeguards for the mother and children. The father should then be encouraged to seek treatment around his relationship difficulties and anger management. If he then succeeds in making a very different and healthier sort of relationship with a partner, there is some prospect of this being non-violent.

However, the enormous difficulties such men have in acknowledging any wrongdoing of any sort means that few seek help at any stage, except perhaps when coerced through court proceedings. Those that do often manage to curb the violence while the input and support is active but return to previous practices when it ceases. Furthermore, the very fact of the woman trying to preserve their relationship in these situations can be seen as a kind of condoning, which does not augur well for a change in the power structure between them. The woman may need considerable support in remaining firm in her decisions and in recovering from her experiences. Many describe rediscovering themselves and a rapid improvement in self-esteem when they successfully end such a relationship, having recognized the extreme disempowerment they underwent. But, similarly to the men, preventing involvement in future similar relationships requires a much more in-depth re-evaluation of themselves and the factors which lead to the forming of such relationships.

Where the couple propose to continue their relationship and seek appropriate help, there are then major issues about whether the child should remain while the couple try to resolve their issues. This requires some prediction of their ability to change and gauging whether the time it may take for significant progress fits with the child's timetable in terms of later rehabilitation. Children remaining in potentially violent households are likely to be under extreme pressures of secrecy and will be aware that any disclosure of violence to involved agencies may result in their removal and the loss of their family.

In order to recover following parental separation, the child needs to find a real sense of security. This means the mother being emotionally available and attentive and providing consistency and continuity. The mother, particularly initially, may not have the emotional resources to meet the child's needs, since it often takes a considerable period for her to regain her sense of worth as a person and as a parent. The child may also have become difficult to manage and, like most children after parental separation, is likely to have mixed feelings about the departure. Support for the mother during this difficult period, when she may still be in fear of her partner and have many uncertainties to resolve about her future, will be all-important in indirectly helping the child. The child may also need support, and at times therapeutic help, in coming to terms with the situation and in understanding the meaning of what has happened for them. Consideration of such interventions should only be considered once some form of stability has been achieved. Meanwhile, the child may benefit from a forum allowing the expression of some feelings, verbally or in a non-verbal form, perhaps with other children who share similar experiences.

The problem of the child's distorted understanding of roles, aggression and parenting is likely to take a long time to adjust and will depend largely on their subsequent experience of parenting and of alternative patterns of interacting. The perpetrator of the violence being able to convey to the child a sincere belief that violence is wrong and that he was wrong to have been violent is potentially an important part of this readjustment.

## CONCLUSIONS

In conclusion, I would argue the following principles.

1  Children should not be allowed to continue to live in situations of repeated violence between their carers.
2  Greater commitment to providing protection for victims of domestic violence is needed through both the courts and resources of a practical (such as refuges and housing) and emotional (in terms of support services) nature.
3  Greater attention should be given by the courts and welfare services to the children in such situations.
4  Statutory removal should be considered when a child is within a domestically violent situation and intervention results in no improvements in the child's situation.
5  When violent parents/partners separate and there are court proceedings to resolve battles about residence or contact, first a finding should be sought as to the presence and perpetration of such violence and, second, if a finding is made against one of the parents, there should be a rebuttable presumption against residence or contact for the violent parent.

6  Attitudes need to change in the common automatic perception that mothers fighting contact applications are in some way unreasonable and obstructive, rather than caring and protective.

7  Children's wishes and views in these situations must be given due weight and so must the fact that over-ruling these has particular implications for them and the way they feel valued.

8  Before granting a divorce the judge should seek to be made aware, in cases where there are children, of whether there is domestic violence and, if there is, to examine plans for the children. An alert list could be used for such a purpose.

9  Networks of services need to be developed, linked to the burgeoning of domestic violence services, which are easily accessible and specifically address the assessment of the children's mental health and the need for protection and treatment.

## References

Andrews, B. and Brown, G.W. (1988) Marital violence in the community: a biographical approach, *British Journal of Psychiatry* 153: 305–12.

Blacklock, N. (2001) Domestic violence: working with perpetrators, the community and its institutions, *Advances in Psychiatric Treatment* 7: 65–72.

Christensen, E. (1995) Families in distress: the development of children growing up with alcohol and violence, *Arctic Medical Research* 54: 53–9.

Crockenberg, S.B. and Forgays, D. (1996) The role of emotion in children's understanding and emotional reactions to marital conflict, *Merrill-Palmer Quarterly* 42: 22–47.

Davies, P.T. and Cummings, E.M. (1994) Marital conflict and child adjustment: an emotional security hypothesis, *Developmental Psychology* 31: 677–84.

Depner, C.E., Leino, E.V. and Chun, A. (1992) Interparental conflicts and child adjustment: a decade review and meta-analysis, *Family and Conciliation Courts' Review* 3: 323–41.

Eckenrode, J., Ganzel, B., Henderson, C.R., Smith, E., Olds, D.L., Powers J., Cole, R., Kitzman, H. and Sidora, K. (2000) Preventing child abuse and neglect with a program of nurse home visitation: the limiting effects of domestic violence, *Journal of the American Medical Association* 284: 1385–91.

Emery, R.E. (1989) Family violence, *American Psychologist* 44: 312–28.

Geffner, R. and Rosenbaum, A. (1990) Characteristics and treatment of batterers, *Behavioral Sciences and the Law* 8: 131–40.

Hamberger, L.K. and Potente, T. (1994) Counselling heterosexual women arrested for domestic violence: implications for theory and practice, *Violence and Victims* 9: 125–37.

Hester, M. and Pearson, C. (1998) *From Periphery to Centre: Domestic Violence in Work with Abused Children*, Bristol: The Policy Press.

Hester, M. and Radford, L. (1996) *Domestic Violence and Child Contact Arrangements in England and Denmark*, Bristol: The Policy Press.

Jacobsen, N.S., Gottman, J.M., Gortner, E., Berns, S. and Shortt, J.W. (1996) Psychological factors in the longitudinal course of battering: when do the couples split up? When does the abuse decrease? *Violence and Victims* 11: 371–92.

Jaffe, P., Wolfe, D., Wilson, S. and Zak, L. (1986) Similarities in behavioural and social maladjustment among child victims and witnesses to domestic violence, *American Journal of Orthopsychiatry* 56: 142–6.

Johnson, J.R. (1994) High-conflict divorce: the future of children, *Children and Divorce* 4: 165–82.

Johnson, J.R. and Campbell, L.E.G. (1988) *Impasses of Divorce: The Dynamics and Resolution of Family Conflict*, New York: The Free Press.

Keilitz, S.L. (1994) Civil Protection Orders: a viable justice system tool for deterring domestic violence, *Violence and Victims* 9: 79–84.

Kolbo, J.R., Blakely, E.H. and Engelman, D. (1996) Children who witness domestic violence: a review of empirical literature, *Journal of Interpersonal Violence* 11: 281–93.

Kyriacou, D.N., Anglin, D., Taliaferro, E., Stone, S., Tubb, T., Linden, J.A., Muelleman, R., Barton, E. and Kraus, J.F. (1999) Risk factors for injury to women from domestic violence, *New England Journal of Medicine* 341: 1892–8.

McCloskey, L.A. and Walker, M. (2000) Post-traumatic stress in children exposed to family violence and single event trauma, *Journal of the American Academy of Child and Adolescent Psychiatry* 39: 108–15.

O'Leary, K.D., Malone, J. and Tyree, A. (1994) Physical aggression in early marriage: prerelationship and relationship effects, *Journal of Consulting and Clinical Psychology* 62: 594–602.

Osofsky, J.D. and Fenichel, E. (eds) (1993/94) Caring for infants and toddlers in violent environments: hurt, healing and hope, *Zero to Three* 14: 1–48.

Pagelow, M.D. (1984) *Family Violence*, New York: Praeger.

Pagelow, M. (1990) Effects of domestic violence on children and their consequences for custody and visitation agreements, *Mediation Quarterly* 7: 347–63.

Ross, S.M. (1996) Risk of physical abuse to children of spouse abusing parents, *Child Abuse and Neglect* 20: 589–98.

Rumm, P.D., Cummings, P., Krauss, M.R., Bell, M.A. and Rivara, F.P. (2000) Identified spouse abuse as a risk factor for child abuse, *Child Abuse and Neglect* 24: 1375–81.

Steinman, S.B., Zemmmelman, S.E. and Knoblauch, T.M. (1985) A study of parents who sought joint custody following divorce: who reaches agreement and sustains joint custody and who returns to court, *Journal of the American Academy of Child Psychiatry* 24: 554–62.

Sternberg, K.J., Lamb, M.E. and Greenbaum, C. (1994) The effects of domestic violence on children's perception of their perpetrating and non-perpetrating parents, *International Journal of Behavioral Development* 17: 779–95.

Sturge, C. (2000) Contact and domestic violence – the experts' court report, *Family Law* 30: 615–29 (in consultation with Dr D. Glaser).

Terr, L (1991) Childhood traumas: an outline and overview, *American Journal of Psychiatry* 148: 10–20.

Tolman, T.R. and Edelson, J.L. (1995) Intervention for men who batter: a review of research, in S.R. Smith and M.A. Straus (eds) *Understanding Partner Violence: Prevalence, Consequences and Solutions*, Minneapolis, MN: National Council on Family Relations.

Voris, M.J. (1991) Civil Orders of Protection: do they protect children, the tag-along victims of domestic violence? *Ohio N.U.L. Review* 17: 599–600.

Walker, L.E. and Meloy, J.R. (1998) Stalking and domestic violence: the psychology of stalking, in J. Meloy (ed.) *Clinical and Forensic Perspectives*, San Diego: Academic Press.

Wilson, M. and Daly, M. (1993) Spousal homicide risk and estrangement, *Violence and Victims* 8: 3–16.

Zalar, R.W. (2000) Domestic violence, *New England Journal of Medicine* 342: 1450–52.

# Chapter 11

# How do mental health problems affect parenting?

*Sylvia Duncan and Peter Reder*

The nature of psychiatric disorder and its impact on parental and family functioning are complex areas for non-mental health practitioners, who may have particular difficulty defining their concerns about a child's welfare. Often, child care professionals have been worried over a period of time but, because the parent's functioning varies, they remain unsure whether there is substantive evidence of significant harm. Their continuing uncertainty means that the threshold for taking child protective measures may not be reached until late in the day. Indeed, mental health professionals can themselves have conflicting ways of understanding the issues involved and this widened professional network increases the potential for differences of opinion or miscommunications. Sometimes, the parent will be known to adult psychiatric services but, in other instances, their mental state has never been examined. Concern about the parent's mental health can become such a focus of attention that it dominates all other issues. A feature of a significant number of such cases is that the parent expresses genuine concern for the welfare of their child: the problem is that they find themself unable to act in ways that consistently satisfy the child's needs.

A number of other dilemmas may arise that will need to be addressed and resolved. The commonest predicament is that the parent's disorder has an episodic course and they fluctuate between good-enough and poor parenting. For quite long periods of time, they are symptom free and provide adequate care but then their mental state deteriorates and they may require enforced admission to hospital. The child's bond with the parent and sense of security is disrupted, both practically and emotionally, sometimes in extremely traumatic circumstances. The question is whether the periods of good parenting can compensate for the episodes of adverse care and so help the child to tolerate them and make progress in all aspects of their development.

Deterioration in the parent's mental state could be linked to their non-compliance with treatment, perhaps because they dislike the neurological or sedating side-effects of medication. Alternatively, they may refuse treatment altogether – whether it be medication or psychotherapy – or oscillate between acceptance and non-cooperation. The effect is that their capacity to provide consistent care for their child can not be ensured over the long term and the dilemma is how to predict the likelihood of them providing islands of satisfactory care and whether, overall, that will satisfy the child's needs.

Another common dilemma is that a psychiatric disorder cannot be diagnosed, despite apparently irrational behaviour from the parent and clear concerns for the child. This may be because the parent consistently refuses to attend for assessment, even if it has been mandated by the court. Alternatively, they cooperate with the assessment process but the mental health team finds insufficient evidence of a formal psychiatric disorder. This problem was highlighted in our recent review of fatal child abuse cases (Reder and Duncan, 1999), where there had been a number of examples of a parent demonstrating apparently delusional thinking or irrational behaviour but a psychiatrist concluded that they did not show evidence of a formal psychiatric disorder on the day of the assessment. All members of the professional network then agreed that no intervention was therefore possible and so the child remained living with the parent who later killed them. We called this process 'assessment paralysis' because no one had been able to assert that the parent's behaviour had been so bizarre or so dangerous that, no matter what label was put to it, the child needed protection from it.

One unfortunate problem occurs when an adult psychiatrist who is invited to contribute to the parenting assessment suggests that, because the prognosis for the adult's disorder is good, there is no reason why they should not care for their child. The opinion suggests that care of a child depends solely on whether the parent does, or does not, have a current psychiatric illness, instead of recognizing that this is only one element in a much larger picture of the ongoing parent–child relationship. It also erroneously implies that care of a child can be understood simply from the parent's perspective, without consideration of the child's perspective.

## GUIDING PRINCIPLES

Assessing the welfare of a child living with a parent who is believed to be suffering from mental health problems can therefore pose special difficulties for child protection networks and for courts. We believe that they can be addressed by recognizing the following guiding principles:

- children are affected emotionally by parental mental health problems;
- some parents with mental health problems neglect or otherwise maltreat their children;
- risk of harm to the child is primarily a function of the parent's behaviour, not their diagnosis;
- substance misuse is the most concerning parental mental health problem;
- the parent–child relationship must be understood from the child's perspective;
- the optimal approach is a coordinated assessment between a child-focused expert and an adult-focused expert;

- psychological conflicts underlying any psychiatric disorder also need to be assessed;
- valid opinions can be offered even when the ideal assessment is not possible.

In discussing each of these premises, we have attempted to overcome any confusion about parameters of psychiatric disorder or diagnostic categories by referring as much as possible to parental 'mental health problems'. Recent literature reviews in many of these areas can be found in Cleaver *et al.* (1999), Jenuwine and Cohler (1999) and Reder *et al.* (2000) and we shall support our arguments with representative citations from the literature. Previous discussions about assessing parenting by adults with mental health problems can also be found in Oates (1984), Göpfert *et al.* (1996), Jacobsen *et al.* (1997) and Henry and Kumar (1999), while Swadi (1994) and Drummond and Fitzpatrick (2000) focused on the assessment of substance misusing parents.

## Children are affected emotionally by their parent's mental health problems

The impact of parental mental health problems on children is now well documented (e.g. Rutter and Quinton, 1984; Cassell and Coleman, 1995; Falkov, 1998; Cleaver *et al.*, 1999; Duncan and Reder, 2000). Children are affected by: the primary symptoms of their parent's disorder – such as irritability, aggressiveness, withdrawal, or bizarre ideas and actions; by its secondary features – such as inability to plan ahead or to follow through with tasks; and by associated psychosocial consequences – such as marital discord and deterioration in living standards and lifestyle.

From a four-year follow-up study of children of psychiatric patients, Rutter and Quinton (1984) concluded that one third showed no emotional or behavioural disturbance, one third showed transient problems and one third exhibited persistent disorders. More recent studies found psychiatric disorder in more than two-thirds of the patients' children (Singer *et al.*, 2000; Falkov, personal communication). The whole range of childhood disorders have been found, including psychosomatic complaints, anxiety, cognitive problems, aggressive or antisocial behaviour, low self-esteem, depression, school non-attendance and poor peer relationships (Pound, 1996).

However, capacity to identify a diagnosable psychiatric disorder in the children is a severe test of whether they are affected emotionally (Angold *et al.*, 1999) and the 1989 Children Act's notion of 'significant harm' is more useful and relevant (see Duncan and Baker, Chapter 5). Clinical experience (e.g. Fredman and Fuggle, 2000), as well as qualitative research (e.g. Singer *et al.*, 2000), suggests that, without appropriate intervention, children's emotional development may be significantly harmed by the primary and secondary symptoms of their parent's disorder and by their own confusion and anxiety about it.

Clearly, the nature and severity of the parent's disturbed behaviour are important factors determining the effect on a child in the family. The child's vulnerability will also depend on their age and whether the parent's breakdown coincides with sensitive periods in their own development. Resilience is also afforded by the support of and sensitivity to the child's dilemmas shown by other adults, both within the family and among the professional network, and by experiences of success in other areas of life, such as at school (Rutter, 1985).

## Parents with mental health problems may maltreat their children

The commonest effect on children living with a parent with a mental health problem is to their emotional development and assessors must establish whether psychological effects have become emotionally detrimental. However, an additional link between parental disorder and child abuse and neglect is increasingly reported (Falkov, 1997; Reder and Duncan, 1999). For example, Glaser and Prior (1997) reviewed the cases of all children whose names were on the Child Protection Registers of four English local authorities. Parental mental illness, including suicidal attempts, anorexia nervosa, depressive psychosis and schizophrenia, was present in 31 per cent of cases and substance misuse in 26 per cent. Cleaver *et al.* (1999) juxtaposed reports of children's contact with protective agencies to demonstrate that the association between parental mental health problems and child maltreatment concerns rose progressively with the level of enquiry. The prevalence of identified mental illness increased at each stage, from referral, to first interview, on to being the subject of a child protection conference, to being looked after by the local authority or to suffering severe maltreatment. The same incremental association appeared with parental substance misuse.

An association is also recognized between fatal child abuse and parental mental health problems, especially substance misuse (e.g. Alfaro, 1988; Falkov, 1996; Wilczynski, 1997; Reder and Duncan, 1999). The New South Wales Child Death Review Team (2000) compared those deaths in which there was a history of parental substance misuse with all the others and found that the substance misuse sub-group contained more than eleven times the number of suspicious or confirmed non-accidental injury deaths.

## Harm to a child arises from their parent's behaviour

Whether we are focusing on adverse effects to the child's emotional well-being or on risks to their physical safety, it is important to recognize that it is the parent's *behaviour* that impacts on the child. For instance, in Rutter and Quinton's (1984) study, the adverse effects on the children were independent of parental diagnosis and it was family discord and hostility that were the principal mediating variables between parental problems and children's difficulties. In other words, the children were primarily affected by their parents' general functioning and behaviour. Other studies have also shown that parental diagnosis is not the determining factor in the outcome for the child and that what does matter is the quality of the parenting they receive (Goodman and Brumley, 1990), the severity/chronicity of the adult's disorder, whatever its nature, and lower socio-economic status (Sameroff *et al.*, 1982).

Schutz *et al.* (1989), Herman (1990) and Budd and Holdsworth (1996) have commented that the focus of parenting assessments when concerns are raised about the parent's mental health should not be on the psychiatric diagnosis as such but on the effect of any psychiatric impairment on the parent–child relationship and the child's welfare. Our solution to the 'assessment paralysis' dilemma discussed earlier is that two different issues must be held in mind, one being the risk to the child and the other being the nature of the parent's disorder. The risk to the child can be appraised by identifying worrying aspects of their parent's behaviour and considering its impact on the child in the past and its likely effect in the future.

In Table 11.1, we have summarized the commonest behavioural manifestations of adult mental health problems and how they are likely to impact on a child. For example, parental withdrawal into self-preoccupation, such as during a depressive or psychotic episode, means that they are available neither emotionally nor practically and this is likely to leave their child anxious or miserable, liable to be neglected or exposed to physical danger, or to develop behaviour problems. The child might resort to self-reliance and pseudo-maturity as protection against their

*Table 11.1* Potential impact on a child of behaviours associated with parental mental health problems

| Parental behaviour | Potential impact on child (in addition to attachment problems) |
| --- | --- |
| Self-preoccupation | Neglected |
| Emotional unavailability | Depressed, anxious, neglected |
| Practical unavailability | Out of control, self-reliant, neglected, exposed to danger |
| Frequent separations | Anxious, perplexed, angry, neglected |
| Threats of abandonment | Anxious, inhibited, self-blame |
| Unpredictable/chaotic planning | Anxious, inhibited, neglected |
| Irritability/overreactions | Inhibited, physically abused |
| Distorted expressions of reality | Anxious, confused |
| Strange behaviour/beliefs | Embroiled in behaviour, shame, perplexed, physically abused |
| Dependency | Caretaker role |
| Pessimism/blames self | Caretaker role, depressed, low self-esteem |
| Blames child | Emotionally abused, physically abused, guilt |
| Unsuccessful limit-setting | Behaviour problem |
| Mental discord and hostility | Behaviour problem, anxiety, self-blame |
| Social deterioration | Neglect, shame |

*Source*: Duncan and Reder (2000).

neglect and isolation. Repeated hospitalizations of the parent, perhaps precipitated by a dramatic crisis or attempted suicide, tend to leave the child anxious and perplexed, as well as prone to neglect if adequate alternative caretakers are not found. However, some children are also exposed to repeated threats of abandonment by irritated parents, through such emotionally damaging comments as: 'You're driving me mad'; 'You'll be the death of me'; or 'I've had enough of you and if you don't do that I'll put you into care.'

A common feature of these parental problems is unpredictable behaviour and chaotic planning, which may endanger young children who need to be met from school or to have food bought for them, as well as interfering with the attachment process. The child's reaction can be insecurity, anxiety or confusion or, in older children, compulsive self-reliance. Inhibition and timidity are a frequent response of children whose parent is irritable or unpredictable, because they fear provoking another eruption of frightening behaviour. Parental psychotic ideation, with distorted expressions of reality and strange beliefs, is usually frightening and confusing to children or else they may feel ashamed of their family. However, some children who are exposed to psychotic beliefs find it increasingly difficult to distinguish reality from the distortions and come to share their parent's ideas.

Physical abuse is a possible consequence of the parental irritability or overreaction to stress that accompanies anxiety and depression; it can also result from a parent's distorted beliefs or aggressive behaviour during psychotic episodes. Unusual parental preoccupations as part of obsessive conditions or phobias may also lead to physical abuse of the children. It is the disinhibition and boundary blurring of substance misuse that increases the risk of child sexual abuse.

The important secondary effects of parental disturbance include unsuccessful limit-setting, marital discord and deterioration in social circumstances, which are liable to lead to behaviour problems, anxiety and shame, together with neglect of the child's emotional needs.

## Parental substance misuse is a particularly concerning problem

Research literature confirms clinical experience that substance misuse is the most worrying of parental mental health problems and it has been particularly identified as a risk factor for child abuse. The most recent reviews of cases brought before the Boston Juvenile Court on Care and Protection petitions (Bishop *et al.*, 2000) found a formal diagnosis of substance misuse in at least one parent in 65 per cent of cases (71 per cent if allegations were included). Araji and Finkelhor (1986) concluded that alcohol misuse is associated with child sexual abuse in up to 50 per cent of cases. Substance misuse is therefore included on many research-based high-risk checklists, such as that proposed by Browne and Saqi (1988).

Whatever the index of concern, when compared with controls or other abusing families, the worst prognosis for a child is when their parent misuses drugs or alcohol. Indices studied have included:

- rates of reported child abuse (Kelley, 1992; Curtis and McCullough, 1993; Wasserman and Leventhal, 1993; Kelleher *et al.*, 1994; Jaudes *et al.*, 1995; Forrester, 2000);
- reports of serious child maltreatment brought to court (Famularo, Stone *et al.*, 1986; Famularo *et al.*, 1992; Murphy *et al.*, 1991; Forrester, 2000);
- rates of re-abuse (Murphy *et al.*, 1991; Wolock and Magura, 1996);
- links with fatal child abuse (Wilczynski, 1997; Reder and Duncan, 1999; New South Wales Child Death Review Team, 2000);
- links with unexplained infant deaths (Davidson Ward *et al.*, 1990; Durand *et al.*, 1990; New South Wales Child Death Review Team, 2000);
- statutory decisions to separate a child from their parent (Famularo, Barnum and Stone, 1986; Kelley, 1992; Sagatun-Edwards *et al.*, 1995);
- children's adverse development if returned to their parent/s (Ornoy *et al.*, 1996);
- non-compliance with court-ordered interventions (Famularo *et al.*, 1989; Murphy *et al.*, 1991);
- children permanently removed from their parent/s by a court (Olofsson *et al.*, 1983; Regan *et al.*, 1987; Murphy *et al.*, 1991; Sagatun-Edwards *et al.*, 1995).

Black and Mayer (1980) and Feig (1998) summarized the spectrum of parenting problems to which children of substance misusing parents may be exposed. The households tend to be chaotic and the lifestyle highly unstructured, so that rules are applied inconsistently and the level of supervision is poor. A parent may react to their child's behaviour in one way when sober and in another when intoxicated. The children therefore tend not to develop a sense of cause and effect and may fail to establish appropriate internal control of their behaviour. The substance abuser spends increasing amounts of time and energy on activities related to their addiction, especially acquiring the drugs and recovering from their after-effects. As a result, children are neglected or expected to assume a parentified role.

Swadi (1994) emphasized how the quality of child care by substance misusing parents crucially depends on their lifestyle and he grouped relevant factors for assessment under the following themes:

- *home environment* (e.g. whether the bills are paid, geographical stability, whether the accommodation is used by other substance misusers and/or for criminal activities);
- *provision of basic necessities* (e.g. food and clothing, meeting emotional needs, supervision, school attendance);
- *pattern of parental substance misuse* (e.g. type, frequency, chronicity, effect on level of consciousness, whether they are responsible for the child when under the influence, disposal of needles, whether the child witnesses drug use, attempts at treatment);
- *effect on parental mental state* (e.g. cognitive state, judgement);

- *procurement of the substances* (e.g. whether the child is left alone meanwhile, whether the child is exposed to violence or danger from suppliers);
- *family's social network* (e.g. whether acquaintances are exclusively substance misusers, extended family support);
- *parental attitude to their substance misuse* (e.g. responsibility, denial, insight, recognition of effect on their child, motivation to change);
- *child's perceptions* (e.g. whether the child feels safe and protected, whether the quality of their care fluctuates in relation to the parental misuse, their attitude to the parent's substance use, whether they feel responsible for the parent).

Clinical experience suggests that the period after a parent has successfully weaned themselves off drugs or alcohol can pose a particular risk to the child for a number of reasons. The parent has to attempt to separate themselves from fellow substance misusers who had previously been the focus of their daily world and they may not have a supportive network available. They no longer have the anxiety-reducing effects of substances to modify the impact of everyday tensions or of their own inner conflicts and unhappiness.

It is generally agreed that the lifestyle associated with misuse of drugs is more disruptive than that shown by alcohol abusers, with greater likelihood of poverty, personal disorganization and continuous preoccupation with obtaining the drugs (Hogan, 1998; Drummond and Fitzpatrick, 2000), all to the detriment of child care.

## The parent–child relationship must be understood from the child's perspective

Parenting is a role that must fulfil the child's emotional and physical needs and therefore the relationship should be understood from the child's perspective. While it is often said that parents with mental health problems can provide good-enough care and demonstrate positive parenting skills, especially between episodes of disorder, we believe that this primarily describes the parenting relationship from the position of the adult. When considered from the child's perspective, the fluctuations from 'good' to 'bad', uncertainties about whether the disturbed times will recur and their actual experiences during those episodes can have major emotional consequences.

When it comes to issues of parenting, the needs of the child must take primacy over the needs of the parent and the principal focus must remain how the child has experienced, and is likely to experience, their parent's behaviour. Therefore, the prognosis of the parent's disorder is only one element of a much larger picture and should not be offered as the sole indicator that the parent can resume care of their child.

## Coordinated assessments are required

In order for the relevance of the parent's mental health problems to contribute appropriately to the larger picture, parallel assessments will be necessary, one from the child's perspective and the other from the parent's. These then need to be co-ordinated to provide a coherent opinion about parenting. The effects of the parent's mental health problems can be addressed through an analysis of their disturbed behaviour, including its severity, duration and frequency. Its impact on the child can then be considered, using information gathered from the child directly and from those who have observed the child's development and functioning, both in everyday circumstances and in formal assessment. The adult-focused assessment can proffer an opinion about the nature, origins and likely repetition of the parent's problems and, clearly, the diagnosis and treatment potential will form *elements* of that prediction. Nevertheless, the absence of a formal psychiatric diagnosis to explain the parent's functioning should not prevent the child-focused assessor describing the parent's behaviour and its past, present and likely future effects on the child.

Drummond and Fitzpatrick (2000) have described the importance of collab-orative assessments between the adult and child specialists when a parent misuses substances, and their comments apply equally to other mental health problems. Their approach is to clarify the different areas which each professional will address, followed by separate assessments. The child specialist considers whether the child has suffered, or is likely to suffer, significant harm as a result of the parenting they have received. The adult specialist assesses the parent's disorder, treatment possibilities and the longer-term prognosis. If providing treatment, they will also review what changes have occurred.

> However, neither of these separate assessments can in itself provide the overall picture and recommendations to the court must arise out of an on-going con-versation between the specialists that bridges their different perspectives. This collaboration should allow them to draw inferences that highlight the adult's behaviour as a parent, the child's experiences of being parented in that way, and the likelihood of the parent's behaviour changing. (Drummond and Fitzpatrick, 2000: p. 142)

This notion of collaborative conversations adds to the areas of exploration recommended by Oates (1984), Göpfert *et al.* (1996) and Jacobsen *et al.* (1997) by enabling each issue to be considered both from the perspective of how it affects the prognosis for the adult and how it impacts on, and is experienced by, the child. We have pooled the areas that these authors considered relevant:

- What is the level of the parent's disturbance, especially impulse control?
- Does the parent present early in any acute phase?
- Has there been appropriate help-seeking behaviour?

- What is their level of compliance with medication?
- Has the parent a capacity to form trusting relationships and use help?
- Is there insight into both the parenting problems and the psychiatric symptoms?
- What is the other parent's (if relevant) attitude to the illness, relationship with the child and commitment to the family?
- What family supports are available at times of crisis?
- What is the quality of functioning of the parent during remission?
- What are the duration of remissions and frequency of relapses?
- Is the child directly involved in behaviours associated with the illness?
- Does the parent acknowledge any risks to the child?
- Has the parent been able to taken steps to reduce the adverse effects of their disorder on the child?
- If the child has been injured by the parents, what stress factors were present at the time?
- Is the parent capable of reading the child's cues or moods accurately?
- Is the parent able to function as a secure base for the child?

These general areas of exploration can be complemented by reference to the more specific parental behaviours and their consequences for the child that we have linked together in Table 11.1.

## Underlying conflicts should also be assessed

In many ways, the core approach to these parenting assessments is no different from that used with other families. For instance, the same questions are needed about the physical and emotional care of the child, the relationship between the parent and child and the child's emotional development, as we have discussed in Chapter 1. Similarly, it is essential to attempt to understand any psychological or interpersonal conflicts of the parent, their historical origins and their relevance for the parent–child relationship. In addition, many mental health problems have a conflictual component or are precipitated by a psychological crisis, and a history of previous emotional trauma may help explain an individual's current difficulties. This understanding has a double relevance, since parenting breakdown also tends to have its origins in adverse childhood experiences (see Reder and Duncan, Chapter 12) and sometimes a common genesis becomes apparent for both the child care and the mental health problems.

There is now impressive evidence that many psychiatric patients have histories of emotional or sexual abuse in childhood (Reder and Duncan, 2000). While we are not suggesting that such experiences explain all psychiatric illness, nor do we ignore the relevance of genetic and biological factors, we believe that the influence of psychological conflicts must be considered when trying to understand the origin or onset of many disorders. Common pathways might then become apparent to both the mental health and the child care difficulties, with intermediary factors being disorders of attachment, low self-esteem and anxiety (e.g. Rogosch *et al.*, 1992). Perhaps the most obvious link is with substance misuse, where the low frustration tolerance, impulsivity, self-centredness, emotional isolation and feelings of inadequacy commonly shown by drug or alcohol dependants (Black and Mayer, 1980; Drummond and Fitzpatrick, 2000) can also explain their problems functioning as a parent. This in turn will have relevance for planning both the therapeutic interventions and the child protection strategies. Treatment is more likely to be successful in the long term if it goes beyond the detoxification or drying-out phase and addresses the adult's underlying psychological problems, while child care and protection are best improved when the underlying psychological conflicts are resolved.

Therefore, even if the parent shows clear evidence of a formal psychiatric disorder, the assessment should not stop with the diagnosis, treatment recommendation and prognosis. An appraisal of psychological conflicts underlying or accompanying their mental health problems will also be relevant to their capacity to parent.

## Valid opinions may be possible in the absence of a psychiatric diagnosis

Occasionally, a psychiatric examination cannot be undertaken because the parent refuses to cooperate and fails to attend all the arranged assessment interviews. Valid opinions about parenting can still be reached in these circumstances, although there is a spectrum of ways in which this can be achieved. Some practitioners are prepared to offer 'paper' assessments, in which they review the background documents and offer a view based on the available information. Other experts believe that it is only appropriate to offer an opinion if they have directly assessed the child and they may instead recommend a Child Assessment Order so that this becomes possible. A number of experts take the middle course and seek additional information and observations from all relevant professionals who have had direct contact with the family, such as a school teacher, health visitor, social worker, general practitioner and/or community psychiatric nurse. As a variation, they may instead offer consultation to the allocated social work team and help them collate together the information already available and also identify the additional facts and observations they will need to seek from other professionals.

However, the same principles apply whatever approach is used, in that descriptions of the parent's behaviour and the contexts in which it occurred, together with evidence of its impact on the child (or hypothesis about its likely impact), can form the basis of the opinion. These might include descriptions of the parent shouting incoherently, hoarding rubbish, living a reclusive existence, demonstrating extreme suspiciousness, or erupting into apparently irrational anger. The reports of other professionals are also likely to provide information about the child's development and emotional status, such as at school, their visible reaction to their parent's behaviour, their general demeanour, and so on. Clearly, it could be argued that psychiatric disorder is only one inference to be drawn from these parental behaviours and that they may just as easily be explained as a variant of normality. However, their significance in these circumstances is not to focus on whether they imply psychiatric disorder or not, but how they impact on the child and have led, or might lead, to significant harm. The report to the court can detail the essential needs of children (see Table 1.4, p. 18) and discuss which of these appear to have been fulfilled or compromised by the parent, together with an account of the likely impact on the child of experiencing their parent's concerning behaviour.

## CONCLUSIONS

In all child care assessments, no one single factor points towards adequacy of parenting and all the different elements need to be weighed against each other. However, a core theme that underpins assessments when a parent may have a mental health problem – which is also central to other instances of parenting breakdown – is that harm to children is a function of their parent's behaviour. The impact on the child can therefore be addressed by identifying the different problematic parental behaviours and how the child has experienced, or is likely to experience, them.

In some families, the parent's behaviour is so extreme, or the danger they pose so evident, that few dilemmas arise. It is commonly acknowledged that the greatest risk is to a child who has become incorporated into their parent's psychotic delusions or hallucinations (Husain and Daniel, 1984; Cassell and Coleman, 1995; Reder and Duncan, 1999). This will become apparent in what the parent says, does or threatens to do, such as talking to the child as though they are a dead relative, or accusing the child of hating them. A severely depressed parent may also talk about their child as though they were an extension of themselves, posing the risk of an altruistic murder of the child as well as suicide by the adult. Some older children have been so exposed to irrational ideas of their parent that they come to share their beliefs and also shun opportunities to test reality through contact with others. Parents who show severe ritualistic behaviour may involve their children in the rituals, as described by Fellow-Smith (2000). Other presentations of concern are the parent whose disorder has become chronic, with unrelenting deterioration in their motivation, self-preoccupation or social functioning, so that their child's practical and emotional needs are persistently neglected.

More complex dilemmas can be resolved by applying the same core principle. The concern might be that the parent refuses treatment, or that they have been able to provide islands of good-enough child care. Within the professional network, the key professionals may have no knowledge of psychiatry, or an adult psychiatrist may offer advice about parenting based solely on their assessment of the parent's current mental state. In all of these circumstances, the first step towards identifying any immediate or long-term risk of significant harm is by describing the parent's behaviour and the child's response to it.

Perhaps the most difficult issue to weigh up is when a child experiences oscillations between 'good' and 'bad' times, with episodes of apparently satisfactory parental care, followed by sudden or gradual deterioration, loss of their parent to hospital and then a temporary resumption of the 'good' times. A child may demonstrate a protective or loyal tie to their parent, despite the many previous disruptions to family life. In some instances, a child's age, resilience and support from the other parent indicates that their development will not be significantly compromised by the episodes of disturbed parental behaviour, even though they inevitably suffer emotionally. With other families, it becomes evident that the 'good' times are not really so, since the child is primarily struggling with uncertainty and a fear that the 'good' times will eventually end, perhaps with a dramatic and frightening detention of their parent in hospital. Detailed accounts of the parent's behaviour during the periods of remission may also reveal that they are unable to focus adequately on the child's needs or empathize satisfactorily with their experiences. The child's loyalty then becomes understandable as a defensive manoeuvre and an attempt to retain some sense of stability in their increasingly chaotic world.

Finally, some dilemmas associated with these cases are not professional or psychological, but ethical. The first author attended a Child Protection Conference about the child of a parent who refused to take her anti-psychotic medication. The chair of the Conference referred to the mother's refusal as 'wilful neglect of the child's needs' and indicated that her compliance with treatment *for herself* would be used as a measure of significant harm to the child. In other words, she would be compelled to accept psychiatric treatment if she wanted to retain care of her child. While this would be consistent with the principle that the child's needs are paramount, it also raises complex issues of human rights, which deserve consideration but are beyond the scope of this chapter.

## References

Alfaro, J. (1988) What can we learn from child abuse fatalities? A synthesis of nine studies, in D.J. Besharov (ed.) *Protecting Children from Abuse and Neglect: Policy and Practice*, Springfield, IL: Charles C. Thomas.

Angold, A., Costello, E.J., Farmer, E.M.Z., Burns, B.J. and Erkanli, A. (1999) Impaired but undiagnosed, *Journal of the American Academy of Child & Adolescent Psychiatry* 38: 129–37.

Araji, S. and Finkelhor, D. (1986) Abusers: a review of the research, in D. Finkelhor and associates, *A Sourcebook on Child Sexual Abuse*, Beverley Hills, CA: Sage.

Bishop, S.J., Murphy, J.M., Hicks, R., Quinn, D., Lewis, P.J., Grace, M. and Jellinek, M.S. (2000) What progress has been made in meeting the needs of seriously maltreated children? The course of 200 cases through the Boston Juvenile Court, *Child Abuse & Neglect* 24: 599–610.

Black, R. and Mayer, J. (1980) Parents with special problems: alcoholism and opiate addiction, in C.H. Kempe and R.E. Helfer (eds) *The Battered Child*, Chicago: University of Chicago Press.

Browne, K. and Saqi, S. (1988) Approaches to screening for child abuse and neglect, in K. Browne, C. Davies and P. Stratton (eds) *Early Prediction and Prevention of Child Abuse*, Chichester: John Wiley.

Budd, K.S. and Holdsworth, M.J. (1996) Issues in clinical assessment of minimal parenting competence, *Journal of Clinical Child Psychology* 25: 2–14.

Cassell, D. and Coleman, R. (1995) Parents with psychiatric problems, in P. Reder and C. Lucey (eds) *Assessment of Parenting: Psychiatric and Psychological Contributions*, London: Routledge.

Cleaver, H., Unell, I. and Aldgate, J. (1999) *Children's Needs – Parenting Capacity: The Impact of Parental Mental Illness, Problem Alcohol and Drug Use, and Domestic Violence on Children's Development*, London: The Stationery Office.

Curtis, P.A. and McCullough, C. (1993) The impact of alcohol and other drugs on the child welfare system, *Child Welfare* 72: 533–42.

Davidson Ward, S.L., Bautista, D., Chan, L., Derry, M., Lisbin, A., Durfee, M.J., Mills, K.S.C. and Keens, T.G. (1990) Sudden infant death syndrome in infants of substance-abusing mothers, *Pediatrics* 94: 124–6.

Drummond, D.C. and Fitzpatrick, G. (2000) Children of substance misusing parents, in P. Reder, M. McClure and A. Jolley (eds) *Family Matters: Interfaces between Child and Adult Mental Health*, London: Routledge.

Duncan, S. and Reder, P. (2000) Children's experience of major psychiatric disorder in their parent: an overview, in P. Reder, M. McClure and A. Jolley (eds) *Family Matters: Interfaces between Child and Adult Mental Health*, London: Routledge.

Durand, D.J., Espinosa, A.M. and Nickerson, B.G. (1990) Association between prenatal cocaine exposure and sudden infant death syndrome, *Journal of Pediatrics* 117: 909–11.

Falkov, A. (1996) *Study of Working Together 'Part 8' Reports. Fatal Child Abuse and Parental Psychiatric Disorder: An Analysis of 100 Area Child Protection Committee Case Reviews Conducted under the Terms of Part 8 of Working Together under the Children Act 1989*, London: Department of Health.

Falkov, A. (1997) Parental psychiatric disorder and child maltreatment, Part II: extent and nature of the association, National Children's Bureau Highlight No. 149.

Falkov, A. (1998) *Crossing Bridges: Training Resources for Working with Mentally Ill Parents and their Children*, London: Department of Health.

Famularo, R., Barnum, R. and Stone, K. (1986) Court-ordered removal in severe child maltreatment: an association to parental major affective disorder, *Child Abuse & Neglect* 10: 487–92.

Famularo, R., Kinscherff, R., Bunshaft, D., Spivak, G. and Fenton, T. (1989) Parental compliance to court-ordered treatment interventions in cases of child maltreatment, *Child Abuse & Neglect* 13: 507–14.

Famularo, R., Kinscherff, R. and Fenton, T. (1992) Parental substance abuse and the nature of child maltreatment, *Child Abuse & Neglect* 16: 475–83.

Famularo, R., Stone, K., Barnum, R. and Wharton, R. (1986) Alcoholism and severe child maltreatment, *American Journal of Orthopsychiatry* 56: 481–5.

Feig, L. (1998) Understanding the problem: the gap between substance abuse programs and child welfare services, in R.L. Hampron, V. Senatore and T.P. Gullotta (eds) *Substance Abuse, Family Violence, and Child Welfare: Bridging Perspectives*. Thousand Oaks, CA: Sage.

Fellow-Smith, L. (2000) Impact of parental anxiety disorder on children, in P. Reder, M.

McClure and A. Jolley (eds) *Family Matters: Interfaces between Child and Adult Mental Health*, London: Routledge.

Forrester, D. (2000) Parental substance misuse and child protection in a British sample: a survey of children on the Child Protection Register in an inner London district office, *Child Abuse Review* 9: 235–46.

Fredman, G. and Fuggle, P. (2000) Parents with mental health problems: involving the children, in P. Reder, M. McClure and A. Jolley (eds) *Family Matters: Interfaces between Child and Adult Mental Health*, London: Routledge.

Glaser, D. and Prior, V. (1997) Is the term child protection applicable to emotional abuse? *Child Abuse Review* 6: 315–29.

Goodman, S.H. and Brumley, H.E. (1990) Schizophrenic and depressed mothers: relational deficits in parenting, *Developmental Psychology* 26: 31–9.

Göpfert, M., Webster, J., Pollard, J. and Nelki, J.S. (1996) The assessment and prediction of parenting capacity: a community-oriented approach, in M. Göpfert, J. Webster and M.V. Seeman (eds) *Parental Psychiatric Disorder: Distressed Parents and their Families*, Cambridge: Cambridge University Press.

Henry, L.A. and Kumar, R.C. (1999) Risk assessments of infants born to parents with a mental health problem or a learning disability, in A. Weir and A. Douglas (eds) *Child Protection & Adult Mental Health: Conflict of Interest?* Oxford: Butterworth-Heinemann.

Herman, S.P. (1990) Special issues in child custody evaluations, *Journal of the American Academy of Child & Adolescent Psychiatry* 29: 969–74.

Hogan, D.M. (1998) The psychological development and welfare of children of opiate and cocaine users: review and research needs, *Journal of Child Psychology & Psychiatry* 39: 609–20.

Husain, A. and Daniel, A. (1984) A comparative study of filicidal and abusive mothers, *Canadian Journal of Psychiatry* 29: 596–8.

Jacobsen, T., Miller, L.J. and Pesek Kirkwood, K. (1997) Assessing parenting competence in individuals with severe mental illness: a comprehensive service, *Journal of Mental Health Administration* 24: 189–99.

Jaudes, P.K., Ekwo, E. and van Voorhis, J. (1995) Association of drug abuse and child abuse, *Child Abuse & Neglect* 19: 1065–75.

Jenuwine, M.J. and Cohler, B.J. (1999) Major parental psychopathology and child custody, in R.M. Galatzer-Levy and L. Kraus (eds) *The Scientific Basis of Child Custody Decisions*, New York: John Wiley.

Kelleher, K., Chaffin, M., Hollenberg, J. and Fischer, E. (1994) Alcohol and drug disorders among physically abusive and neglectful parents in a community-based sample, *American Journal of Public Health* 84: 1586–90.

Kelley, S.J. (1992) Parenting stress and child maltreatment in drug-exposed children, *Child Abuse & Neglect* 16: 317–28.

Murphy, J.M., Jellinek, M., Quinn, D., Smith, G., Poitrast, F.G. and Goshko, M. (1991) Substance abuse and serious child mistreatment: prevalence, risk, and outcome in a court sample, *Child Abuse & Neglect* 15: 197–211.

New South Wales Child Death Review Team (2000) *1998–99 Report*.

Oates, M. (1984) Assessing fitness to parent, in *Taking a Stand: Child Psychiatrists in Custody, Access, and Disputed Adoption Cases*, London: British Agencies for Adoption and Fostering.

Olofsson, M., Buckley, W., Andersen, G.E. and Friis-Hansen, B. (1983) Investigation of

89 children born by drug-dependent mothers, *Acta Paediatrica Scandinavica* 72: 407–10.

Ornoy, A., Michailevskaya, V., Lukashov, I., Bar-Hamburger, R. and Harel, S. (1996) The developmental outcome of children born to heroin-dependent mothers, raised at home or adopted, *Child Abuse & Neglect*, 20: 385–96.

Pound, A. (1996) Parental affective disorder and childhood disturbance, in M. Göpfert, J. Webster and M.V. Seeman (eds) *Parental Psychiatric Disorder: Distressed Parents and their Families*, Cambridge: Cambridge University Press.

Reder, P. and Duncan, S. (1999) *Lost Innocents: A Follow-up Study of Fatal Child Abuse.* London: Routledge.

Reder, P. and Duncan, S. (2000) Abuse then and now, in P. Reder, M. McClure and A. Jolley (eds) *Family Matters: Interfaces between Child and Adult Mental Health*, London: Routledge.

Reder, P., McClure, M. and Jolley, A. (eds) (2000) *Family Matters: Interfaces between Child and Adult Mental Health*, London: Routledge.

Regan, D.O., Ehrlich, S.M. and Finnegan, L.P. (1987) Infants of drug addicts: at risk for child abuse, neglect, and placement in foster care, *Neurotoxicology & Teratology* 9: 315–19.

Rogosch, F.A., Mowbray, C.T. and Bogat, G.A. (1992) Determinants of parenting attitude in mothers with severe psychopathology, *Development and Psychopathology* 4: 469–87.

Rutter, M. (1985) Resilience in the face of adversity: protective factors and resistance to psychiatric disorder, *British Journal of Psychiatry* 147: 598–611.

Rutter, M. and Quinton, D. (1984) Parental psychiatric disorder: effects on children, *Psychological Medicine* 14: 853–80.

Sagatun-Edwards, I.J., Saylor, C. and Shifflett, B. (1995) Drug exposed infants in the social welfare system and juvenile court, *Child Abuse & Neglect* 19: 83–91.

Sameroff, A.J., Seifer, R. and Zax, M. (1982) Early development of children at risk for emotional disorder, *Monographs of the Society for Research in Child Development* 47 (7, Serial No. 199).

Schutz, B.M., Dixon, E.B., Lindenberger, J.C. and Ruther, N.J. (1989) *Solomon's Sword: A Practical Guide to Conducting Child Custody Evaluations*, San Francisco: Jossey-Bass.

Singer, J., Tang, S. and Berelowitz, M. (2000) Needs assessment in the children of parents with major psychiatric illness, in P. Reder, M. McClure and A. Jolley (eds) *Family Matters: Interfaces between Child and Adult Mental Health*, London: Routledge.

Swadi, H. (1994) Parenting capacity and substance misuse: an assessment scheme, *ACPP Review & Newsletter* 16: 237–44.

Wasserman, D.R. and Leventhal, J.M. (1993) Maltreatment of children born to cocaine-dependent mothers, *American Journal of Diseases of Children* 147: 1324–8.

Wilczynski, A. (1997) *Child Homicide*, London: Greenwich Medical Media.

Wolock, I. and Magura, S. (1996) Parental substance abuse as a predictor of child maltreatment re-reports, *Child Abuse & Neglect* 20: 1183–93.

# Chapter 12

# Would exploration of unresolved conflicts inform parenting assessments?

*Peter Reder and Sylvia Duncan*

A central component of our parenting assessments is the attempt to understand personal and interpersonal conflicts which have intruded into the adults' relationships with their family-of-origin, their partner/s, their children and involved professionals. In this chapter, we shall describe the concept of 'unresolved care and control conflicts', a theme that emerged from two studies we have undertaken into fatal child abuse. We shall propose that the concept has a wider application than child fatalities and is relevant to child maltreatment in general. As such, it can help us understand the functioning of many parents whose care of their children has become the subject of family proceedings. While not suggesting that these unresolved conflicts explain all child maltreatment, or are the only relevant contributor to parenting breakdown, we do believe that they should be specifically addressed as one important aspect of the overall assessment.

## UNRESOLVED CARE AND CONTROL CONFLICTS IN FATAL ABUSE

Two reviews of fatal child abuse cases that we have undertaken (Reder *et al.*, 1993a; 1993b; Reder and Duncan, 1999a; 1999b; 2001) suggested a common theme to the functioning of many of the parents. There was clear evidence of childhood abuse, neglect or rejection in the histories of approximately half of these caretakers and we presumed that, because of the limited information available in some of the reports, this was an under-representation. In adult life, they often showed violence or criminality, domestic violence, threatening behaviour towards professionals, problems of alcohol and/or drug misuse and considerable ongoing difficulties prioritizing their children's needs. Two core themes were apparent, which frequently coexisted: tensions about being cared for and caring for others, which we called 'care conflicts', and tensions about self-control, wishing to control others and fearing control by them, which we referred to as 'control conflicts'.

'Care conflicts' appeared to arise out of actual experiences of abandonment, neglect or rejection as a child, or feeling unloved by parents. They showed in later life as excessive reliance on others and fear of being left by them or, its counterpart, excessive distancing from others and intolerance of other people's dependency. 'Control conflicts' seemed to be based on childhood experiences of feeling helpless in the face of sexual abuse, physical abuse or neglect, an internalized model of relationships based on aggression and coercion, or poor self-discipline because of inappropriate limit-setting. In adult life, they were enacted through excessive proneness to violence, a determination to dominate partners, poor self-control and misperceptions of others' behaviour as controlling.

Fear of being abandoned was a feature of many of the adults' relationships, sometimes played out through mutual threats to leave one another, followed by reconciliations. A reverse side of the coin was shown by the parents who recurrently shied away from intimate relationships, presumably to avoid the risk of being hurt if the other should ever leave. This pseudo-independence or 'flight', appeared to be an attempt to assert mastery over closeness with others and gain some sense of control over their own lives. Many of the adult partnerships were characterized by violence, not exclusively male to female. Violence tended to be used as a means of dominating others and aggressive threats were commonly made if a partner tried to leave a liaison. A number of the men were also suspicious of other people and feared that their partner might become more interested in another man and leave them, so that they became mistrustful, possessive and imprisoning.

Once adults from such backgrounds conceived a child, these residual conflicts inevitably impinged on their attitudes towards the pregnancy. Failure to attend for antenatal appointments, with minimal preparation for the arrival of a dependent baby, was a major theme. Absence of postnatal care also featured significantly, including refusal to attend clinics or admit health visitors for developmental checks. We inferred that this represented an inability to prioritize the infant's needs for care and we were particularly struck by the number of mothers who inappropriately tried to wean their babies on to solids when only a few weeks old, as though wishing them to be older than they were.

Many of the parents were more liable to abuse when they felt rejected or abandoned, especially by their own parents or by a partner. This might have come about through actual separation, emotional distancing or simply the threat of being left. Escalation of an abusing couple's arguments appeared to exacerbate both care and control conflicts by raising the prospects of abandonment and/or unrestrained violence and the reports revealed that such episodes frequently coincided with increasing abuse of the child. Mounting aggression between a couple, accompanied by increasing substance misuse, seemed particularly dangerous for the same reasons. Parent–child interactions appeared particularly stressed by increases in dependency demands upon the parents, such as when a mother realized that she was pregnant again or when she gave birth to a new baby. Refusing antenatal and postnatal care, or neglecting the baby's basic needs, seemed to represent a denial of the expected or actual extra demands for care.

Frustration with children's normal infantile needs was noted in some reports, with one father resenting his baby's crying and a mother slapping her baby for urinating whilst she was changing the nappy. Information about the moments leading up to the fatal assault, where recorded, suggested that intolerance of an infant's uncontrollable behaviour, such as inconsolable crying or grisliness, was crucial. We inferred that these represented a moment-to-moment care crisis because the child needed extra comforting but rejected the parent's efforts. They also represented a control crisis because the parent experienced the child's needs for care as demanding and controlling.

A number of discussions about fatal child physical abuse and neglect lend support to our framework. Tuteur and Glotzer (1966) noted that all of the 'murdering' mothers they interviewed had grown up in emotionally cold and rejecting environments and usually showed extreme dependency needs, which they carried into their marriage union and which were seldom satisfactorily met. In Wilczynski's (1997) study of child homicide suspects, 44 per cent had suffered maltreatment or family disruption in childhood, including having been made the subject of a Care Order, experienced abuse or neglect, witnessed significant parental conflict or violence, or been separated from a parent before the age of 15 years. Crimmins *et al.* (1997) coined the term 'motherless mothers' for many of the convicted women murderers they studied. The women's mothers had been unavailable to them emotionally or had been absent during their childhood, had subjected them to prolonged abuse and/or had suffered from alcoholism and other mental health problems. The majority of the women who had killed their children gave such histories, had also been involved with an abusive partner and had abused drugs or alcohol.

Motz (2001) reported the case of a mother who had killed her 11-month-old son. The woman had never known her father and her mother had been recurrently hospitalized with depression. During her childhood, she had lived in numerous children's homes, where she had been sexually abused, twice by residents and once by a member of staff. She had learned to stifle her anger by speaking in a whisper. When pregnant, she had never been able to conceptualize herself as capable of mothering and the infanticide occurred soon after her estranged husband had petitioned her for divorce, which had left her feeling devastated and abandoned.

Precipitants of fatal assaults on children have also been discussed by others. Krugman (1985) found clear triggers in 19 of 24 cases of fatal abuse, particularly toileting accidents, messy nappy changes or inconsolable crying. Korbin (1987) reported that perceptions of rejection underlay fatal assaults following the child's crying or food refusal and Brewster *et al.* (1998) found that the child's crying immediately preceded the fatal assault in over half of the cases studied. Byrne and Jones (1998: p. 300) described a near-fatal assault by a father who 'battered his baby son when he vomited, causing skull fractures. He had lost his own mother when he was one year old and his father blamed him for her death and physically abused him. The father was anxious his baby would choke on his vomit and felt helpless, infuriated and persecuted by his rejection of food.'

## RELEVANCE TO CHILD ABUSE IN GENERAL

Even though the concept of unresolved care and control conflicts emerged from reviews of fatal child abuse cases, descriptions of parents who maltreat their children to a lesser degree of severity provide essentially the same picture. In an early paper, Green *et al.* (1974) described mothers who found that their child's nurturant demands intensified their own unsatisfied dependency feelings and they relied on the child to satisfy these unmet needs. They also showed poor impulse control. Green (1979) reported that child-abusing fathers have experienced harsh punishment and rejection in childhood resulting in impaired impulse control, feelings of worthlessness and alcohol misuse. They often abuse their children while reluctantly having to take over child care duties at a time of tension between the couple, when the child's mother has withdrawn from the child and from him. In addition, it was suggested that actual or threatened loss of employment may have coincided and compromised his self-esteem, while a difficult-to-care-for child, such as one who was irritable or colicky, may have threatened his sense of competence.

Pianta *et al.* (1989: p. 207) inferred that 'Women who have not resolved inter-personal issues of trust, dependency, and autonomy are likely to be considerably stressed when faced with the demands of a highly dependent child . . . They may also find themselves seeking to meet their own emotional needs in the context of the parent–child relationship and may experience hostility toward the child when those needs are not met.' Garbarino *et al.* (1986) identified psychologically mal-treating parents as: having themselves been psychologically abused as children; often relying on their children to satisfy their own unsatisfied dependency needs; being impulsive; tending to blame their children and the environment for their own failures; frequently being addicted to drugs or alcohol; and usually involved in parent–child power struggles.

Haugaard and Reppucci (1988) summarized the available knowledge about parents who sexually abuse as follows:

> Although descriptions of the typical incestuous family vary, they have some factors in common. One or both of the parents may have been sexually or physically abused when they were children or may come from families in which they were abandoned or otherwise neglected . . . The relationship between the parents in an incestuous family is often characterised by a marked difference in power and prestige, although it may be either of the parents who is the more powerful. (p. 127)

Authors have continued to identify a compulsion for control in those who sexually abuse children, where their sense of powerlessness when abused or emotionally neglected in childhood leads to a need to dominate others and a sexualization of closeness, intimacy, aggression and power (e.g. Finkelhor and associates, 1986; Glasser, 1988; Bentovim, 1993; Beck-Sander, 1995). The compensatory use of sexual fantasies when feeling humiliated or rejected (e.g. O'Callaghan and Print, 1994) and the disinhibiting role of alcohol in the commission of sexually abusive acts is also widely noted.

## EQUIVALENTS IN PSYCHODYNAMIC AND ATTACHMENT MODELS

Where authors have based their analysis of child abuse on psychodynamic or attachment theories, central themes emerge which have close parallels with our descriptions of unresolved care and control conflicts.

Steele (1987) considered that the same patterns of psychic functioning underlie all forms of child maltreatment and that, if interviewed appropriately, all mal-treating parents would reveal personal histories in which they felt uncared for as a child. This might have taken the form of explicit physical abuse, exposure to violence, rejection, neglect, insecure attachments, humiliation, or failure to protect. As adults and parents, such individuals feel their deepest needs have never been met, are dependent, lack basic trust and so fear that the very people to whom they look for support and help will be the ones most likely to attack them, and are suspicious of authority. At times of stress, such as when they feel especially inferior or unloved, they give priority to their own needs, often expecting their child to satisfy them, and have unrealistic expectations of the child's developmental capa-cities. Acts of abuse were said to occur through a shift in super-ego identification to the parent's own punitive parent. Motz (2001) explained infanticide by a mother in the following way:

> She has powerfully identified with the helplessness of the child, and has found her own inability to provide for the needs of the infant intolerable . . . The inability to tolerate dependence in the child and the memory of her own inability to have her needs met by her mother generate a life or death struggle between mother and child. The infant's needs are perceived as life-threatening attacks which must be defended against. (pp. 114–15)

Crittenden and Ainsworth (1989) and Howe *et al*. (1999) have described how hostile or rejecting caretaking can produce *avoidant* insecure attachment styles in children, who grow up to become remote, self-reliant and 'in control' of their emotional life. As parents, they may resort to physical punishment to control their children and tend to withdraw from their demands for closeness. Emotionally un-predictable or underinvolved parenting can give rise to an *ambivalent* attachment pattern in individuals, whose emotions dominate their lives, especially when concerned if others care about them and whether they are unlovable or worthless. They cling excessively when threatened with losing a partner, blame others for upsetting them, may be jealously possessive and use threats of leaving to con-trol the partner's availability. Physically abusive experiences may generate a *disorganized* attachment pattern and individuals who learn to use punitive aggressiveness or submissive compliance to control the predictability of their environment. As parents, they fear losing control of their children and resort to using power, punitive hostility and rejection when the child's attachment needs trigger their own anxieties.

Crittenden (1996) integrated these various models, describing members of violent families as behaving as if they believed that important resources (e.g. love, attention, money) were in short supply and were acquired through the exercise of power. They expect relationships to be based on issues of conflict, control, coercion, victimization and rejection. Anger at a baby's crying might occur because the parent perceives the baby as monopolizing their attention. Neglectful parents were described as often appearing depressed and preoccupied about powerlessness and helplessness. They believe that others will not meet their needs or that they can elicit satisfying help and support from others. Sexually abusing parents were identified as often excessively anxious about relationships and, even though they fear abandonment by those close to them, their interactions are distancing and rejecting. Whatever the nature of their abusive tendency, such personal and interpersonal problems render these parents especially sensitive to stresses in their lives, which in turn increase their potential to repeat abusive acts.

## CONSTELLATIONS OF PROBLEM BEHAVIOURS

It is important to emphasize that we are describing a *constellation* of problem behaviours resulting from the same core conflicts, for which there is some supporting evidence. A significant overlap between physical abuse of children and other forms of family violence has been reported by Giles-Sims (1985), Ross (1996) and Rumm *et al.* (2000), while a link between substance misuse, family violence and child maltreatment is discussed in Kantor and Straus (1990) and Hampton *et al.* (1998). The association between child abuse and deficient perinatal care is reported in a number of studies (e.g. Benedict *et al.*, 1985; Anderson, 1987; Egan *et al.*, 1990).

Furthermore, equivalents to our model of unresolved conflicts can be found in the literature on male violence to female partners. In a multi-level discussion, Goldner *et al.* (1990) argued that the violence is both wilful and impulse-ridden, representing a conscious strategy to control the woman and a frightening loss of self-control. The man maintains an illusion of personal power and psychic autonomy by denying his dependency needs and controlling any evidence of independence in his partner, since he fears disintegration were she to leave him. If she does assert her right to be cared for, he is terrified that her needs will be insatiable and he either threatens to leave her (asserting that he is, after all, independent) or becomes violent (reasserting his power). The woman becomes 'hypnotized' by his underlying vulnerabilities, which become more overt when he craves her forgiveness. Goldner *et al.* suggested that the couple's relationship is founded on a mutual wish for magical rescue from ambivalent loyalty bonds to their own rejecting or abusive parents.

Dutton (1998) identified a similar cyclical theme. He suggested that the man typically experiences high levels of depression and anxiety, often self-treated by alcohol or drugs, but their internal tensions progressively build, to be dissipated by uncontrolled violence, followed by contrition and pleas for forgiveness. They desire intimacy and demand closeness but are mistrustful and fear rejection, instead blaming their partner for not soothing their high anxiety levels and feeling compelled to control her so that she does not show an interest in another man. McGee (2000) concluded that a core feature of domestic violence is the man's compulsion to control all aspects of the woman's life, including using a calculated strategy of increasing her fear and uncertainty. In addition, children in the household are subjected to the same intimidation and psychological domination, with threats of harm to either the mother or the child used as a means of controlling one or both of them.

## RELEVANCE TO RESILIENCE

The literature on resilience to the consequences of childhood maltreatment consistently highlights a number of key protective factors (Rutter, 1985; 1989; Egeland *et al.*, 1988; Scott Heller *et al.*, 1999; Reder and Duncan, 2000). These are: the availability of an emotionally supportive relationship with a non-abusing adult during childhood; a stable relationship with a partner in adult life; success in an unrelated area of life, such as at school; and a sense of self-efficacy, with control over their life. The capacity for reflection is the other significant factor, variously reported as 'cognitively confronting and reflecting on one's experiences', 'acknowledging the details of the earlier abuse and summoning the appropriate affect', 'objectifying or gaining a perspective on the past abuse and integrating it into their view of themself', and 'being able to forgive the abusing parent' (e.g. Main and Goldwyn, 1984; Emde, 1988; Fonagy *et al.*, 1994; Himelein and McElrath, 1996). Furthermore, psychotherapy was one of the factors identified as proffering resilience by Egeland *et al.* (1988).

All these factors readily translate into care–control conflict concepts. For example, a supportive relationship with a non-abusing adult and/or a current partner implies actual experiences of being cared for and cared about, which helps compensate for other uncaring or rejecting relationships. A sense of success in one area of life can be understood as combating feelings of helplessness arising from abusive experiences and mitigating against perpetuation of unresolved control conflicts. Similarly, reflectiveness, including through psychotherapy, offers an opportunity to resolve conflicts engendered by childhood maltreatment.

## RELEVANCE OF A CARE AND CONTROL CONFLICTS MODEL TO PARENTING ASSESSMENTS

In summary, many authors have identified an equivalent constellation of personal and interpersonal difficulties in abusive families that link adverse childhood experiences of the parents, their violent and/or fragile relationships, and the maltreatment of their children. We have suggested that the term 'unresolved care and control conflicts' usefully summarizes these difficulties by directing attention towards inner personal tensions and interpersonal stresses. Not all maltreating families will necessarily show evidence of these conflicts but we believe that they occur with enough frequency to suggest they should be borne in mind during all parenting assessments.

While the model is framed in terms of *conflicts*, it also emphasizes *interaction* and *meaning* by linking the impact of past events and experiences, an individual's view of themselves and other people, and the pattern of relationships that they tend to form through their lives. In parenting assessments, it enables the assessor: (a) to attribute meaning to events in the parent's life when reviewing their history; (b) to hypothesize links between stressful past experiences and episodes of abuse to their child, as well as to postulate future risks of harm; (c) to highlight wider areas of exploration during the assessment; and (d) to identify areas of therapeutic need.

### Attributing meaning to events and behaviour

History taking in parenting assessments has a different emphasis from that usually undertaken in everyday psychiatric practice. Although psychiatrists customarily elicit a history of symptoms and signs and a chronology of significant events in the person's life, their ultimate purpose is to arrive at a diagnostic formulation and treatment recommendation, so that the individual's history is described more factually and primarily weighed up in support of the diagnosis. Since parenting is a process and a relationship that can not be described in diagnostic terms, understanding its evolution requires a more interactional perspective on the parents' histories. Emphasis is placed on the significance that events have had for them and the meaning that they have attributed to those experiences, such as the impact on their self-esteem or their beliefs about themself.

> For example, in one case, all of the assessment reports on a father contained in the court papers mentioned the same fact about his history – that he had had asthma throughout his time at school. However, nothing more was reported about this aspect of his life. When his history was reviewed again by another assessor, more information was sought about this, through such questions as: 'how did that affect you?' This led to his revealing that he was

mercilessly ridiculed at school for being weak and different, that he had very few friends throughout his childhood, felt alone and an outsider and failed at his school work. However, he had never been able to reveal this to his parents because they were emotionally distant. He had grown up feeling unloved and uncared for, lonely and miserable. His subsequent history of forming dependent relationships with older women and finding it anxiety-provoking to care for a prematurely born infant began to make more sense.

Such a framework also helps the assessor describe an individual's behaviour in terms of interactional patterns, based on formative relationships and further shaped by later experiences, rather than immutable inherent characteristics. Similarly, an assessment which concludes that a parent 'is violent' would be much more useful if it elucidated circumstances in which that person showed poor impulse control, to whom, precipitated by what, and so on.

The relative advantages are well illustrated by the case of Susan Aukland (Inquiry Report, 1975; Reder *et al.*, 1993a), a 15-month-old child who was fatally assaulted by her father, John Aukland.

At the age of 3, John Aukland was 'involved in a childhood incident which resulted in both his feet being broken'. He developed a chronic infection, requiring him to spend long periods in hospital, and he was pushed around in a pram until he was 9 years old. Throughout his adult life, he behaved as a chronic invalid, having long periods off work and becoming reliant on prescribed drugs, sick notes, his parents and his wife. He denigrated the woman he married and regarded her as incompetent and immature, yet he was also emotionally and practically dependent on her. Their marriage was characterized by intimidation and violence by him, especially when drunk, and frequent arguments, separations and reconciliations. John Aukland suffered from chronic anxiety and psychosomatic complaints, which worsened at the times his wife left him and also at the birth of each of their four children. He was referred to a local psychiatrist six weeks after the birth of their first child, Marianne, having admitted that he was afraid of injuring his wife and the baby. The psychiatrist described the problem as 'hysterical emphasis on reactive depression in a vulnerable personality' but also identified that Marianne's birth had exacerbated his recurrent anxieties and depression.

Three weeks later, John Aukland fatally assaulted Marianne after she had started to cry and he described that 'this thing came over me like some evil, and I started banging her'. An expert psychiatric opinion to the court identified a 'combination of constitutional factors and environmental pressures' but, at his trial, a prison medical officer advised the court that he had recovered from his depression, although remaining 'of weak character', and that the prospect of him similarly reoffending was 'very remote indeed'.

During the mother's pregnancy with their third child, John Aukland was referred with a psychosomatic skin complaint to the same local psychiatrist who had originally seen him. This time, his assessment concluded that he was 'a plausible hysterical psychopathic personality' and an 'irresponsible psychopath who lacked self-criticism' and the case lapsed when he failed to attend the next appointments.

When Susan, their fourth child, was nearly I year old, her mother left the home because of the father's heavy drinking and cruelty, leaving him to care for three young children. Four months later, after a night of heavy drinking, John Aukland killed Susan. Her body showed evidence of numerous assaults over the previous two weeks and the next youngest child, aged 28 months, was also bruised.

Whereas two early psychiatric assessments had identified interactional factors which linked the father's personal difficulties, critical transitional events and the risks to his children, the other formulations focused exclusively on a diagnosis, as though it were an inherent attribute unrelated to his family circumstances or the children's safety.

## Identifying past stressors and future risks

The Susan Aukland case also illustrates that history taking, which highlights past conflicts and the meaning of events within an interactional framework, also has the potential to link periods of psychological stress for the parent with episodes of abuse to the child. This also can provide interactional pointers towards future risk. Thus, in certain families, the risk will be increased when there are crises in parental relationships precariously organized around dependency or domination – such as the birth of another dependent child, or threats of, or actual, separation between the parental couple.

The model particularly adds a new dimension to risk factors commonly identified in high-risk checklists. It draws attention to the meaning of certain attributes for the individual concerned and how they may have impacted on their subsequent relationships and view of themselves as a person and as a caretaker. For instance, it is often said that bearing a first child at a young age increases the risk of future abuse to children in the family (e.g. Browne and Saqi, 1988). In our view, the relevance of this factor lies not in its statistical associations but in the interpersonal experiences that could have led to the early pregnancy and may continue to operate (see Reder and Fitzpatrick, Chapter 8). Therefore it might pose questions about whether the young mother tended to sexualize relationships following sexual abuse in childhood, whether her risk-taking behaviour indicated an impoverished sense of identity, whether she left home in a crisis to escape severe family tensions, and whether she desired a baby in the hope that the infant would provide love and compensation for emotional deprivation in her own childhood.

## Highlighting wider areas of exploration

This model of unresolved conflicts is part of a general framework that understands parenting as a relationship that is both influenced by personal history and sensitive to current experiences. Over time, patterns may be discerned in an individual's style of relating and the model guides an assessor to explore the parent's relationship history as well as their current interactions with others. Sometimes, it indicates areas to be examined that might not otherwise have been considered relevant.

For example, the concept has been particularly useful when a question arises about whether a child should be rehabilitated to the care of a grandparent (for example, their maternal grandmother) rather than a parent (such as their mother). The social worker's assessment has usually suggested that the mother is unable to provide reliable care because of continuing adverse factors (which we translate as representing unresolved care and/or control conflicts). We believe that the assessment needs to be extended to consider the three-generational link between the mother's current incapacity to care for her child and the parenting that she received from her own mother, i.e. the grandmother, as a child – in other words, whether the mother's caretaking difficulties can be traced back to equivalent problems of the grandmother. For instance, if the grandmother had been rejecting, abusive or neglectful at that time, or repeatedly entered into relationships with violent or abusive partners, the basis of *her* conflicts needs to be understood, together with an appraisal of whether sufficient resolution has occurred during the intervening years, since this will impact on her capacity to look after her grandchild.

## Addressing therapeutic need and potential

The notion of unresolved conflicts also has relevance for identifying areas of therapeutic need and planning components of therapeutic interventions for parents who have abused. The reported outcomes of therapeutic programmes for maltreating families suggest that multidimensional interventions that address a combination of behaviour patterns, relationships, psychological processing and living circumstances are probably the most effective (e.g. Crittenden, 1991; Gough, 1993; Iwaniec, 1995; Stevenson, 1998; Jones, 1997; Byrne and Jones, 1998; Macdonald, 2001). Within such programmes, individual counselling using cognitive-behavioural approaches or reflective psychotherapy for the parent/s is considered important. In addition, some parents are only able to move on in their functioning as a person and as a parent through more formal individual psychodynamic psychotherapy.

Steele (1997) has described the principal issues that are liable to emerge during such therapy, all of which can be translated into the model of care and control conflicts. The therapist needs to recognize that the parent's inability to be empathically sensitive to their children directly results from the unempathic care that they themselves received in early years. Many parents are likely to repeat in the therapy a helpless dependency, based on either their fear of punishment or an inner emptiness and yearning for love that is a residue of their emotionally deprived childhood. The disregard that they experienced from insensitive caretakers leaves them particularly sensitive to abandonment or inattention by the therapist. Their sense of emotional emptiness will often have led to role reversal in which the child has been expected to supply love, pleasure and approval. Hence the therapist should also endeavour to orient them towards sources of satisfaction in their own social contacts. On the other hand, some parents initially present as angry, rebellious, uncooperative and denying, transferring on to the therapist and other authorities long-lasting feelings towards their parents that originated in their childhood. Steele suggested that the objective of the therapy is to help the parent recognize the residues of their early experiences and thereby avoid following the old patterns, instead learning new patterns of interpersonal relationships that are under their own control and in the interests of themself and their child.

Reder and Fredman (1996) have also discussed how individuals may repeat in their encounters with professional 'helpers' the same experiences that they had with their formative caretakers, a process which they called 'the relationship to help'. They

> were particularly struck by a number of mothers who indicated that they had been sexually abused as children and were still suffering the sequelae but, despite our concerned offers of help, never engaged with us. Many of them made an initial loud cry of distress, but did not attend the appointments offered or only came sporadically . . . We had the sense that this pattern recapitulated the woman's childhood experiences: for instance, desperately wanting to turn to someone but feeling frightened by the abuser's threats; fearing that they did not deserve to be rescued; or doubting that the non-abusing parent could be trusted to support and protect them . . . These formative experiences then laid down their expectations of any type of help from anyone in the future, so that their relationships with professionals recreated the same belief that help was both desperately wanted but could not be relied upon. (Reder and Fredman, 1996: p. 459)

With these understandings of the possible course of psychotherapeutic treatment, the assessor can identify how the parent's earlier experiences of unresolved care and control conflicts appear to have impacted on their later functioning and to consider whether such conflicts are potentially available for reflection and resolution in therapy.

## INCLUDING CARE AND CONTROL CONFLICTS IN THE ASSESSMENT

A core feature of assessments of parental figures is a detailed review of their personal history. The aim is not only to obtain a chronological account of significant events in their lives but also to elicit what meaning those experiences had for them and how they were affected by them. The assessor tries to discover who has been important to them, either in a positive or an unpleasant way, and how relationships with those people developed and evolved. In other words, it is a history of the individual as a developing person who has grown up in the context of their family and wider relationships, all of which have shaped their view of themselves and way of relating to others. Even though the task of the interview is assessment, our exploratory approach has some similarities to the systemic therapeutic style described by Boscolo and Bertrando (1996) when working with individuals.

The most useful way to elicit this history is by compiling the family genogram with them (see McGoldrick *et al.*, 1999). It is an advantage to have available in the room a large white-board, so that the genogram can be visibly drawn up as the story emerges. Experience has taught that the history should be sought in a chronological manner, starting with the individual's family-of-origin and tracing through subsequent events. Alongside enquiring about factual details (e.g. names and ages of parents and siblings, age at starting school) are questions about caretaking experiences and family relationships, together with their impact. Obviously, each prompt must be appropriate to the emerging story and responses to previous questions but examples might include:

> 'Which parent were you closer to?';
> 'How did that come about?';
> 'How were you looked after?';
> 'How did your parents discipline you?';
> 'Did that happen to [your siblings] as well?';
> 'What was that like for you?';
> 'How did that affect you?';
> 'Were you able to tell anyone about that?';
> 'Do you think you have ever got over that?'.

The chronology might continue through such non-specific questions as:

> 'What happened after that?'; and
> 'What was the next major thing that happened to you?'

to targeted enquiries such as:

---

'Were there any emotional problems in any of your family members as you were growing up?';
'Were you ever in trouble with the police?';
'How old were you when you left home?';
'What were the circumstances of this?;
'Were there any issues left not sorted out with your parents when you left?';
'When you first met [your partner], what did s/he seem like to you?';
'What do you think [your partner] was attracted to in you?';
'How did your relationship together develop?';
'Were alcohol or drugs involved?';
'Have you ever separated?';
'What was your reaction when you discovered you were pregnant?';
'What was [your partner's] reaction?';
'Did you attend for antenatal care?';

---

and so on.

There is no element of this exploration that specifically considers care and control conflicts *per se*. Each person's history is unique and some parents report no experiences of rejection, maltreatment or neglect. We would press them further in order to examine whether dissociation, denial or idealization has distorted their memory of past traumata, especially if the court papers suggest a different version of events. However, it would be entirely contrary to an impartial assessment process to presume that all positive accounts are false. On the other hand, many of the adults involved in family proceedings do have traumatic backgrounds and the process of taking their history often reveals adverse childhood experiences that have left their mark on them as an individual and as a caretaker.

## CONCLUSIONS

Each case that comes to family proceedings could be considered to be complex, in the sense that it requires an appraisal of formative experiences, personal dilemmas, relationships between numerous people and the way that all of these have impacted on the well-being of children in the family. Assessors therefore need to have a framework which helps them integrate the potentially overwhelming volume of information available. We have found that the notion of unresolved care and control conflicts from the past impacting on current parenting behaviour is a useful explanatory hypothesis to hold in mind when assessing families, especially where maltreatment is suspected. Of course, there will be some families where this concept does not seem to be relevant and we must organize our understanding of the case in a different way. Nonetheless, for the majority, we find that it helps connect different elements of a complex story, suggests a meaning for various events and offers a coherent means of understanding the presenting problems.

For example, although child neglect can be particularly difficult to define and assess, it may be possible to identify patterns in the parents' personal histories that suggest a continuing impact of past conflicts on their everyday functioning such that they are unable to prioritize the children's needs. Tracing through the history of the case then highlights how chronic neglect of the children became interspersed with more severely neglectful episodes, which coincided with crises in these conflicts, such as the birth of another child, an illness in the family or parental separation.

In a more speculative way, we would like to suggest that our discussion about triggering events to serious physical child abuse might contribute an element of understanding to a group of particularly complex and concerning cases. These are where a parent steadfastly denies allegations that they have shaken or otherwise severely assaulted their infant and the child is much too young to be interviewed, has suffered major brain damage or even died. In these circumstances, the mental health expert is initially reliant on medical opinions and police investigations as to the likely cause of the injuries, their timing, which caretakers were present at the time, and so on, and then on the court's 'findings of fact' as to how, and by whom, the child was injured. The value of mental health opinions comes at the second stage in considering the future care of surviving children.

We have been involved in a number of such cases and discussed others with colleagues, and have noted a theme common to some of them. The accused parent describes a sequence of events leading up to the crisis in which they admit shaking or smacking the infant but *after* the child had developed a breathing problem or lost consciousness: the shake or smack is explained as an attempt to revive the collapsed child, not the cause of it. One father offered the following story: he was feeding the child with a bottle; the child spat out some milk; then coughed and cried; then turned blue and stopped breathing; he patted the child firmly on the back; then he shook her briefly in an attempt to revive her; he soon had to yell for someone to call an ambulance. The father maintained this account, even after the court had made a finding of fact against him. The triggering events described in the literature, such as the infant crying, vomiting, urinating or defecating, suggest that there was a missing fragment to his account, or that he had reversed the order of events in his own mind, perhaps because of his horror at what he had done or through dissociation. His personal history contained many indicators of unresolved care–control conflicts, which, in the light of the medical, forensic and legal findings, enabled the assessor to hypothesize a sequence through which the events may have happened and to weigh up the risk he was likely to pose to other children.

The notion of unresolved conflicts, then, can be useful in a significant number of cases by offering a way to integrate the emerging information, to understand the functioning of the parents, to identify aspects of risk and to aid the assessment of therapeutic needs. However, it must be emphasized again that the theme may not apply to some families, is never taken as the sole focus of the assessment and needs to be integrated with other factors in the assessment scheme, as outlined in Chapter 1, in order to provide a comprehensive assessment of parenting.

## References

Anderson, C.L. (1987) Assessing parenting potential for child abuse risk, *Pediatric Nursing* 13: 323–7.

Beck-Sander, A. (1995) Childhood abuse in adult offenders: the role of control in perpetuating cycles of abuse, *Journal of Forensic Psychiatry* 6: 486–98.

Benedict, M.I., White, R.B. and Cornely, D.A. (1985) Maternal perinatal risk factors and child abuse, *Child Abuse & Neglect* 9: 217–24.

Bentovim, A. (1993) Why do adults sexually abuse children? *British Medical Journal* 307: 144–5.

Boscolo, L. and Bertrando, P. (1996) *Systemic Therapy with Individuals*, London: Karnac Books.

Brewster, A.L., Nelson, J.P., Hymel, K.P., Colby, D.R., Lucas, D.R., McCanne, T.R. and Milner, J.S. (1998) Victim, perpetrator, family, and incident characteristics of 32 infant maltreatment deaths in the United States Air Force, *Child Abuse & Neglect* 22: 91–101.

Browne, K. and Saqi, S. (1988) Approaches to screening for child abuse and neglect, in K. Browne, C. Davies and P. Stratton (eds) *Early Prediction and Prevention of Child Abuse*, Chichester: John Wiley.

Byrne, G. and Jones, D. (1998) Severe breakdown in the parenting of infants, in J. Green and B. Jacobs (eds) *In-patient Child Psychiatry: Modern Practice, Research and the Future*, London: Routledge.

Crimmins, S., Langley, S., Brownstein, H.H. and Spunt, B.J. (1997) Convicted women who have killed children: a self-psychology perspective, *Journal of Interpersonal Violence* 12: 49–69.

Crittenden, P.M. (1991) Treatment of child abuse and neglect, *Human Systems* 2: 161–79.

Crittenden, P.M. (1996) Research on maltreating families: implications for intervention, in J. Briere, L. Berliner, J.A. Bulkley, C. Jenny and T. Reid (eds) *The APSAC Handbook on Child Maltreatment*, Thousand Oaks, CA: Sage.

Crittenden, P.M. and Ainsworth, M.D.S. (1989) Child maltreatment and attachment theory, in D. Cicchetti and V. Carlson (eds) *Child Maltreatment: Theory and Research on the Causes and Consequences of Child Abuse and Neglect*, Cambridge: Cambridge University Press.

Dutton, D.G. (1998) *The Abusive Personality: Violence and Control in Intimate Relationships*, New York: The Guilford Press.

Egan, T.G., Monaghan, S.M., Muir, R.C., Gilmore, R.J., Clarkson, J.E. and Crooks, T.J. (1990) Prenatal screening of pregnant mothers for parenting difficulties: final results from the Queen Mary Child Care Unit, *Social Science & Medicine* 30: 289–95.

Egeland, B., Jacobvitz, D. and Sroufe, L.A. (1988) Breaking the cycle of abuse, *Child Development* 59: 1080–8.

Emde, R.N. (1988) The effect of relationships on relationships: a developmental approach to clinical intervention, in R.A. Hinde and J. Stevenson-Hinde (eds) *Relationships within Families: Mutual Influences*, Oxford: Clarendon.

Finkelhor, D. and associates (1986) *A Sourcebook on Child Sexual Abuse*, Beverley Hills: Sage.

Fonagy, P., Steele, M., Steele, H., Higgitt, A. and Target, M. (1994) The theory and practice of resilience, *Journal of Child Psychology and Psychiatry* 35: 231–57.

Garbarino, J., Guttmann, E. and Wilson Seeley, J. (1986) *The Psychologically Battered Child*, San Francisco: Jossey-Bass.

Giles-Sims, J. (1985) A longitudinal study of battered children of battered wives, *Family Relations* 34: 205–10.

Glasser, M. (1988) Psychodynamic aspects of paedophilia, *Psychoanalytic Psychotherapy* 3: 121–33.

Goldner, V., Penn, P., Sheinberg, M. and Walker, G. (1990) Love and violence: gender paradoxes in volatile attachments, *Family Process* 29: 343–64.

Gough, D. (1993) *Child Abuse Interventions: A Review of the Research Literature*, London: HMSO.

Green, A.H. (1979) Child-abusing fathers, *Journal of the American Academy of Child Psychiatry* 18: 270–82.

Green, A.H., Gaines, R.W. and Sandgrund, A. (1974) Child abuse: pathological syndrome of family interaction, *American Journal of Psychiatry* 131: 882–6.

Hampton, R.L., Senatore, V. and Gullotta, T.P. (eds) (1998) *Substance Abuse, Family Violence, and Child Welfare: Bridging Perspectives*, Thousand Oaks, CA: Sage.

Haugaard, J.J. and Reppucci, N.D. (1988) *The Sexual Abuse of Children: A Comprehensive Guide to Current Knowledge and Intervention Strategies*, San Francisco: Jossey-Bass.

Himelein, M.J. and McElrath, J.A.V. (1996) Resilient child sexual abuse survivors: cognitive coping and illusion, *Child Abuse & Neglect* 20: 747–58.

Howe, D., Brandon, M., Hinings, D. and Schofield G. (1999) *Attachment Theory, Child Maltreatment and Family Support: A Practice and Assessment Model*, Basingstoke: Macmillan.

Inquiry Report (1975) *Report of the Committee of Inquiry into the Provision and Co-ordination of Services to the Family of John George Aukland*, London: HMSO.

Iwaniec, D. (1995) *The Emotionally Abused and Neglected Child: Identification, Assessment and Intervention*, Chichester: Wiley.

Jones, D.P.H. (1997) Treatment of the child and the family where child abuse or neglect has occurred, in R.E. Helfer and R.S. Kempe (eds) *The Battered Child*, 5th ed., Chicago: University of Chicago Press.

Kantor, G.K. and Straus, M.A. (1990) The drunken bum theory of wife beating, in M.A. Straus and R.J. Gelles (eds) *Physical Violence in American Families*, New Brunswick, NJ: Transaction Books.

Korbin, J.E. (1987) Incarcerated mothers' perceptions and interpretations of their fatally maltreated children, *Child Abuse & Neglect* 11: 397–407.

Krugman, R.D. (1985) Fatal child abuse: analysis of 24 cases, *Pediatrician* 12: 68–72.

Macdonald, G. (2001) *Effective Interventions for Child Abuse and Neglect: An Evidence-based Approach to Planning and Evaluating Interventions*, Chichester: Wiley.

McGee, C. (2000) *Childhood Experiences of Domestic Violence*, London: Jessica Kingsley.

McGoldrick, M., Gerson, R. and Shellenberger, S. (1999) *Genograms: Assessment & Intervention*, 2nd ed., New York: Norton.

Main, M. and Goldwyn, R. (1984) Predicting rejection of her infant from mother's representation of her own experiences: implications for the abused-abusing inter-generational cycle, *Child Abuse & Neglect* 8: 203–17.

Motz, A. (2001) *The Psychology of Female Violence: Crimes against the Body*, London: Brunner/Routledge.

O'Callaghan, D. and Print, B. (1994) Adolescent sexual abusers: research, assessment and treatment, in T. Morrison, M. Erooga and R.C. Beckett (eds) *Sexual Offending against Children: Assessment and Treatment of Male Abusers*, London: Routledge.

Pianta, R., Egeland, B. and Erickson, M.F. (1989) The antecedents of maltreatment: results of the Mother-Child Interaction Project, in D. Cicchetti and V. Carlson (eds) *Child Maltreatment: Theory and Research on the Causes and Consequences of Child Abuse and Neglect*, Cambridge: Cambridge University Press.

Reder, P. and Duncan, S. (1999a) *Lost Innocents: A Follow-up Study of Fatal Child Abuse*, London: Routledge.

Reder, P. and Duncan, S. (1999b) Conflictual relationships and risks of child abuse, *Journal of Child Centred Practice* 6: 127–45.

Reder, P. and Duncan, S. (2000) Abuse then and now, in P. Reder, M. McClure and A. Jolley (eds) *Family Matters: Interfaces between Child and Adult Mental Health*, London: Routledge.

Reder, P. and Duncan, S. (2001) Abusive relationships, care and control conflicts and insecure attachments, *Child Abuse Review* 10: 411–27.

Reder, P., Duncan, S. and Gray, M. (1993a) *Beyond Blame: Child Abuse Tragedies Revisited*, London: Routledge.

Reder, P., Duncan, S. and Gray, M. (1993b) A new look at child abuse tragedies, *Child Abuse Review* 2: 89–100.

Reder, P. and Fredman, G. (1996) The relationship to help: interacting beliefs about the treatment process, *Clinical Child Psychology & Psychiatry* 1: 457–67.

Ross, S.M. (1996) Risk of physical abuse to children of spouse abusing parents, *Child Abuse & Neglect* 20: 589–98.

Rumm, P.D., Cummings, P., Krauss, M.R., Bell, M.A. and Rivara, F.P. (2000) Identified spouse abuse as a risk factor for child abuse, *Child Abuse & Neglect* 24: 1375–81.

Rutter, M. (1985) Resilience in the face of adversity: protective factors and resistance to psychiatric disorder, *British Journal of Psychiatry* 147: 598–611.

Rutter, M. (1989) Intergenerational continuities and discontinuities in serious parenting difficulties, in D. Cicchetti and V. Carlson (eds) *Child Maltreatment: Theory and Research on the Causes and Consequences of Child Abuse and Neglect*, Cambridge: Cambridge University Press.

Scott Heller, S., Larrieu, J.A., D'Imperio, R. and Boris, N.W. (1999) Research on resilience to child maltreatment: empirical considerations, *Child Abuse & Neglect* 23: 321–38.

Steele, B. (1987) Psychodynamic factors in child abuse, in R.E. Helfer and R.S. Kempe (eds) *The Battered Child*, 4th ed., Chicago: University of Chicago Press.

Steele, B. (1997) Further reflections on the therapy of those who maltreat children, in R.E. Helfer and R.S. Kempe (eds) *The Battered Child*, 5th ed., Chicago: University of Chicago Press.

Stevenson, O. (1998) *Neglected Children: Issues and Dilemmas*, Oxford: Blackwell Science.

Tuteur, W. and Glotzer, J. (1966) Further observations on murdering mothers, *Journal of Forensic Sciences* 11: 373–83.

Wilczynski, A. (1997) *Child Homicide*, London: Greenwich Medical Media.

# Chapter 13

# Does the past predict the future?

*Peter Reder*

The degree to which the future can be predicted is central to most child care cases. Relevant questions include: whether the parent has the potential to change through therapy; the prospect that the child is likely to suffer significant harm; or whether future contact with a non-custodial parent will be in the child's interest. A particularly common concern is whether parental figures have changed their functioning and style of relationships and can be relied upon in the future to offer the child a different caring environment.

Some parents assert that they have changed their previous pattern of unstable relationships, violent behaviour or substance misuse and have settled down with a committed and caring partner. Or, they may suggest that the birth of their first child has given them a different attitude to life and to responsibilities. It is not that they deny problems, since they readily admit that they had difficulties in the past, but they insist that they have managed to bring about a change in their lives and have permanently altered a habitual pattern of turbulent interactions with others. The claim is for a transition in functioning that has come about *without any therapeutic intervention*. This poses a challenge for the expert witness, who needs to assess what degree of validity can be placed on this assertion and to clarify what factors, if any, might have led to such a transition.

These questions are among the most difficult for mental health professionals to answer, since our capacity to predict the future is limited. Despite numerous attempts at devising risk protocols as general screening measures, their prognostic capacity in individual cases remains uncertain (Browne *et al.*, 2002). Therefore, in order to offer useful opinions to courts, psychiatrists and psychologists tend to rely on theoretical principles and factors associated with either repetition or change reported in the research literature and then apply these to the specific features of the case. This chapter will first review research evidence for the repetition of antisocial behaviour or abusive parenting. Then, some of the principal psychological frameworks of human behaviour will be considered in order to identify which aspects support or refute the proposal that transitional change is possible in the course of a person's life. The processes which are relevant to developmental resilience and to change in personal functioning will be identified, together with the implications for parenting assessments.

## REPETITION OF ABUSIVE BEHAVIOURS

The three most pertinent measures of repetition over time are: reported rates of re-abuse to children remaining with their families; intergenerational continuities of abuse; and recidivism by those who violently offend.

Rates of re-abuse of children by their parents are generally reported to be high, despite professional interventions. Herrenkohl *et al*. (1979) found that, among families in which physical abuse had occurred, 54 per cent showed repeat incidents in up to 10 years of follow-up (the figure was 44 per cent for gross neglect). Murphy *et al*. (1992) noted a one third recidivism rate when two years later they followed up maltreated children who had been restored to parental custody. Similar rates for all child abuse were reported by Browne (1986) and Alexander *et al*. (1990). Corby (1987) studied families receiving casework following child physical abuse and neglect and found a recurrence rate of 28 per cent. Farmer and Owen (1995) discovered that 25 per cent of children whose names had been entered on the Child Protection Register for all kinds of abuse had been re-abused within 20 months. Cleaver and Freeman (1995) found a re-abuse rate of 26 per cent over two years, Thorburn *et al*. (1995) reported an actual or suspected re-abuse rate within six months of one in five children and Gibbons *et al*. (1995) found a re-abuse rate following physical abuse of 20 per cent over 10 years. Bools *et al*. (1993) concluded that at least one in three parents who induced illnesses in their children re-abused them in a similar way once they were rehabilitated home (over a mean follow-up of 5.6 years), while Davis *et al*. (1998) reported likely re-abuse rates of 40 per cent by parents who deliberately poison their child and of 50 per cent by those who abuse by deliberate suffocation.

Paedophilia is usually considered to be a compulsive addiction and adult abusers are shown to have started early in adolescence and abused numerous children in the years that followed. In Elliott *et al*.'s (1995) study of 91 convicted child sex offenders, one third had been under the age of 16 when they first became sexually attracted to children and 70 per cent of the 91 had committed offences against up to 9 children, 23 per cent against between 10 and 40 children and 7 per cent against up to 450 children. However, reported reconviction rates in untreated child sex offenders show a wide variation, ranging from 15 per cent over four years in one study to 64 per cent in another (see Browne and Lynch, 1998). Finkelhor (1986) and Fisher (1994) reviewed evidence that intrafamilial child sex offenders have a lower recidivism rate, of up to 10 per cent, although this is possibly only because of lessening opportunity as their daughters grow older. Furthermore, as shown by Goodwin *et al*. (1983), in later years they may go on to abuse a grand-daughter or niece.

Forensic psychiatrists have long recognized that the best indicator of repetition by an adult who has committed a violent crime is their history of previous violence. However, it is also acknowledged that their capacity to predict dangerousness remains poor, especially because such behaviours tend to be context-related (Scott, 1977; Gunn, 1993). Even so, the Cambridge longitudinal study of delinquency

(Farrington, 1995) found a significant continuity in offending and antisocial behaviour from childhood to adulthood, which was believed to be a function of the individuals rather than their environments, and reoffending could be predicted over the years with surprising accuracy. Generally, the delinquent behaviour increased up to the age of 17 and decreased thereafter, with marital and employment stability significantly fostering desistance from offending. The criminal careers of the most persistent severe offenders started at an early age and these men continued to show a spectrum of other antisocial behaviours, including drug taking, excessive drinking and domestic violence.

A link between maltreatment in childhood and later violent behaviour is demonstrated by the backgrounds of young people in secure accommodation because of serious violent offences (Falshaw and Browne, 1997). The majority (72 per cent) of these young people had originated from abusive and neglectful family environments, including witnessing violence between their parents or being the victims of physical or sexual abuse. Lewis (1992) and Perry (1997), among others, have made similar observations. However, Lewis *et al.* (1989) pointed out that perhaps only 20 per cent of abused children go on to become delinquent but that there is a correlation between the degree of violence inflicted on them as children (especially if the parent seemed to be severely psychiatrically disturbed) and the level of violence in their later antisocial behaviour.

In terms of intergenerational repetition of abuse, approximately one third of abused children go on to become an abuser of their own offspring (Kaufman and Zigler, 1989; Buchanan, 1996). Oliver (1993) suggested that, while one third of abused parents will abuse their child, a further one third remain vulnerable to repeating abusive care, depending on extrafamilial pressure. Domestic violence has also been shown to be intergenerationally repetitive (see Belsky and Pensky, 1988).

Taken together, these findings reveal a significant repetition of abusive, aggressive or antisocial behaviour. However, they also suggest that a proportion of those who have abused their child do not repeat such behaviour and that childhood experiences of maltreatment do not automatically lead to abusive behaviours towards the next generation. The next questions are whether models of psychological development are consistent with these inferences and whether those frameworks enable us to identify the factors most relevant to developmental change and therefore those which need to be included in parenting assessments.

## THEORETICAL MODELS

Detailed reviews of even the principal theories of human personality and relationships, or of the research evidence which supports them, is not possible here. Instead, representative contributions will be considered in what is inevitably an oversimplified and selective account.

## Personality and experience

Individuals change little in observable personality traits over their lifetime (Block, 1971; McCrae and Costa, 1984) but, although heredity plays a significant part in shaping personality, an adult's mode of interacting with others also depends on other developmental processes. As Rutter (1985; 1999) and Caspi *et al.* (1990) described, there is a continuous interplay between an individual's own personality traits and their early and later experiences. Adversity sets in motion a chain of events, the meaning of which varies according to the young person's temperament and stage of development, while different people will expose themselves to different experiences. Belsky and Pensky (1988) therefore envisaged personality as a dynamic self-system with interpersonal consequences, in which individuals are predisposed to attend to certain stimuli and to react in characteristic ways, all of which elicit responses from the social world that maintain the emotional and interpersonal proclivities of that individual. Thus, 'insofar as the family is concerned, past is often prologue to the future. Developmental history appears to shape personality development and, thereby, future functioning' (p. 206).

However, proponents of the social constructionist school view personality not as something which exists inside someone as traits but as the ongoing product of social encounters and relationships. People are seen as having a multiplicity of potential identities, any version of which might emerge through different encounters, the meanings that each participant attributes to the other's behaviour and culture-bound assumptions about each person. Individuals are said to construct 'narratives' as self-referential descriptions of their identity, which are subject to negotiation because they must be compatible with the versions held by other people who figure in the accounts. Change could come about through personal agency and choice if individuals were to analyse critically the narratives which frame their lives, since this would open up the possibility of alternative identities (White and Epston, 1990; Burr, 1995).

Caspi and Elder (1988) and Rutter (1989) offered an equivalent interactional model within which to understand intergenerational consequences of childhood maltreatment. They argued that there is a cumulative risk of serious parenting breakdown over a person's life cycle, which stems from a long chain of indirect connections. Each adverse experience creates a set of circumstances that makes it more likely that another adverse experience will occur. For instance, a hostile family environment may lead to family breakdown and an inability to plan in life, so that partners are chosen who themselves have personal problems and these relationships are unstable and unsupportive, early pregnancies occur, and so on. However, although new experiences are incorporated into previous schemata, these schemata can be adapted in response to environmental demands and also become progressively more sophisticated through identifiable stages of development. Hence, it is possible for an individual to alter previous patterns of behaviour and interaction.

## Internal schemata

The notion of internal schemata is central to many developmental models, although the degree to which they are believed to impact on later functioning varies. The psychoanalytic concept of 'transference', 'internal working models' of attachment theory and 'life scripts' of intergenerational family processes will be briefly considered.

### Repetition compulsion and transference

Freud wrote of the 'repetition compulsion' in which people tended to repeat earlier, usually childhood, patterns over and over again (see LaPlanche and Pontalis, 1973). However, Sandler *et al.* (1973) pointed out that this refers only to a *tendency*, not to a *compulsion*. Even so, at each new phase of a person's psychic development, it is suggested that earlier developmental conflicts and forms of adaptation must be reworked, so that all forms of psychological phenomena, although superseded by later forms, remain potentially active and repetition in psychic functioning is common (Tyson and Tyson, 1990). 'Transference' was considered by Freud to be a prime example of repetition, because the patient repeated repressed attitudes and emotions in the contemporary context of their relationship with the therapist instead of remembering it as something belonging to the past (see LaPlanche and Pontalis, 1973). Some later writers considered that transference elements enter, to a varying degree, into all everyday relationships, often prompted by a characteristic of the other person which represents an attribute of a significant figure from the past (e.g. Greenson, 1965; Sandler *et al.*, 1973; Sandler *et al.*, 1980).

Most psychoanalytic writings have assumed that an individual's personality (including customary modes of relating to others) emerges through internalization of experiences with principal caretakers during the very earliest years, if not months, of life and that development of psychic systems effectively ceases at adolescence. However, some authors were more optimistic about the possibility for change in personality in adult life and Settlage *et al.* (1988) proposed that certain life events in adulthood can act as developmental challenges and a stimulus for further psychic reorganization because they create a disequilibrium, a motivational tension towards adaptive structure reorganization and resolution through a change in the individual's sense of identity. Furthermore, there is evidence that the effects of early traumata can be reversed to a considerable extent (e.g. Skuse, 1988; Clarke and Clarke, 1992; Iwaniec and Sneddon, 2001).

### Internal working models

Attachment theory proposes that an 'internal working model', or mental representation of self and others, develops during the formative years out of attachment experiences (see Holmes, 1993; Howe *et al.*, 1999). Failure by the parent to provide protection and a secure base results in the child developing anxiety, insecurity, poor self-esteem and distorted expectations of future important relationships. Attachment styles assessed in infancy do tend to correlate with those in later childhood, adolescence and adulthood (Rothbard and Shaver, 1994) and Holmes (1993) described the insecurely attached child as seeing themselves as unworthy of love and viewing the world as a dangerous place in which other people are to be treated with great caution. Such assumptions are considered to be relatively enduring and those built up in the early years of life particularly persistent and unlikely to be modified by subsequent experience, probably playing an important part in choices of partner and relationships with them.

However, cognitive development of later childhood and adulthood offers the potential for attachment experiences to be understood and mastered and Belsky and Pensky (1988) acknowledged that, although internal models have a strong propensity to resist change, they are susceptible to revision. Byng-Hall (1995) wrote of active experimental manoeuvres that the mind makes in planning some future event based on knowledge of what has happened in the past, and internal working models being experimented with and adapted over time. Pearson *et al.*'s (1994) notion of 'earned security' allows for the possibility that facilitative relationships at any time in a person's life can help to disconfirm an insecure working model. The individual becomes able to access their feelings and understand their contribution to relationships, thereby controlling their feelings rather than being controlled by them. One further factor of significance for attachment theory is that infants have a hierarchy of attachment figures, albeit that the mother is usually the most important, so that adverse experiences with one can be mitigated by positive experiences with another.

### Life scripts

Byng-Hall (1995) used family 'scripts' as a metaphor for schemata in the present based on the influence of beliefs, attitudes, expectations or experiences from the past. The individual's response to these influences can be to create for themself either a '*replicative*' or a '*corrective*' script, although there is usually a tension between the different scripts. For example, 'the parent who was obsessively disciplined as a child, and has vowed not to discipline his or her children in the same way. This may indeed produce a new, permissive form of discipline . . . But under moments of stress, he or she may replicate exactly the same ferocious discipline, sometimes saying and doing precisely the same things as his or her parent did' (p. 43). Child abuse victims may identify with either the aggressor or the victim (or both) but the experiences may be repressed and therefore be unavailable for review, so that the child becomes involved in similar abusive contexts in the future – as an abuser, as a victim, or as both at different times. An alternative is that the person identifies with the role of rescuer, actual or imagined, or else they adopt a corrective script involving isolation from all relationships.

Choosing a partner usually involves the opportunity to re-enact both replicative and corrective scripts. For Byng-Hall, the key to re-editing family scripts lies in the adequate exchange of information between everyday experience of family life and the meanings attributed to the way family members interact, so that belief systems can alter. The capacity to refrain from taking repetitive action based on a replicative script depends on the capacity to reflect and what he called 'interactive awareness', a capacity to monitor one's own processes and the feedback from others. Byng-Hall used Bowlby's notion of 'defensive exclusion' to suggest that some parents attempt to bury their past by operating a massive corrective script and trying to live completely new lives. However, he believed that there is always a risk for them of some unfortunate aspects of replicative scripts surfacing, triggered by particular cues in certain contexts. Discontinuous change, through trying to write a completely new script, is unrealistic but old scripts can be re-edited if continuity between past and present is acknowledged.

## Family life cycle and transitional phases

The theories discussed so far point towards individuals carrying psychological 'baggage' from the past which influences their development and style of relationships but they are not inevitably stuck in repetitive patterns from which there is no escape. The concept of the family life cycle (Carter and McGoldrick, 1980) adds a systemic dimension to personal development by describing transitional points in a family's history, such as births, deaths, marriages, leaving home, the phase of adolescence, major illnesses, and so on, to which all family members must adjust. These transitions give each individual the opportunity to break free from the past and some families adjust well to the new experiences but others do not and inadvertently try to maintain outmoded relationship patterns. Factors which influence the negotiation of life cycle transitions include personal beliefs about identity and role within the family, flexibility of the family's relationship patterns in order to allow emotional conflicts to be resolved and each person's ability to appreciate a connection between past and present functioning (Boscolo and Bertrando, 1996).

The birth of a first child is commonly cited as the turning point in the parents' lives, changing their behaviour, peer relationships, view of themself and sense of responsibility. In child care court cases, the child's father may allege that there is now a marked contrast between his previously transient relationships or violent and antisocial behaviour and his current avowed investment in the child.

There is some theoretical support for the birth of the first child acting as a critical agent for change in an individual. Antonucci and Mikus (1988) concluded that the child's birth ushers in a period of disequilibrium and personal reorganization for the parents and is usually an event marking a complete change in life approach. The child's birth makes the parent not only a mother or a father but also an adult. For the mother, the first pregnancy marks a particular transitional point in her female identity and also in her relationship with her family-of-origin, since she must move from a primary sense of herself as a daughter to her mother to a realization that she is herself a mother to her child. In this way, motherhood reawakens the original mother–daughter relationship, so that earlier childhood identifications with the mother are measured against the reality of the new mother's relationship with her own child (Pines, 1972). Thus, the new parental role reawakens any dormant conflicts, such as about dependency, control, autonomy, intimacy, sexuality or aggression (Coleman and Coleman, 1971).

This regressive pull is usually offset by opportunities for personal growth and resolution, since the individual can deal with the conflict as an adult who has more psychological resources than when they were a child and also has the possibility of re-experiencing the issue through the eyes of their own child. Nonetheless, encounters with unresolved emotional issues can be distressing and the capacity to reprocess prior developmental conflicts probably varies from individual to individual, depending on their tolerance for ambiguity and arousal, as well as their flexibility and the availability of external supports (Antonucci and Mikus, 1988).

Many new parents contemplate a notion of 'the future' for the first time and, instead of living in the here-and-now, experience an anticipation for what might be, both for themselves and for their child. This sense of future offers them an opportunity to revise their view of themselves and the meaning of their life and seems to represent what Markus and Nurius (1986) termed 'possible selves', the individual's wished for (or feared) conception of themselves as they might become. The child's birth allows the parent to evaluate their 'possible parent self', which is probably based on the role models provided by their own parents, with their 'actual parent self' and make adjustments, with consequent boosts to their self-esteem. However, the ability to reduce the dissonance will depend on their capacity for self-reflection.

## Developmental resilience

These theoretical frameworks all point to cognitive processes as being a crucial variable between continuities or transformations in behaviour. Does our understanding of developmental resilence add further detail to this picture?

According to Rutter (1985), the key elements which determine whether a person will overcome adversity are their sense of self-esteem and self-efficacy. The availability of another close, affectionate and supportive person, whether it be a non-abusing parent or mentor outside the family, is crucial in providing this self-esteem. This, in turn, increases the possibility of the individual forming a satisfying partnership in adult life, which is itself another protective factor. Experience of success in any other area of life as a child, such as at school, contributes to the sense of self-efficacy and an internal locus of control, leading on to a propensity to act positively. A sense of helplessness and being a victim of circumstance, on the other hand, will increase the likelihood that one adversity will lead to another, and so on.

This is supported by the protective factors that have repeatedly emerged from studies of resilience following child abuse. These are: highly developed cognitive skills; a positive self-concept; an internal locus of control for positive experiences (together with an external attribution of blame for the maltreatment); support from the non-offending care-giver; and evidence of a secure early attachment (Conte and Schuerman, 1987; Kendall-Tackett *et al.*, 1993; Romans *et al.*, 1995; Spaccarelli and Kim, 1995; Scott Heller *et al.*, 1999). These factors are clearly interactive, since higher intelligence is likely to lead to raised self-esteem from academic success and a sense of competence and capacity to influence one's life. It is also suggested that availability of support from people other than the abusing parent sets the stage for the use of external support in adulthood (Scott Heller *et al.*, 1999). Furthermore, Himelein and McElrath (1996) concluded that successful resolution of child sexual abuse involves some component of cognitively confronting and reflecting on one's experience. However, resilience may be fluid over time and the impact of different protective and risk factors may change at different life phases.

Nonetheless, there is a consistent pattern to the factors which mitigate against a transgenerational repetition of abuse and these are equivalent to those described as affording children resilience generally to adverse experiences. Egeland *et al.* (1988) reported that 'exception' mothers significantly differed from 'continuity' ones in: having had an emotionally supportive adult available during childhood; having undergone therapy (of over one year's duration) at any time in their lives; and in describing their relationship with their partner as stable, satisfying and supportive. Cognitive processes are repeatedly cited as significant protective factors, including an ability to acknowledge the details of the earlier abuse and to summon the appropriate affect, to gain a perspective on it and to integrate it into their view of themselves (e.g. Hunter and Kilstrom, 1979; Main and Goldwyn, 1984; Egeland *et al.*, 1987; Grossman *et al.*, 1988).

Despite this, Bandura (1982) and Caspi and Elder (1988) were prepared to accept that chance plays a part in enabling individuals to change and that, at times in their lives, an individual emerges, or a fortuitous event is encountered, that intervenes in the developmental process rather than simply confirming an established mode of relating to others. Such reorganization is considered to be especially likely during the assumption of new roles, such as marriage, since these events open up wide opportunities for disconfirming and then reconstructing definitions of self and others. For Bandura (1982), a strong sense of personal agency expands a person's freedom of action at these choice points and enables them to serve as personal contributor to their own life course.

Again, even though a high correlation has been shown between a mother's attachment status (as measured on the Adult Attachment Interview) and their child's, Main *et al.* (1985) found a minority group of parents who had disrupted and traumatic childhoods but securely attached children. These mothers most commonly showed coherence of their narrative – i.e. an understandable account of their childhood experiences, recalled with appropriate affect and empathy for their own parents' difficulties. Ricks (1985) suggested that the capacity to break a cycle of insecure attachment from one generation to the next involves a change in the person's underlying mental representation of self and of others due to change within the formative relationships over time, positive alternative relationships and particularly strong experiences within one relationship. Points of transition in the life cycle also allow for reorganization of internal working models (equivalent to Byng-Hall's 'corrective scripts') to occur: for example, an adolescent reviewing their parents' behaviour, an adult finding a partner or having a child and reviewing their own upbringing, vowing to behave differently and finding that the other person supports a change in script.

## IMPLICATIONS FOR THE ASSESSMENT OF PARENTING

The psychological models reviewed here suggest that while one adverse experience is likely to lead the individual into further harmful contexts, this is not inevitable and there are many opportunities to change over time. Significant intermediaries at each possible transitional point are at least one positive 'other' relationship and the meaning that the individual attributes to their experiences, past and present. Particular themes emerge from this review with sufficient consistency to indicate the factors that need to be addressed in parenting assessments when there is a history of abusive relationships.

### Psychological mindedness

The ability to undergo transitions in personal functioning and move on from adverse experiences seems to be crucially linked to a *capacity to reflect* on the past. It is necessary to be able to recall past experiences, with the appropriate affect, and to acknowledge a continuity between past and present: in other words, to realize that previous hurts remain in the memory and have an effect on present and future relationships. This is not necessarily the same as the psychoanalytic notion of insight, which implies the need for repeated working through of the experience before the transition is secure (Sandler *et al.*, 1973). It is more akin to what Fonagy (1991) referred to as a 'mentalizing capacity', an internal representation of the person's own, or others', states of mind, especially in relation to emotions.

The important facet is the individual being able to put into some perspective the *meaning* that other people and experiences have had for them, both in the past and in the present. It may well be that the abused child realizes that their experiences, however dreadful, were survivable and that they have managed to endure them with a relative sense of intactness. Instead of disowning them through dissociation (Egeland and Susman-Stillman, 1996; Sing Narang and Contreras, 2000), the knowledge and memories of childhood remain available to psychic awareness and integrated as part of the sense of self. This capacity for self-awareness is likely, in turn, to increase the individual's capacity to evaluate others when they come into contact with them and therefore to form judgements about their capacity for intimacy, tendency for violence, their risk to the child, and so on. A self-monitoring capacity will also enable the person to contain their own feelings instead of translating them into impulsive acts, whether directed towards their child, partner or self.

At assessment, parents with limited psychological mindedness give superficial accounts of their history, with significant gaps and minimal affective content. Answers are given in a matter-of-fact way and they may become irritated when the interviewer focuses on emotional issues. There is no evidence that they can use the interviewer's curiosity or suggestions to reflect on possible links between events during their life and, if they do offer any explanations, they tend to be concrete or blaming of others. Examples include parents who say that they cannot remember anything in their childhood prior to 6 or 7 years of age, or who claim that there were no problems at all as they grew up, either for themself or other family members. When their early history includes events that, in principle, could be expected to have a major impact on a developing child (such as being moved from family to family), they claim that there were no emotional repercussions for them: 'it just happened, and that's all there is to it', or 'I missed my mum a bit but got over it.' They give a similar account of their adult life, such as saying that a pregnancy made no difference to them or to their relationship as a couple. One young adult explained his many offences during adolescence as 'I was bored.' If problems are admitted to, they are minimized; such as a mother who referred to severely violent conflict between herself and her partner as 'a rough patch' and the incident in which their son was injured during one of their fights as 'one split second of loss of control'. Characteristically, they reply that they do not think that any help is needed in the future, except perhaps some concrete provision, such as money.

## A supportive relationship

A history of a positive and supportive relationship with at least one adult figure in the past seems to be crucial in enabling a person to overcome a negative relationship with one parental figure. This would be equivalent to the psychoanalytic notion of having an 'internalized good object' or, in attachment language, the provision of a 'secure base'. Additionally, the relationship with the current partner should be sufficiently supportive to reinforce the person's self-esteem and enable transitions in self-identity to be experimented with and consolidated from a position of security. In psychoanalytic terms, the partner does not respond as others have done to certain transference phenomena, while in behavioural terms they do not reinforce unwanted behaviours.

Clearly, the contribution of the partner to the relationship needs to be directly assessed before any opinion can be valid. Sometimes, the current partner does, indeed, seem to have a different quality from others in the past and to hold out the potential for a supportive contribution to their relationship. For instance, a mother's new cohabitee may be clearly less impulsive or consistently more affectionate than her many previously aggressive partners and he may be tolerant of her changing moods, unprovoked by emotional crises and determined to work towards a settled relationship. However, in other cases, the new partner has a history of similar personal and interpersonal problems and the relationship is based on a fragile mutual dependency rather than a sense of reliable supportiveness. Their relationship continues to be characterized by intermittent cycles of violence or recurrent threats to leave each other in which past conflicts are played out in the present without resolution (Reder and Duncan, 2001).

## Reinforcements to self-esteem

A cluster of factors can be subsumed under the general heading of reinforcements to self-esteem (in addition to the presence of a supportive partner). A history of *success* in other areas of life, such as at school, at work or in leisure pursuits, is likely to help that person overcome adverse parenting experiences. Allied to this is a sense of *personal agency*, a belief that they are capable of influencing events in their lives rather than being a passive victim of circumstance and of other people's whims. Such parents accept responsibility for their contribution to past problems, such as their care of the child, but also balance that with a realistic appraisal of the part played by other people. Similarly, they do not blame themself for causing any abuse that they may have suffered in childhood.

Parents with a poor sense of personal agency fail to conceptualize relationships in terms of mutual contributions and lack ownership of the part that they have played in encounters with others. They may offer numerous practical reasons why it was not possible for them to have behaved differently. This factor is also related to their degree of psychological-mindedness, since individuals who automatically ward off uncomfortable feelings or deny ambivalence are unlikely to be able to judge other people, anticipate their future behaviour, or monitor their own attitude to them. One young mother returned to live with a violent man after she talked with a friend who 'let me see his good side'.

In some cases, a parent conveys that their self-esteem is entirely dependent on being allowed to retain care of their baby. A young mother with a long history of physical, emotional and sexual abuse in childhood, followed by violent offending in young adolescence, spoke of her baby having changed her life because it was the only good thing she had ever produced and she described him as 'perfect'. However, she also said at interview that the existence of her baby had kept her sane, made her feel safe and was all that she had to live for. In other words, she appeared to preserve an idealized image of the baby which was her only source of self-esteem and was the provider of comfort to her, a relationship that could be considered fragile and of potential risk to the child.

## Timing

One additional factor is relevant to this aspect of parenting assessments. It is that transitions in personal identity or relationship patterns take time to be negotiated and consolidated. Mathers (1974) suggested that it takes between one and two years for a critical life experience to be subjectively recognized and acknowledged as bringing about a change in that person's self-identity. If the parent who is the subject of the assessment is claiming that a personality adaptation has occurred, then it seems to be important to have the evidence of at least one year's alternative functioning to underpin their assertion. This will need to be weighed against whether such a delay is within the child's time scale for stability.

## CONCLUSIONS

There is evidence that past patterns of behaviour and relationships have a strong tendency to be repeated, but also that a significant number of people manage to break free of such patterns. The principal psychological models used by mental health professionals provide, to varying degrees, explanations for this. A person's cognitive processes act as the critical intermediary, so that a more appropriate aphorism than Byron's 'the best prophet of the future is the past' (*Letter*, 28 January 1821) seems to be 'those who cannot remember the past are condemned to fulfil it' (Santayana, G., *The Life of Reason*, vol. 1, 1905, ch. 12).

There will be some cases in which the likelihood of a parent repeating abusive behaviour is strong. For instance, their threatening or violent behaviour has persisted unabated and, in tracing their history through with them, it is clear that their relationships continue to be transient, or pervaded by the same unresolved conflicts. They are more likely to show temperamental irritability, to have grown up in chaotic homes where they have not gained an understanding of social cause and effect, developed a planning ability, or acquired an internal locus of control (Clarke and Clarke, 1992). They may only offer mechanical or concrete evidence of change, such as having moved home, or having recently turned up regularly for contact visits (even though the visits were emotionally empty or distressing for the child), or having verbally agreed to cooperate with the social worker (even though their compliance coincides with the imminence of the court hearing). They are not psychologically minded and may even belittle attempts at reflectiveness in others. They blame others for any problems and cannot consider what aspects of other people they would need to judge in order for their relationship together not to be a recapitulation of previous ones.

Equally, there will be a few cases in which the prospect of lasting change seems good. The parent has a conscious wish for a different lifestyle and a sense of what difference they are aiming towards. As their history unfolds during the assessment interviews, they are aware of the impact of past traumas on them subsequently and can tolerate the emotions that accompany the memories. Their current partner is evidently supportive and they have managed to remain together for some time, such as one year. They accept responsibility for their contribution to past problems and also demonstrate a sense of self-esteem and capacity to control their lives.

There will be many more cases in which the future prospects are unclear. However, the likelihood of an individual repeating previous abusive relationships is only one element in a comprehensive parenting assessment and, in all cases, it will be necessary to integrate this theme with all other aspects of the case (as discussed by Reder, Duncan and Lucey in Chapter 1). For instance, current circumstances and attitudes are equally important as past experiences and a history of supportive relationships in previous years, which is known to be a significant contributor to resilience, should not be allowed to outweigh the question of current supportive networks and whether the parent is able to access them and make constructive use of them. Current concerns about risk of abuse may apply to a different child from the one who was previously removed into foster care; this child may be older, have a different temperament and a different psychological meaning to the parent, and therefore the parent–child relationship will be different. In other words, the dimension focusing on the parent's propensity to repeat past patterns of behaviour will need to be integrated in a multidimensional assessment that takes account of current as well as past contexts.

# References

Alexander, R., Crabbe, L., Sato, Y., Smith, W. and Bennett, T. (1990) Serial abuse in children who are shaken, *American Journal of Disease of Children* 144: 58–60.

Antonucci, T.C. and Mikus, K. (1988) The power of parenthood: personality and attitudinal changes during the transition to parenthood, in G.Y. Michaels and W.A. Goldberg (eds) *The Transition to Parenthood: Current Theory and Research*, Cambridge: Cambridge University Press.

Bandura, A. (1982) The psychology of chance encounters and life paths, *American Psychologist* 37: 747–55.

Belsky, J. and Pensky, E. (1988) Developmental history, personality, and family relationships: toward an emergent family system, in R.A. Hinde and J. Stevenson-Hinde (eds) *Relationships within Families: Mutual Influences*, Oxford: Clarendon Press.

Block, J. (1971) *Lives through Time*, Berkeley, CA: Bancroft.

Bools, C.N., Neale, B.A. and Meadow, S.R. (1993) Follow up of victims of fabricated illness (Munchausen syndrome by proxy), *Archives of Disease in Childhood* 69: 625–30.

Boscolo, L. and Bertrando, P. (1996) *Systemic Therapy with Individuals*, London: Karnac.

Browne, D.H. (1986) The role of stress in the commission of subsequent acts of child abuse and neglect, *Journal of Family Violence* 1: 289–97.

Browne, K.D. and Lynch, M. (1998) Editorial: protecting children from sex offenders, *Child Abuse Review* 7: 369–78.

Browne, K.D., Hanks, H., Stratton, P. and Hamilton, C. (eds) (2002) *Early Prediction and Prevention of Child Abuse: A Handbook*, Chichester: John Wiley.

Buchanan, A. (1996) *Cycles of Child Maltreatment: Facts, Fallacies and Interventions*, Chichester: John Wiley.

Burr, V. (1995) *An Introduction to Social Constructionism*, London: Routledge.

Byng-Hall, J. (1995) *Rewriting Family Scripts: Improvisation and Systems Change*, New York: The Guilford Press.

Carter, E.A. and McGoldrick, M. (eds) (1980) *The Family Life Cycle: A Framework for Family Therapy*, New York: Gardner.

Caspi, A. and Elder, G.H. (1988) Emergent family patterns: the intergenerational construction of problem behaviour and relationships, in R.A. Hinde and J. Stevenson-

Hinde (eds) *Relationships within Families: Mutual Influences*, Oxford: Clarendon Press.

Caspi, A., Elder, G.H. and Herbener, A.S. (1990) Childhood personality and the prediction of life-course patterns, in L.N. Robins and M. Rutter (eds) *Straight and Devious Pathways from Childhood to Adulthood*, Cambridge: Cambridge University Press.

Clarke, A.M. and Clarke, A.D.B. (1992) How modifiable is the human life path? *International Journal of Research in Mental Retardation* 18: 137–57.

Cleaver, H. and Freeman, P. (1995) *Parental Perspectives in Cases of Suspected Child Abuse*, London: HMSO.

Coleman, A. and Coleman, L. (1971) *Pregnancy: The Psychological Experience*, New York: Bantam Books.

Conte, J.R. and Schuerman, J.R. (1987) Factors associated with an increased impact of child sexual abuse, *Child Abuse & Neglect* 11: 201–11.

Corby, B. (1987) *Working with Child Abuse: Social Work Practice and the Child Abuse System*, Milton Keynes: Open University Press.

Davis, P., McClure, R.J., Rolfe, K., Chessman, N., Pearson, S., Sibert, J.R. and Meadow, R. (1998) Procedures, placement, and risks of further abuse after Munchausen syndrome by proxy, non-accidental poisoning, and non-accidental suffocation, *Archives of Disease in Childhood* 78: 217–21.

Egeland, B., Jacobvitz, D. and Papatola, K. (1987) Intergenerational continuity of abuse, in R.J. Gelles and J.B. Lancaster (eds) *Child Abuse and Neglect: Biosocial Dimensions*, New York: Aldine de Gruyter.

Egeland, B., Jacobvitz, D. and Sroufe, L.A. (1988) Breaking the cycle of abuse, *Child Development* 59: 1080–8.

Egeland, B. and Susman-Stillman, A. (1996) Dissociation as a mediator of child abuse across generations, *Child Abuse & Neglect* 20: 1123–32.

Elliott, M., Browne, K. and Kilcoyne, J. (1995) Child sexual abuse prevention: what offenders tell us, *Child Abuse & Neglect* 19: 579–94.

Falshaw, L. and Browne, K. (1997) Adverse childhood experiences and violent acts of young people in secure accommodation, *Journal of Mental Health* 6: 443–55.

Farmer, E. and Owen, M. (1995) *Child Protection Practice: Private Risks and Public Remedies*, London: HMSO.

Farrington, D.P. (1995) The development of offending and anti-social behaviour from childhood: key findings from the Cambridge Study in Delinquent Development, *Journal of Child Psychology & Psychiatry* 36: 929–64.

Finkelhor, D. (1986) Abusers: special topics, in D. Finkelhor and associates, *A Sourcebook on Child Sexual Abuse*, Beverley Hills, CA: Sage.

Fisher, D. (1994) Adult sex offenders. Who are they? Why and how do they do it? in T. Morrison, M. Erooga and R.C. Beckett (eds) *Sexual Offending against Children: Assessment and Treatment of Male Abusers*, London: Routledge.

Fonagy, P. (1991) Thinking about thinking: some clinical and theoretical considerations in the treatment of a borderline patient, *International Journal of Psycho-Analysis* 72: 639–56.

Gibbons, J., Gallager, B., Bell, C. and Gordon, D. (1995) *Development after Physical Abuse in Early Childhood*, London: HMSO.

Goodwin, J., Cormier, L. and Owen, J. (1983) Grandfather-granddaughter incest: a trigenerational view, *Child Abuse & Neglect* 7: 163–70.

Greenson, R.R. (1965) The working alliance and the transference neurosis, *Psychoanalytic Quarterly* 34: 155–81.

Grossman, K., Fremmer-Bombik, E., Rudolph, J. and Grossman, K.E. (1988) Maternal attachment representations as related to patterns of infant-mother attachment and maternal care during the first year, in R.A. Hinde and J. Stevenson-Hinde (eds) *Relationships within Families: Mutual Influences*, Oxford: Clarendon.

Gunn, J. (1993) Dangerousness, in J. Gunn and P.J. Taylor (eds) *Forensic Psychiatry: Clinical, Legal and Ethical Issues*, Oxford: Butterworth-Heinemann.

Herrenkohl, R.C., Herrenkohl, E.C., Egolf, B. and Seech, M. (1979) The repetition of child abuse: how frequently does it occur? *Child Abuse & Neglect* 3: 67–72.

Himelein, M.J. and McElrath, J.A.V. (1996) Resilient child sexual abuse survivors: cognitive coping and illusion, *Child Abuse & Neglect* 20: 747–58.

Holmes, J. (1993) *John Bowlby & Attachment Theory*, London: Routledge.

Howe, D., Brandon, M., Hinings, D. and Schofield, G. (1999) *Attachment Theory, Child Maltreatment and Family Support: A Practice and Assessment Model*, Basingstoke: Macmillan.

Hunter, R.S. and Kilstrom, N. (1979) Breaking the cycle in abusive families, *American Journal of Psychiatry* 136: 1320–2.

Iwaniec, D. and Sneddon, H. (2001) Attachment styles in adults who failed to thrive as children: outcomes of a 20 year follow-up study of factors influencing maintenance or change in attachment style, *British Journal of Social Work* 31: 179–95.

Kaufman, J. and Zigler, E. (1989) The intergenerational transmission of child abuse, in D. Cicchetti and V. Carlson (eds) *Child Maltreatment: Theory and Research on the Causes and Consequences of Child Abuse and Neglect*, Cambridge: Cambridge University Press.

Kendall-Tackett, K.A., Williams, L.M. and Finkelhor, D. (1993) Impact of sexual abuse on children: a review and synthesis of recent empirical studies, *Psychological Bulletin* 113: 164–80.

LaPlanche, J. and Pontalis, J.-B. (1973) *The Language of Psycho-Analysis*, London: Hogarth.

Lewis, D.O. (1992) From abuse to violence: psychophysiological consequences of maltreatment, *Journal of the American Academy of Child & Adolescent Psychiatry* 31: 383–9.

Lewis, D.O., Mallouh, C. and Webb, V. (1989) Child abuse, delinquency, and violent criminality, in D. Cicchetti and V. Carlson (eds) *Child Maltreatment: Theory and Research on the Causes and Consequences of Child Abuse and Neglect*, Cambridge: Cambridge University Press.

McCrae, R. and Costa, P. (1984) *Emerging Lives, Enduring Disposition: Personality in Adulthood*, Boston: Little & Brown.

Main, M. and Goldwyn, R. (1984) Predicting rejection of her infant from mother's representation of her own experiences: implications for the abused-abusing inter-generational cycle, *Child Abuse & Neglect* 8: 203–17.

Main, M., Kaplan, N. and Cassidy, J. (1985) Security in infancy, childhood, and adulthood: a move to the level of representation, in I. Bretherton and E. Waters (eds) *Growing Points of Attachment Theory and Research*, Chicago: University of Chicago Press.

Markus, H. and Nurius, P. (1986) Possible selves, *American Psychologist* 41: 954–69.

Mathers, J. (1974) The gestation period of identity change, *British Journal of Psychiatry* 125: 472–4.

Murphy, J.M., Bishop, S.J., Jellineck, M.S., Quinn, D. and Poitrast, F.G. (1992) What happens after the care and protection petition? Reabuse in a court sample, *Child Abuse & Neglect* 16: 485–553.

Oliver, J.E. (1993) Intergenerational transmission of child abuse: rates, research, and clinical implications, *American Journal of Psychiatry* 150: 1315–24.

Pearson, J.L., Cohn, D.A., Cowan, P.A. and Cowan, C.P. (1994) Earned- and continuous-security in adult attachment: relation to depressive symptomatology and parenting style, *Development and Psychopathology* 6: 359–73.

Perry, B.D. (1997) *Maltreated Children: Experience, Brain Development and the Next Generation*, New York: Norton.

Pines, D. (1972) Pregnancy and motherhood: interaction between fantasy and reality, *British Journal of Medical Psychology* 45: 333–43.

Reder, P. and Duncan, S. (2001) Abusive relationships, care and control conflicts and insecure attachments, *Child Abuse Review* 10: 411–27.

Ricks, M.H. (1985) The social transition of parental behaviour: attachment across the generations, in I. Bretherton and E. Waters (eds) *Growing Points of Attachment Theory and Research*, Chicago: University of Chicago Press.

Romans, S.E., Martin, J.L., Anderson, J.C., O'Shea, M.L. and Mullen, P.E. (1995) Factors that mediate between child sexual abuse and adult psychological outcome, *Psychological Medicine* 25: 127–42.

Rothbard, J. and Shaver, P.R. (1994) Continuity of attachment across the life span, in M.B. Sperling and W.H. Berman (eds) *Attachment in Adults: Clinical and Developmental Perspectives*, New York: The Guilford Press.

Rutter, M. (1985) Resilience in the face of adversity: protective factors and resistance to psychiatric disorder, *British Journal of Psychiatry* 147: 598–611.

Rutter, M. (1989) Intergenerational continuities and discontinuities in serious parenting difficulties, in D. Cicchetti and V. Carlson (eds) *Child Maltreatment: Theory and Research on the Causes and Consequences of Child Abuse and Neglect*, Cambridge: Cambridge University Press.

Rutter, M.L. (1999) Psychosocial adversity and child psychopathology, *British Journal of Psychiatry* 174: 480–93.

Sandler, J., Dare, C. and Holder, A. (1973) *The Patient and the Analyst: The Basis of the Psychoanalytic Process*, London: George Allen & Unwin.

Sandler, J., Kennedy, H. and Tyson, R.L. (1980) *The Technique of Child Psychoanalysis: Discussions with Anna Freud*, London: Hogarth.

Scott, P.D. (1977) Assessing dangerousness in criminals, *British Journal of Psychiatry* 131: 127–42.

Scott Heller, S., Larrieu, J.A., D'Imperio, R. and Boris, N.W. (1999) Research on resilience to child maltreatment: empirical considerations, *Child Abuse & Neglect* 23: 321–38.

Settlage, C.F., Curtis, J., Lozoff, Ma., Lozoff, Mi., Silberschatz, G. and Simburg, E.J. (1988) Conceptualizing adult development, *Journal of the American Psycho-Analytic Association* 36: 347–69.

Sing Narang and Contreras, J.M. (2000) Dissociation as a mediator between child abuse history and adult abuse potential, *Child Abuse & Neglect* 24: 653–65.

Skuse, D. (1988) Extreme deprivation in early childhood, in K. Mogford and D. Bishop (eds) *Language Development in Exceptional Circumstances*, London: Churchill Livingstone.

Spaccarelli, S. and Kim, S. (1995) Resilience criteria and factors associated with resilience in sexually abused girls, *Child Abuse & Neglect* 19: 1171–82.

Thorburn, J., Lewis, A. and Shemmings, D. (1995) *Paternalism or Partnership? Family Involvement in the Child Protection Process*, London: HMSO.

Tyson, P. and Tyson, R.L. (1990) *Psychoanalytic Theories of Development: An Integration*, New Haven, CT: Yale University Press.

White, M. and Epston, D. (1990) *Narrative Means to Therapeutic Ends*, New York: Norton.

# Part IV

# Recommendations

# Chapter 14

# Is it possible to work with parental denial?

*Arnon Bentovim*

## INTRODUCTION

Denial by parents who are considered to be responsible for abuse of their children is a pervasive reality in working in the field. At the Great Ormond Street Hospital for Children in London, we studied 98 children referred to our treatment service following consensus amongst professionals (including civil courts) that they had been sexually abused (Hyde *et al.*, 1995; Monck *et al.*, 1996). Only 9 per cent of the adult abusers took full responsibility for their actions; a further 16 per cent took a degree of responsibility for what was alleged but minimized the severity; and 75 per cent took no responsibility, denying that abuse had occurred and blaming the child for creating a false reality or a professional for encouraging false allegations. Thirty seven per cent of the partners accommodated to the abuser's denials and could not accept that abuse had occurred; 33 per cent could not decide whether to believe the child or the abuser; while 30 per cent were convinced that abuse had taken place and took a protective stance.

Dale *et al.* (2002) have researched severe physical abuse and reported the frequency of infants with 'serious injuries and discrepant parental explanations'. They describe the significant challenges of managing such cases, where risks are high and the outcome can be fatal. Indeed, examination of fatal cases also reveals discrepant histories and delays in seeking help (Krugman, 1985). The risk is that professionals will accommodate to the explanations given, accept them and return the children home without adequate protection, to suffer further injuries.

## THE RELEVANCE OF PARENTAL DENIAL

The return of a child who has been seriously maltreated to a family where there is no understanding of how the abuse occurred is clearly risky. A number of areas are relevant.

## Psychological impact on the child

In the Great Ormond Street Hospital research, those sexually abused children whose testimony continued to be rejected by the presumed abuser and the other partner had the most serious and worrying mental health problems. Although relieved not to live in a family where they were disbelieved and rejected, at the same time they felt an intense sense of grief at the loss of the only family they had known.

In our view, the pernicious effect of disbelief, disavowal and rejection is profound and can undermine personality functioning in later life. The impact on these young people's distress often has the paradoxical effect of confirming the disbelief of the parents, whose tie to each other and mutual loyalty is strengthened in the face of statements that can be dismissed as coming from a disturbed child. A resolution for some children is to subscribe to the denial and demand to return home where they now state that they were not abused. A similar pattern can be seen in physically abused and rejected children, where 'traumatic bonding' (an enmeshed, intense attachment to the perpetrator of abuse) can take precedence in their own minds over the risk and fear to which they have been exposed.

## Maintenance of dysfunctional family relationships

In families in which parents avoid conflict between themselves, abuse may occur when they displace their anger on to the children. As described above, collusive denial of abuse by parents, especially if believed by others, further cements the relationship between the parents and helps them avoid conflict and differences. Together, they can face the world, reject professional opinions and ignore the views of courts. Since such powerful denial systems remain closed to external influence, there is the risk of progressive failure to adapt to children's needs, with diminishing emotional support for them, blunting of communication and continuing poor care. Little change is possible and the children remain at risk.

## Impossibility of identifying triggers to assaults and abuse

If denial persists, the implication is that it is not possible to understand the process by which abuse occurred and the factors which triggered the parent's irritation, anger or sexual feelings. Hence, there can be no way of developing an abuse-free life for the child or other children in the family. Often, the processes leading to an explosion or abusive act represent a complex chain of interacting factors, such as personality characteristics, interpersonal responses between parents or the extended family, a sense of overload linked with privation, or illness. Without acknowledgement of such processes, it is impossible to understand events which caused the abuse, develop appropriate protective strategies and therefore prevent repetition in the future.

## Inability to believe in the parent's truthfulness or cooperation

Parental refusal to contemplate that their child's state is their responsibility makes it extremely difficult for professionals to build up a sense of trust, openness and partnership with them. The professionals cannot know whether the parents can be relied on to share stressful moments or times when they feel themselves to be a danger towards their child. Since it is extremely difficult for a parent to admit to themself that loving feelings can turn to anger and a desire to hurt, professionals must be able to trust that such fluctuations in feelings would be shared so that protective action can be taken. If a partner is supporting the process of denial, then the professional's difficulties are increased and the risk of marginalization and of a closed family system is greater, with increasing risk to the child.

## IS ACKNOWLEDGEMENT A PREREQUISITE FOR CHANGE?

Questions are often raised as to whether changes in parenting require acknowledgement that there are problems and the part that the parents played in them. There is an ongoing professional debate about how much responsibility is required as a prerequisite for keeping a child safe. Some have argued that denial is a contraindication to rehabilitation (e.g. Dale *et al.*, 1986; Reder and Lucey, 1995; Jones, 1998), whilst others have suggested that it may be possible to tolerate an initial lack of acceptance of responsibility and work therapeutically with some parents towards that goal (e.g. Fitzpatrick, 1995; Essex *et al.*, 1996; Robinson and Witney, 1999).

In my view, if a parent had such a capacity, it would be unlikely that the child would have been abused in the first place, since such a level of self-reflectiveness and self-knowledge would indicate other pathways towards coping. It seems that abuse occurs in the absence of a high degree of self-reflection, based on overwhelming impulses which are then rationalized. The question is whether a parent can be expected to stand back far enough to begin to look at themself, try to understand the problem and ask questions with a degree of curiosity about how such a problem could have come about, and what part they or their partner have played.

Parents often find it extremely difficult even to contemplate that they could have had any part in causing an injury. Using Prochaska and DiClemente's (1982) comprehensive model of change, Morrison (1998) described the complex processes necessary for parents to create a safe context for children when abuse has occurred. In the earliest stages, when agencies are making enquiries following a report of abuse, families are anxious, scared, defensive, angry and reluctant to look at difficulties within. The next stage is one of 'contemplation', where families begin to consider the possibility that there is a problem and explore whether they feel able to tackle it and make progress. There are then seven further steps of contemplation, with moves from: acceptance that there is a problem; acceptance of some responsibility for it; feeling some discomfort about the problem; believing that things must change; being able to see that they can be part of the solution, can make a choice and can see the next steps towards change. This is a painful and potentially arduous process, which needs a good deal of determination and support to achieve.

The debate will be explored in this chapter and it will be argued that there may be scope to work in circumstances of doubt or where there is a degree of denial present. However, what is essential is a full and detailed assessment of individuals and their family context in order to make judgements about how safe the parent can keep their child. Since children who have been abused, disbelieved and rejected need help to manage their emotional distress, to rebuild attachments and to readjust their precarious sense of self as a victim who feels responsible for everything that has happened to them, this chapter will ask whether another way forward is possible in such intractable denial situations.

## UNDERSTANDING THE DENIAL PROCESS

It is important to understand denial, not only as an individual process but as a relationship issue in terms of who needs to be convinced that denial is the 'correct' construction in order to maintain relationships within the family and with those outside it.

### Psychological and social denial

Trepper and Barrett (1989) have pragmatically described two forms of denial: psychological and social. They allied the notion of psychological denial to 'repression', the apparent absence of any conscious memory of having abused, even when the evidence of such action was strong. Social denial, by comparison, involves a degree of awareness that the individual was responsible for abusive acts but, at the same time, they minimize and attempt to render the facts meaningless. This is frequently associated with blaming a child for exaggerating or blaming professionals for implanting ideas that serious abuse took place. An assertion might be made that there was harmless touching with no inappropriate intent, or the life-threatening nature of a shaking injury becomes minimized once the child recovers. A parent may argue that the infant's leg must have caught in the cot's bars, or the infant must have fractured it themselves, the anal dilation must be due to constipation or the sexualized behaviour could have arisen through viewing pornographic material. Other professionals and adults may be appealed to to create an alliance to strengthen such assertions, or else the action may be said to have been 'a one-off', out of character and not justifying such serious concerns. Alternatively, the parent may accept that the child was abused but claim that the wrong person has been named, as a result of confusion, jealousy or a grievance. Some perpetrators state categorically that, whilst there may have been abuse, they have absolutely no memory of it because of drunkenness, being in a drugged state or 'forgetting'.

It is, of course, difficult to differentiate psychological and social forms of denial, since the absence of memory can only be established through the subjective report of the alleged perpetrator. However, recent writings about memory (e.g. Epstein and Bottoms, 2002), whilst applying to specific memories of abusive experiences, speculate that there can be forceful forgetting, repression and later recollection of apparently repressed memory. This could also apply to memories of abusive actions, so that perception of the effect of the acts on the victim 'traumatize' the perpetrator, leading to a similar process of forced forgetting, repression and dissociation.

## Development of a sense of conscience

By definition, psychological or social forms of denial require a stage of personal development where the individual has acquired a social conscience and can distinguish between what is right and wrong, appropriate and inappropriate. There is a possibility that some individuals fail to develop an adequate social conscience, either because of severe personality disorder or markedly impaired intellectual functioning. They may blur issues of truth, honesty and reality, based on value systems involving a powerful anti-authority stance and rejection of ordinary standards.

## Avoidance of punishment

Alternatively, denial may represent an avoidance of the likelihood of punishment, in the knowledge that abuse of a child is not only a failure of care but also a criminal act. Herein lies a paradox, for persistent denial in the criminal court renders it more likely that responsibility cannot be proven beyond a reasonable doubt and so the parent is advised that they should not incriminate themself. However, at the same time, within the civil court context, for a parent not to accept responsibility may mean that the child is less likely to be returned to their care. Caught in such a bind, the self-protective instinct may well be a factor which maintains denial, despite the parent being quite aware of the nature of their actions.

## Trauma organized systems as a model to understand denial processes

I have put forward the view that 'trauma organized systems' could be a key theory to help us understand denial processes in families where physical and sexual abuse have occurred (Bentovim, 1992). The framework is a socio-cultural one, society being seen as a context in which women and children are looked at as requiring protection yet also as appropriate objects for violence and punishment. Thus, the family can be an organization that protects, nurtures and facilitates children's development and growth, but it can also be one which constrains and abuses the children's development in the name of discipline, control and loyalty.

Families where abuse occurs are characterized by high levels of traumatic and stressful experiences throughout the lives of the parents, which have cumulative effects on the children. For example, in our research on the origins of abusive behaviour (Skuse *et al.*, 1998), we noted that young people who behave in a sexually abusive manner often have had significant exposure to violence and mal-treatment, perpetrated both against themself and against maternal figures. They are prone to react to stress with abusive behaviour. Similar patterns can be seen in young people who abuse physically and use physical violence. Furthermore, such individuals also become the parents who physically and sexually abuse in adult life. An important study by Midgely (1997) demonstrated significant levels of dissociative phenomena in young people who abuse others and findings from Adult Attachment Interviews that parents who induce illness in their children have dismissive attachment patterns (Bluglass, 2001) can also be linked to an inter-generational pattern of denial and dismissal of reality.

An explanation is that traumatic events overwhelm defensive capacities by evoking intense affective arousal, a sense of helplessness and extreme distress. They may well be registered in the brain in ways that maintain arousal, fight and flight. They can also result in post-traumatic stress, with re-enactments and flash-backs, nightmares and distressing memories of abuse precipitated by stimuli associated with the original events. A key element of the post-traumatic response is the avoidance limb, which includes dissociation, restriction of thought and blanking out. These responses can have a profound and pervasive effect on all aspects of emotional life, including attachment relationships and sense of self, and result in a spectrum of denial tendencies, from psychological to social.

The notion of 'organized systems' relates to the use of language used by individuals to define and make sense of the situations. If the language is one of absence, blame on others and refusal to accept responsibility, then such thinking organizes others within the family to comply with the denial of abuse, in the same way that there was compliance with the fact of abuse. The reasoning associated with the abusive act itself may be to blame the child or the partner for causing the adult to lose their temper, behave sexually, block the child's airway or administer medication. Thus, traumatic events from the past are processed in ways which come to organize thinking, and from which narratives, beliefs and convictions emerge.

## ASSESSMENT IN THE CONTEXT OF DENIAL

The *Framework for Assessment of Children in Need and their Families* (Department of Health *et al.*, 2000), with its comprehensive eco-systemic model, is an important contribution to assessing parenting and the potential for change. The observational instruments – the *Home Observation* (Caldwell and Bradley,

1984; Cox and Walker, 2001) and the *Family Assessment* (Bentovim and Bingley-Miller, 2001) – are two evidence-based approaches to assessing parents which will also assist in the process of appraising treatability. Assessments which look at family strengths as well as difficulties are essential if professionals are not to be organized by denial systems (Bentovim and Bingley-Miller, 2001). During the assessment, it is crucial to evaluate the nature of the abuse itself and construct the reality of what must have happened, expecting some degree of denial or minimizing by the parent. However, the conclusions must take into account all aspects of the family's functioning and not focus exclusively on the presence or absence of denial, which is only one element of a much larger assessment.

When we are asked if it is possible to work with individuals who state that they have no memory of abusive behaviour, our approach is to use a sequence of hypothetical questions (Jenkins, 1990; Boscolo *et al.*, 1987) to try to move them from the 'pre-contemplative stage' to the 'contemplative stage' (Morrison, 1998). For instance, we ask the alleged abuser: 'What would your response be if the following morning you woke up and realized that there was a grain of truth in the allegation and had a sudden return of memory of abusive actions?'; 'What would happen if you recalled an act which may have caused fractures, bruising or sexual contact?'; 'Could you live with yourself?'; 'Might you feel so distressed that you might take some action against yourself?'; 'Do you think such behaviour would be understandable?'; 'Would someone who acted in this way be open to treatment?'; 'Could that individual have a child in his or her care eventually?'

Very frequently, parents say that they could not tolerate themself if they had indeed been responsible for such an act; they do not think that individuals who abuse children can be helped; and a child should not be allowed to live with such a parent. We then connote the failure to recall as being, perhaps, a way of ultimately protecting the child. We would say that if a court believed a child had been abused and if a parent had no distinct memory of their actions and no understanding of the antecedent factors leading to moments of overwhelming rage or sexual arousal, then the court would not be happy for a child to be in that individual's care. As the parent would also reject an individual responsible for such behaviour and does not feel help can be given to them, then recollection of abusive action could lead to even greater difficulty for them. In such circumstances, maintenance of 'denial' may help the child remain in a 'safe' situation.

We attempt to normalize frustration with children, to talk about the fact that people who abuse often have great love, affection and a deep wish to care. Perhaps the way they were abused when they were children leads parents to find crying, fussing and anger difficult to cope with. Alternatively, we explain that there can be historical unconscious forces, which are not part of their 'normal' selves, which lead people to see children as sexual beings: actions then occur which are totally out of character for those parents. We try to paint abusive actions as an 'understandable' response to frustration, or a troubled personal history as having meaning rather than being associated with monstrously cruel behaviour (which may be their own construction). In painting a picture of how a parent might behave under stress, we attempt to create an alliance with them and help them shift from a denial stance, particularly when the denial is more social than psychological.

There are some parents, however, who remain absolutely adamant. They state that this description does not fit them in any way, or that they have no such recollection. Indeed, their stance may be to attack the observer who considers that their child has been abused, which can often result in extensively hard-fought court cases and persisting denial, whatever the decision of the court. There is increasing reliance in the UK family proceedings courts on initial causation hearings, to assess whether abuse has occurred (on the balance of probability), followed by a later disposal hearing. This does provide an opportunity for parents to reconsider their stance once all the information has been rehearsed and a judgment made. However, many parents remain in absolute denial, despite the fact that the court has adjudicated that serious abuse occurred. Perhaps their need to maintain alliances with important figures who remain unconvinced, such as partners, parents or family networks, continues to be more important than the truth about their child. Unfortunately, the adversarial legal system, which urges parties into opposing realities, leaves little room for shifting positions and may reinforce denial. The court may also contribute to the process by asserting that the more serious the allegation, the less likely is it to be real, and so the stronger the evidence needs to be – an interesting variation on the truth/denial theme.

## CASE EXAMPLES

Some parents or families are suitable for a 'hypothesizing' approach to their difficulties, while others prove not to be able to use such strategies. This is illustrated by the following case examples.

### Psychological denial

We accepted an abusive father's request for hypnosis, as he had no conscious memory of the abuse of his children, for which he had been prosecuted. He proved to be a good subject for hypnotic regression but, as he returned in memory to the phase when he was living with his wife and step-children, he became profoundly depressed and suicidal. The process of regression was stopped because of a concern that he might make an attempt on his own life.

The children had no wish to see their father and gave a coherent and credible account of their abuse, which was believed by their mother. With no possibility that the father would recollect his abusive behaviour, there could be no therapeutic work to ensure that he could be a safe parent.

## Social denial

The importance of the 'network' in maintaining or dissolving social denial was noted in one case. Professionals agreed that a mother was responsible for a Munchausen by proxy situation, by inducing cyanotic episodes and administering Aspirins to her child. She maintained absolute denial of responsibility, remaining convinced that her son had been physically ill. Her two children were placed with her mother and a subsequent child was placed with his father. Extensive psychiatric assessments did not alter the mother's belief in the 'illness states' of her child. She met another partner and the child of this relationship was removed for 'further assessment'. On this occasion, following supportive and collaborative social work, the mother was able to say in a family/network meeting that she accepted responsibility for inducing the cyanotic attacks in her previous child. She asked whether she was going to be arrested and told us that her earlier denial had partly been motivated by her fear of punishment, an intolerable sense of profound guilt and a fear of her then partner's violence. She was aware that, without taking some responsibility, there could be no treatment and she would also lose her youngest child. The most important factor was that her current partner was able to explain that her admission of abusive behaviour would not alienate him, as she had felt it must.

The forces which 'maintained' and 'rewarded' denial were outweighed by the potential losses and she took the risk of beginning to admit some responsibility.

## A lifetime of social denial

A man who had served an 8-year prison sentence for sexually abusing one of his two daughters stated that he had no recollection of the events. He informed us that he drank a bottle of whisky every day and had no memory of any abusive behaviour. His wife, who was prosecuted as a co-defender, also claimed no memory, as she was drunk. It was discovered unexpectedly that he had fathered three of his other daughter's children and that he and she used to go drinking together. Her partner was said to be fed up with the amount of time they spent together. The other daughter, the mother of the three children, acknowledged that the DNA tests must have been correct but she, too, had no recollection of any action which could have led to the pregnancies: indeed, there had never been any sexual contact. She said, 'We would not have had the test if we suspected what the results might be.' Her mother, the children's grandmother, said that she felt very angry about what had been revealed but she had not expressed her feelings to her husband. Instead, they were living somewhat separate lives from each other but remained a couple.

In this case, it was impossible to work therapeutically to break through the pervasive denial.

## Confronting social denial

A 5-year-old presented with severe vaginal bleeding and was found to have evidence of vaginal penetration and a vaginal tear. This was claimed to be either a straddle injury or caused by a sibling playing with a toy car and penetrating his sister's vagina. Although there was no immediate satisfactory explanation, the family seemed to be open and cooperative and the child was discharged home with a care plan to work closely with social services. However, social workers were excluded as soon as the child returned home. It was only our insistence that we could not assess the child unless she was living in a neutral context that led to the court ruling that she spend a period of time in a foster home, with no family contact. With considerable resistance, she was able to disclose that her father had perpetrated the abuse. Only later could the mother reveal the violence of his style of relating, the oppressive force which he used to control the family and how he had organized the family to his belief that a sibling was responsible.

Removal of the child enabled the mother to relinquish her denial, but the vehemence of the father's denial was unshakeable and it was not possible to work therapeutically with him.

## Shaking injury in a trauma organized system

An infant sustained a severe shaking injury resulting in subdural haemorrhages and serious visual problems. He was the first son of the father and the fourth of the mother. The injury was initially explained as being caused by one of the older siblings behaving in a jealous and rough way towards him. Such was the absolute certainty of the father that he convinced his partner and persuaded the local child protection team to interview the boys. Nonetheless, because the injury was not adequately explained, the infant was taken into care. The father then received a period of counselling to help him deal with the stress that 'his only infant had been removed from his care'. During this therapeutic work, he began to acknowledge responsibility and, as it were, think the unthinkable. He was subsequently able to demonstrate with a doll his frustration with the infant's crying and acknowledge that, even though he had been able to steer a 30-ton tank around narrow tracks when he was in the military, he felt that he had no capacity to cope with a small infant. We learned that the mother had encouraged him to handle the infant and to provide care for him, both to give him a task while he was not working and to allow him to bond with the infant. This was the father's first stable relationship and he was terrified of losing his partner if he admitted feeling overwhelmed and unable to cope. Therefore, he tried to blame the sibling. Because of his determination to accept responsibility, even though it led to a conviction, he was able to assuage his considerable sense of guilt. He was able to describe 'something snapping' when he lost control, seeing the impact of his shake and being overwhelmed by what he had done.

Eventually, he revealed that, during childhood, he had seen his brother being severely punished and it became apparent that his own baby's inconsolable crying had triggered the same sense of helplessness and a desire for revenge. This was projected on to the infant and, for a moment, the father had felt like a child and perceived the infant to be a punitive parent.

## Induced illness in a trauma organized system

A similar situation was seen in another family where the mother had induced a life-threatening illness in her first child by administering substances whilst she and the newborn baby were still in hospital. The mother, who could not accept the findings of the causation hearing, separated from her husband and infant and subsequently bore another child. The court was asked to consider the risk to the second child. The mother was a woman with a considerable sense of competence and, during a series of individual assessment meetings, it emerged that, at the time, she had been too ashamed to admit that she had wanted to remain in hospital to avoid caring for the infant at home. Furthermore, an unexpected death of one of her siblings had coincided with that infant's birth. This had caused a traumatic grief reaction and a numbness, with absence of any feelings for the newborn baby, who was experienced as a burden, especially if needing to be cared for alone. Admitting a failure of competence had been impossible for this mother, given the fragile nature of her then relationships.

Acknowledgement of grieving enabled this mother to accept her hidden need for care as a mother in hospital rather than facing the loneliness of being a mother at home.

## OTHER SYSTEMIC FAMILY THERAPY APPROACHES TO DENIAL

There have been a number of similar attempts to develop approaches to families who show denial, especially when the prognosis is in doubt.

### The Bristol 'resolutions' model (Essex et al., 1999)

This model was developed by the Avon NSPCC and mirrors our own approach (Bentovim *et al.*, 1988) in making protection the central issue. They argue that an exclusive focus on responsibility issues, rather than taking a broader view which centralizes protection, can lead to children living in care unnecessarily without the prospect of rehabilitation home, which is contrary to the spirit of the Children Act. They note the dilemma inherent in competing criminal and civil structures. If a parent takes responsibility for a severely abusive act, then prison is a feared consequence. If responsibility is not taken in the civil court, then the risk is that the child will not be returned to the parent's care. The Bristol team leave room for a parent to make partial admissions of responsibility during the course of the work.

Their approach in both severe sexual and physical abuse cases is to restrict and control the power of an alleged abuser, as well as to strengthen the protective capacity of the non-abusing parent. Structured reunification is attempted if all relevant professionals agree that there are sufficient strengths in the family to build on. Criteria for this work include: families where one carer is deemed not to have been directly involved in the abuse and wants to explore family reunification; the child shares this view; the family displays positive strengths; and there have been no previous concerns regarding child care.

The approach follows a number of stages. The first stage requires that the family (and extended family, if appropriate) develops a safety plan through changes in behaviour and organization of family life. The safety plan is drawn up without the alleged abuser being present and then shared with him so that he has the opportunity to suggest modifications. The essence of the work is openness, sharing widely and regular feedback between the family, therapeutic group and care system, main-taining a focus on the mechanisms of abusive action without confrontation. The second phase involves working in the hypothetical. Adults are put in roles of 'a similar family' in which abuse has been confirmed. They are encouraged to look at the issues from the points of view of respective members of this hypothetical family, to express feelings which they might experience and to tell each other what might be going through their minds. Responses, which reflect those seen in families where abuse has occurred, become available for further exploration and 'resolution' can occur. Preventive psycho-educational work for children and young people is offered and counselling provided for the carer, while other agencies work with the alleged abuser. The authors report that the approach is successful but requires a maternal figure who is protective, as it would be more difficult to follow if the mother were responsible for the abuse.

In my view, this approach confirms that a therapeutic plan can be followed with some families. There need to be sufficient flexibility and strengths, a reasonable relationship with care authorities and the absence of personal problems which would be highly resistant to change. This model offers a way forward but would need considerable professional support and monitoring, with alternative care plans being available in case of failure.

## 'Exploring safe uncertainty' model (Robinson & Whitney, 1999)

An alternative strategy has been developed by a child and adolescent mental health team.

The authors describe a case referred to them by social services in order to confirm that three young children with unexplained fractures required alternative long-term care. The children stated that they were frightened of their step-father. The parents denied responsibility for the fractures, were angry with social services and were initially resistant to the mental health team. The team offered them the possibility 'to work together to demonstrate to the Local Authority and Court that the concerns expressed were perhaps unfounded, to change their parenting and to demonstrate they could meet the needs of the children, should the Court give them the opportunity' (p. 266). They hoped to achieve a balance between protection of children and supporting families through the provision of 'safe uncertainty' (Mason, 1989; 1993). This requires agreement about clear boundaries and parameters, whilst respectfully exploring how the family may wish to be. This was an invitation the family 'could not refuse' (Jenkins, 1990).

The family described was one with a history of long-standing abuse experienced by the mother and a partner who presented as confrontational to professionals. Despite opposition by the social services department, who had had a lengthy negative experience of the family, the Guardian and the court agreed to support the team's recommendations. A period of successful therapeutic work followed, focusing on safety and encouraging the mother and step-father to develop their parenting skills, including a limited acknowledgement that their parenting difficulties had led to the children being injured.

Kolko (1996) has described the value of similar structured family therapy and cognitive therapy approaches to physical abuse, and the advantages of focused approaches to support in the community.

## OUTCOME

We are able to define those parents with a *hopeful prognosis* for rehabilitation (Bentovim *et al.* 1987). These are situations where a reasonable level of responsibility is taken, there is the potential for restoring attachments and family relationships, individual and parenting difficulties are amenable to change, the necessary resources are available, and there is reasonable collaboration with social services.

At the other extreme are circumstances where the *prognosis is poor* and we feel hopeless about rehabilitation. We find a combination of denial of any responsibility for abuse, a refusal to contemplate the possibility that a partner may have perpetrated it, serious parental health problems which are not changeable within the child's time frame (such as addictions, serious learning difficulties, intractable psychiatric disorders or recurrent domestic violence), requirements for therapeutic input which is not available or the parents lack the motivation to use it, and a pervasively negative response to protective agencies. Other factors contributing to a sense of hopelessness about neglectful families are numerous unsuccessful attempts to intervene, lack of recognition of the professionals' profound concerns and a weight of interlinked problems, even where a degree of responsibility has been taken.

We also see situations where the *prognosis is in doubt*, often because of uncertainty whether parental responsibility is being taken or not and whether the non-abusive parent truly believes the child or is siding with the abuser's denial. In situations of doubt, one may see the paradox of a parent who is perfectly willing to describe issues known to be risk factors for abusive behaviour, such as stress associated with childbirth, marital tensions or conflict with extended family, and yet where the fact of abuse is not accepted. In such cases, the principle of therapeutic assessment work may play an important role in determining whether a doubtful situation is hopeful or hopeless. Placement within Family Units can have this function, as exemplified by the work of the Marlborough Hospital in London (Asen *et al.*, 1989), which offers an extended period of assessment over several weeks. The role of denial in such assessments is important, although not necessarily organizing its outcome. It is necessary to develop approaches for families which identify their strengths as well as the risks in order to try to build on the strengths. Asen *et al.* (1989) described approximately 30 per cent of families where abuse was severe and where the child could not be rehabilitated back, denial being one aspect of the total picture, but a striking 70 per cent of cases could be recommended for rehabilitation.

In the Great Ormond Street Hospital child sexual abuse study (Hyde *et al.*, 1995; Monck *et al.*, 1996), at the time of referral, about one third of the children were living with the protective parent who believed them, whilst the remainder were living in a foster or residential home because of their parents' denial. As a result of therapeutic work, 70 per cent were able to live with a family member, while 30 per cent remained living elsewhere because the non-abusing parent chose to ally themselves with the abuser's continued denials rather than with the child.

## RISK FROM INDIVIDUALS WITH PREVIOUS CONVICTIONS

Adults with previous convictions for child abuse are of concern when they acknowledge abusive behaviour in the past but state categorically that this is not a present concern and there is no risk that they would abuse again. There may not be direct evidence of current maltreatment of any child and their parenting may even appear to be positive. The issues are: how likely is harm to recur and can treatment programmes be delivered in the presence of denial of risk?

A number of studies (e.g. Marshall, 1994) have demonstrated that this is feasible and that there is the potential for change in the absence of acknowledgement of abuse itself. G. Willis (personal communication) described the use of hypothetical approaches to work with sexually abusing individuals, asking: 'If abuse had occurred, what would be the sort of way in which it would occur?'; 'What would be the sort of ways of grooming a child?'; 'What would be the steps in an abusive cycle?' The aim is to stress that safety is based on knowledge, and the more understanding that they show about how abuse can occur, the more the local authority would trust them. It is possible, even in the hypothetical, to explore how resentment that a young child is being better cared for than they had been can lead to jealousy of them. Discussions are possible about emotional loneliness experienced by individuals who grow up in an abusive context, which could lead to a need for emotional closeness with a child. Eventually, there may be acceptance of the need to teach children self-protection skills and for partners to understand what circumstances could lead to abuse. Therefore, building up knowledge in the hypothetical might help individuals convince local authorities that they can be safe and move the prognosis from one of doubt into one which is more hopeful.

## KEEPING CHILDREN SAFE

The core issue in working in the abuse field is to keep children safe. I am often asked how does one keep a child safe in a family where there is denial. My initial response is to ask whether the principles of keeping children safe in the context of *acceptance* of responsibility of abuse are understood.

It is helpful to think in terms of stages of treatment or rehabilitation work. The first stage, when abuse is initially revealed, is to establish immediate protection of the child. This includes assessing the extent of the abuse itself and a full understanding of the context in which it has taken place (including all the factors described above guiding how hopeful or doubtful is the situation). A decision often needs to be taken at this initial stage as to whether the child is safe within the family, particularly whether the non-abusing parent understands the process by which the abuse occurred and therefore can protect the child within the home. Very frequently, this will require separation of the abuser and the child, such as the abuser leaving the home. If neither parent takes responsibility for serious abuse and does not understand its origins, the child would need to be placed in a context of safety outside the family. A full assessment is then required to see whether the situation is one of doubt and, therefore, whether therapeutic work can be recommended whilst the child lives in an alternative setting.

The second stage of a care plan requires that therapeutic work takes place within a context of safety for the child, whether living separately, with the protective parent, or through developing a protective plan. Therapy may be offered to individual parents or to the couple if it remains unknown who was responsible for the abusive act. This is where the 'resolutions' approach (Essex *et al.*, 1996) would try to establish whether a continuing safety plan can be developed. The Great Ormond Street Hospital sexual abuse treatment programme (Bentovim *et al.*, 1988) requires a perpetrator to be in group therapy, with an expectation that he would begin to take appropriate responsibility so that there was a fit between the victim's and abuser's statements. At the same time, the protective parent would be participating in a group in order to develop her understanding of the ways that abusers work and so be able to develop an increasingly protective approach. Robinson and Witney's 'exploring safe uncertainty' approach (1999) would be to develop appropriate ways of dealing with parental conflict and behavioural management and to develop an increasingly collaborative partnership around protecting the children.

Through increasing work with the parents together as a couple, and being open about growing understanding of how the abuse may have occurred, it becomes possible to contemplate whether the third stage of work can begin. This third stage is towards rehabilitation and is an important transition. Decisions to rehabilitate to a carer who now believes that abuse has occurred and takes a protective stance require close collaboration, openness and trust between therapeutic and care systems. As Furniss (1991) has pointed out, the therapeutic task is to help the family convince the care agency, and through them the courts, that protection can be assured.

## CONCLUSIONS

Abusive actions are a symptom of the cumulative interaction between historical and current stress and relationship difficulties. Denial, and the failure to take responsibility for abusive behaviour, is an integral aspect of thinking which sees children as deserving of punishment, neglect, rejection or sexual contact. The urge to abuse may be overwhelming but, at the same time, the abusive thoughts are negated. A variety of therapeutic approaches and strategies can ally with the parent to help them face the unfaceable and acknowledge what cannot be acknowledged. Once intergenerational experiences of abuse and current stresses can be confronted, it becomes possible for them to accept responsibility for the abuse of their children and to begin to reverse, even partially, the processes which led to it. Denial is integral to the process and needs to be worked with actively, not regarded as necessarily the enemy of change.

# References

Asen, K., George, E., Piper, R. and Stevens, A. (1989) A systems approach to child abuse: management and treatment issues, *Child Abuse & Neglect* 13: 45–58.

Bentovim, A. (1992) *Trauma Organised Systems: Physical and Sexual Abuse in Families*, London: Karnac.

Bentovim, A. and Bingley-Miller, L. (2001) *The Family Assessment: Assessment of Family Competence, Strengths and Difficulties*, Brighton: Pavilion.

Bentovim, A., Elton, A., Hildebrand, J., Tranter, M. and Vizard, E. (eds) (1988) *Sexual Child Abuse within the Family*, London: Wright.

Bentovim, A., Elton, A. and Tranter, M. (1987) Prognosis for rehabilitation after abuse, *Adoption & Fostering* 11: 26–31.

Bluglass, K. (2001) Treatment of perpetrators, in G. Adshead and D. Brooke (eds) *Munchausen's Syndrome by Proxy: Current Issues in Assessment, Treatment and Research*, London: Imperial College Press.

Boscolo, L., Cecchin, G., Hoffman, L. and Penn, P. (1987) *Milan Systemic Therapy: Conversations in Theory and Practice*, New York: Basic Books.

Caldwell, B.M. and Bradley, R.H. (1984) *Home Observation for Measurement of the Environment – Administration Manual (Revised Edition)*, Arkansas: University of Arkansas.

Cox, A. and Walker, S. (2001) *Home Observation for Measurement the Environment – UK Version*, Brighton: Pavilion.

Dale, P., Davies, M., Morrison, T. and Waters, J. (1986) *Dangerous Families: Assessment and Treatment of Child Abuse*, London: Tavistock.

Dale, P., Green, R. and Fellows, R. (2002) *What Really Happened? Child Protection Case Management of Infants with Serious Injuries and Discrepant Parental Explanations*, London: NSPCC.

Department of Health, Department for Education and Employment and Home Office (2000) *Framework for the Assessment of Children in Need and their Families*, London: The Stationery Office.

Epstein, M.A. and Bottoms, B.L. (2002) Explaining the forgetting and recovery of abuse and trauma memories: possible mechanisms, *Child Maltreatment* 7: 210–25.

Essex, S., Gumbleton, J. and Luger, C. (1996) Resolutions: working with families where responsibility for abuse is denied, *Child Abuse Review* 5: 191–201.

Fitzpatrick, G. (1995) Assessing treatability, in P. Reder and C. Lucey (eds) *Assessment of Parenting: Psychiatric and Psychological Contributions*, London: Routledge.

Furniss, T. (1991) *The Multi-professional Handbook of Child Sexual Abuse: Integrated Management, Therapy and Legal Intervention*, London: Routledge.

Hyde, C., Bentovim, A. and Monck, E. (1995) Some clinical and methodological implications of a treatment outcome study of sexually abused children, *Child Abuse & Neglect* 19: 1387–99.

Jenkins, A. (1990) *Invitations to Responsibility*, Adelaide: Dulwich Centre Publications.

Jones, D.P.H. (1998) The effectiveness of intervention, in M. Adcock and R. White (eds) *Significant Harm: Its Management and Outcome*, Croydon: Significant Publications.

Kolko, D.J. (1996) Individual cognitive-behavioral treatment and family therapy for physically abused children and their offending parents: the comparison of clinical outcomes, *Child Maltreatment* 1: 322–42.

Krugman, R.D. (1985) Fatal child abuse: analysis of 24 cases, *Pediatrician* 12: 68–72.

Marshall, W.L. (1994) Treatment effects on denial and minimisation in incarcerated sex offenders, *Behaviour Research & Therapy* 32: 559–64.

Mason, B. (1989) *Handing Over*, London: Karnac.

Mason, B. (1993) Towards positions of safe uncertainty, *Human Systems* 4: 189–200.

Midgely, N. (1997) Dissociation and Abuse: A Study of Dissociation among Sexually and Physically Abused Adolescent Boys, unpublished MSc. thesis, University College, London.

Monck, E., Sharland, E., Bentovim, A., Goodall, G., Hyde, C. and Lwin, R. (1996) *Sexually Abused Children: A Descriptive and Treatment Outcome Study*, London: HMSO.

Morrison, A. (1998) Partnership, collaboration and change under the Children Act, in M. Adcock and R. White (eds) *Significant Harm: Its Management and Outcome*, 2nd ed., Croydon: Significant Publications.

Prochaska, J.O. and DiClemente, C.C. (1982) Transtheoretical therapy: toward a more integrative model of change, *Psychotherapy: Theory, Research & Practice* 19: 276–88.

Reder, P. and Lucey, C. (1995) Balanced opinions, in P. Reder and C. Lucey (eds) *Assessment of Parenting: Psychiatric and Psychological Contributions*, London: Routledge.

Robinson, G. and Witney, L. (1999) Working systemically following abuse: exploring safe uncertainty, *Child Abuse Review* 8: 264–74.

Skuse, D., Bentovim, A., Hodges, J., Stevenson, J., Andreou, C., Lanyardo, M., New, M., Williams, B. and McMillan, D. (1998) Risk factors for development of sexually abusive behaviour in sexually victimised adolescent boys: cross-sectional study, *British Medical Journal* 317: 175–9.

Trepper, T.S. and Barrett, M.J. (1989) *Systemic Treatment of Incest: A Therapeutic Handbook*, New York: Haworth.

# Chapter 15

# What contact arrangements are in a child's best interests?

*Clare Lucey, Claire Sturge, Liz Fellow-Smith and Peter Reder*

## INTRODUCTION

Psychiatrists or psychologists may be asked by a court to provide an opinion about a child's contact with their non-resident parent. This most commonly occurs in the context of persistent disputes between separated or divorced parents or during family proceedings after the child has been removed from their parent's care as the result of significant harm.

In this chapter, we offer a theoretical and practical framework to help experts and courts address this question. Although we shall discuss general principles, recommendations in any particular instance must be case-specific and reflect the unique features of the child and their overall circumstances. They must also address the range of options available to the court: from no contact, to varieties of indirect contact, to infrequent direct and supervised contact, and on to more flexible arrangements. We shall elaborate on the types of possible contact and comment on the indications for their use. For ease of discussion, we shall focus on disputes between separated or divorced parents but the principles are applicable to all other contexts where child–parent contact is an issue, such as family proceedings under the Children Act 1989 and long-term fostering or adoption, and examples will also be given to illustrate this.

## THEORETICAL PRINCIPLES

We conceptualize the child as an individual growing up in the context of a family group and a wider network of significant relationships (Hoffman, 1982; Gorell Barnes, 1985), in which account must be taken of the child's personal characteristics, their developmental stage, their past experiences and their current interpersonal relationships. Within this framework, the following factors are important (see Goldstein *et al.*, 1973; Kelmer Pringle, 1975; Minuchin, 1974; Rutter, 1985; Wolkind and Rutter, 1985; Bowlby, 1988; Black, 1988; Baker, 1995; Schaffer, 1998; and Golombok, 2000).

## The part played by innate factors

Children have individual differences in temperament, such as reactivity, sociability, adaptability and ease of mood, which influence, for example, how easy it is for their parents to care for them, their relationship with each parent, their responses to stress and their tolerance of change.

## The child's emotional and cognitive development

Young children are emotionally sensitive to psychological traumata, including losses of important figures or unpredictability in their caretakers. As they grow up, children gradually develop a more mature repertoire of emotional reactions and a more advanced range of cognitive skills, which enable them to understand and evaluate their experiences. Even so, they will be stressed by exposure to significant family and personal conflict.

## The child's vulnerability and resilience

Children with different temperaments have different capacities to withstand psychological stress. Good early relationships, including secure attachment, a sense of self-efficacy and positive experiences with at least one significant adult enhance this resilience to adversity.

## History of the parent–child relationship

The future of a child's relationship with a parent will significantly depend on whether they have had a positive relationship in the past and whether that parent has adequately met the child's developmental needs.

## Impact of discordant family relationships

Unresolved discord between parents is one of the major stressors for a child, potentially affecting all aspects of their emotional life, and continuing disharmony is consistently shown to have more adverse effects than parental separation of itself. The child may become embroiled in the parental disputes and 'triangulated' between them as demands for loyalty are pressed on them from both sides.

If separated/divorced parents do not agree and continue their disputes through arrangements about the child, contact is likely to be a conflictual and traumatic experience for the child (e.g. Wallerstein *et al.*, 1988; Connell, 1988; Jenkins and Smith, 1991; Cummings and Davies, 1994; Hetherington and Stanley-Hagan, 1999; Sturge and Glaser, 2000). The parent who has maltreated their child but continues to deny their responsibility, or who groundlessly suggests to the child that 'I'll soon get you back', will undermine the child's current placement and sense of stability.

How much the child understands will depend on their age, developmental stage and emotional state (Reder and Fitzpatrick, 1998; Reder and Duncan, Chapter 7) but even young children realize when their family has broken up that their life has changed and that their parents are in dispute, and they are likely to be distressed by it. They will experience the pain of loss and separation and the upset of being caught between angry parents. Because they do not fully comprehend this, and because of their natural tendency to blame themselves for events, they can experience a strong sense of guilt in addition to other feelings of anger, sadness, loss, powerlessness, vulnerability, and fear about their safety and for the future. The child is likely to feel that their life is in turmoil but that their parents are too preoccupied with their own disputes to notice or to help.

There are times in such circumstances when the child feels almost unbearable pulls on their loyalty and demands that they make impossible choices. The child may not want to upset either parent, or may have mixed feelings of love and hurt towards both of them, yet feel that it is up to them to decide which parent 'wins'. They may want to continue seeing their other parent but fear the impact of this on the one with whom they are living, even worrying that that parent might become hostile and not want to continue caring for them. These anxieties about family life will feel even greater if they coincide with other life cycle changes, such as moving home, changing school or the birth of a sibling.

Children removed from their parents following significant harm have had to tolerate considerable emotional stress and conflict (see Briere, 1992; Reder and Duncan, 2000a). For example, their self-esteem will have been undermined and they often feel responsible for causing the abuse that they suffered. They can have a range of psychological symptoms, including post-traumatic stress disorder and psychosomatic complaints, and may show evidence of dissociation and self-destructive behaviour. Their sense of helplessness may be considerable, so that, as with children of separated/divorced parents, uncertainty about their future living or contact arrangements is likely to exacerbate these problems.

## CONTACT DISPUTES

Why do some parents continue to dispute contact arrangements, even years after their separation or divorce? For some, the justifications are appropriate, reasoned and child-centred: they have a primary concern for their child's welfare and good grounds for believing that the non-resident parent would not satisfy the child's needs. However, other parents are intent on holding on to the remnants of a past relationship with their ex-partner, however unhappy it may have been, either to avoid acknowledging the loss or in order to seek psychological compensation for their hurt. They may wish for revenge, for a sense of power and control over the other, or for confirmation that the other was to blame in order to protect their self-esteem (e.g. Mattinson and Sinclair, 1979). A number of separated couples become 'addicted' to the interpersonal and legal battle, especially to the excitation and arousal that accompanies it, or, because of egocentricity, stubbornly refuse to compromise and risk 'losing face'.

Care plans presented to courts by local authorities applying to remove a child from their parent's care because of significant harm should always consider future contact arrangements. Hence, they are open to debate and dispute during the court process. There are different possible reasons why a parent might continue to challenge contact arrangements after their child has been removed from their care by a court. They may still care about the child, want to continue playing a part in the child's life and consider that they have something to offer in the future. It may also be in order to diminish their guilt by demonstrating to the child that 'I did everything to keep you'; or they may try to preserve a belief that their child will eventually return to their care. Alternatively, they may find it difficult to adjust their view of themself and accept the loss inherent in no longer being the child's carer; they may want to have an opportunity to continue their abusive behaviour; they may want to try to triumph over professionals; or they might want to maintain a sense of 'ownership' of the child, as though a piece of property, and prevent anyone else getting what 'belongs' to them.

In order to resolve such disputes, or to rule on contact within a proposed care plan, the court is able to consider different forms of contact arrangements.

## DIFFERENT FORMS OF CONTACT

Children may benefit from different forms of contact, depending on their needs, the family circumstances and the purposes of the arrangement. The main distinctions are between direct (face-to-face) and indirect (through an intermediary) contact and within these categories are a range of possible options, as summarized in Table 15.1.

*Unsupervised Direct* contact is possible when the parents agree sufficiently on arrangements and continue to prioritize the child's needs. It may last anything from a few hours to many days of 'staying contact'. A range of intensities of *Supervised Direct* contact are possible, depending on the degree of concern about the child's physical or emotional safety when meeting the non-resident parent. *Guided Supervised Direct* contact involves an intermediary taking an active, facilitating role in addressing specific issues with the child and parent before, during and after the meeting, in a focal therapeutic manner (this is illustrated through a vignette in the final section of the chapter). *Indirect* contact requires the active role of an intermediary, who may be either a member of the family or a professional, so that communications between the child and parent can proceed in the absence of face-to-face meetings. Varying intensities of communication monitoring by this intermediary are possible. In *Guided Indirect* contact, the intermediary meets at different times with the child and non-resident parent in order to encourage more appropriate communications between them. *No* contact may be a necessary recommendation if the child's welfare would be compromised by further meetings with the non-resident parent.

Table 15.1 Types of contact, their function and practical implications

| Type of contact | Description | Function | Practice implications |
|---|---|---|---|
| **Direct** Unsupervised | May be for short or long periods, including overnight/holidays; by mutual agreement or Court Order | Maintaining and promoting a positive, conflict-free relationship | Is the usual arrangement for children after parental separation, when court intervention is not required; can be flexible, fixed/frequent or infrequent |
| Supervised (a) Low intensity | Minimal supervision, e.g. at the start and end of contact, or intermittent | Structuring/providing a context for contact; ensuring the parent is in a fit state (e.g. not drunk or disturbed) | Professional requires experience rather than training; can occur in a naturalistic setting (e.g. with a relative supervising) |
| (b) Medium intensity | Neutral adult present to observe/ monitor the meeting and/or to be available to the child | Supervisor in a supportive role and alert to the child's needs; provides reassurance to resident parent about child's safety during contact | (as above) |
| (c) High intensity | Closely supervised at all times | Protecting the child from physical, sexual or emotional risk | Trained professional required; is unlikely to be suitable as a long-term arrangement but may be useful as a transitional stage |
| Guided | Supervisor takes an active role with a planned piece of work and manages the contact throughout | Focusing on specific problems which need to be overcome in order for the child to negotiate their future life | Requires a professional with a wide range of facilitative skills; has a short-term aim of effecting change, in order to clarify the viability of future contact arrangements |

continued

Table 15.1 continued

| Type of contact | Description | Function | Practice implications |
|---|---|---|---|
| **Indirect** Unmonitored | Non-resident parent writes/sends gifts directly to the child and/or vice versa | Keeping in touch | Resident parent needs to be supportive to the child about the arrangements |
| Monitored: (a) Medium intensity | Corrrespondence is vetted by a third party before reaching the child | Keeping in touch while ensuring child's welfare is not compromised | Intermediary may be the resident parent but is usually a social worker or other professional |
| (b) High intensity | 'Post-box' contact in which communication is entirely through a third party and infrequent (e.g. annually) | Allowing information to the child or information exchange | Normally managed by social services |
| Guided | 'Proxy' contact in which an intermediary meets the child and non-resident parent separately to consider what communications/ questions/responses should be made, to be passed on directly by the 'proxy' person or indirectly in writing | Enabling meaningful indirect contact which has the potential to address issues important to the child or for reparation through more active interchanges | May be transitional: i.e. leading to the child wishing for closer contact; appropriate resources can be difficult to find |
| **No contact** | Absence of any contact | Clarifying that contact is not in child's interests; providing the opportunity for a fresh start | Will need to be reconsidered if the child requests contact or the circumstances change substantially (e.g. the child is unable to remain with the 'resident' parent) |

## PRINCIPLES OF CONTACT

We believe that the following principles apply to decisions about contact arrangements, whatever the nature of the case:

- the purpose of any proposed contact must be overt and clear;
- contact must be for the benefit of the child and therefore take account of the child's perspective and emotional reactions;
- contact should ensure the safety and well-being of the child at all times;
- consensus is preferable;
- contact arrangements can only emerge in the context of decisions about the child's living arrangements;
- contact plans will need to be monitored and reviewed;
- contact arrangements should be suited to the unique needs and circumstances of each individual child.

### Purpose of contact must be clear

Contact can have different purposes and these must be defined for each child and made overtly clear to all those involved in the decision and carrying it out, including, of course, the parent and the child.

One purpose of contact can be to provide an opportunity *to impart information* to the child about their family-of-origin and their own life so far. Information made available to the child is likely to promote a sense of self and identity through an understanding of their origins, roots and life history. For example, the contact could enable discussion about the reasons for the parental separation and why the child is living with one parent and not the other, or why the child is no longer able to live with their birth family. The child has an opportunity to ask questions and make sense of why there have been changes in their living arrangements. The child can also satisfy any curiosity about their family's past history and has the opportunity to test the reality of family mythologies, including raising concerns about the possible inheritance of medical or psychiatric disorders.

Explanations from the parent about the family changes also give them the chance *to express remorse* and, in the longer term, *to begin a process of reparation* of the broken relationship or other emotional damage experienced by the child, where possible.

Contact can help to provide the child with experiences that *facilitate their healthy emotional growth*. This includes the opportunity to experience concern, tenderness, warmth, acceptance and continuity of a meaningful relationship. The child is able to spend time with another family member who may introduce them to different interests and outlooks, enabling them to learn from new and stimulating experiences, and who lets them know that they have remained the focus of love, attention and concern.

A particularly important aspect of emotional growth that can be afforded by contact is the opportunity *to form and build relationships*. For an infant, this might mean developing a relationship from a basis of no previous knowledge. Where there has been a lengthy gap, contact may facilitate the rekindling of a positive relationship. Hence, in some cases, the contact will help *assess the feasibility of a return* to the parent's care, or help strengthen the relationship prior to a return.

When future contact between the child and parent is not envisaged, a period of contact may serve the very different purpose of *facilitating a clear end to the relationship*. The child and parent would be aware that they are meeting in order to say good-bye, so that the encounters may need to be facilitated, allowing their feelings during and afterwards to be acknowledged. The goals are to make the ending explicit, to allow for good-byes and explanations, and to enable the child to move on to a different stage in their life and invest in other relationships. In addition, the parent could be helped to move on in their life, which further frees the child to forge new relationships.

## Contact must be for the benefit of the child

Children are developmentally immature and dependent on adults to recognize their practical and emotional needs and ensure that they are met. This includes providing a sufficiently safe, reliable and caring constellation of relationships around them, even if the family has become dislocated. Children are also reliant on adults to acknowledge their predicaments and promote their welfare, including speaking for them. Hence, in conflictual divorces, it is important that the child's needs are recognized and addressed and their own views elicited.

When it comes to decisions about contact, the needs of the child must be prioritized and the family dilemmas addressed from the child's perspective. This includes taking into consideration the child's emotional reactions to the family break-up, the parental disputes and, most especially, to the prospect of future meetings with the non-custodial parent. In addition, the aims of the contact must be identified from the child's perspective and in the light of whether they fulfil the child's needs. The primary aim must be to promote the child's development.

Another consideration is that contact arrangements should ensure the safety and well-being of the child at all times, and especially ensure their protection from abuse, conflict or distorted messages.

## Consensus is best

Agreement between the parties inevitably reduces conflict and stress for the child. When agreement is achieved, the contact itself is liable to be more rewarding and the adults will be more reliable in their commitment to the arrangements. This is less likely if the plans have to be imposed by the court following prolonged litigation and counter-accusations between the parties. In particular, the child's needs will be best served when the resident parent supports the final plan.

## Plans for the child's living arrangements should provide the context for decisions about contact

Decisions about the child must primarily address the child's needs and consider their perspective. Even though contact arrangements may be the sole preoccupation of the parents, or the focus of protracted arguments in court, the priority is for the child to know where and with whom they will be living. This placement decision should guide how the other needs of the child are fulfilled, including for contact with the non-resident parent. This is especially relevant to family proceedings cases, where the care plan addresses all aspects of the child's living circumstances. Clearly, there will be some circumstances in which details about the child's placement depend on contact intentions. Nonetheless, as a general principle, proposals for the child's living arrangements should provide the context within which decisions about contact are made.

## Contact plans will need to be monitored and reviewed

Over time, children's development means that their needs change, while their family or other circumstances may also become modified. The child's feelings towards their non-custodial parent may also change as a result of contact between them. Hence, contact plans will need to be monitored and reviewed over time to acknowledge such changes and consider whether the identified aims are still being fulfilled or whether other support structures are necessary. Where the parents can not be relied upon to tailor arrangements to the child's changing needs, a review by the court itself may be required or, in order to progress beyond an adversarial setting, review by an independent agency sanctioned by the court.

## Contact arrangements should be suited to the unique needs and circumstances of each child

The choice between the different forms of possible contact depends on which arrangements are best suited to the child's needs and circumstances, where each child is considered as a separate individual with unique characteristics, experiences and requirements. Table 15.2 collates the essential needs of children that must be satisfied through parental care, some of which have greater primacy at a particular stage of development, while the child's temperament may influence how easy it is to satisfy others. Contact arrangements should also meet these same needs. Hence, consideration must be given to such factors as the child's age, their ability to understand the issues involved, the child's wishes and feelings, which adults appear to be sensitive to them, the child's emotional and physical health, their resilience to parental discord, their capacity to tolerate long journeys in order to fulfil the arrangements, and so on. This may therefore mean that different siblings from the same family will require different contact arrangements with their separated parent.

*Table 15.2* Essential needs of children that must be met through parental care

| Physical needs | Behavioural needs | Emotional needs |
|---|---|---|
| Nutrition | Stimulation/interaction | Affection/empathy |
| Warmth/shelter | Exploration/learning | Availability |
| Health/cleanliness | Socialization/role model | Consistency |
| Safety | Limit-setting/disciplining | Reality testing |
| Contact/comfort | Rest | Building of self-esteem |
| | | Attachment/autonomy |
| | | Individual identity |
| | | Advocacy |

*Source:* Adapted from Reder and Duncan (2000b).

Careful consideration of the interplay between each of these essential needs and the child's individual circumstances will enable a recommendation to be made about the most suitable contact arrangements.

## FACTORS GUIDING THE OPINION

A number of factors can be identified as particularly relevant to decisions about contact. We shall describe them here as a series of dimensions, where evidence of strong positives along any axis suggest that contact arrangements could be successful, while strong negatives are indicators against it – see Figure 15.1. These dimensions are intended as a guide to the assessment, since some factors will be more relevant to one case than another or may change over time.

## Meaning of the relationship

Just as every child has a different meaning for each of their parents (Reder and Duncan, 1995), each parental figure will have a different psychological significance for a child. Some adults will have always been an important figure for the child because they were one of their principal caretakers, played a major part in their upbringing and were one of their main emotional supports during difficult times. Others, although frequently absent, may have continued to provide a sense of reliability as someone who always kept in touch, thought and cared about the child and made them feel important. On the other hand, some adults mean very little to the child because they have provided neither practical nor emotional input or were absent for long periods. An adult may also have a negative meaning because they were unkind, hostile or abusive and they represent all the unpleasant experiences from which the child is desperate to move on.

Contact is likely to be in a child's interests if it enables them either to maintain a relationship with a parental figure who has had a positive meaning for them, or offers the potential to build one.

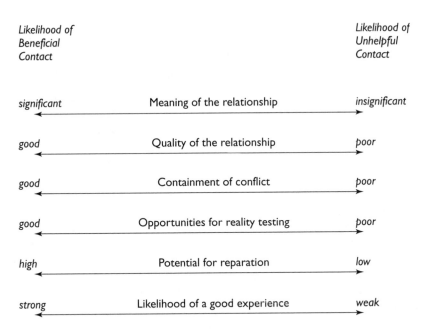

Figure 15.1 Principal dimensions guiding whether contact will be beneficial or harmful

## The quality of the relationship

The quality of the relationship will be multi-determined by such factors as the child's temperament, the fit between characteristics of the child and the adult, the impact of various events through the history of that relationship, the child's vulnerability or resilience to adversity, the influences of others around them, the parent's responses to the child (such as warmth or criticism) and their readiness to meet the child's needs.

It will be especially influenced by the child's early experiences and patterns of closeness. However, the notion of attachment has come to be used loosely by some professionals involved in child care cases (Reder and Duncan, 2001; Baker, Chapter 4). Instruction letters from solicitors often ask mental health professionals to assess the child's attachment to their parent when it is the closeness of relationship between them generally, and the child's sense of trust and security, that are being referred to. Attachment is an important concept but should be reserved for that aspect of early parenting which provides the child with a secure base and an opportunity for proximity when under threat (Howe et al., 1999). If the parent was unresponsive to the early attachment demands, the child is likely to have developed anxiety, and a sense of personal insecurity and an expectation that other people cannot be relied upon. However, these consequences could have been modified in later years as the result of more positive experiences.

Derivatives of the attachment dynamic have relevance for contact in a number of ways. If the non-resident parent was an attachment figure who provided the child with a sense of security, the child will experience a loss following prolonged absence; denial of contact between them may threaten the child's continuing security and identity. On the other hand, the adult may have been a transient or peripheral figure during the child's infancy, so that attachment was forged with other, more available, adults. Current age is also relevant, since the child may still be young enough to depend on proximity to an attachment figure for their sense of security and well-being. If they are older, such as in later childhood or early adolescence, they would have moved on from needing the availability of selected attachment figures and instead only require adults to reinforce their self-esteem from time to time.

Contact is more likely to meet a child's needs when the parent has been an attachment figure and continues to facilitate age-appropriate closeness and security. The child will derive a sense of well-being from their presence since the parent acts reliably, consistently and sensitively towards them. A non-resident parent, while not able to function as a 'secure base' attachment figure who is available practically and emotionally whenever needed, can provide a degree of emotional security by, for example, being sensitive to the child's emotional states and keeping promises that they have made.

## Containment of conflict

We do not use the term conflict here to mean strife or physical violence between people, but instead refer to psychological dissonance, tension or 'unease' within a relationship. All interpersonal relationships contain some degree of emotional conflict, even if it is transient or intermittent, because of different personal per-spectives, discrepant expectations, or incompatible unresolved issues from each person's past. Following family break-up, there are bound to be residual issues of loss, hurt, anger, anxiety, disappointment, or blame, most especially between the parents but perhaps also between the child and one or both parents. The greatest risk for a child of separated/divorced parents is to be caught as the triangulated figure (Minuchin, 1974) between parents whose unresolved conflicts are enacted through them, particularly in the process of implementing contact arrangements.

Contact is more likely to meet a child's needs when there are fewer of these tensions between those involved, or there is an effective mechanism for containing and resolving them.

## Opportunities for reality testing

Children are entitled to the facts about themselves, such as who their parents were, the reasons why certain events occurred to them, and who else has been relevant to their lives, even if such information may be emotionally upsetting. Children also need to be taught about the everyday world so that they can test their ideas and learn how to weigh up alternative possible explanations. Without this opportunity, children are liable to avoid thinking about their personal experiences, construct distorted beliefs or harbour unnecessary fears. Hence, reality testing is both a cognitive and an emotional necessity. Cognitively, the child needs to be able to validate facts or beliefs in order to maintain a coherent perspective on their history and experiences. Emotionally, reality testing is a means by which children validate their feelings and attitudes towards other people and also confirm that they are entitled to have such feelings.

Parents play a crucial role in helping children test reality, by giving them truthful information, supporting their emotional reactions to it and encouraging them to observe their world and think about it. This may be a non-verbal process in which the parent acts in a supportive, interested and tolerant manner, as well as a verbal exchange. Following family break-up, the child may need the opportunity to reduce distorted beliefs about that parent by testing out the stories given to them by the other parent. This may be particularly important when the child has protected themself from the upset of family discord by adopting polarized views, idealizing one parent and denigrating the other.

Contact is more likely to meet the child's needs when each parent does not give a distorted picture of the other. However, if this does occur, the non-resident parent needs to allow the child to develop their own views by being sympathetic to their dilemma, being truthful to the child about the family story and encouraging them to continue to ask questions if and when they want.

## Potential for reparation

Reparation is a process whereby an individual comes to terms with negative feelings about an event or another person so that they can integrate that experience constructively. It does not imply behaving as though they never had those feelings, which would be an erroneous negation. Instead, it means no longer being vulnerable to feelings from the past invading and distorting new experiences. For a child whose family has broken up, or who has been maltreated, it can be helpful to confront a parent about upsetting words or actions and to receive acknowledgement, perhaps with some degree of apology. In this way, angry or painful feelings can be balanced with more positive ones and create the opportunity for a different relationship to evolve in the future. However, there will be some children who, because of their experiences or personality, do not readily reflect on their feelings and relationships in this way and allowance must be made for them. There will also be some family circumstances, such as relentless child sexual abuse or severe violence between the parental couple, where the potential for reparation does not exist.

Contact will usually be beneficial if the non-custodial parent facilitates a child's readiness to repair past emotional traumata. To do so, they must admit to, and feel genuine remorse for, any wrongs they have done and be emotionally available to engage with the child in a gradual process of reparation.

## Likelihood of a good experience

Since most forms of contact are concerned with retaining elements of a relationship, its content is relevant to the likelihood of success. It needs to be more than a mechanical or routine arrangement which only provides for physical proximity but little in the way of an emotional encounter.

Contact is more likely to satisfy the child's needs if it is enjoyable, if it extends the child's experiences and enables the child to feel important to that parent.

## CONTACT FOLLOWING PARENTING BREAKDOWN

We have mainly concentrated our discussion on disputes between separated parents in order to illustrate the psychological and practical issues relevant to contact. However, exactly the same considerations apply to other circumstances, such as cases heard under the Children Act, in which a child has been removed from their parent's care because of significant harm. Since it has been shown that contact for a child temporarily or permanently looked after away from their birth parent can be beneficial (Quinton *et al.*, 1997; Howe, 1998; Sykes, 2001), the same factors will need to be assessed. For example, the primacy of the child's needs, the importance of clarifying the purpose of contact, and the need to weigh up the relative merits of different forms of contact are identical. If separation has followed abuse or neglect by that parent, there will be the same concerns about whether reparation is possible, the likelihood of a good experience at the meeting, or if indirect contact through an intermediary is the only viable option. Similarly, Harris Hendricks *et al.* (1993) identify very similar principles to guide whether contact is in the child's interests after one parent has killed the other parent.

## ASSESSMENT AND OPINION

Whatever the nature of the case, the recommendations to the court must be based on a careful reading of the background documentation, collation of collateral information from other observers, and a detailed direct assessment. Each relevant adult will need to be interviewed, followed by observation of parent/s and child/ren meeting each other. This will contribute to understanding who is important to the child, to whom they turn when upset, and how sensitive the adult is to the child's thoughts and feelings. Direct interviews with the child should be able to elicit further details about this as well as their views on what decision they would like the court to make (even though the court may not always follow their wishes; see Reder and Duncan, Chapter 7).

Opinions and recommendations to courts are achieved through a balancing act, in which all available information about the case is weighed against theoretical principles, practice experience and guidance from the research literature. We start from the premise, demonstrated by much research (e.g. Lund, 1984; Mitchell, 1988; Wallerstein *et al.*, 1988), that it is preferable for children to have contact with a non-resident parent if possible. We would then ask ourselves, 'Is it clear that contact would be for the child's benefit?'; 'Would indirect contact be better than direct?'; 'Is there evidence that contact would facilitate resolution of conflicts or exacerbate them?'; 'Would the child be helped to test reality or be fed false stories about their past and unrealistic expectations about their future?'; 'Would contact be a good experience?'

In disputes between separated parents, a brief attempted mediation between the couple may indicate whether change is possible and whether further mediation work should be recommended in order to increase the potential for beneficial arrangements. A consistent message from research is that children are more affected by persistent and severe parental conflict than by their separation (e.g. Rutter, 1971; Johnson *et al.*, 1987; Wallerstein *et al.*, 1988; Hetherington, 1989). Therefore, if it becomes apparent that the parents remain locked in their battle and that contact would be unworkable, then, sadly, it may be that the child has to 'lose' contact with the non-resident parent rather than continue to be embroiled in the dispute. Of course, the passage of time may alter this picture and contact arrangements would then need to be reviewed.

Other considerations follow from the core judgements about whether contact is in the child's interests and, if so, of what nature. Particularly common debates in court concern the frequency, duration and venue of contact. We do not believe that there are good psychological determinants for any of these, beyond taking into account the child's age and developmental status. Frequency of contact should be guided by its function and the child's experiences of it. If the relationship has been meaningful and it is anticipated that it will continue, the frequency should be at a level which ensures that this is possible. A reduced frequency makes sense if the child is to be given time and space to forge links with new or other carers or if its function is essentially to impart information. Fine tuning the frequency and deciding between, say, once every three months or every four months is more a pragmatic than a psychological issue. Again, offering guidance on how long the meetings should last is of a similarly pragmatic order, with obvious consideration being given to the child's age and temperament, to the purpose and context of the meeting, and general support for it. Smaller children may tire or become bored sooner and their needs for food and rest must be considered. Older children may lose interest when the meeting venue is artificial. Difficulties can be minimized when there is clarity about such mechanical details but also a willingness to review them if the underlying purpose is not being achieved or if circumstances change. Ideally, the parents can themselves make reasonable adjustments to contact arrangements by mutual consent but, in some divorce cases, it will require mediation or, unfortunately, further litigation.

## CASE EXAMPLES

Disputed contact cases can be fraught and complex and pose dilemmas for courts as well as those advising them. For instance, it can be particularly difficult to weigh up whether similar contact arrangements would serve the needs of different siblings, or to promote the welfare of children whose parents appear implacably hostile (we prefer not to use the pseudo-scientific term 'parental alienation syndrome'; see Faller, 1998; Sturge, 2000; Sturge and Glaser, 2000). The boundary between virulent contact manipulation and emotional abuse of the child can be particularly difficult to define. The following (disguised) case vignettes illustrate how it may be possible to address such dilemmas.

### Case 1: sibling contact

The family consisted of mother, father and four children aged 5, 4, 2 and 1. The family proceedings followed a non-accidental injury to the baby and significant neglect of the 2-year-old. Assessment revealed that the parents had moderate alcohol misuse problems, that the two eldest children had not suffered significant harm, and that the two youngest children had been most vulnerable because of the extra dependency demands that they placed on their parents. The children's need for stable care of a reasonable quality could not be achieved if the parents continued to care for all of their children and so the sibling group had to be separated. The court was particularly exercised about the need for the two youngest children to have contact with their elder siblings. The expert's recommendation was based on the principles, dimensions and children's needs that we have outlined above and was reached by identifying hierarchies of decision making, presented as a series of steps:

- establish a safe alternative place for the two youngest children to live (a foster family);
- develop a long-term care plan for them (adoption);
- develop a long-term care plan for the two older children (remain with their parents);
- consider issues of contact between the non-resident children and their parents (the purpose would be to maintain knowledge about their natural family);
- discover whether the prospective adoptive parents would be able to support the children's contact with their parents and consider what help might be needed to enable both sets of parents to achieve this;
- only then could contact between the youngest children and their other siblings be addressed.

Since very young children lack the developmental capacity for enduring selective attachments or cognitively to imbue others with special meanings (Rutter, 1985), it was considered that the meaning of the sibling relationships for the two youngest ones lay more towards the 'insignificant' end of that dimension (see Figure 15.1). Therefore, there were no significant additional purposes to such contact beyond the intermittent need to maintain up-to-date information. Clearly, this was different for the elder two children, who had experience and memory, but the adoptive placement stability needed to take precedence.

## Case 2: implacable hostility

Three years after the parents of a 7-year-old girl had divorced, her mother became concerned that sexual abuse was occurring during contact visits with the father. The mother repeatedly questioned the girl at length about her suspicions and remained unconvinced by her denials. Eventually, the mother stopped all contact and managed to obtain an assessment by the local child protection team, who found no evidence that abuse had ever taken place. However, instead of reassuring the mother, this prompted her to interrogate her daughter more frequently, to the point that the girl developed physical complaints and was referred to a child mental health service. At assessment, the girl spoke positively of her father but was clearly distressed by her mother's continuing preoccupations. Family therapy (for mother and daughter) was recommended but conversation about the fraught relationships proved impossible. An offer was made of some individual work with the girl but her mother first insisted on knowing everything that she said in the session and then refused to let her be seen without the mother being present. The mother's behaviour was now considered to have reached the threshold of emotional abuse and the case entered the child protection system. Concurrently, the father applied for continuing contact with his daughter.

The opinion given to the court was that the child had, indeed, suffered significant harm as the result of her mother's care and that the decision about contact could only be addressed once the child's living circumstances were clear. Consistent with Glaser's (1995) suggestions about the need for a primarily therapeutic response to emotional abuse, it was recommended that there should be a trial of therapy with the mother to see if her preoccupations could moderate. Failing this, a review was recommended of the father's capacity to care for the daughter on a full-time basis.

## Case 3:  guided contact

A mother was killed in a road traffic accident after she and her 6-year-old daughter, Rachael, had been living with her new partner, Martin, for four years. Rachael's natural father, Philip, had had no contact with her since she was a year old. Martin wished to assume responsibility for Rachael's care after her mother's death and was reluctant to allow Philip to become more involved in her care or to see her. As neither 'father' held parental responsibility, the local authority obtained an Interim Care Order, which was followed by rival applications by Martin and Philip for residence and contact.

Assessment included an evaluation of the relationship between Martin and Rachael and concluded that it was meaningful and loving and that she should therefore remain living with him. In addition, however, Rachael could benefit by building a closer relationship with her natural father. Philip agreed to this proposal once it was suggested to him that he would be helped to develop a relationship with his daughter through guided contact, and this recommendation was approved by the court.

To begin with, work was undertaken with Martin on his fears of losing Rachael, having already lost her mother, and his feelings of rivalry with Philip. Meetings with Philip explored his absence from Rachael's life so far, his motivation and commitment to her, and helped him understand more about children's developmental needs. A time was allocated to see Philip and Martin together without Rachael and separate sessions were arranged with Rachael to help prepare her to meet her natural father.

The guided contact session itself temporarily turned the assessor into a therapist and capitalized on aspects of structural family therapy (e.g. Minuchin, 1974; 1984) and mediation (e.g. Robinson, 1993) techniques. The 'therapist' took an active and controlling role, negotiating the meeting's rules and boundaries, prompting and regulating the traffic of communications between participants and managing anxieties as they emerged so that overt conflict did not erupt. The 'therapist' organized the room and seating arrangements, provided refreshments, made the introductions, had already planned with Philip the activities that he could use to engage Rachael, prompted these at appropriate times during the session, intervened in awkward moments and decided when to draw the session to a close.

A final session was arranged to debrief all participants, to allow everyone's respective positions to be acknowledged and for agreement to be reached about the next steps. The 'therapist' was then able to report these resolutions back to the court.

# References

Baker, T. (1995) What constitutes reasonable contact? in P. Reder and C. Lucey (eds) *Assessment of Parenting: Psychiatric and Psychological Contributions*, London: Routledge.

Black, D. (1988) Annotation. The bereaved child, *Journal of Child Psychology & Psychiatry* 19: 287–92.

Bowlby, J. (1988) *A Secure Base: Clinical Applications of Attachment Theory*, London: Routledge.

Briere, J.N. (1992) *Child Abuse Trauma: Theory and Treatment of the Lasting Effects*, Newbury Park, CA: Sage.

Connell, H.M. (1988) Effect of family break-up and parent divorce on children, *Australian Paediatric Journal* 24: 222–7.

Cummings, E.M. and Davies, P.T. (1994) *Children and Marital Conflict: The Impact of Family Dispute and Resolution*, New York: The Guilford Press.

Faller, K.C. (1998) The parental alienation syndrome: what is it and what data support it? *Child Maltreatment* 3: 100–15.

Glaser, D. (1995) Emotionally abusive experiences, in P. Reder and C. Lucey (eds) *Assessment of Parenting: Psychiatric and Psychological Contributions*, London: Routledge.

Goldstein, J., Freud, A. and Solnit, A.J. (1973) *Beyond the Best Interests of the Child*, New York: The Free Press.

Golombok, S. (2000) *Parenting: What Really Counts*, London: Routledge.

Gorell Barnes, G. (1985) Systems theory and family theory, in M. Rutter and L. Hersov (eds) *Child and Adolescent Psychiatry: Modern Approaches*, 2nd ed., Oxford: Blackwell.

Harris Hendricks, J., Black, D. and Kaplan, T. (1993) *When Father Kills Mother: Guiding Children through Trauma and Grief*, London: Routledge.

Hetherington, E.M. (1989) Coping with family transitions: winners, losers, and survivors, *Child Development* 60: 1–14.

Hetherington, E.M. and Stanley-Hagan, M. (1999) The adjustment of children with divorced parents: a risk and resiliency prospective study, *Journal of Child Psychology & Psychiatry* 40: 129–40.

Hoffman, L. (1982) A co-evolutionary framework for systemic family therapy, *Australian Journal of Family Therapy* 4: 9–21.

Howe, D. (1998) *Patterns of Adoption: Nature, Nurture and Psychosocial Development*, Oxford: Blackwell.

Howe, D., Brandon, M., Hinings, D. and Schofield, G. (1999) *Attachment Theory, Child Maltreatment and Family Support: A Practice and Assessment Model*, Basingstoke: Macmillan.

Jenkins, J.M. and Smith, M.A. (1991) Marital disharmony and children's behaviour problems: aspects of a poor marriage that affect children adversely, *Journal of Child Psychology & Psychiatry* 32: 793–810.

Johnson, J., Gonzalez, R. and Campbell, L.E.G. (1987) Ongoing post-divorce conflict and child disturbance, *Journal of Abnormal Child Psychology* 15: 493–509.

Kelmer Pringle, M. (1975) *The Needs of Children*, London: Hutchinson.

Lund, M. (1984) Research on divorce and children, *Family Law* 14: 198–201.

Mattinson, J. and Sinclair, I. (1979) *Mate and Stalemate: Working with Marital Problems in a Social Services Department*, Oxford: Blackwell.

Minuchin, S. (1974) *Families and Family Therapy*, London: Tavistock.

Minuchin, S. (1984) Patterns of divorce, in *Family Kaleidoscope*, Cambridge, MA: Harvard University Press.

Mitchell, A. (1988) Children's experience of divorce, *Family Law* 18: 460–3.

Quinton, D., Rushton, A., Dance, C. and Mayes, D. (1997) Contact between children placed away from home and their birth parents: research issues and evidence, *Clinical Child Psychology & Psychiatry* 2: 393–413.

Reder, P. and Duncan, S. (1995) The meaning of the child, in P. Reder and C. Lucey (eds) *Assessment of Parenting: Psychiatric and Psychological Contributions*, London: Routledge.

Reder, P. and Duncan, S. (2000a) Abuse then and now, in P. Reder, M. McClure and A. Jolley (eds) *Family Matters: Interfaces between Child and Adult Mental Health*, London: Routledge.

Reder, P. and Duncan, S. (2000b) Children's experience of major psychiatric disorder in the parent: an overview, in P. Reder, M. McClure and A. Jolley (eds) *Family Matters: Interfaces between Child and Adult Mental Health*, London: Routledge.

Reder, P. and Duncan, S. (2001) Abusive relationships, care and control conflicts and insecure attachments, *Child Abuse Review* 10: 411–27.

Reder, P. and Fitzpatrick, G. (1998) What is sufficient understanding? *Clinical Child Psychology & Psychiatry* 3: 103–13.

Robinson, M. (1993) A family systems approach to mediation during divorce, in J. Carpenter and A. Treacher (eds) *Using Family Therapy in the 90s*, Oxford: Blackwell.

Rutter, M. (1971) Parent-child separation: psychological effects on the children, *Journal of Child Psychology & Psychiatry* 12: 233–60.

Rutter, M. (1985) Resilience in the face of adversity: protective factors and resistance to psychiatric disorders, *British Journal of Psychiatry* 147: 598–611.

Schaffer, H.R. (ed.) (1998) *Making Decisions about Children*, 2nd ed., Oxford: Blackwell.

Sturge, C. (2000) Contact and domestic violence – the experts' court report, *Family Law* 30: 615–29.

Sturge, C. and Glaser, D. (2000) Divorce and separation: impact of parental factors on children, in N. Wall (ed.) *No Fault or Flaw*, London: Jordan Press.

Sykes, M.R. (2001) Adoption with contact: a study of adoptive parents and the impact of continuing contact with families of origin, *Journal of Family Therapy* 23: 296–316.

Wallerstein, J.S., Corbin, S.B. and Lewis, J.M. (1988) Children of divorce: a 10 year study, in E.M. Hetherington and J.D. Arasteh (eds) *Impact of Divorce, Single Parenting and Step-parenting on Children*, Hillsdale, NJ: Erlbaum.

Wolkind, S. and Rutter, M. (1985) Separation, loss and family relationships, in M. Rutter and L. Hersov (eds) *Child and Adolescent Psychiatry: Modern Approaches*, 2nd ed., Oxford: Blackwell.

# Chapter 16

# Long-term foster care or adoption?

*John Triseliotis*

The intention of long-term fostering is for the child to live in the household on a 'permanent' basis until they reach adulthood, and possibly beyond, so that the child forms a psychosocial base in their life. Because of this expectation, long-term fostering is often referred to as 'permanent'. However, there is widespread confusion in social services departments as to what exactly is meant by the terms 'long-term fostering' and 'permanence' (Triseliotis *et al.*, 2000; Lowe and Murch, 2001). In fostering, parental responsibility usually continues to be held by the local authority or the birth parent/s and the child can be removed at the instigation of a number of parties. An Adoption Order, on the other hand, confirms permanence through its legality, with all parental responsibilities being transferred to the adoptive family and the child can only be removed, as with any other child, if the adopter/s are found to be neglectful or abusive.

A key question when considering the future of children who cannot live with their birth families is whether it matters which form of substitute parenting they go to. The research literature will be reviewed in order to contrast a number of variables relating to this:

* placement stability;
* child's adjustment;
* child's sense of security and belonging;
* child's personal and social functioning; and
* substitute parent's perspective.

A more detailed literature analysis can be found in Triseliotis (2002).

## REVIEW OF RESEARCH

There is a dearth of studies on long-term fostering that go beyond the snap-shot type of approach. By contrast, because of the much greater stability associated with adoption, populations of adopted children and adopted adults have become the target of numerous researchers. In addition, it can be difficult to compare studies because of significant methodological disparities, including absence of controls or before-and-after baselines, the dearth of longitudinal studies, the exclusion of some categories of children (e.g. those with disabilities), variable durations of follow-up, and reliance on memories or sole judgements of social workers in establishing breakdown rates. Contrasts with past studies are also made more difficult because the social context between then and now has changed, as have policies and practices in relation to children and families. As an example, most of the children in foster care now would, in the past, have gone to residential establishments because of their 'special needs', such as emotional and behavioural problems and/or physical or mental disabilities. Those who went into foster care in the past do not even come into the care system now but are looked after at home with support from a range of services. Because many children adopted now have special needs and are older at placement, considerable overlaps in characteristics and circumstances can be expected between them and those going in to long-term foster care (see Holloway, 1997a; 1997b; Quinton *et al.*, 1998; Rushton *et al.*, 2001).

## Placement stability

When a placement is made in either long-term fostering or adoption, the expectation is that it will last until the child reaches adulthood. The overall breakdown rate noted by a number of key studies in *long-term fostering* for all age-groups, between two and five years after the placement was made, is around 43 per cent (Parker, 1966; George, 1970; Berridge and Cleaver, 1987; Rowe *et al.*, 1989; Thoburn, 1991; Strathclyde Regional Council, 1991; Holloway, 1997a; 1997b; Rushton *et al.*, 2001). The average ranges from 60 per cent found by one study at a time when mostly non-problematic children went into fostering (George, 1970) to 27 per cent found by a more recent survey of far more difficult children (Thoburn, 1991). This trend is also supported by Rowe *et al.* (1989) and Rushton *et al.* (2001), who suggest an improved delivery of foster care services.

The overall *adoption* breakdown rate for children with special needs is around 19 per cent, for follow-up periods ranging between two and eight years after placement (Kadushin, 1970; Tremitiere, 1984; Boyne *et al.*, 1984; Nelson, 1985; Festinger, 1986; Barth and Berry, 1988; Rowe *et al.*, 1989; Thoburn, 1991; Borland *et al.*, 1991; Strathclyde Regional Council, 1991; Lowe *et al.*, 1999; Cabinet Office, 2000; Rushton *et al.*, 2001). Around 4 per cent of children return to care annually after the Adoption Order is granted (Department of Health, personal communication). Overall breakdown rates, however, disguise differences due to the age of the child at placement, which is known to be a crucial factor in placement stability. It is therefore necessary to analyse breakdown rates by age groups.

### (i) Children placed prior to one year of age

Three studies give an average of 30 per cent breakdown rates after three to five years for children placed in *long-term fostering* when aged 0–1 year (Parker, 1966;

George, 1970; Berridge & Cleaver, 1987). More recent surveys, though, found hardly any breakdowns for either *adoption* or *long-term fostering* 30 months to 6 years after placements had been made (Thoburn, 1991; Rushton *et al.*, 2001). A summary of nine USA studies of *adoption* found the overall breakdown rates to be just under 2 per cent (Kadushin, 1970), while two recent British studies reported that, of children placed when under a year old, none had broken down within a five- to six-year period (Holloway, 1997a; 1997b; Castle *et al.*, 2000).

### (ii)  Children placed in the pre-school period

For the slightly older pre-school age group, *adoption* studies from about 1980 onwards have consistently shown an average breakdown rate of around 5 per cent, between two and five years following placement (Kadushin, 1970; Tremitiere, 1984; Boyne *et al.*, 1984; Kaye & Tipton, 1985; Barth & Berry, 1988; Rowe *et al.*, 1989; Thoburn, 1991; Borland *et al.*, 1991; Lowe *et al.*, 1999). *Long-term fostering* breakdowns, for the same age group and approximately the same follow-up period, average 22 per cent, ranging between 39 per cent (Parker, 1966; George, 1970; Berridge & Cleaver, 1987) and 4 per cent (Rowe *et al.*, 1989; Thoburn, 1991), which is broadly the same as adoption. In fact, the recent Rushton *et al.* (2001) study covering both *adoption* and *long-term fostering* found no breakdowns amongst children placed when under 6 years old, six years after the placements were made.

Overall, if we were also to include past studies, then breakdowns amongst the *adoption* group have been significantly lower compared to the *fostering* group. However, if we were to include studies carried out in only the last 10 years or so, then hardly any differences can be found. One possibility is that this can be attributed to improved policies and practices.

### (iii)  Children placed between the ages of 5 and 12 years

Up to the mid-1980s, three studies had reported the overall rate of *long-term fostering* breakdowns for this age group to be over 50 per cent (Parker, 1966; George, 1970; Berridge & Cleaver, 1987). Three subsequent surveys suggested a significant drop (Rowe *et al.*, 1989; Thoburn, 1991; Rushton *et al.*, 2001), but a fourth recorded again high rates of 52 per cent (Holloway, 1997a; 1997b). Since about 1980, *adoption* breakdowns for a broadly similar age group of special needs children average 15 per cent (Rushton *et al.*, 1988; Rowe *et al.*, 1989; Thoburn, 1991; Borland *et al.*, 1991; Lowe *et al.*, 1999; Rushton *et al.*, 2001). The main surprise here is the high breakdown rate of 27 per cent found by the Rushton *et al.* (2001) study, which followed up the children six years into their placement.

If studies carried out before about 1990 were to be included, then they would show that *long-term fostering* results in significantly higher breakdown rates compared to *adoption*. However, if only more recent studies are considered, they show that *fostering* breakdowns are still higher but the gap between these two forms of substitute parenting is narrowing. What some recent studies reflect, however, is the increasing number of very problematic children being placed in both types of alternative care.

### (iv) Placement of adolescents

Far more adolescents are likely to be placed in long-term fostering than in adoption. Of the 2,700 children who left care through *adoption* in 1999/2000, 179 (or 6.6 per cent) were aged 10 and upwards (Department of Health, 2001). Whether placed in *long-term fostering* or *adoption*, the breakdown rates for adolescents can be very high and between one third and more than a half are likely to disrupt within a three- to five-year period (see Parker, 1966; Berridge and Cleaver, 1987; Rowe *et al.*, 1989; Thoburn, 1991; Holloway, 1997a; 1997b; Rushton *et al.*, 2001 for fostering studies; and Strathclyde Regional Council, 1991; Borland *et al.*, 1991; Holloway, 1997a; 1997b; Lowe *et al.*, 1999; Rushton *et al.*, 2001 for adoption studies).

Though the overall breakdown rate suggests somewhat lower breakdowns in favour of *adoption*, this disguises the fact that a proportion of older children are adopted by their foster carers after the placement stabilizes. Possibly because of the high breakdown rates expected, agencies appear cautious nowadays about placing adolescents for adoption. For example, the number of adolescents placed between 1996 and 2000 was halved (Department of Health, 2001). Whilst it cannot always be presumed that the breakdown of a placement does not involve some benefits to a child, nevertheless, the real challenge is in being able to recognize which 50 per cent or so can profit from either type of placement without exposing children to unnecessary failures.

In summary, the overall picture that emerges about breakdowns is a mixed one. Whilst some recent studies suggest a narrowing of the gap between breakdown rates of adoption and long-term fostering, a sombre message comes from Sinclair (Sinclair *et al.*, 2000; Sinclair, 2001), who concluded that foster care rarely offers permanence. In their sample, only 3 per cent of placements lasted eight years or more, with breakdowns of around 20 per cent a year, and the likelihood of breakdown reduced very little with length of placement.

## Child's adjustment

Identifying and measuring children's behavioural and emotional difficulties is often complex and imprecise and made more so by the absence in most studies of 'before-' and 'after-' placement baseline measures. A further dilemma is whether to look for intermediary outcomes (i.e. during childhood) or for more final ones (after the child reaches adulthood).

Two early snap-shot type studies, which took place mostly at a time when it was thought that only non-problematic children went into foster care, reported that around one third of them was 'disturbed', some seriously, compared with 7 per cent in the general population (Thorpe, 1974; Rowe *et al.*, 1984). More recent studies suggest that around half of the children in fostering display high levels of emotional and behavioural problems (Minis, 1999; Holloway, 1997a; 1997b; Sinclair *et al.*, 2000; Triseliotis *et al.*, 2000; Schofield *et al.*, 2000). Some of the studies report that the difficulties were irrespective of the child's age. Brand and Brinich (1999) noted from their analysis of extensive statistical data in the USA that young children in foster care had significantly higher scores on the behaviour problem scale than children in any other placement type.

Most studies report that adoptive children placed as infants or when young hardly differ in adjustment from the general population (Seglow *et al.*, 1972; Lambert and Streather, 1980; Plomin and DeFries, 1985; St Claire and Osborne, 1987; Bohman and Sigvardsson, 1990; Maughan and Pickles, 1990; Brodzinsky, 1993). A somewhat discordant note is struck by a New Zealand study (Fergusson *et al.*, 1995), which found that adopted children were more likely to have higher rates of 'externalizing', but not 'internalizing', behaviours. When it comes to the adoption of older children and those with special needs, as with fostering, between a third and a half have been found to display problems of some intensity, with little improvement being noted after a year (Holloway, 1997a; 1997b; Howe, 1997; Quinton *et al.*, 1998; Rushton *et al.*, 2001). On the other hand, within a two-year period, the under 2-year-olds adopted from Romanian institutions had made excellent progress, in spite of the gross deprivations to which they had been exposed (Rutter *et al.*, 1998).

In summary, as with breakdown rates, 'adjustment' in childhood as an outcome variable is now becoming less useful for contrasting long-term fostering and adoption because the more recent studies have found very high adjustment problems in both groups (Holloway, 1997a; 1997b; Quinton *et al.*, 1998; Rushton *et al.*, 2001). Rushton and colleagues also reported that, whilst the long-term foster children in their study had some differences in their pre-placement backgrounds, their problem profile was very similar to the adopted group.

## Child's sense of security and belonging

Attention was drawn in the early 1980s to findings suggesting that *long-term fostering*, unlike adoption, appeared to leave the children feeling unusually insecure and lacking a full sense of belonging to their substitute family (Triseliotis, 1983). Subsequent studies were to confirm this finding (Rowe *et al.*, 1984; Hill *et al.*, 1989; Bohman and Sigvardsson, 1990; Triseliotis and Hill, 1990). These and other studies (e.g. Tizard, 1977) have identified two key areas around which these insecurities are concentrated: (i) anxiety and uncertainty on the part of the child and their carers arising from the impermanence of the situation; and (ii) ambiguity of position.

## (i) Uncertainty

Because of the lack of legal security which could result in the termination of the placement, many children and foster carers are left in a continuous state of anxiety about what might come next. The foster child's insecurity is further emphasized by more recent studies, which report that a small group of carers indicate that if the child's behaviour were to get much worse, or their own children seemed to suffer as a result, then the foster child might have to go (Sinclair *et al.*, 2000; Triseliotis *et al.*, 2000; Schofield *et al.*, 2000). This appears to contrast with the reported perseverance demonstrated by most adoptive parents. Rowe *et al.* (1984) also highlighted the child's justifiable feelings of insecurity when in long-term fostering, as evidenced by the number of changes that occurred while the study was in progress, plus the fact that nearly half of the placements had been in some jeopardy at some stage. Bohman and Sigvardsson (1990) attributed the poorer performance of formerly fostered young people to the same insecurities, adding that there was no guarantee that the child might not some day return to the biological parent/s. The foster carers also expressed concerns about their insecure position and the researchers considered that this insecurity inevitably influenced the relationship between foster parents and the children.

## (ii) Ambiguity

The ambiguous position of children in long-term fostering appears to make many of them feel that they 'belong' to nobody. Though they do not live with their parents and often are no longer in touch with them, their carers are not their 'parents', neither can they call them 'mum' or 'dad' by right. This ambiguity appears to lead to a sense of unusualness and difference, which is especially experienced in school and at play. Other likely events in their lives reinforce this sense of difference, such as having a separate surname, anxieties about being moved, and the comings and goings of short-stay children in the household (Triseliotis, 1983; Hill *et al.*, 1989; Triseliotis and Hill, 1990; Bohman and Sigvardsson, 1990).

Although around 375,000 *adopted* adults (possibly half of the total) have so far searched for more information about their origins and/or sought reunions with birth relatives, the evidence also suggests that this is not because they wish to replace their adoptive parents. For most of them, the adoptive parents retained a firm place in their relationships and affections (Triseliotis, 1973; Howe and Feast, 2000).

We can conclude that, even when *long-term fostering* lasts, the children still feel less secure and have a weaker sense of belonging compared to those who are adopted. This is possibly the main defining differences between the two forms of substitute parenting.

## Child's personal and social functioning

One series of studies concluded that, compared with those who had been adopted, adults who had been *long-term fostered* were: 'somewhat' less able to form relationships or carry out the parenting role; less likely to continue their education beyond the statutory school-leaving age; and more liable to be unemployed and draw social security benefits and/or be homeless. However, around one in ten in both groups had seen a psychiatrist during their adult life or had criminal convictions since the age of 16 (Triseliotis, 1980; Triseliotis and Russell, 1984; Triseliotis and Hill, 1990). These findings were largely confirmed by Bohman and Sigvardsson's Swedish longitudinal study (1990).

Dumaret's earlier (1985) French study, which also contrasted long-term fostering and adoption, reported that the *adopted* group fared better on all measurements. However, a later study concluded that those *fostered* did not differ in terms of social functioning and integration from the rest of the population (Dumaret and Coppel-Batsch, 1998). A much less 'rosy' picture is painted by a retrospective USA cohort study (Benedict *et al.*, 1996), which found high levels of unemployment, homelessness, drug abuse, arrests, and violence towards or received from partners amongst adults who were formerly in *long-term fostering*.

In my own series of studies (Triseliotis, 1980; Triseliotis and Russell, 1984; Triseliotis and Hill, 1990) contrasting their perceptions of coping and well-being in adults who had grown up in *long-term fostering* with those of adults who had been *adopted*, the adoption group emerge as doing significantly better. Ninety per cent of those adopted rated their 'coping with current life' as 'very good' to 'good', compared with 57 per cent of those formerly fostered, while 90 per cent of those adopted rated the 'feelings of well-being' as 'very good' or 'good', compared to 35 per cent of the fostered group. The adoptive 'experience' was rated positively by 82 per cent, the fostering 'experience' as positively by 62 per cent. Only 2 per cent of those adopted rated their 'current closeness to their former carers' as 'very poor' or 'poor', compared to 27 per cent of those formerly fostered. Where children in long-term foster care became integrated into their foster family and continued to live there beyond the age of 16 or 18 as members of the family, then levels of satisfaction could be high. However, a significant number had left their carers once they reached the age of 16 and one third had lost all contact with them. They largely drifted between different birth relatives or joined the group of young homeless. A quarter of them had joined the armed forces, compared to none from the adopted group.

Similarly, in Owen's (1999) study, around 85 per cent of those *adopted* when aged between 6 and 11 and now grown up said that they had been shown physical affection and were still getting on well with their single parent, which contrasted with only around 70 per cent from a community sample.

## Substitute parent's perspective

Levels of carers' satisfaction amongst those who *adopt* infants and young children averages around 80 per cent (Kornitzer, 1968; Raynor, 1980; Howe, 1996). Adopted people featuring in 'search and reunion' studies have expressed similar levels of satisfaction with their adoption (Howe and Feast, 2000). One study asked foster carers to rate their experience of *long-term fostering* when the children were aged around 21 (Triseliotis, 1980). Over half (55 per cent) expressed satisfaction with how the placement had worked out. In most cases, the foster child had become part of the family and found a family for life. The remaining 45 per cent were split equally between those expressing less of a long-term commitment to the specific child and more investment in their role as a foster carer, and those who felt that the placement had not worked out.

Few studies have yet elicited the retrospective views of those who adopted children with special needs. However, Owen (1999) reports that high levels of satisfaction were expressed by single parents *adopting* older children, noting that children with disabilities did particularly well. Thoburn *et al.* (2000) found that just over three-fifths (63 per cent) of those who had *adopted* or *fostered* long-term children of minority ethnic origin, some of them transracially, were also positive about the experience, while only 12 per cent felt negatively. Howe (1996) reported that 93 per cent of *adopters* said that, although the child's growing up period proved most challenging, they nonetheless had 'positive parent–child relationships'. It should not come as a surprise if subsequent studies into the long-term outcome of adoption for children with special needs show lower levels of satisfaction, either from the adopters' or from the adoptive person's perspective.

## PRACTICAL IMPLICATIONS

The weight of evidence examined suggests that adoption confers significant advantages on children who cannot live with their birth families, mainly in terms of emotional security, legality and sense of belonging. However, long-term fostering still can be the plan of choice, especially:

- for children who are clear that they do not want adoption;
- for children closely attached to their carers and for whom a move would not be in their interests;
- where there is a high level of continuous birth family involvement;
- for some children, especially older ones, and their carers who might require time to get to know each other before making a final commitment or decision.

Other things being equal, the ideal for children in long-term fostering who cannot return to live with their birth families is to be adopted by their foster carers, assuming that this is also the expressed wish of the older child and their carers. Such adoptions can spare children the trauma arising from a move and also provide them with legal security. Some 13 per cent of carers adopt or express a wish to adopt their foster children each year (Sinclair *et al.*, 2000). Where old enough, the children must be consulted, listened to and their views seriously considered and respected (see Reder and Duncan, Chapter 7). This is also the best predictor of placement stability (Triseliotis *et al.*, 1995; Sellick and Thoburn, 1996). Some older children will be clear that they do not want adoption, or that they do not want to leave their foster homes. Others still may prefer the benefits that evidently go with adoption. For young children, who cannot express a clear view, others will have to make the decision on their behalf, after considering the facts and the empirical evidence available.

For the child's natural parents, long-term fostering keeps the door open to the possibility of rehabilitation and also largely safeguards continuing face-to-face contact. They may therefore ask the court to rule against placing the child for adoption. The reality is that, once the child has been in care for around two years, the chance of rehabilitation to their parents is distant (see Prime Minister's Review, 2000: p. 84). Over the years, a number of judges have come to recognize the advantages of adoption over long-term fostering, but one reason given for not granting an Adoption Order is where hopes of rehabilitation are still expressed or there is continuing frequent contact between the child and members of their birth family. The preferable recommendation in circumstances where there is still such a meaningful link is for the emotional and genealogical continuity to be preserved by providing for post-adoption contact.

Possibly the biggest planning dilemma occurs when the foster parents express a commitment to care long-term but not to adopt, perhaps for financial reasons. Given some of the unpredictabilities inherent in long-term fostering, the question is whether it is preferable to move a young child to an adoptive placement, thus breaking up their attachments, or to leave them where they are. The important factor is that uprooting can be very traumatic to the child. A similar concern is when a foster carer offers to look after a young child for the rest of their life, only to decide to give up some years later when it is almost impossible to find an adoptive home for the child, especially if a boy. The scenario that usually follows is a succession of temporary fostering placements with the child eventually growing up without a family to call their own and no social base in life.

## CONCLUSIONS

Allowing for the methodological difficulties in contrasting the two different forms of substitute care, differences in breakdown rates and levels of adjustment of the children are diminishing. In some age groups they are evening out. However, at least one recent study (Sinclair, 2001) concluded that foster care rarely offers permanence because its placements are too liable to break down, it offers less security than adoption and a less enduring psychosocial base in life for those who cannot live with their birth families.

The main limitation of long-term fostering is its unpredictability and the uncertain and ambiguous position in which the children find themselves. Taken together, these conditions appear to generate long-standing feelings of insecurity and anxiety in children and, sometimes, in their carers. It is possible, of course, that this is because of the different expectations placed on adopters and foster carers and the different commitments that the two groups of substitute parents bring to the task. For example, studies suggest that when difficulties arise adopters tend to persevere against the odds whilst long-term foster parents may be readier to give up (Howe, 1996; 1997; Quinton *et al.*, 1998; Triselioitis *et al.*, 2000; Sinclair *et al.*, 2000; Schofield *et al.*, 2000).

It is still too early to predict the impact of the Special Guardianship Order proposed in the 2001 Adoption (England and Wales) Bill, which is intended to provide for greater security to children and their carers through a provision somewhere between long-term foster care and adoption. It remains to be seen whether the Order will eventually be used to fulfil this expectation, or whether it will be used for some children who are currently being adopted. Much will also depend on the circumstances under which the Order can be reversed.

Finally, when deciding between these two different forms of substitute care, account has to be taken of each child's individual needs and circumstances, as well as those of their carers and the range of resources available in prospective placements. Adoption is not the answer for every child who cannot live with, or eventually return to, their birth family and long-term fostering still has a place in planning for the needs of some children. The main defining differences found between these two alternative forms of substitute parenting appear to be the legality of adoption and higher levels of emotional security, sense of belonging and general well-being expressed by those growing up adopted. A significant number of those whose fostering placements last do find a family for life, albeit lacking some of the more intense qualities found with adoption. Finally, all decisions in child placement involve an element of risk. It is only possible to minimize it by balancing the child's age, levels of adjustment, current attachments, wishes (where old enough), and the strength of their carer's commitment.

## References

Barth, R.P. and Berry, M. (1988) *Adoption and Disruption: Rates, Risks and Responses*, New York: Aldine de Gruyter.

Benedict, M.I., Zuravin, S. and Stallings, R.Y. (1996) Adult functioning of children who lived in kin versus non-relative family foster homes, *Child Welfare* 75: 529–49.

Berridge, D. and Cleaver, H. (1987) *Foster Home Breakdown*, Oxford: Basil Blackwell.

Bohman, M. and Sigvardsson, S. (1990) Outcome in adoption: lessons from longitudinal studies, in D.M. Brodzinsky and M.D. Schechter (eds) *The Psychology of Adoption*, New York: Oxford University Press.

Borland, M., O'Hara, G. and Triseliotis, J. (1991) Permanency planning for children in Lothioan Region, in Social Work Services Group (eds) *Adoption and Fostering*, Edinburgh: Scottish Office.

Boyne, J., Denby, L., Kettering, J.R. and Wheeler, W. (1984) *The Shadow of Success: A Statistical Analysis of Outcomes of Adoptions and Hard-to-Place Children*, Westfield, NJ: Spaulding for Children.

Brand, E.A. and Brinich, M.P. (1999) Behaviour problems and mental health contacts in adopted, foster and nonadopted children, *Journal of Child Psychology & Psychiatry* 40: 1221–9.

Brodzinsky, D.M. (1993) Long-term outcomes in adoption, *Future of Children* 3: 153–66.

Cabinet Office (2000) *Adoption: A New Approach*, White Paper, London: Department of Health.

Castle, J., Beckett, C. and Groothues, C. (2000) Infant adoption in England, *Adoption & Fostering* 24: 26–35.

Department of Health (2001) *Annual Statistics of Looked After Children*, London: Department of Health.

Dumaret, A. (1985) IQ, scholastic performance and behaviour of sibs raised in contrasting environments, *Journal of Child Psychology & Psychiatry* 26: 553–80.

Dumaret, A. and Coppel-Batsch, M. (1998) Effects in adulthood of separations and long-term foster care: a French study, *Adoption & Fostering* 22: 31–9.

Fergusson, D.M., Lynskey, M. and Horwood, L.J. (1995) The adolescent outcomes of adoption: a 16-year longitudinal study, *Journal of Child Psychology & Psychiatry* 36: 597–616.

Festinger, T. (1986) *Necessary Risk: A Study of Adoptions and Disrupted Adoptive Placements*, New York: Child Welfare League of America.

George, V. (1970) *Foster Care*, London: Routledge & Kegan Paul.

Hill, M., Lambert, L. and Triseliotis, J. (1989) *Achieving Adoption with Love and Money*, London: National Children's Bureau.

Holloway, J.S. (1997a) Outcome in placements for adoption or long-term fostering, *Archives of Disease in Childhood* 76: 227–30.

Holloway, J.S. (1997b) Foster and adoptive mothers' assessment of permanent family placements, *Archives of Disease in Childhood* 76: 231–5.

Howe, D. (1996) Adopters' relationships with their adopted children from adolescence to early adulthood, *Adoption & Fostering* 20: 35–43.

Howe, D. (1997) Parent-reported problems in 211 adopted children: some risk and protective factors, *Journal of Child Psychology & Psychiatry* 38: 401–11.

Howe, D. and Feast, J. (2000) *Adoption, Search and Reunion*, London: The Children's Society.

Kadushin, A. (1970) *Adopting Older Children*, New York: Columbia University Press.

Kaye, E. and Tipton, M. (1985) *Evaluation of State Activities with Regard to Adoption Disruption*, Washington, DC: Office of Human Development Services.

Kornitzer, M. (1968) *Adoption and Family Life*, London: Putnam.

Lambert, L. and Streather, J. (1980) *Children in Changing Families*, London: Macmillan.

Lowe, N., Murch, M., Borkowski, M., Weaver, A., Beckford, V. and Thomas, C. (1999) *Supporting Adoption: Reframing the Approach*, London: British Agencies for Adoption and Fostering.

Lowe, N. and Murch, M. (2001) *The Plan for Children: Adoption or Long-term Fostering*, Report to the Department of Health.

Maughan, B. and Pickles, A. (1990) Adopted and illegitimate children growing up, in L.N. Robins and M. Rutter (eds) *Straight and Devious Pathways from Childhood to Adulthood*, Cambridge: Cambridge University Press.

Minnis, H. (1999) *Results of the Foster Carers Training Project*, pamphlet, Glasgow.

Nelson, K. (1985) *On the Frontiers of Adoption: A Study of Special Needs Adoptive Families*, Washington, DC: Child Welfare League of America.

Owen, M. (1999) *Novices, Old Hands and Professionals: Adoption by Single People*, London: British Agencies for Adoption and Fostering.

Parker, R.A. (1966) *Decision in Child Care: A Study of Prediction in Fostering*, London: George Allen & Unwin.

Plomin, R. and DeFries, J.C. (1985) *Origins of Individual Differences: The Colorado Adoption Project*, New York: Academic Press.

Prime Minister's Review (2000) *Adoption*, London: Cabinet Office.

Quinton, D., Rushton, A., Dance, C. and Mayes, D. (1998) *Joining New Families: A Study of Adoption and Fostering in Middle Childhood*, London: Wiley.

Raynor, L. (1980) *The Adopted Child Comes of Age*, London: George Allen & Unwin.

Rowe, J., Cain, H., Hundleby, M. and Keane, A. (1984) *Long-term Foster Care*, London: Batsford.

Rowe, J., Hundleby, M. and Garnett, L. (1989) *Child Care Now*, London: British Agencies for Adoption and Fostering.

Rushton, A., Treseder, J. and Quinton, D. (1988) *New Parents for Older Children*, London: British Agencies for Adoption and Fostering.

Rushton, A., Dance, C., Quinton, D. and Mayes, D. (2001) Personal communication.

Rutter, M. and the English and Romanian Adoptees (ERA) Study Team (1998) Developmental catch-up and deficit following adoption after global early privation, *Journal of Child Psychology & Psychiatry* 39: 465–76.

St Claire, L. and Osborne, A.F. (1987) The ability and behaviour of children who have been 'in care' or separated from their parents, *Early Child Development and Care* 28, 3 (Special Issue): 187–353.

Schofield, G., Beek, M., Sargent, K. with Thoburn, J. (2000) *Growing up in Foster Care*, London: British Agencies for Adoption and Fostering.

Seglow, J., Kelmer Pringle, M. and Wedge, P. (1972) *Growing-up Adopted: A Long-term National Study of Adopted Children and their Families*, Windsor: NFER.

Sellick, C. and Thoburn, J. (1996) *What Works in Family Placement*, London: Barnardos.

Sinclair, I. (2001) Paper delivered at British Agencies for Adoption and Fostering Research Symposium, London, 29 November.

Sinclair, I., Wilson, K. and Gibbs, I. (2000) *Supporting Foster Placements*, Interim Report to the Department of Health.

Strathclyde Regional Council (1991) Fostering and adoption disruption, in Social Work Services Group (eds) *Adoption and Fostering*, Edinburgh: Scottish Office.

Thoburn, J. (1991) Family placement, in J. Fratter (ed.) *Family Placement*, London: British Agencies for Adoption and Fostering.

Thoburn, J., Norford, L. and Rashid, S. (2000) *Permanent Family Placement for Children of Minority Ethnic Origin*, London: Jessica Kingsley.

Thorpe, R. (1974) The Social and Psychological Situation of the Long-term Foster Child with Regard to his Natural Family, unpublished PhD thesis, Nottingham University.

Tizard, B. (1977) *Adoption: A Second Chance*, London: Open Books.

Tremitiere, B. (1984) *Disruption: A Break in Commitment*, York: Tressler-Lutheram.

Triseliotis, J. (1973) *In Search of Origins*, London: Routledge & Kegan Paul.

Triseliotis, J. (1980) *Growing up Fostered*, Report to the Social Science Research Council, London.

Triseliotis, J. (1983) Identity and security in long-term fostering and adoption, *Adoption & Fostering* 7: 22–31.

Triseliotis, J. (2002) Long-term foster care or adoption? The evidence examined, *Journal of Child & Family Social Work* 7: 23–34.

Triseliotis, J., Borland, M. and Hill, M. (2000) *Delivering Fostering Services*, London: British Agencies for Adoption and Fostering.

Triseliotis, J., Borland, M., Hill, M. and Lambert, L. (1995) *Teenagers and the Social Work Services*, London: HMSO.

Triseliotis, J. and Hill, M. (1990) Contrasting adoptive, foster care and residential care, in D.M. Brodzinsky and M.D. Schechter (eds) *The Psychology of Adoption*, New York: Oxford University Press.

Triseliotis, J. and Russell, J. (1984) *Hard to Place: The Outcome of Adoption and Residential Care*, London: Gower.

# Part V

# Judgments

# Chapter 17

# How does a judge weigh up a case?

*The Rt Hon. Lord Justice Thorpe*

The topic which I am asked to address is one of great amplitude. Therefore, in order to set reasonable boundaries, I begin by postulating the nature of the case, my choice resting upon assumptions as to my readers. So, the hypothetical case in question is a local authority application for a Care Order listed for trial before either a High Court judge in the Family Division or before the designated circuit judge in the local care centre. The case raises many issues of disputed fact, particularly historic fact. The local authority's application is opposed by one or both parents and perhaps other family members. The child or children of course have the benefit of an experienced children's guardian, who has instructed a solicitor from the children's panel, who in turn has instructed an experienced barrister. The application for a Care Order is supported by a care plan that directs the child or children to a new family and seeks to limit or terminate contact with the birth family. Of course the care plan is fundamentally irreconcilable with the family's opposition to the Care Order application but it has the support of the guardian, in general if not in detail. The local authority rely on expert evidence as to historic fact and also expert evidence as to what is best done for the future. The parents rely on expert evidence as to historic fact and the guardian calls expert evidence to support the amendment of the care plan for which he contends.

Having spent one day reading the statements and the reports, five days listening to oral evidence and half a day listening to closing submissions from the barristers, the judge must now order his thoughts and explain his conclusions. This he may do in an *extempore* judgment which will be recorded for the purposes of subsequent transcription. Alternatively he may choose to take time to write a judgment which will subsequently be handed down to the parties. Whichever course he chooses, the same discipline must be adopted.

## ISSUES OF HISTORIC FACT AS TO WHICH THERE IS NO EXPERT EVIDENCE

The case might be that the single mother has a drink problem. In consequence, on repeated occasions she has exposed the children to danger by taking them with her on a binge or by leaving them alone and unsupervised in her flat or by drinking herself into a stupor at home. The case for the local authority consists of some direct evidence from social workers, one incident involving the police and some gossipy contributions from neighbours. The mother's case is that she likes a drink from time to time ('who doesn't?') but she has always put the children first. Her case is vehemently supported by her mother.

Here the judge's task should follow the following path. First, he should remind himself of what is agreed between the parties: in the instance which I have given the answer would be not much. Second, he should look for what is incontrovertible. For instance, within social work records there may be clear entries showing that on such and such a date there was a home visit or perhaps that on some other date the mother's application for a move to a different housing estate was refused. Similarly there may be incontrovertible facts established by the police records: for instance, the mother may have been breathalysed and blood-tested.

Akin to incontrovertible fact there may be other contemporaneous records. The mother's general practitioner's notes may reveal consultations and prescriptions. Within the police records there may be a statement by the mother, either as noted in the constable's pocket book or, more formally, a signed statement under caution. Even the former is likely to carry greater weight with the judge than subsequent statements on oath in the witness box, tinged with conscious or subconscious determination to exonerate past failings.

From these relatively scant stepping-stones the judge must move through fast-running and possibly even deep water before he reaches the bank of conclusion. The evidence of the neighbours may be of little assistance, amounting to little more than rumour and lacking direct observation. But where there is a direct conflict of primary evidence the judge must measure each version for inconsistency with surrounding facts that are either conceded or established. He should then test each contribution for internal inconsistency. In some cases reliance may be placed upon inconsistency with matters not otherwise relevant to the case, introduced under the advocate's licence to cross-examine as to facts which, although not directly relevant, may reveal a tendency to deceive. Here the judge must be cautious. Unless the tendency revealed is gross and persistent, credit points outside the factual area under direct investigation generally do not resolve much. So, too, must he be cautious when approaching another well-known aid, the demeanour of the witness. Of course, the judge has the unparalleled advantage of absorbing the atmosphere of the case from beginning to end, of observing the behaviour of individuals in court over the course of days, not only when under the spotlight in the witness box but also in their comings, their goings and their reactions to the events of hearing. There must be a thin partition between the observation of demeanour and the judge's intuitive conviction that A is credible and B is not, or perhaps only that A is reliable and B is not. Of course, in this last task of determining reliability the judge should rely not so much on intuition as an intelligent appraisal of what is more likely and therefore more credible. We all know that improbable events occur but the judge will hesitate before franking an improbable account.

## THE ASSESSMENT OF CHARACTER AND PERSONALITY

Where it is the responsibility of the court to make decisions in the field of child care and protection, the proceedings are not strictly adversarial but partially inquisitorial. The assessment of the capacity to parent is often crucial to the placement decision. What assessment of the capacity to parent would be complete if it ignored a survey of the attributes and qualities which form part of the general character or personality of the individual? Those qualities and attributes distinguish one individual from the next and permit predictions as to future behaviour founded upon patterns of past behaviour (Thorpe, 1993; 1994; see also Reder, Chapter 13). Over the course of the last 40 years, the permissibility of a judicial assessment of character in the context of the capacity to parent has developed from rejection to acceptance. In modern times, the trial judge is not only entitled but obliged to base outcome at least in part upon his assessment of the personality of the adults contending for the responsibility to care for the child whose future is in question.

But beside this generalization, two strong caveats must be entered. The first is that abnormality or disorder of personality constitutes one of the descending steps from mental health to mental illness. Therefore, judges would do well to read and to think about what mental health experts have to say in an area of expertise which is particularly theirs. But, even that preparation is insufficient in any case in which any of the adults contending for care fall within or approach the classification of abnormal or disordered personality. In those cases, the trial judge would generally be wise to require the introduction of an expert assessment from a suitably qualified mental health expert (see Cordess, Chapter 9). By that I mean an expert whose professional emphasis is upon the welfare of the child exposed to risk. There is an inevitable tendency for the adult psychiatrist in patient relationship to focus on issues of diagnosis and classification in order to arrive at a conclusion that the individual is fit to have the care of the child. Whatever may be the clinical classification of the abnormal personality, in the end the professional must use his or her own judgement in assessing the potential impact on the family and child.

The second caveat is that any judicial assessment of personality, unaided by expert advice, must be founded upon principles established in psychological medicine and must reflect past patterns of behaviour established in the evidence. Trial judges are not entitled to make snap assessments of personality, based upon little more than intuition and personal prejudice, applied to relatively brief observation of the individual attempting to express himself or herself under pressure and in the unfamiliar setting of the witness box. Judges are inevitably both prejudiced and fallible and perhaps nowhere are they more fallible than when confronted with such an intangible, complex and subtle factor as personality.

However, there are safeguards against judicial fallibility in this field. First, there is accumulated professional experience. Public law cases may be tried at the higher levels only by judges who have been specially trained and selected for the task. The vast majority will have had many years' experience accumulated during a specialist practice as either barristers or solicitors, followed by assignment to family work on the bench. The second safeguard is self-knowledge. The more the judge recognizes and comes to terms with his own emotions and psychological instabilities the better able he will be both to recognize and guard against his own prejudices and also to understand the emotional and psychological mainsprings within others. The third safeguard is detachment. That virtue is most easily demonstrated by emphasizing the dangers of its opposite, attachment. Attachment may be on more than one level, physical, emotional or psychological. Those professions that are directly involved with the litigants in their homes and in their lives are more exposed to the risk of inappropriate involvement. Obviously, the wall between the judge and the litigant is a sufficient safeguard against anything but the fantasy of attachment. The judge who is not fulfilled in his emotional and personal life is at greater risk. In that event, insight is particularly necessary to maintain circumspection.

Judges must recognize that the task of assessing personality is formidably difficult. Many human beings are strongly psychologically defended and their social presentation may be assured and convincing. But what must be judged is not just what they choose to reveal but also what they strive to hide. We are all influenced to action and emotion by the unconscious, the repressed and what is denied. It is within the sphere of the unconscious and the repressed that dangerousness and the capacity to harm are at work. How is that to be registered and measured during the witness box exposure? The judge will not have had the advantage of a home visit, which, although prearranged, may have given the court reporter or the expert an opportunity to gauge subtle impressions of the home and also of the family's internal and social relationships. The judge's vital contribution is to establish the patterns emerging from the history. One of the most important functions of the litigation process is to establish the history through the statements filed during the adversarial preparations and then explored during the oral evidence. This is the vital judicial function and, until it is complete, expert assessment may need to remain provisional or conditional.

## HISTORICAL FACT AS TO WHICH THERE IS A CONFLICT OF EXPERT EVIDENCE

To illustrate what I mean in this section I instance the case of a child admitted to hospital with a series of injuries that subsequently prove fatal. As well as multiple complex injuries to the skull and brain, X-rays demonstrate a number of healing fractures of different ages and examination shows abrasions and bruising, the significance of which is open to more than one interpretation. Here, the lay evidence is unlikely to amount to much. The parents' position is incomprehension and denial. On the other side, there is nothing prior to the reception at hospital accident and emergency department. All depends upon expert evidence from paediatricians and paediatric radiologists. Here, I would suggest, the judge's task is more cerebral.

Again he will start with what the experts agree, confining himself to what may be limited but crucial areas of disagreement. Obviously, the experts, in finding their way to an agreed statement of the issues in dispute between them, will have fully harvested the field of incontrovertible fact and contemporaneous record. But expert witnesses are essentially honest witnesses. They may be misguided, they may be using their instruction in the case as an opportunity to ride some professional hobbyhorse, but they will not be out to deceive the judge. So the orthodox view is that demeanour is simply not an aid to resolving a conflict of expert opinion. I would not myself adopt that orthodox view as absolute. If an expert's contribution is tainted by some extra agenda, that flavour may emerge from his presentation in the witness box or even when in court but not in the witness box. But that will be the exceptional case. In the routine case the judge must subject each expert's evidence to a scrutiny both for internal consistency and also for consistency with surrounding circumstances or opinions that are incontrovertible or established with something approaching certainty. Cases in which the rival opinions are equally consistent and convincing will be rare. When they occur, the judge must endeavour to discern which has the greater scientific and rational force, conscious of his own fallibility and with it the possibility that he will make the wrong choice.

## APPLYING THE LAW

To this stage of the judicial task, the use of judicial discretion is impermissible. The facts must be found in accordance with the evidence and not otherwise. The judge's next task is to apply the law to the facts and equally in its execution there is no room for judicial discretion. That the Children Act 1989 can give rise to very difficult questions of law is simply demonstrated by reference to the cases of *Re H* (1996) and *Lancashire County Council v B* (2000), the first of which required the House of Lords to establish the burden of proof in cases of sexual abuse and the second of which tackled the even more difficult questions created by the extension of opportunity to adjoining families to inflict serious head injuries on a child. Equally it is decisions of the House of Lords which have explained and clarified the judicial task in deciding in the individual case whether or not the Section 31 threshold has been crossed (see in *Re M*, 1994; *Lancashire County Council v B*, 2000). Thus, the individual trial judge has much more than the bare words of Parliament: he has the ultimate judicial guidance helping him to distinguish between what is sufficiently substantial to satisfy the test and what fails to rise above the level of indefinable suspicion and anxiety.

Reference to the standard of proof in sexual abuse cases requires something on the role of the expert in this area. More than a decade ago, physical signs and symptoms described and interpreted by paediatricians gave rise to huge difficulties in litigation, in health services, in social services and police services. Thankfully, those difficulties were overcome and instances in which the judge is presented with any crucial dispute as to the interpretation of signs and symptoms are probably extremely rare. But what seems to many a dangerous aspect of the family justice system is that it is extremely rare for the child or adolescent victim to give direct evidence. In most cases the nearest equivalent will be a video-taped 'Memorandum' interview. Additionally, the child may have described past experiences to foster carers, social workers and to a consultant child and adolescent psychiatrist. Each one of these may have a view as to the veracity of the victim and thus the accuracy of what is described. Interviewing children and interpreting their words is something that a lay person may do well through experience and a natural aptitude. But, as has been rightly pointed out, interviewing children who have been damaged by past experiences is not the straightforward task that some believe it to be (see Schofield, 1998). What they describe may be distorted by very complex factors. Thus the safest interviewer and the safest interpreter of the narrative is, in my opinion, the child and adolescent psychiatrist or the clinical psychologist who has had the highest degree of training amplified by experience. Accordingly I was relieved by the decision of my court in *Re M and R* (1996) which established that the evidence of such an expert as to the credibility of the child is admissible and may be taken into account by the judge. Prior to that decision there had been some tension surrounding the role of the expert witness and the role of the judge. Since the judge alone decides issues of veracity and fact it was contended that for an expert witness to express an opinion as to veracity was to trespass on the judicial function. The proper answer to that contention was found in the Civil Evidence Act 1972.

## THE CHILD'S FUTURE

Once the judge has completed his preliminary tasks of finding the facts and applying the law to the facts, he must approach the most difficult and the most crucial part of his job: deciding outcome. In some instances, a clear decision on the facts may in turn be decisive of outcome. Obviously, if a judge concludes that the natural parents are fundamentally dangerous and the child at risk is of an ideal age for adoption, the outcome may be indisputable. But equally common will be the cases where, on the facts found, the choice between two starkly different outcomes is extremely finely balanced. In those instances there may be conflicting expert evidence. The child and adolescent psychiatrist called by the local authority or the children's guardian may advise the judge that the risks attendant upon rehabilitation are too great to be contemplated. On the other hand, the child and adolescent psychiatrist called by the parents may advise that given a sustained period of psychotherapy, the availability of which may itself be in doubt, the risks can be contained to give the child a safe life within the home to which he belongs. How is the judge to evaluate such rival opinions? He may scrutinize each opinion to see whether the relevant past fact as found, perhaps by a judgment on a preliminary issue, has been sufficiently but not excessively brought into account. Obviously, any assessment of future risk, who ever makes it, must be reflective of past events and balanced. A practice of split hearings has become common place. Many cases raise a crucial issue of past fact: for instance was a child sexually abused and, if so, by whom; alternatively, how did the child sustain the injuries revealed by X-ray? Any expert appraised of future placement and any formulation of the local authority's care plan depend crucially on the resolution of the disputed history. So it is often sensible to arrange one full hearing to decide the disputed factual issue followed, at a suitable interval, by a second to decide the child's future and thus conclude the case.

Then the judge may look to the expert's letter of instruction to see whether the right issue was fairly put. Equally he may look to any account of discussion or other communication between the experts. Experts, like judges, are vulnerable to bias, prejudice and an obstinate inability to shift, particularly when their *amour propre* is at stake. Partisanship may be the product of erroneous or unreliable instruction. Equally it may arise subconsciously as a result of exposure to a particularly tragic case. Joint instructions or instructions from the guardian alone are some safeguard against partisanship. But the judge must always have a nose for this flaw. In no other category of case is it more important that the judge should feel that the expert is there to help him and that the expert proffers the same opinion to the parent as he would offer to the children's guardian, if his instructions came from that source.

The Children Act 1989 was preceded by the most intense public consideration and discussion before any parliamentary debate. Thus, there was no room for doubt as to the parliamentary intention, namely a clear division of power and responsibility between the family justice system and the social services system. The judge alone could make the Care Order but the care plan underpinning it was the responsibility of social services, for both formulation and implementation. This undoubtedly created difficulties and tensions. Only by way of example: there were cases in which the care plan provided for a rehabilitation which the judge regarded as fundamentally dangerous: or the care plan might provide for adoption when the judge was convinced that long-term fostering held better welfare prospects: alternatively there were instances in which the future seemed too uncertain to permit the judge to forgo control but where otherwise the Care Order was clearly justified. The advent of the Human Rights Act 1998 has come to provide an impetus for change which mere debate had failed to achieve. The decisions of our court in *Re W and Re W&B* (2001) have redrawn the boundary of responsibility between judge and local authority. Whether that decision will be questioned on appeal or how it will be given practical development remains to be seen.

## CONCLUSION

In the end whatever value the judge attaches to the expert advice, he knows that the responsibility for outcome, and it is indeed a heavy one, is upon him alone. He alone must evaluate the risks. He alone must decide for the child which is the least adverse outcome. There is perhaps no other area of judicial work where the judicial discretion is more extensive. The more finely balanced the choice the more difficult will it be to appeal his decision. If a judge has made careful findings of fact without error, has correctly applied the law, has rightly defined the choice between, say, rehabilitation and long-term care as extremely finely balanced, how can it be said on appeal that the preference for one against the other was plainly wrong? This sense of being in effect the ultimate arbiter inevitably increases the responsibility of the decision. He is fortunate if he can feel that he has shared that responsibility with wise experts.

My endeavour has been to give some insight into how the judge should discharge his responsibility in contested public law cases brought under the Children Act 1989. I have not attempted to state the law but only to show where the judge finds his directions as to the law. For an introduction to cardinal principles I would commend Allen (1998). Equally, I have not sought to advise experts as to how they should perform their crucial function. Here, I would commend Black *et al.* (1998) and Wall (2000).

The President's Interdisciplinary Family Law committee is committed to maintaining and improving forensic services to the family justice system. One recent initiative, in conjunction with the Royal College of Psychiatrists, the Royal College of Paediatrics and Child Health and the British Psychological Association, has been the creation of a network of courts offering mini pupillages with a specialist judge to those seeking to expand their experience and confidence in court work. I am in no doubt that the readiness of specialist judges to contribute in this way is an acknowledgement of the huge contribution that mental health professionals and paediatricians make to the family justice system.

## References

Allen, N. (1998) *Making Sense of the Children Act*, 3rd ed., Chichester: Wiley.

Black, D., Harris-Hendricks, J. and Wolkind, S. (eds) (1998) *Child Psychiatry and the Law*, 3rd ed., London: Gaskell.

Lancashire County Council v B (2000) *Family Law Reports* 1: 563.

Re H (Minors) (Sexual Abuse: Standard of Proof) (1996) *Appeal Cases* 4: 563.

Re M (Minor) (Care Orders: Threshold Conditions) (1994) *Appeal Cases* 2: 424.

Re M and R (Minors) (Sexual Abuse: Expert Evidence) (1996) *All England Reports* 4: 239.

Re W and Re W&B (2001) *Family Court Reporter* 2: 450.

Schofield, G. (1998) Making sense of the ascertainable wishes and feelings of insecurely attached children, *Child & Family Law Quarterly* 10: 363–75.

Thorpe, The Hon. Mr Justice (1993) The assessment of personality: its contribution to judicial decisions in the field of child care and protection, *Family Law* 23: 293–96.

Thorpe, The Hon. Mr Justice (1994) Personality assessment, *Family Law* 24: 257–60.

Wall, Mr Justice (2000) *A Handbook for Expert Witnesses in Children Act Cases*, Bristol: Family Law.

# Index

Page numbers in **bold** type refer to figures and tables.